Lease Accounting with SAP®: IFRS 16 and ASC 842

Hanno Hofmann, Pamela Lim, Joy Mabborang, Louis Teunissen

# Lease Accounting with SAP®: IFRS 16 and ASC 842

SAP RE-FX and SAP Lease Administration by Nakisa

Rheinwerk Publishing

**Editor** Emily Nicholls
**Copyeditor** Yvette Chin
**Cover Design** Graham Geary
**Photo Credit** Shutterstock.com/56666983/© Ambient Ideas
**Layout Design** Vera Brauner
**Production** Graham Geary
**Typesetting** III-satz, Husby (Germany)
**Printed and bound in** the United States of America, on paper from sustainable sources

**ISBN 978-1-4932-1689-5**

1st edition 2018

**Library of Congress Cataloging-in-Publication Data**
Names: Hofmann, Hanno, author. | Lim, Pamela, author. | Mabborang, Joy, author.
Title: Lease accounting with SAP : IFRS 16 and ASC 842 : SAP RE-FX and SAP lease administration by Nakisa / Hanno Hofmann, Pamela Lim, Joy Mabborang, Louis Teunissen.
Description: 1st Edition. | Boston : Rheinwerk Publishing, [2018] | Includes index.
Identifiers: LCCN 2017061072 (print) | LCCN 2018002023 (ebook) | ISBN 9781493216901 (ebook) | ISBN 9781493216895 (alk. paper)
Subjects: LCSH: Lease and rental services--Accounting. | SAP ERP.
Classification: LCC HF5686.L42 (ebook) | LCC HF5686.L42 H63 2018 (print) | DDC 657/.75--dc23
LC record available at https://lccn.loc.gov/2017061072

# Contents at a Glance

# Dear Reader,

I am a lessee.

For the moment, at least. My partner and I have concluded that, as we navigate the intersection of life plans and financial realities, renting our apartment makes sense. Of course, having a responsive landlord means our snowy sidewalks get shoveled promptly and our 100-year-old plumbing is someone else's headache. But more importantly, having an at-will lease agreement means that our household of two can stay agile for a little while longer before we hire a realtor and a lawyer. (Plus, have you *seen* the real estate market in Boston?!) We'll revisit the question of when to rent versus when to own in another year.

Organizations around the world have always done this kind of calculus for their property and their equipment. However, starting soon, they'll be doing another kind of math as they transition to the new lease accounting regulations set by the IASB and FASB. Figuring out how to account for which leases and when is a tall order with a tight deadline. Fortunately, SAP's two leasing solutions are here to help—and the experienced author team behind this IFRS 16 and ASC 842 book can pave the way.

What did you think about *Lease Accounting with SAP: IFRS 16 and ASC 842*? Your comments and suggestions are the most useful tools to help us make our books the best they can be. Please feel free to contact me and share any praise or criticism you may have.

Thank you for purchasing a book from SAP PRESS!

**Emily Nicholls**
Editor, SAP PRESS

*emilyn@rheinwerk-publishing.com*
*www.sap-press.com*
Rheinwerk Publishing · Boston, MA

# Contents

# Foreword

Ten years have passed since the credit crisis.

Out of this crisis came calls for improved financial transparency. One result of this goal that should have a positive impact are International Financial Reporting Standard 16 and Accounting Standards Codification 842—accounting regulations to move leased assets from disclosures directly onto a company's balance sheet. This task will not be trivial, as an estimated $3 to $4 trillion in leased assets worldwide occupy corporate balance sheets.

Almost every company has leased assets of property and moveable assets across their portfolio. But at SAP, we know that leasing can be a very tricky business, since different business processes are needed for real property and for movable assets. In addition, during our initial product research, we spoke to over 500 customers, but only one reported having the ability to truly view all their leased assets immediately, and another reported having leases spread across 700 finance departments globally. Suffice to say, most companies have a lot of work ahead of them to achieve full visibility.

Further, corporate finance stakeholders will be watching very carefully when these rules change. By January 1, 2019, most public companies around the world will need to report leased assets under the new IFRS 16 and ASC 842 rules. The same will apply for most private companies by January 1, 2020.

Previous experience with accounting compliance topics has shown us that the time and effort required to adopt new regulations are always underestimated. Our experience working with lease accounting since 2011 is that most companies will start too late to effectively prepare for upcoming changes. Customers adopting IFRS 16 and ASC 842 have reported encountering more complexity than they originally forecasted throughout their projects.

Due to the complexities of IFRS 16 and ASC 842 in practice, along with real-world complexities and customer feedback after adopting other regulations like IFRS 15 and ASC 606, SAP has developed a best-of-breed approach for providing software solutions that assist customers in their efforts to become compliant: SAP Flexible Real Estate Management (SAP RE-FX) handles lease accounting of real property assets and related business scenarios, while SAP Lease Administration by Nakisa handles lease accounting of equipment assets and related business scenarios.

To guide readers through implementing and using these solutions, SAP PRESS has assembled an all-star cast:

- Hanno Hofmann from Walldorf Consulting is a leasing expert who gained a tremendous amount of experience implementing on the lessor side of the lease accounting business. He has since been involved in many IFRS 15 and 16 projects and—together with Pamela Lim, Joy Mabborang, Louis Teunissen, Pui Pui Wong, and Heiko Roth—brings that invaluable experience to our readers.
- Tom Anderson from SAP was an SAP RE-FX implementation consultant for years, and is now the solution manager for SAP RE-FX—a solution with hundreds of IFRS 16 projects underway and thousands expected through 2019 for property assets.
- Imran Mia from Nakisa is an accountant by trade who has been breathing the new lease accounting standards for equipment for the last few years. Together with Zeina Dabbagh and Puja Mehta, he has been visiting one customer at a time to introduce the SAP Lease Administration application, which now has over 100 customers and hundreds more expected in 2018.

To any reader, our recommendation is to start working on IFRS 16 and ASC 842 now. You should perform an accounting assessment upfront followed by an assessment of systems impact. Ideally, your project team should be as cross-functional and as diversified as this author team.

I want to thank the experts from SAP, Nakisa, Walldorf Consulting, and SAP PRESS for their contributions in making this book possible! We hope that readers will quickly comprehend the basics challenges of lease accounting and take tangible action towards successful outcomes for their organizations.

**Pete Graham**
Director, Finance Solutions and Mobility
SAP

# Preface

In the last few years, over the course of many revenue recognition implementation projects, my team at Walldorf Consulting has collaborated with project leads who were stumped. They needed a resource that not only talked about the solution implementation, but also explained the theory behind it. Because at the end of the day, they told us, accounting folks need to understand the new regulations in the same way that the IT folks need to understand the results of whatever the software is calculating.

Fast forward to more guidance from the IASB and the FASB, and another round of IFRS and ASC updates. Looking ahead to leasing projects, we set out to write that book for lease accounting—a book that would span the project spectrum, explaining not only the principles behind lease accounting, but also how SAP's two systems get implemented, and then what to do after SAP Flexible Real Estate Management and SAP Lease Administration by Nakisa implementations go live.

In other words, our objective has been to go beyond configuration, and to do the following:

- Outline the differences between the new standards and their predecessors (Introduction)
- Give a solid explanation of the leasing basics (Chapter 1)
- Walk through compliance readiness checks (Chapter 2)
- Demystify common project management challenges (Chapter 3)
- Step through the key configuration activities for both SAP Lease Administration (Chapter 4) and SAP RE-FX (Chapter 5)
- Describe transition accounting (Chapter 6)
- Explain how to manage leases using SAP Lease Administration (Chapter 7) and SAP RE-FX (Chapter 8) after go-live
- Remind readers of the new disclosure requirements and how to use out-of-the-box reporting functionality in both solutions (Chapter 9)
- Review common business cases for three representative industries (Chapter 10)

Why did we put so much content around the main configuration chapters? Because we truly believe that IFRS 16 and ASC 842 implementation projects will only be successful when the implementation teams not only understand the necessary

Customizing activities, but also have mastered the theory behind those activities in SAP Lease Administration and SAP RE-FX. It's important to enable everyone from the executive decision-makers to the consulting and IT professionals, project teams, and managers, to the lease managers, lease administrators, and field operators to set up and work in these systems.

In this book we have attempted here to showcase both systems; each solution has advantages and disadvantages, and your organization should evaluate which one is a better fit on a case-by-case basis. In combination, though, they are certainly powerful enough to cover all industry requirements across the SAP customer installed base.

Before we dig into the leasing content in this book, I'd like to recognize some of the people who contributed to its creation and offer my thanks. First, to the entire Walldorf Consulting team—Louis, Pam, Joy, Lyle, Jaime, Pui Pui, and Heiko—who made this possible with the countless extra hours beyond normal Walldorf project work. Second, to the folks from SAP and Nakisa who were always committed to the success of this book; thank you, Tom, Imran, Puja, and Zeina. Third, to Pete Graham, who, as an SAP sales director, is deeply engaged with leasing projects and who helped assemble the team for this book. Fourth, to the entire Rheinwerk Publishing team, and in particular to Emily Nicholls, who was able to work around our notoriously late deliveries and never lost her patience. And finally, to my family, who never lets me forget that there is more to life than just work.

**Hanno Hofmann**
Spring 2018

# Introduction

Leasing is a financing mechanism prevalent across most major industries. Leasing allows companies to obtain the right to use assets through regular rental payments instead of having to incur large cash outflows. Valuable assets such as equipment, machinery, or real estate can be used by a business without an outright purchase, which may not be the best use for a company's working capital.

The way organizations account for their leases has a significant impact on their financial profiles. To govern this documentation, two financial standards boards, the International Accounting Standards Board (IASB) and the United States' Financial Accounting Standards Board (FASB), periodically issue standards to guide their adherents' accounting practices. In some cases, the two boards are able to agree on a new universal standard; in others, as with leasing, they each issue their own rules, which vary in similarity.

The IASB and FASB do not specify any penalties for International Financial Reporting Standards 16 and Accounting Standards Codification 842 non-compliance. Organizations that adhere to these standards do so not from fear of the consequences, but rather as a demonstration of professionalism and dedication to best practices to interested third parties. The indirect fall-out could include the wavering of debt covenants or credit line agreements or diminished stakeholder confidence.

In this chapter, we'll explain regulatory changes around lease accounting and discuss the regulations' impact on lessees' business processes and IT systems. We'll examine how the SAP Lease Administration by Nakisa (hereafter, SAP Lease Administration) and SAP Flexible Real Estate Management (SAP RE-FX) solutions play pivotal roles in assisting entities in transitioning to the new standards. Note that we'll go into more detail on lease accounting in Chapter 1, on disclosures and reporting in Chapter 9, and on SAP's two leasing systems throughout the book.

## The Shift: Regulatory Changes at a Glance

Let's begin by examining how IFRS 16 and ASC 842 compare to their predecessor standards.

## IFRS 16 vs. IAS 17

In January 2016, the IASB released IFRS 16 (Leases), replacing its previous standard IAS 17 (Leases), with an effective date of January 1, 2019. IFRS 16 provides an accounting model for the identification of lease arrangements and their impact on the financial statements. The new standard will bring several leases onto the balance sheet for lessees, while lessor accounting will remain largely unchanged. Financial metrics such as earnings before interest, taxes, depreciation, and amortization (EBITDA); operating profit; and net income have been redefined with the elimination of using operating leases as a method of off-balance sheet accounting. Where lessees are faced with substantial change to their business processes, lessors must also align their offerings to new requirements and behaviors, such as shorter lease terms or new service opportunities.

IFRS 16 and IAS 17, which govern multinational public and private companies who report under international standards, are similar in scope. Leases of all assets are affected by the new standard, with the following exceptions:

- Licenses of intellectual property granted by a lessor
- Leases of non-regenerative resources
- Leases of biological assets
- Service concession arrangements
- Rights held by lessees under licensing agreements

IFRS 16, however, introduces a new definition of a lease. The standard provides a detailed guide to assess if a contract is a lease, a service, or both. (This definition is different from International Financial Reporting Interpretations Committee [IFRIC] 4 guidance where an operating lease or service is not clearly distinguished.)

The current IAS 17 approach is to distinguish between operating and finance leases. Leases transferring substantially all risks and rewards of asset ownership were classified as finance leases, while all others were operating leases. This classification method was subjective and allowed entities to classify leases that were substantially finance leases as operating leases to keep assets off-balance sheet. IFRS 16 was introduced to ensure that lessees would present lease-related assets and liabilities on their financial statements in a manner truer to their lease transactions. By eliminating off-balance sheet financing entirely, IFRS 16 produces greater clarity of how lease transactions affect a company's assets and liabilities.

The primary impact of the new standard on financial statements will see the "risk and rewards" model being replaced with a "right-of-use" model, where lessees will recognize a right-of-use asset (ROU asset) and a lease liability on the balance sheet. Lease liabilities will be measured in relation to an estimated lease term and as the present value of future lease payments. These payments refer to fixed, interminable payments for lease components, and lease terms shall include optional lease periods where an entity may extend a lease in a manner that is "reasonably certain."

Additionally, contingent rent or irregular lease payments must be considered in the evaluation of a lease asset and liability and determined to be either fixed payments in substance or payments dependent on an index or rate.

Let's look at changes to the standard in a few key places.

***Lease Identification***

IFRS 16 introduces a new definition of a lease. Under the new standard, a distinction is made between a service contract and a lease contract. Previously, distinguishing between the two was not crucial, and many companies would account for both types of contracts in the same way (e.g., as a simple expense in a profit and loss statement).

Going forward, IFRS 16 takes a closer look at whether a contract contains an underlying, identifiable asset. Only where this criterion is met can a contract be considered to contain a lease. Otherwise, where no asset can be identified, a contract will be said to not contain a lease.

**Example**

Two companies enter into separate five-year rental contracts with a warehouse owner to use a space to store their goods.

Company A is entitled to occupy a certain square footage for storage. The owner of the warehouse will, however, identify the specific place to be used based on decision criteria such as the space available and frequency of goods movement. The owner can change the location of the space allocated to Company A at his discretion.

Company B will use a specific storage unit in the east wing of the warehouse. This allocated storage space is fixed for the duration of the contract.

Company A's option will not contain a lease as no asset can be identified—the warehouse owner holds the right to change the allocated space without Company A's approval at any given time, and the warehouse owner derives economic benefit from substituting the space. Company A is party to a service arrangement with the warehouse owner, whereas Company B has entered into an operating lease.

Other key questions to determine whether a contract contains a lease include the following:

- Whether the lessee has the right to obtain substantially all of the economic benefits
- Who has the right to direct how and for what purpose the asset is used
- Whether the lessee can operate the asset without the supplier changing those operating instructions
- Whether the lessee designed the asset in a way that predetermines how and for what purpose it will be used

We'll take a closer look at these conditions in Chapter 1.

***Lease Elements and Non-Lease Components***

Because the accounting for an operating lease and the accounting for a service arrangement have similar impacts on the financial statements, many entities do not separate operating lease components in their contracts.

Moving forward, as all leases will be brought on-balance sheet per IFRS 16, rental and lease payments must be split into lease and non-lease elements because entities are required to do two things:

- Account for a lease component as a lease (if the criterion is met under IFRS 16)
- Account for a service component as they did previously (as a simple expense in a profit and loss statement)

These lease elements may include services provided by the lessors such as maintenance and repairs. Nevertheless, if an activity does not transfer a good or direct service to the lessee, the activity shall not be regarded as a lease component.

The separation of components is required by lessees and lessors where:

1. The lessee derives benefits from the use of the asset alone or in combination with other resources (which may have arisen from another event).
2. The underlying asset in the contract is neither related to nor dependent on other underlying assets.

Lessors must then allocate to each component a standalone selling price (SSP) per IFRS 15 (Revenue from Contracts with Customers). Observable information should be used as much as possible to identify these components and arrive at discernable SSPs. In some cases, lessors may not have distinguished said components in prices quoted to customers, which would make past data non-existent for lease and non-lease components. In these instances, entities are required to estimate component SSPs using three approaches provided by IFRS 15:

1. The adjusted market assessment approach
2. The expected cost plus margin approach
3. The residual approach

**Example**

Let's return to Company B's scenario. The agreement consists of a monthly payment of $6,000, which includes the storage unit rental and the fortnightly cleaning fee.

The payment must be separated into the lease component and the maintenance services based on observable SSPs. The standalone prices for each can be determined based on similar lease and maintenance contracts that were entered separately. For example, Company B may find that it could rent a similar unit in another warehouse for $5,000 and pay a separate cleaning and maintenance fee of $1,000 per month. In the scenario where no observable prices are available, Company B is required to estimate the SSPs of these components.

#### *Lessee Accounting*

Beginning with IFRS 16, lessees no longer need to classify leases at inception, prescribing a single accounting model for every lease. With every ROU asset identified, a corresponding liability based on the discounted payments must be recognized on the balance sheet. The asset's depreciation will be treated accordingly in the profit and loss statement and the liability amortized over the lease duration.

The new lessee accounting model has two exceptions:

- Short-term leases (lease of an asset for 12 months or less). If a lease contains a purchase option, however, the exception does not apply.
- Leases of low-value assets (furniture, low-value IT equipment, etc.). The absolute value of the lease asset would be approximately $5,000 or less.

#### *Lessor Accounting*

Lessors, on the other hand, will not see any change to the dual lease accounting model, where lease classification tests will continue to observe guidance from IAS 17 criteria.

When comparing IFRS 16 to IAS 17, no substantial change in the definitions of each lease type has occurred. However, explicit guidance on certain areas of lease accounting has been outlined in greater detail in IFRS 16:

1. Sale-and-leaseback transactions
2. Subleases
3. Lease modifications
4. Lessor disclosures

## ASC 842 vs. ASC 840

In February 2016, the FASB released its own standard, ASC 842, which replaces ASC 840.

ASC 842 provides new guidance on accounting for leases. In this regulation, FASB introduces a new definition of a lease: a contract, or part of a contract, that conveys the right to control the use of identified property, plant, or equipment (an identified asset) for a period of time in exchange for consideration. Under ASC 842, a contract is said to contain a lease if the lessee receives two things:

- The right to obtain substantially all of the economic benefits from the use of the identified asset
- The right to direct the use of the identified asset

In contrast, ASC 840 more simply defines a lease as an agreement that conveys the right to use an asset for a period of time.

Like ASC 840, ASC 842 offers dual classification, on-balance sheet lease accounting for lessees, requiring most leases to be classified as either operating or finance leases, but without the "bright line" tests of FAS 13. Lessors, on the other hand, are required to classify leases as either operating, direct financing, or sales-type leases.

ASC 842 will have far-reaching implications on almost every entity across major industries. Like IFRS 16, ASC 842 will entail a bigger change for lessee accounting—where effectively all leases will be brought on-balance sheet and consequently, an ROU asset and lease liability must be recognized—but will not result in fundamentally changes to lessor accounting.

The new standard's impact on the financial statements will see similar income statement patterns between finance and operating leases as between capital and operating leases. (Capital leases are similar to finance leases, but require property purchased through capital loans to be recorded as taxable assets.)

Finance leases would typically be front-loaded, meaning that lease payments would be higher in earlier periods and lower as the lease period approaches its end. Operating leases, on the other hand, would have straight-line lease payments.

#### *Lease Definition*

ASC 842 defines leases as a contract or partial contract that entails a right of use of property, plant, and equipment (PP&E) for a stipulated duration in exchange for consideration. The standard does not apply to the following leases:

- Leases of intangible assets
- Leases of biological assets
- Leases of inventory
- Leases of non-regenerative resources, such as oil, natural gas, and minerals
- Leases of assets under construction

#### *Lessee Accounting*

ASC 842 provides a guideline for the proper accounting for short-term, finance, and operating lease classifications. The lessee will typically recognize an ROU asset and a lease liability for every lease. These recognition requirements, however, may be optional for short-term leases where lessees will recognize lease payments in income statements over the lease term.

Initial recognition of the ROU asset and lease liability, as well as the measurement of the subsequent lease liability, remains unchanged for operating and finance leases. The new standard, however, includes new guidance for the subsequent measurement of the ROU asset.

For operating leases, the treatment is similar to ASC 840 where periodic lease expenses are recognized on a straight-line basis.

Finance leases, on the other hand, require lessees to separate the interest expense component from the lease liability and separate amortization expense on the ROU asset. What this entails are income statement patterns like that of capital leases under ASC 840. The separation of components will result in front-loaded expense recognition on income statements.

#### *Short-Term Leases Recognition and Measurement Exemption*

A lessee may opt to exempt from ASC 842 a lease with a term of 12 months or less where the option to purchase the underlying asset does not exist. Entities that apply this exception will not recognize short-term leases on the balance sheet but will recognize related lease expenses over the period of the lease on a straight-line basis.

#### *Lessor Accounting*

ASC 842, paragraph 30, specifies the proper accounting by lessors of leases classified as sales-type leases, direct financing leases, or operating leases. For sales-type and direct financing leases, the lessor should de-recognize the underlying asset and recognize or defer additional profits and expenses associated with the lease. For operating leases, the lessor should defer initial direct costs at commencement of the lease and recognize lease payments and initial direct costs over the lease term.

This approach is similar to ASC 840's guidelines on sales-type lease accounting. Lessors de-recognize an underlying asset's carrying amount and recognize or defer additional profits and expenses derived from the lease. Where the collection of payments and guaranteed residual value from the lessee is not probable at the commencement of the lease, the lessor shall not derecognize the asset nor recognize the lease net investment. The lessor should instead continue to recognize the underlying asset according to US Generally Accepted Accounting Principles (US GAAP) guidance and account for both variable and fixed lease payments received as a deposit liability up until the point where:

- It is probable that the entity will receive lease payments in addition to any amount required to fulfill the guaranteed residual value provided by the lessee.
- The contract is terminated, and the lessor's lease payments cannot be refunded, or the underlying asset is repossessed, and the contract contains no other obligation to the lessee and the lessee's lease payments cannot be refunded.

The accounting treatment of direct financing leases is similar to that of sales-type leases where collectability is probable. Selling profit, however, will be deferred at the start of the lease and be incorporated in the measurement of the net investment of the lease.

Interest income will be recognized over the lease term, affecting a periodic discount on the net investment's remaining balance. Similar to ASC 840, ASC 842 will see lessors recognize the underlying asset as well as the lease payments on a straight-line basis. That said, if the collectability of lease payments is not probable at an operating lease's commencement date, then the lease income will be either the lower of the straight-line amount or the lease payment.

#### *Sale-and-Leaseback Transactions*

A sale-and-leaseback transaction is where an entity transfers an asset to another (known as the *buyer-lessor*) and leases the asset back from the buyer-lessor. Under ASC 842, the majority of leases will be brought on-balance sheet, which eliminates entities' ability to use sale-and-leaseback transactions as a source of off-balance sheet financing.

If the transfer of an underlying asset involves passing its control to the buyer-lessor, then the transfer will be deemed a sale and a lease by both seller and buyer. The seller-lessee should then do four things:

1. Recognize the transaction price for the sale at the point in time the buyer-lessor obtains control of the asset
2. Adjust the transaction price for any off-market terms and recognize the entire gain/loss on the sale of the asset
3. Derecognize the carrying amount of the underlying asset
4. Account for the lease in accordance with ASC 842

The buyer-lessor recognizes the asset purchase in accordance with other ASC guidelines and account for the lease per ASC 842.

#### *Leveraged Lease Arrangements*

Leverage leases are leases that meet the criteria in ASC 840. This guidance, however, is not brought forward to ASC 842 and will require lessors to continue applying ASC 840 to leases commencing prior to ASC 842's effective date.

The new standard will only see the classification of operating, sales-type, or direct financing leases. New leases will no longer be allowed to be accounted for as leveraged leases. Upon adoption of ASC 842, lessors may continue to use the leveraged lease accounting approach for leveraged leases that have been grandfathered.

### Compliance Timelines and Transitions

For organizations that hold leases, the clock is ticking.

IFRS 16 is effective on periods commencing on or after January 1, 2019, and ASC 842 is effective for periods beginning after December 15, 2018. These new standards will entail large-scale changes for several entities. Preliminary assessments should be conducted to determine how lease accounting will change, and reliable data must be gathered to effectively facilitate the implementation of IFRS 16 and/or ASC 842 across an entity's operations. Entities may need to consider differences in economic, legal, and operational requirements when preparing systems to store and update lease information on a regular basis.

Early adoption is possible with IFRS 16; however, you cannot apply the new standard before adopting IFRS 15 (Revenue from Contracts with Customers). In transitioning to the new standard, lessees are required to apply either a *full retrospective approach* or a *modified retrospective approach* to their entire lease portfolios.

Lessors need not pass any adjustments in the transition to IFRS 16 for their leases and should recognize those leases based on the new standard's effective date. Additionally, sale-and-leaseback transactions entered into before IFRS 16 applies should be exempt from reassessment when determining if a sale has occurred. Reassessment need not take place for both lessees and lessors for contracts upon transition—if a contract was determined to not have a lease under IAS 17, then reassessment is not necessary under IFRS 16.

We'll go into greater detail about transition accounting using the full and modified retrospective approaches in Chapter 6, but for now, note that the full retrospective approach shown in Figure 1 requires the new leasing standard to be applied retroactively in accordance with IAS 8 (Accounting Policies, Changes in Accounting Estimates, and Errors). As a lessee, an entity shall:

- Apply the standard to all leases
- Restate prior financial information and statements
- Adjust equity at the beginning of the earliest comparative period presented

Entities will need to have extensive and reliable information on their lease accounting and transactions before the standard can be retroactively applied. Historical information about fixed and variable lease payments, discount rates, as well as information used by management in passing judgments and estimates, are imperative. Information required at lease commencement may include the following:

- Lease terms
- Reasonable certainty in exercising a purchase option
- Expected amounts to be paid under guaranteed residual value
- Impairment and amortization of the ROU asset
- Additional disclosures required by IAS 8

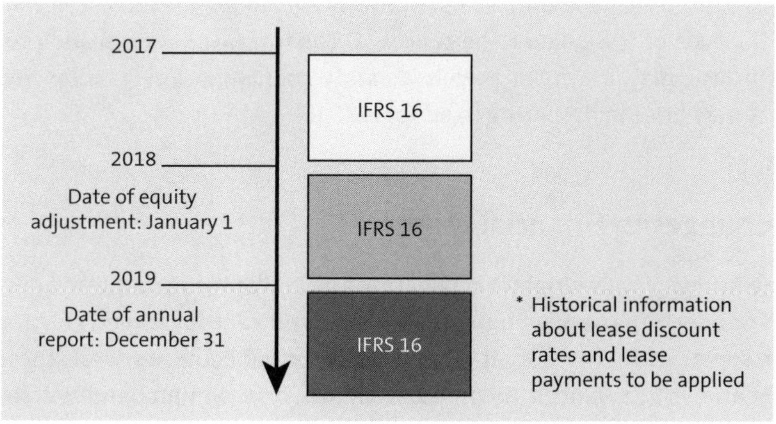


**Figure 1** Full Retrospective Approach

In contrast, when using the modified retrospective approach, shown in Figure 2, entities shall apply the standard from the beginning of the current period. Under this approach, lessees are not required to restate comparative information. The requirements for the adoption of this approach are as follows:

- Recognize lease assets and liabilities at the beginning of the current period per IFRS 16 guidelines
- Account for the effects of initial application by passing adjustments in equity to its opening balance as of January 1, 2019
- Make additional disclosures as required by IAS 8

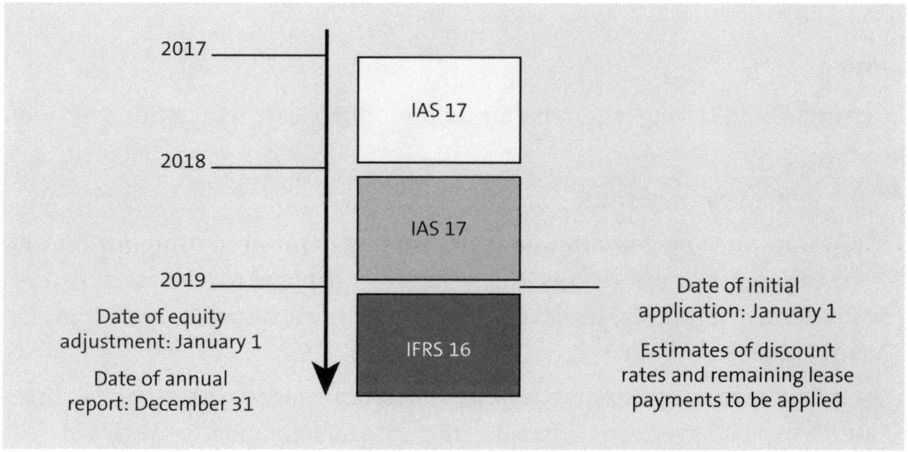


**Figure 2** Modified Retrospective Approach

You should keep in mind that the transition approach you adopt will have a significant impact on the type of lease data to be collected. The timing of system and process changes will also play a critical part in flexibly managing any unexpected complexities that may arise in preparing to adopt IFRS 16.

## The Impact: Changes to Financial Processes

Good project governance is essential for navigating any challenges brought by IFRS 16 and ASC 842. The effects of the new standards will be significant for several entities, inflating balance sheets with the recognition of new assets and liabilities, while these positions will not always be balanced. Income statements, on the other hand, will see front-loaded lease expenses with entries for depreciation and interest more so than operating expenses. Entities must be prepared for several key performance indicators, such as EBITDA and cash flow statement patterns, to be impacted. In summary, the major impacts of IFRS 16 and ASC 842 will include:

- The importance of gathering reliable and complete lease data
- Financial metrics changes
- New thresholds and judgments
- Increased volatility of financial position
- New contract terms
- System and process changes

Now that we've gone over the new regulations broadly, let's next focus on accounting.

### Accounting

IFRS 16 creates the following requirements for presenting lease transactions and their balances:

1. Statement of financial position
   - ROU assets must be presented as their own line items or in combination with PP&E with separate disclosures. This requirement applies to ROU assets defined as investment property; however, these assets must be grouped with investment property.
   - Lease liabilities must be separately presented or included with other liabilities. Line items that have been included in the lease liability must be disclosed.

2. Income statement
   - Amortization of ROU assets must be booked, and amortization expenses must be disclosed in the notes based on the class of the underlying assets.
   - Interest expense must be recognized.
3. Statement of cash flows
   - Lease liabilities cleared with cash payments must be accounted for as financing activities.
   - Cash payments for interest must be accounted for in line with IAS 7 guidelines.
   - Variable, low-value, and short-term lease payments must be recognized as operating activities.

#### Lessee Accounting

An example of the initial journal entries for lessees is as follows:

1. Lessee takes an asset under a lease:
   - Debit ROU asset
   - Credit lease liability
2. Lessee accounts for contract consulting fees:
   - Debit ROU asset
   - Credit supplier
3. Cost of removal discounted to the present value:
   - Debit ROU asset
   - Credit provision for asset removal

In the subsequent measurement of the two elements, the lessee shall recognize the ROU asset using a cost model according to IAS 16 (Property, Plant, and Equipment). The lessee must then depreciate the asset over the lease term. An example of the relevant entries is as follows:

- Debit profit and loss for depreciation
- Credit accumulated depreciation of ROU asset

The lessee may apply IAS 40 (Investment Property) if the ROU asset is an investment property and applies a fair value model. The IAS 16 revaluation model may also be applied if the ROU asset applies the revaluation model and relates to the class of PP&E.

In recognizing interest on the lease liability, the lessee will pass the following entries:

- Debit profit and loss interest expense
- Credit lease liability

Lease payments may also be recognized to reduce the lease liability:

- Debit lease liability
- Credit cash/bank

Lease liabilities must be remeasured if lease terms, lease payments, or discount rates are changed.

#### Lessor Accounting (Finance Leases)

When a lease term commences, the lessor will account for a lease receivable in the balance sheet, where the receivable amount should be equal to the net investment in the lease. The journal entries are as follows:

- Debit lease receivable
- Credit PP&E (the underlying asset)

Subsequently, the lessors shall recognize the lease payments as finance income:

- Debit lease receivable
- Credit profit and loss finance income

The lease receivable must then be reduced by the cash payments received:

- Debit cash/bank
- Credit lease receivable

The finance income received will be accounted for based on a constant periodic rate of return on the lessor's net investment in the lease.

#### Lessor Accounting (Operating Leases)

Lessors will continue recognizing the underlying asset in the balance sheet. Lessors shall also account for the lease income from operating leases over a straight-line basis over the lease term.

**Example**

Let's look at an example to compare the effect the new standard will have on an entity's financial position and income (see Table 1, Table 2, and Figure 3). IFRS 16 will result in a shift in key metrics, and the overall timing of expenses recognized in the income statement will also change.

Entity A has a 5-year lease for a storage unit beginning January 1, 2019, with no option to purchase nor any guaranteed residual value. Payments are $10,000 annually with a rate implicit to the lease of 5%. Depreciation is recognized on a straight-line basis over the lease term, and the present value of the lease payments is $43,295. While net profit under both IFRS 16 and IAS 17 will remain the same, the ROU model alters the presentation of an operating lease's lease payments, resulting in a change in the profit and loss statement. Depreciation and interest expense will be accounted for separately instead of simply presenting the operating expense for both the lease and maintenance under IAS 17. The pattern of lease expense recognition, as noted before, will become front-loaded despite the fact that the cumulative effect on net profit will remain unchanged.

| | Jan. 2019 | Dec. 2019 | Dec. 2020 | Dec. 2021 | Dec. 2022 | Dec. 2023 | Total |
|---|---|---|---|---|---|---|---|
| ROU asset | 0 | 0 | 0 | 0 | 0 | 0 | |
| Lease liability | 0 | 0 | 0 | 0 | 0 | 0 | |
| Operating expense—lease | 0 | 10,000 | 10,000 | 10,000 | 10,000 | 10,000 | 50,000 |
| Net income | 0 | (10,000) | (10,000) | (10,000) | (10,000) | (10,000) | (50,000) |

**Table 1** Impact of IAS 17 on Balance Sheet and Income Statement

| | Jan. 2019 | Dec. 2019 | Dec. 2020 | Dec. 2021 | Dec. 2022 | Dec. 2023 | Total |
|---|---|---|---|---|---|---|---|
| ROU asset | 43,295 | 34,636 | 25,977 | 17,318 | 8,659 | 0 | |
| Lease liability | (43,295) | (35,459) | (27,232) | (18,593) | (9,523) | 0 | |
| Depreciation | 0 | 8, 659 | 8, 659 | 8, 659 | 8, 659 | 8, 659 | 43,295 |
| Interest expense | 0 | 2,164 | 1,772 | 1,361 | 929 | 476 | 6,705 |
| Net income | 0 | (10,823) | (10,431) | (10,020) | (9,588) | (9,135) | (50,000) |

**Table 2** Impact of IFRS 16 on Balance Sheet and Income Statement

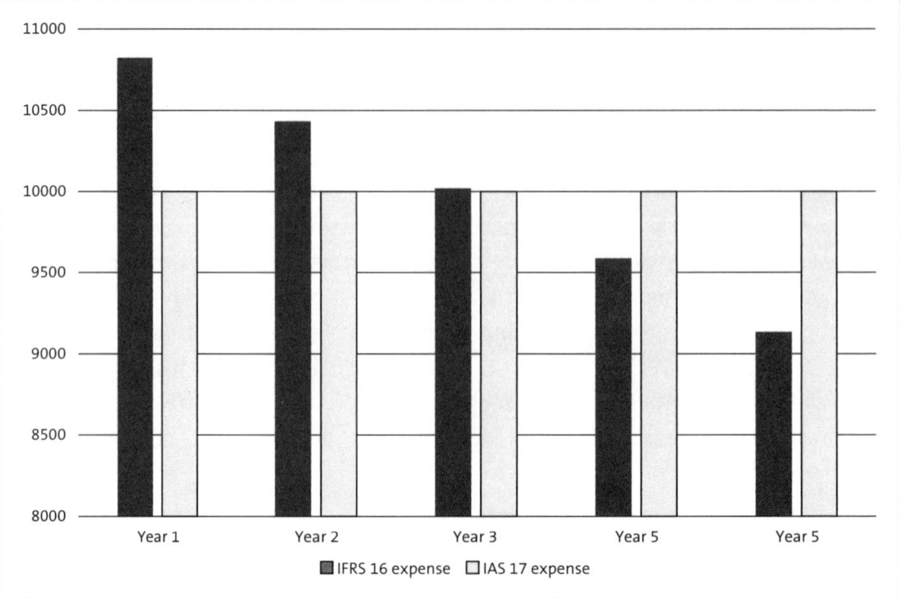


**Figure 3** Operating Expense Comparison

The new accounting treatment under IFRS 16 will result in changes to key financial ratios and metrics. The more commonly affected ratios are:

- Net debt increases
- A higher EBITDA
- An increase in invested capital for the lessee (which will also lower return on invested capital)

Be mindful of these considerations when performing results analysis or when reviewing current regulatory calculations.

### Disclosures and Reporting

New disclosure requirements are particularly relevant to leases in which the entity is a lessee. The transition approach adopted by the entity will impact the disclosures it is required to make.

Under the full retrospective approach, entities must make disclosures about transitioning under IFRS 16 and IAS 8, as shown in Table 3.

| Disclosure Requirements under IFRS 16 | Disclosure Requirements under IAS 8 |
|---|---|
| ■ If IFRS 16 is adopted early, the entity shall disclose this fact.<br>■ If the entity uses practical expedients for lease definition, it must disclose this fact. | ■ The adoption of IFRS 16 must be disclosed, including:<br>– The nature of the changes made to accounting policy<br>– Transitional provisions<br>■ For the current period, prior periods' adjusted amounts to each financial statement line item affected.<br>■ For the current period, prior periods' adjusted amounts of basic and diluted earnings per share.<br>■ The adjusted amount in relation to practicably earlier periods.<br>■ In the scenario where retrospective application is impracticable, the case must be accompanied with an explanation and how IFRS 16 shall be applied. |

**Table 3** Full Retrospective Disclosure Requirements

Similarly, the disclosures shown in Table 4 are required under the modified retrospective approach.

| Disclosure Requirements under IFRS 16 | Disclosure Requirements under IAS 8 |
|---|---|
| ■ If IFRS 16 is adopted early, the entity must disclose this fact.<br>■ If the entity uses practical expedients for lease definition, it must disclose this fact, including:<br>– A statement of any practical expedients that have been used in relation to operating leases<br>– The incremental borrowing rate used in measuring lease liabilities at initial application<br>– Explanations for differences arising between the present value of operating leases disclosed in the previous financial statements, the discounted rate used in the calculation of lease liabilities at initial application, and lease liabilities that were recognized then. | ■ The adoption of IFRS 16 must be disclosed, including:<br>– The nature of the changes made to accounting policy<br>– Transitional provisions<br>– The adjusted amount in relation to practicably earlier periods |

**Table 4** Modified Retrospective Disclosure Requirements

Preparing and presenting these disclosures will involve time and resources and may uncover gaps or pitfalls that exist in your previous disclosures under IAS 17. You must prioritize accuracy and completeness of current disclosures regarding operating leases because analysts and stakeholders rely on these greatly. The impact of adopting the new lease standards should also be comprehensibly and clearly made regardless of the transition approach.

## The Solution: Leasing Systems from SAP

Current processes undertaken by companies (e.g., tracking lease activities through spreadsheets) are inadequate in handling copious amounts of information in an accurate manner. Often, these processes fail to provide:

- Collaboration and communication between the lease administrator, lease accountants, and other stakeholders
- Consistent management of leases across business units
- Automated financial postings arising from lease transactions that are complaint with new standards
- Parallel accounting for IFRS and US GAAP

With majority of leases now being brought on-balance sheet for lessees, entities face huge challenges with disparate processes as they risk inaccurate reporting and noncompliance.

In addition to gathering reliable lease data in preparation for the transition to IFRS 16, companies may also need to update their systems to store new lease information and update them on an ongoing basis in a compliant manner. Processes must also be revisited, and the ability to keep track of ongoing assessments determined. In evaluating readiness, management needs to carefully consider the lease management tools available and determine which would be best for handling their leasing portfolio or if leasing strategies need to be amended at all.

Both SAP Lease Administration and SAP Flexible Real Estate Management (SAP RE-FX) are solutions that facilitate lease administration processes by combining lease abstraction and lease accounting capabilities, thereby allowing entities to fully grasp the impact of several accounting valuations for various standards, in addition to IFRS 16 and ASC 842. However, these two solutions aren't identical: SAP RE-FX is designed to support payment, calculation, and valuation postings for real property leasing, whereas SAP Lease Administration is ideal for handling end-to-end lease contract management and lease lifecycle events.

### SAP Lease Administration by Nakisa

SAP Lease Administration by Nakisa complements SAP Financials solutions, offering functionalities such as lease abstraction, data collection, visualizations, and accounting valuations that collect and consolidate contract information from a myriad of sources. SAP Lease Administration offers a streamlined approach to lease administration; the solution can unify relevant lease information in a single repository, utilizing several data collection formats that offer flexibility in capturing custom attributes for each company's unique processes.

SAP Lease Administration can classify contracts under ASC 840 or IAS 17 and evaluate contracts under ASC 842 and IFRS 16. Lease information can be accurately analyzed against global compliance and accounting standards to bolster better decision-making for your lease portfolio. SAP Lease Administration provides an interface to enter and maintain contractual attributes found in leases and related underlying assets, offering:

- End-to-end lease contract management
- Lease accounting and regulatory compliance with ASC 842 and IFRS 16
- Lease lifecycle events such as extensions, terminations, buy-outs, and reassessments
- Analytics and reporting
- Built-in integration capability with SAP ledgers
- The ability to integrate with other ledger systems

SAP Lease Administration's architecture provides real-time, bidirectional integration with SAP—a sophisticated way to help you avoid redundancies and input errors. SAP Lease Administration can integrate with SAP's financials and logistics modules, namely in the areas of Asset Accounting (AA), SAP General Ledger (GL), Accounts Payable (AP), Material Management (MM), and Investment Management (IM). Of course, you'll need to make configuration decisions for these areas, such as whether new General Ledger accounts need to be created for recognizing ROU assets and lease liabilities, or if new asset classes need to be created in Asset Accounting.

The lease administration process is a complex one, involving several departments in the discussion and planning of business decisions. Make sure you plan for how leases are to be structured and discuss issues involving reporting and conversion. The expertise of implementation teams with experience in SAP finance solutions and SAP Lease Administration is essential to ensure the successful adoption of IFRS 16. Nevertheless, SAP Lease Administration is a powerful tool in data collection and validation, laying a solid foundation for compliance with ASC 842 and IFRS 16. Its functionalities also allow users to grasp the big picture of an entity's leasing portfolio through its reporting and analytics mechanisms.

### SAP Flexible Real Estate Management

A subcomponent of SAP Financials, SAP Flexible Real Estate Management (SAP RE-FX) is another solution that allows entities to manage full lease contract lifecycles. While the module primarily provides the option of processing and managing real estate-related activities and business transactions, SAP RE-FX can also manage IFRS and ASC leasing through the optimization of global lease portfolios.

SAP RE-FX provides greater visibility to its users through a comprehensive view of business transactions on both a macro-level perspective and a granular, individual lease level. SAP RE-FX offers the following:

- Management of real estate: dual master data view that allows for the management of ROU assets
- Contract management: allowing for the management of all contracts in your lease portfolio
- Space management: particularly useful for irregular usage or usual architectural space
- Lease-in: provides greater control of cash flows through a credit side view of the lease-in process
- Control of business processes such as asset management postings and reports

Like SAP Lease Administration, SAP RE-FX streamlines a portfolio of assets globally and offers a centralized repository for lease contract data collection and validation, triggering financial postings derived from valuation calculations.

Lease accountants will be able to evaluate the impact of each lease on financial statements and generate validation postings in accordance with ASC 842 and IFRS 16. With the present value of a lease calculated by the system, an ROU asset and lease liability are automatically created. Thereafter, the system will recognize monthly depreciation of the ROU asset as well as separate the lease payments and interest portions of the payment. Should any rates such as the consumer price index (CPI) increase, the system will immediately revalue the lease—the user will have visibility over incremental differences and track all calculations and postings for a given period.

Fully integrated with SAP Financials, SAP RE-FX can handle entries that have been passed for several lease accounting standards simultaneously, regardless of whether parallel accounting is activated or whether a general ledger account is used. Accountants can run simulations to observe and evaluate the impact an accounting standard may have on a single lease or evaluate its cumulative impact on an entire lease portfolio.

Further, SAP RE-FX's real-time valuation of finance leases reduces the number of applications existing within the system landscape. The complete integration of SAP RE-FX and SAP ERP Financial Accounting has a significant impact in minimizing the risks of data inaccuracy and non-compliance.

With SAP RE-FX, entities can enjoy a system architecture that offers a streamlined integration with SAP modules, reducing risks of input errors or obsolete information. In unifying lease data in a centralized repository, data extraction and validation can occur in a more efficient manner, bolstering better decision-making across business units.

## Summary

You know your organization will be impacted by leasing regulatory changes, and you know what leasing solutions offered by SAP can help you become compliant. But where do you begin?

In Chapter 1, we'll dive deeper into the fundamentals of lease accounting so that you can better understand your organization's requirements and begin to implement SAP Lease Administration and SAP RE-FX.

# Chapter 1
# **Lease Accounting Basics**

*Though a treatise on accounting is outside the scope of this book, this refresher on basic leasing concepts will help with your SAP Flexible Real Estate Management or SAP Lease Administration by Nakisa implementation.*

Before we dive more deeply into implementing SAP's software solutions to reconcile the new leasing requirements International Financial Reporting Standards 16 and Accounting Standards Codification 842, let's review the fundamentals of leasing in Section 1.1. Then, in Section 1.2 and Section 1.3, respectively, we'll differentiate between procedures for lessees and for lessors as we walk through the accounting processes for each role.

## 1.1 Building Blocks of a Lease

A lease is defined as a binding legal contract that outlines the terms and conditions of an agreement for the use of a specific asset for a period of time for a defined amount of regular payments. IFRS 16 and ASC 842 regulate all leases and subleases except for those relating to intangible assets, biological assets, exploration (or the use of non-regenerative resources such as oil and gas), inventory, and assets under construction.

So how do you know if a contract is a lease contract? In this section, we'll walk through the various decision points, continuously referring back to the basic lease contract identification workflow shown in Figure 1.1.

In some cases, leases are broken into multiple lease components. All components of a lease must be part of the contractual agreement and must meet the same criteria. Further, two additional criteria must be met to determine whether the right to use an underlying asset is a separate lease component (per IFRS 16, paragraph B32):

1. The lessee can benefit from use of the underlying asset either on its own or together with other resources that are readily available to the lessee. For example,

if you lease a computer and a separate monitor, you can either use these items on their own or lease another computer/monitor from the same supplier or a different supplier.

2. The underlying asset is neither highly dependent on, nor highly interrelated with, the other underlying assets in the contract. For example, if you buy specific software for a computer that only works on that computer's operating system, then the software is dependent on the computer.

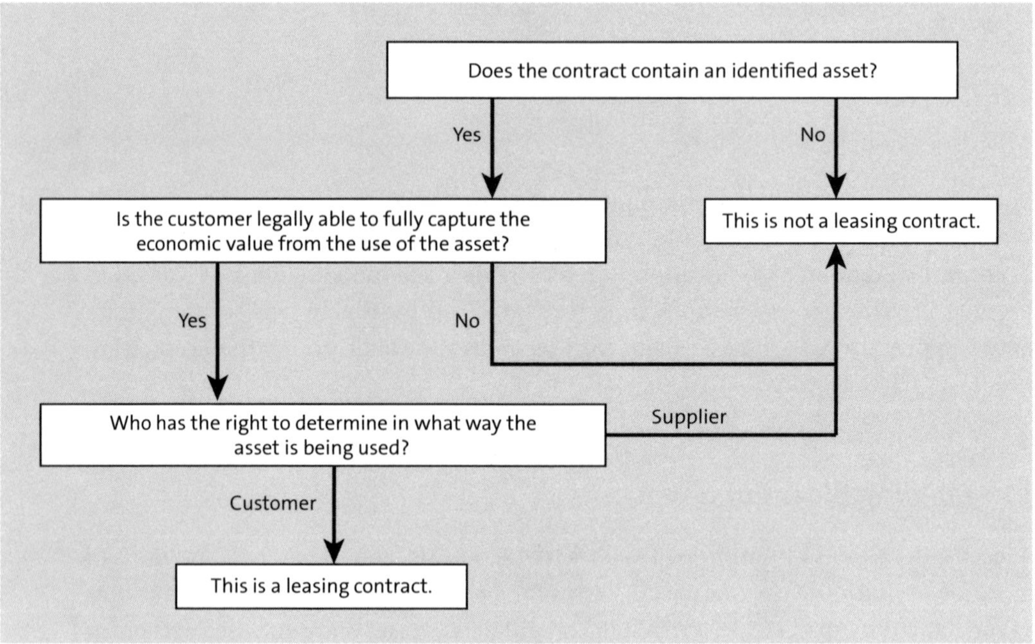


**Figure 1.1** Lease Contract Identification Process

The lease contract identification process looks for two lease components: the identified asset and the right of use of that asset. Let's look at each.

### 1.1.1 Identified Asset

The first question in Figure 1.1 is whether the contract contains an *identified asset*—so let's investigate that term in more detail.

The *identified asset* of a contract can either be explicitly defined in the contract, or it can be implicitly defined when the asset is made accessible for the lessee. Sometimes an asset can also contain another identified asset—for example, when a part of an asset that defines certain capabilities is physically distinct (e.g., the monitor of a computer). We can also identify non-physically distinct parts of an asset, which would be the case if the part substantially represents the entire capability of the whole asset; for example, if a telecommunications provider leases an antenna, that antenna substantially represents the whole asset.

Understanding that, from now on, leases need to be handled differently from service contracts is important. The key distinction is that a lease provides a customer with the right to control the use of an asset, whereas the supplier retains control in a service contract.

### 1.1.2 Right of Use of an Asset

If a contract contains an identified asset, we'll proceed through the flowchart shown in Figure 1.1 to consider whether the contract includes the *right of use* for that asset.

To determine the right of use, your company needs to evaluate whether the lessee has permission to do two things:

- Achieve the full economic benefits of using the identified asset throughout its contractually agreed period. These benefits granted to the lessee would include the economic benefits from commercial transactions with a third party (such as subleasing the asset).
- Define the following:
  - How the asset will be used: The lessee may define the use of an asset by restricting access to its economic benefits to a certain user group or person. In this scenario, the lessee, now entering into a sublease with a third party, only receives economic benefit from the use of the asset by specific group of users (the sublessee) but not from the economic activities (i.e., sales) of the sublessee.
  - Who holds the *right* to direct the use of the identified asset (customer or supplier): In other words, who can decide *what*, *when*, *where*, and/or *how* much type of output is produced?

These decision-making rights are relevant because they affect the economic benefit that can be derived from the use of the asset.

*Protective rights* are the terms and conditions included in the leasing contract that protect the supplier's interest in the identified asset (and/or its related assets and personnel) and ensure that suppliers stay legally compliant with the terms of the lease. Examples of protective rights are terms that define when and/or how much the asset may be used (which would be a limitation of the scope of use). Also, the lessee may be obligated to inform the lessor if the originally intended use changes. Nevertheless, the right to the direct use of the asset would remain unchanged.

### 1.1.3 Lease Modification

A *lease modification* is defined as a change in the terms and conditions of a contract that has implications on the scope of a lease or the financial consideration for a lease. An example of a lease modification would be the addition or termination of the right-of-use to one or more of the underlying assets, or the extension or shortening of the lease term. As shown in Figure 1.2, we must distinguish between restructuring lease payments and changing prices, which would lead to the increase or decrease of the value of the leasing contract. If the lease value decreases, we'll need to remeasure the lease liability; if the lease value increases, the lease modification might require an additional lease contract.

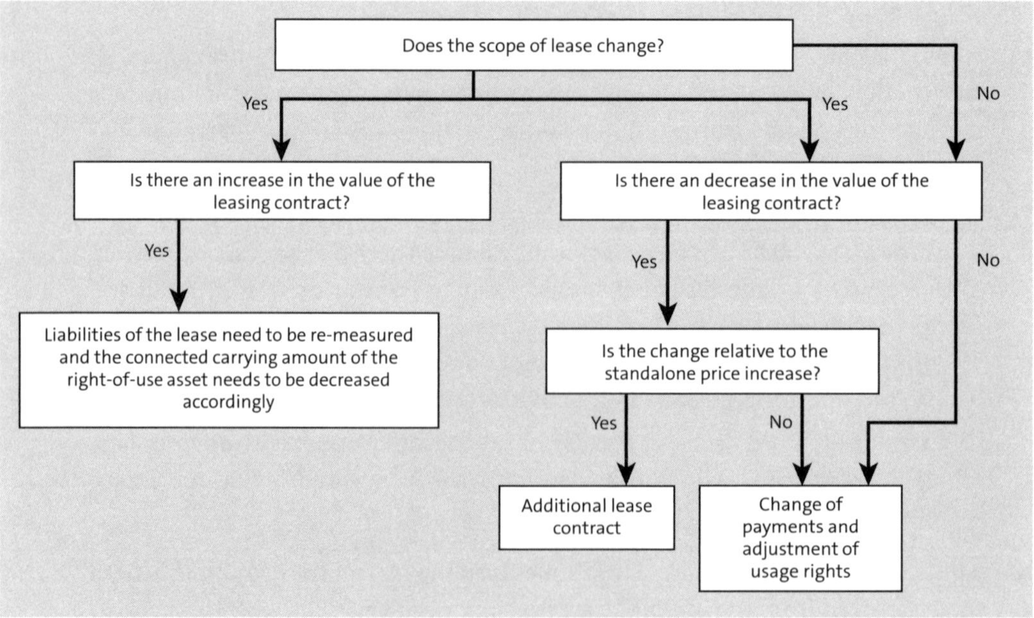


**Figure 1.2** Modification of a Lease

Now that we've defined the lease, let's consider how, depending on whether you're the lessee (the entity using the asset) or the lessor (the entity that owns the asset), lease accounting procedures differ.

## 1.2 Lessee Accounting

This section highlights the new requirements under IFRS 16 and ASC 842 and their implications on lessee accounting. We'll discuss the various accounting treatments adopted by lessees for classification, initial recognition, subsequent measurement, and impairment.

Per IFRS 16, as the lessee, you are not required to differentiate between finance lease contracts (shown on the balance sheet) and operating lease contracts (kept off the balance sheet). The lessee must identify the right-of-use asset (ROU asset) and the corresponding lease liability for nearly all lease contracts, on the economic basis that a lease contract is the acquisition of a right to use an underlying asset with the purchase price paid in installments.

In other words, the new lessee accounting model under IFRS 16 follows a single lease accounting model without a lease classification test. In practice, most leases will be reflected *on* the balance sheet, as shown in Figure 1.3: The lessee recognizes the ROU asset and the lease liability, which is recorded as the purchase of an asset on a finance basis. The lessee will also recognize the interest on the lease liability and the depreciation on the ROU asset in its profit and loss statement.

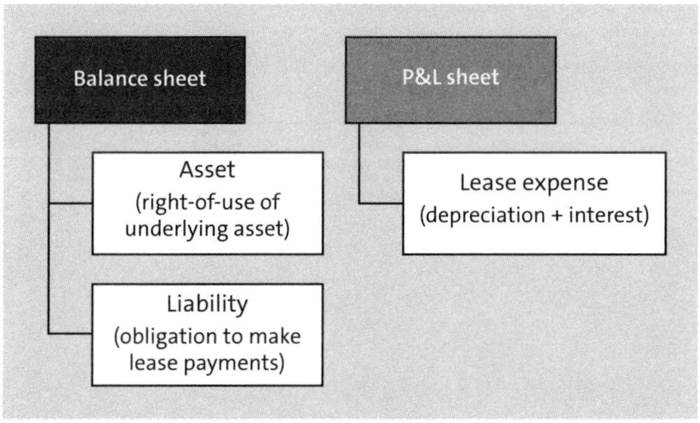


**Figure 1.3** Balance Sheet vs. Profit and Loss Statement

### 1.2.1 Lease Classification

Lease classification—or the determination of the lease type—affects how the lessee recognizes the lease expense on its profit and loss statement after the initial recognition. Figure 1.4 walks through the five criteria of the lease classification for the lessee.

If the answer to any of these questions is "yes," then the lease is a finance lease; otherwise, the lease is an operating lease.

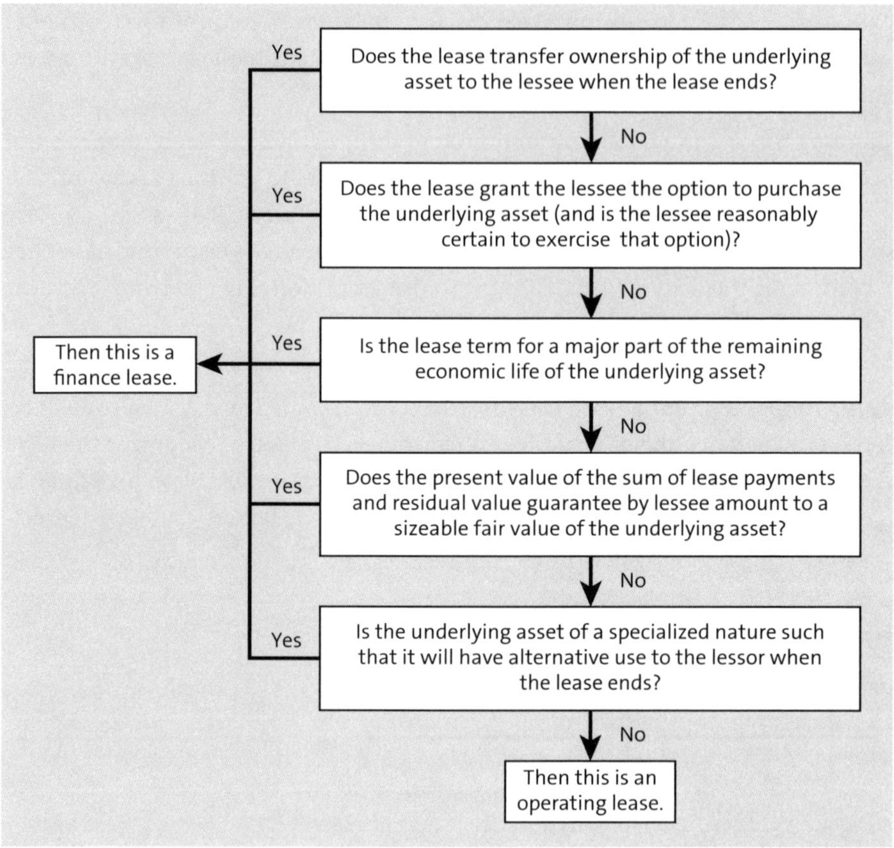


**Figure 1.4** Lease Classification for the Lessee

Let's look at each criterion more closely.

### Transfer of Ownership

The lessee classifies the lease as a finance lease when a *transfer of ownership* of the underlying asset to the lessee will occur by the end of the lease term—for example, when you lease a car for 12 months and then own it outright. A finance lease includes the automatic transfer of legal title under the lease agreement or under a side agreement. This criterion is also met when the lessee is obliged to pay an additional nominal fee for the legal transfer of ownership.

However, if the lessee can decide *not* to pay the nominal fee (resulting in the lessee having the option *not* to purchase the underlying asset), this provision does not meet the criteria on the transfer of ownership.

#### Purchase Option

The lease offers an option to purchase the underlying asset at an expected price lower than the fair value, and the lessee is reasonably certain to exercise it under the significant economic incentive.

In some lease arrangements, a lessee's parent company (instead of the lessee) is reasonably certain to try to exercise the option to purchase the underlying asset at a low value at the end of the lease term. If *only* the lessee has the right of use of the underlying asset, but not the parent company, then the lease is classified as a finance lease.

#### Lease Term

The lease term is defined as the non-cancellable period of the lease. In addition, periods may be included that cover an option to extend or to terminate—if the lessee is reasonably certain to exercise these options. The lease term is reassessed in only very limited circumstances.

To address concerns over possibly controversial interpretations of the term "reasonably certain" under IAS 17, then under IFRS 16, the lessee must consider all relevant facts and circumstances that bring an *economic incentive* to exercise or forfeit the options to extend and/or terminate early.

When the lease term is for the major part (defined as at least 75%) of the remaining economic life of the underlying asset, the lessee has the right to purchase the underlying asset, and the lease will be classified as finance lease. If the lease start date is at or near the end of the economic life of the underlying asset, this criterion does not apply.

#### Present Value

The present value is the sum of the lease payments and guaranteed residual value by the lessee and any other amounts already contained in the lease payments. If the present value is equal to or greater than 90% of the fair value of the underlying asset, this criterion is met. The guaranteed residual value excludes amounts that are already recorded in the lease payments. The attributes that make up a lease payment will be covered shortly.

### Leased Asset of a Specialized Nature

The lease of the underlying asset is of such a specialized nature that the asset affords no alternative use to the lessor at the end of the lease term (e.g., chemical catalysts that only a lessee with the appropriate equipment can use). When this criterion is met, the lessee will classify the lease as a finance lease. Otherwise, the lessee will treat the lease as an operating lease.

## 1.2.2 Initial Recognition and Measurement

On the start date of the lease, the lessee is to recognize the ROU asset and the lease liability. However, this recognition is subject to optional exemptions: short-term leases, portfolio-level leases, and leases of low-value or underlying assets.

Table 1.1 lists the optional recognition exemptions under IFRS 16. For short-term leases, the lessee is to consider the outcome options to extend or to terminate. The lessee will also have to record the lease as a new lease if the lease is modified or the lease term changed (i.e., extending beyond 12 months). On the other hand, the lessee and lessor may decide to apply a portfolio approach for leases on the condition that a material difference is not created in comparison with lease accounting at the contract level. Additionally, leases that share similar characteristics (e.g., small IT office equipment or some office furniture of "low-value assets or underlying assets") can be grouped.

| Short-Term Leases | Portfolio-Level Leases | Low-Value or Underlying Asset (International Accounting Standards Board only) |
|---|---|---|
| ▪ The lease term is less than or equal to 12 months.<br>▪ Exemptions apply to all leases with the same class of underlying assets.<br>▪ Excludes leases with the option to purchase. | ▪ Leases with similar characteristics, i.e., share reasonably expected results that do not materially differ among the individual leases.<br>▪ May apply to lessees and lessors. | ▪ The asset value is less than or equal to USD $5,000 when new.<br>▪ Selection on lease-by-lease basis.<br>▪ Excludes assets highly dependent or interrelated with other assets and head lease |

**Table 1.1** IFRS 16 Optional Recognition Exemptions

When the lessee decides to apply the optional exemption for short-term leases or for leases of low-value/underlying assets, the lease payments are recorded as an expense on a straight-line basis over the lease term or another systematic basis.

### Right-of-Use of Asset

According to IFRS 16, on the start date, the lessee defines the *right-of-use asset* at cost. Figure 1.5 shows the cost equation for the ROU asset: the total sum of lease liabilities, prepaid lease payments, initial direct costs, and estimated costs to dismantle/remove/restore (measured per IAS 17) *less* the lease incentive receivables.

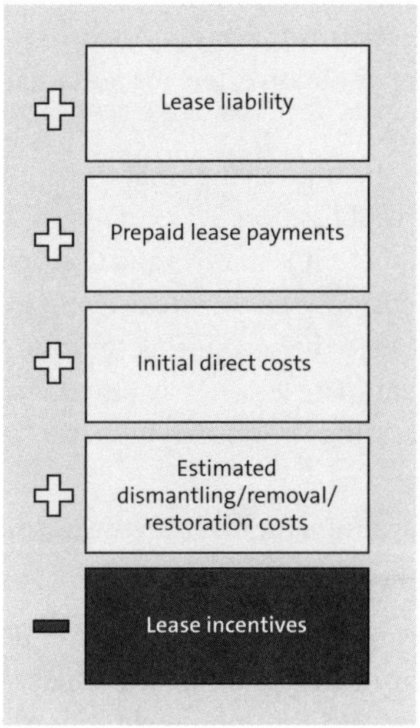


**Figure 1.5** Right-of-Use Asset at Cost Equation

Pausing for a moment our discussion of lease liability, let's look at each element of the cost equation:

- Any *prepaid lease payments* made before the start date of the lease (for use of the underlying asset) are to be recorded as prepaid rent. The prepaid amount is to be reclassified to the ROU asset on the lease start date. As a result, the ROU asset is increased for any lease payments made by the lessee at or before the start date of the lease.

- *Initial direct costs* are additional costs in the lessee's ROU asset, not part of the lease liability. These costs incur when the lease is executed. However, direct or indirect costs relating to the lease negotiation and arrangement are not part of the initial direct cost.
  - The following costs are *included* in the initial direct costs: commissions, legal fees and lease document preparation costs (after lease execution), payables to existing tenants for moving, and consideration paid for the guaranteed residual value by an unrelated third party.
  - The following costs are *excluded* from the initial direct costs: general overhead (employee salaries), internal engineering costs, legal fees for services rendered and negotiation of lease term and conditions (before lease execution), advertising, depreciation, and costs related to an idle asset or obtain offers for potential leases.
- *Restoration costs* are what the lessee pays to restore the underlying asset to a specific condition for the lessor. The lessee records this obligation by recognizing a provision in accordance with IAS 37 (Provisions, Contingent Liabilities and Contingent Assets). The initial carrying amount of the provision is taken into account in the initial measurement of the ROU asset, which links to the accounting for restoration costs in IAS 16 (Property, Plant and Equipment). The lessee may also incur *dismantling/removal costs* for taking apart and relocating the underlying asset to the lessor's original site.
- *Lease incentives* are the payments received or the reimbursements from the lessor to the lessee during the lease term.

Generally, the initial measurement of the ROU asset is similar to most other non-financial assets that are measured initially at cost—for example, to asset measurement per IAS 16 (Property, Plant and Equipment) and IAS 38 (Intangible Assets). However, no clear definition of an ROU asset is in the scope of IAS 16 or IAS 38 by IFRS 16 because ROU assets constitute a new group of assets introduced in the scope of IFRS 16.

**Example**

A lessee has signed a contract for a ten-year term with a lessor to lease a high-speed train on July 1, 2018. The lease begins on August 1, 2018, with initial direct costs of $2,600 incurred. The lessee pays a monthly lease of $20,000 and receives an incentive of $80,000 in cash when the lease takes effect.

For initial lease liability, the lessee computes the present value of lease payables with the discount rate (*if any*): $880,000.

**ROU asset computed by lessee:**

Initial recognition of lease liability *$880,000*

Lease payables at or before start date *$20,000*

Initial direct costs *$2,600*

*Less* lease incentives received *–$80,000*

Therefore, initial recognition of ROU asset *$822,600*

**Journal entry on the lease effective date, July 1, 2018, recorded by the lessee:**

*Dr. Prepaid Rent $20,000*

*Cr. Cash $20,000*

[To record the initial lease payment upon which the lease begins]

*Dr. Cash $100,000*

*Cr. Lease Incentive $80,000*

*Cr. Prepaid Rent $20,000*

[To record the lease incentives received from lessor]

**Journal entry on the lease start date, August 1, 2018, recorded by the lessee:**

*Dr. ROU asset $880,000*

*Cr. Lease Liability $880,000*

[To record the ROU asset and lease liability]

*Dr. Lease Incentive $80,000*

*Cr. ROU asset $80,000*

[To reclassify the lease incentives as an offset to the ROU asset]

*Dr. ROU asset $2,600*

*Cr. Accrued Expenses $2,600*

[To record the initial direct costs]

### Lease Liability

According to IFRS 16, at the start date, the lessee defines the lease liability as the sum of the lease payments and the expected payments until the lease ends at the present value. Figure 1.6 shows the equation for the present value of the lease liability.

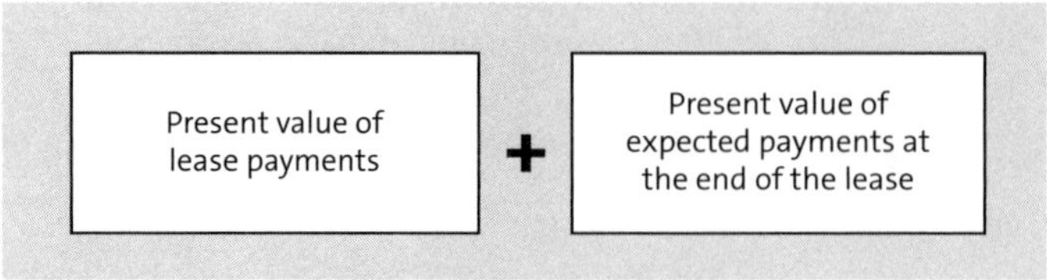


**Figure 1.6** Present Value of the Lease Liability

*Lease payments* defined in the initial measurement of the lease liability include fixed payments (including in-substance fixed payments) minus any lease incentive receivables, variable lease payments that depend on an index or rate, guaranteed residual value amounts expected to be payable by the lessee, the exercise price of purchase options (if the lessee is reasonably certain to this option), and termination option penalties (if the lease term shows the lessee exercising this option).

On the other hand, the following types of payments are excluded in the lease liability: variable lease payments that depend on sales or usage of the underlying asset and payments for non-lease components, unless the lessee decides to combine lease and non-lease components.

The discount rate is part of the total lease payment. The lessee uses the *implicit interest rate* in the lease to compute the present value of the lease payment. This rate is the amount that results in the equilibrium of the sum of the present value of the lease payment and the guaranteed residual value versus the sum of the fair value of the underlying assets and the initial direct costs (by the lessor).

When the implicit interest rate is unavailable, the lessee uses an *incremental borrowing rate* (IBR), which is defined as the rate the lessee pays on the first day of the lease for "a loan" with the same terms and security.

IFRS 16 states the *guaranteed residual value* must reflect the reasonable expectation of the amount payable by the lessee. In contrast, under IAS 17, the lessee must include the maximum amount guaranteed in the lease liability, for instance, in a finance lease. However, the standard does *not* indicate whether the expectation should be based on a probability-weighted approach or on the most probable outcome.

**Example**

A lessee has signed a lease contract with the lessor to lease an industrial machine of which the lease term is ten years. Additionally, the lessee and the lessor settle on a guaranteed residual value: If the fair value of the industrial machine when the lease term ends is below $1,000, then the lessee shall pay the lessor an amount equal to the difference between $1,000 and the fair value of the industrial machine.

At the start of the lease, the lessee expects the fair value of the industrial machine is $1,000 when the lease term ends. The lessee thus includes a zero amount in the lease payments for calculating the residual value portion of the lease liability. The lessee subsequently measures the fair value of the industrial machine when the lease term ends. The lessee then remeasures the lease liability, if the expected fair value of the industrial machine is below $1,000, to take into account the amount expected to be payable (as the actual residual value owed) using an unchanged discount rate.

*Fixed payments* defined by IFRS 16 are the amount the lessee pays the lessor for the right-of-use of the underlying asset during the lease term. Variable lease payments are excluded from this definition, but mandatory "in-substance" fixed lease payments are included under IFRS 16 even though these payments may be unpreventably varied.

**Example**

A lessee has signed a lease contract of six years for commercial equipment, with $60,000 *fixed payables* on the last day of each year. The lessee records all yearly payments at the present value during the initial recognition of the lease liability. If the lessee uses a discount rate of 6%, the lease liability on the lease's start date can be calculated as shown in Table 1.2.

| ($) | Y1 | Y2 | Y3 | Y4 | Y5 | Y6 |
|---|---|---|---|---|---|---|
| **Lease Payments** | 60,000 | 60,000 | 60,000 | 60,000 | 60,000 | 60,000 |
| **Discount** | 56,400 | 53,016 | 49,835 | 46,845 | 44,034 | 41,392 |
| *Lease liability on the start date* | | | | | | **$291,522** |

**Table 1.2** Commercial Equipment Lease Liability

*Variable lease payments (in-substance fixed/index/rate)* comprise mainly of in-substance fixed payments, variable lease payments depending on index or rate, and other kinds of payments.

**Example**

A lessee rents one floor unit of a commercial office for a six-year lease term with an initial $80,000 annual payment. Starting in the second year, and then for each subsequent year, this payment rises by 2.5% of the lessee's sales or 5% of the former lease payment rate on each lease start date.

For the purposes of lease classification, the lease payments are *fixed annual lease payments* of $80,000 with additional 5% hikes. Regardless of sales revenue, the lessee is obliged to pay an additional 5% each year. Henceforth, this increment level is an *in-substance fixed lease payment.*

Common types of indices that lease payments may depend on include the consumer price index (CPI), producer price indices (PPIs), retail prices indices (RPIs), house price indices (HPIs), and average earnings indices.

**Example**

A lessee rents several floor units in SoHo (commercial/residential mixed-use) for a lease term of six years. The lease involves an initial $680,000, payable on an annual basis, to be evaluated annually and incrementally changed according to the consumer price index (CPI) and the house price index (HPI).

This rental lease covers *variable lease payments* depending on indices. Thus, the lease liability on the lease's start date is calculated as shown in Table 1.3.

| ($) | Y1 | Y2 | Y3 | Y4 | Y5 | Y6 |
|---|---|---|---|---|---|---|
| **Lease Payables** | 680,000 | 748,000 | 822,800 | 905,080 | 995,588 | 1,095,147 |
| **CPI (4%)** | - | 29,920 | 32,912 | 36,203 | 39,823 | 43,805 |
| **HPI (6%)** | - | 44,880 | 49,368 | 54,305 | 59,735 | 65,708 |
| | 680,000 | 822,800 | 905,080 | 995,588 | 1,095,147 | 1,204,661 |
| *Lease liability plus variables* | | | | | | **$5,703,276** |

**Table 1.3** SoHo Lease Liability plus Variables

### 1.2.3 Reassessment and Subsequent Measurement

After the lease start date, the lessee and lessor may agree to modify the lease to change the lease extension or termination terms, to change the payment schedule, or to lease additional space in the same property.

Figure 1.7 shows how the lessee analyzes a change in the lease; the outcome is either a new lease separate from the original lease or a single modified lease. Note that the accounting approach for the original lease is not impacted by the modification.

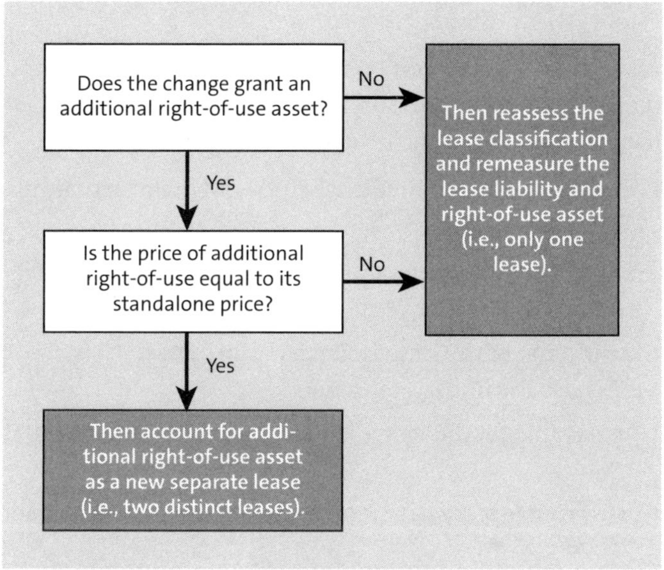


**Figure 1.7** Lessee Analysis of a Change in the Lease

For a modified lease, the lessee will reassess the lease classification and remeasure the lease liability and ROU asset. A modified lease may also contain multiple components.

**Example**

After the start date of a two-year lease term for 1,000 square meters at $20,000 per month, the lessee and lessor decide to expand the lease space by 500 square meters on the floor unit for the remaining lease term for an extra $5,000 per payment. Thus, the lessee will pay $25,000 monthly after the lease modification.

Therefore, the lessee should account for this lease modification as a new and separate lease since the *additional right-of-use asset* is being granted at a *price equal to the standalone price* for the extra lease space.

On the new lease start date, the lessee now has two separate leases: the initial lease for 1,000 square meters for two years and a new lease for the extra 500 square meters for 1.5 years, once extra space is available for use.

**Lease Liability**

According to ASC 842, the lessee must reassess certain assumptions made at the lease start date (e.g., whether exercising a renewal or purchase option is reasonably certain); remeasure the lease liability; and adjust the related ROU asset.

You'll need to reassess and remeasure lease elements when the following situations arise:

- The lease contract was modified to the extent that the combined contract is accounted as one lease.
- A trigger event affected the certainty of the lessee exercising an option to renew or terminate the lease or to purchase the underlying asset.
- The amount expected to be payable by the lessee under the guaranteed residual value changed.
- The contingency upon which variable lease payments were required was resolved.

As shown in Figure 1.8, each of these situations requires a specific reassessment workflow.

**Example**

A lessee has signed a non-cancellable lease contract with the lessor to lease a commercial office floor unit of the Main Tower building in Frankfurt, Germany. The lease term is for an initial period of six years at $1,000,000 paid annually. The lessee has a renewal option of an additional four years at similar rental price as a lease extension.

The lessee includes these factors to identify and derive the lease term:

- The lessee plans to carry out business in the same district for a minimum of 12 years. The Main Tower location is convenient and ideal for establishing strong relationships with business clients and vendors.

- The market rental forecast for a comparable building in the same district like the Japan Center involves 6% increases over the 10-year time frame covered by the lease. Lease rentals are in line with the current rental market trends at lease start.

Based on these factors, the lessee concludes that a *significant economic incentive for lease extension/renewal* exists. Hence, for the purposes of accounting for the lease, the lessee also uses a lease term of 10 years.

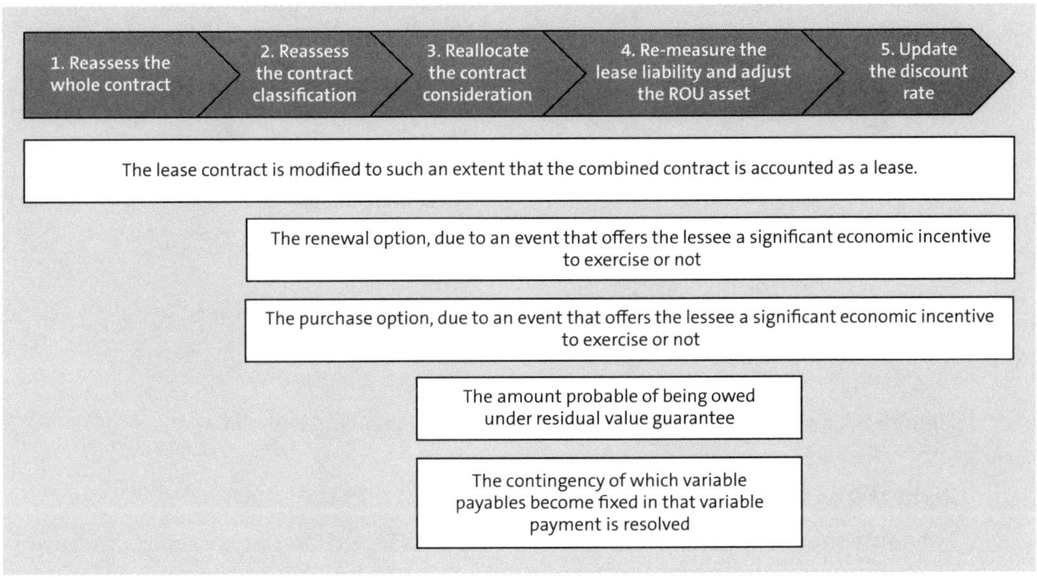


**Figure 1.8** Reassessment and Remeasurement of a Lease

After the start date, the lease liability will be subsequently measured by certain changes in the amount of liability being carried, while the ROU asset is measured using a cost model. Subsequently, the lessee is *not* allowed to measure the lease liability at fair value. And the remeasurement in the lease liability will affect the ROU asset to be adjusted accordingly.

Figure 1.9 describes the changes in the carrying amount of lease liability leading to a right-of-use adjustment or to the recognition of a profit or loss:

- IFRS 16 permits an exceptional reassessment of the discount rate during the lease term if a change in the lease terms or a reassessment relating to the purchase option occurs.

- The lessee is to reassess variable lease payments that are determined by reference to the index or rate only when cash flow would change due to a change in the reference index or rate (e.g., a change in the future lease payments resulting from a change in the index or rate used to determine those payments).

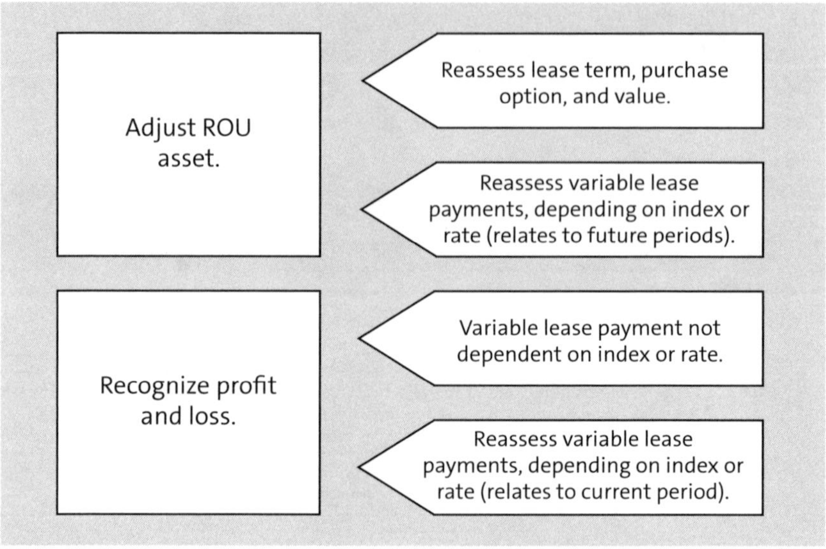


**Figure 1.9** Changes in Carrying Amount of Lease Liability

### Right-of-Use Asset

For subsequent measurement, the lessee records ROU assets at cost minus accumulated depreciation and accumulated impairment losses and adjusts the remeasurement of the lease liability.

ROU asset depreciation under IAS 16 follows straight-line deprecation cost methods and shows consumption patterns reflecting the future economic benefits for the ROU asset.

ROU asset depreciation starts at the lease start date. These factors affect the period of coverage for asset depreciation.

When the ownership of the underlying asset is transferred to the lessee or a purchase option may reasonably be exercised by the lessee, then the depreciation period lasts until the end of the underlying asset's useful life; otherwise, the depreciation period lasts until the earlier of the end of the ROU assets' useful life or the end of the lease term.

### 1.2.4 Capital Lease/Asset Impairment

The lessee determines whether a lease is either a financed purchase or an arrangement to obtain usage rights to an asset for a specified period. The lessee classifies the lease as a finance lease when one or more lease classification criteria under ASC 842, paragraph 10-25-2, are met.

For finance leases, the lessee must measure the ROU asset and lease liability at the present value of the lease payments on the balance sheet. Interest on the lease liability is recognized separately from the amortization of the ROU asset in the income statement. The statement of cash flows also records the repayments of principal portion of lease liability (financing activities), interest payments of lease liability (operating activities), and variable lease payments (operating activities).

On the lease start date, the lessee measures the lease liability as the present value of the future lease payments and the ROU assets at cost.

**Example**

A lessee has signed a lease contract with a lessor to lease a commercial property (land included). The lease term is 20 years, with a 10-year renewal option. The lease payment $1,000,000 is per year, with 10% annual increases, at beginning of each year. The fair value of the underlying lease asset is $10,000,000, with an expected economic life of 40 years. The lessee has received $500,000 in incentives in Year 5, for normal tenant improvements. The discount rate is estimated at 10%. Other features in this lease include provisions that the title to the property would not automatically be transferred to the lessee when the lease expires; that no guaranteed residual value or initial direct costs for the underlying asset can be incurred by the lessee; and that the lessee bears the costs of maintenance, taxes, and insurance separately from lease payments.

The schedule of lease payments on yearly basis ($'000) is shown in Table 1.4. In Year 5, the lessee received $500k in lease incentives.

| Y1 | Y2 | Y3 | Y4 | Y5 | Y6 | Y7 | Y8 | Y9 | Y10 |
|---|---|---|---|---|---|---|---|---|---|
| 1,000 | 1,100 | 1,200 | 1,300 | 900* | 1,500 | 1,600 | 1,700 | 1,800 | 1,900 |
| **Y11** | Y12 | Y13 | Y14 | Y15 | Y16 | Y17 | Y18 | Y19 | Y20 |
| 2,000 | 2,100 | 2,200 | 2,300 | 2,400 | 2,500 | 2,600 | 2,700 | 2,800 | 2,900 |
| Total | | | | | | | | **$38,500,000** | |

**Table 1.4** Commercial Property Lease Payment Schedule

The lessee classifies this lease as the finance lease per classification criteria.

**Analysis the lessee uses to measure and record this finance lease:**

PV of lease payments, less incentives ($'000) $13,743,79

PV of purchase option at the end of the lease term ($'000) $22,124,81

Total lease liability ($'000) $35,868,61

**Journal entry on the lease start date recorded by the lessee:**

*Dr. ROU asset ($'000) $35,868,61*

*Cr. Lease Liability ($'000) $35,868,61*

Over the lease's term, the lessee amortizes the ROU asset and enters the interest expenses on the lease liability on the lease start date. Subsequent measurements on the income statement and the lease depend on the lease classification.

**Example**

A lessee has signed a lease contract with a lessor to lease a commercial property. The lease term is ten years, with $680,000 payable annually on the last day of the year. The lessee's incremental borrowing rate (effective interest rate) is 10%, and the initial recognition for lease payments is $6,120,000.

At the end of Year 1, the lessee makes the first annual lease payment of $680,000 to the lessor. Of this payment, the interest expense is $6,120,000 × 10% = $612,000, and the principal payment is $680,000 – $612,000 = $68,000. Thus, the lease liability has decreased by $68,000. At the start of Year 2, the carrying amount of the lease liability is $6,120,000 – $68,000 = $6,052,000.

A lessee can adopt IAS 36 (Impairment of Assets) to identify and account for ROU asset impairment, if any. When an impairment loss has been recognized, the lessee also adjusts the future depreciation costs for the ROU asset to revise the amount of liability being carried.

When a lessee records an impairment cost on an ROU asset associated with a finance lease, it should revise the amortization expense by calculating a new straight-line amortization based on the revised asset value.

**Example**

A lessee signed a lease contract for an industrial machine for factory operation over a non-cancellable period of eight years. The ROU asset's initial carrying amount ($800) is later measured at cost and on a straight-line depreciation over the eight-year period. In other words, the annual depreciation cost is $100.

On the last day of Year 6, an impairment to the cash-generating unit including the ROU asset occurs. An allocation of $80 in impairment costs is made for the ROU asset.

Prior to the impairment, the ROU asset's carrying amount was $600. After the impairment, the carrying amount is reduced to $520 and imminent annual depreciation cost is recalculated as $260 ($520 ÷ 2 years remaining on the lease).

### 1.2.5 Operating Lease

The lessee classifies the lease as an operating lease when none of the criteria found in ASC 842, paragraph 10-25-2, are met.

**Example**

A lessee has signed a lease contract with a lessor to lease commercial equipment. The lease term is ten years with no renewal option. The lease payment is $1,000,000 at the beginning of each month. The lessee has the option to purchase the equipment at fair market value when the lease expires. The economic life of the equipment is ten years. Other features in this lease include provisions that the title to the equipment remains with the lessor, that the fair value of the equipment is $50,000 with no guaranteed residual value when the lease expires; that neither incentives nor initial direct costs will be incurred by the lessee; and that the lessee bears all maintenance costs separately from the lease payments.

Let's walk through the analysis the lessee uses to measure and record this operating lease. The lessee first computes the lease liability—i.e., (12 months × 10 years) × $1,000,000 = $120,000,000—the present value of the monthly; and the fixed lease payments over the entirety of the lease term.

The present value of the ROU asset is equal to the lease liability since, on or before lease start date, initial direct costs, prepaid lease payments, or lease incentives do not need to be adjusted.

**Journal entry on the lease start date recorded by the lessee:**

*Dr. ROU asset $120,000,000*

*Cr. Lease Liability $120,000,000*

If, after remeasurement, the classification of an operating lease does not change, then the lessee should to calculate the single lease expense after the remeasurement as the total sum of future, undiscounted cash flows and ROU asset minus the lease liability at the remeasurement date divided by the remaining lease term.

When the original finance lease is remeasured and reclassified as an operating lease, the lessee must consider any differences between the carrying amount of the ROU asset after recording the remeasurement adjustment and the carrying amount of the ROU asset that would have resulted from initial classification of the lease *as an operating lease* (e.g., a rent prepayment or a lease incentive).

Now that we've gone over how lessees account for lease contracts, let's change gears and discuss lessor accounting.

## 1.3 Lessor Accounting

When compared to IAS 17, IFRS 16 does not contain any substantial changes to lessor accounting. The lessor still must classify leases as either finance or operating leases, depending on whether all risks and rewards incidental to owning the underlying asset are to be substantially transferred.

For a lessor, the most important task is to determine which set of accounting rules must be applied to a lease by executing a lease classification according to IAS 17 classification rules. Generally, as shown in Figure 1.10, due to the dual lessor accounting model, the outcome of such a classification will be either an operating lease or a finance lease.

For a finance lease, the lessor recognizes a receivable at an amount equal to total net investment, which is the present value of the aggregate of lease payments receivable by the lessor and any unguaranteed residual value.

For an operating lease, the lessor continues to recognize the underlying assets. However, some changes to current requirements are worth mentioning. Especially when considering the requirements under IFRS 15, the lessor will have to incorporate some new requirements surrounding revenue recognition in the accounting rules.

For a finance lease, lessors are required to capitalize receivables in the balance sheet amounting to the total net investment. Outstanding lease payments are treated by the lessor as principal repayments and financial income.

For an operating lease where the lessor is the legal and economic owner of the leased asset, the lessor must capitalize the leased asset in its balance sheet. The valuation at initial recognition is at acquisition or production cost.

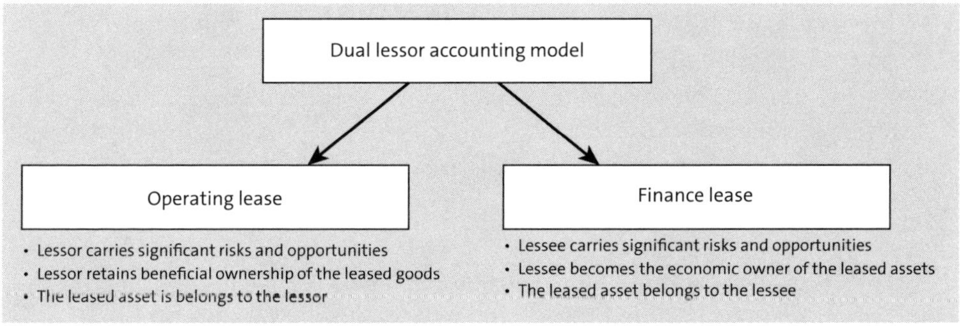


**Figure 1.10** Lease Classification for Lessors

### 1.3.1 Lease Classification

IAS 17 distinguishes between finance leases and operating leases. For lease classification in accordance with IAS 17, the economic content of the contractual relationship is more important than its legal structure. Therefore, understanding the guidelines from the International Accounting Standards Board (IASB) to narrow the scope for accounting policy measures is important. Figure 1.11 shows the relevant classification steps for lessors to identify the kind of lease they have to account for.

To suggest a better financial position on the balance sheet, lessees are usually anxious to outsource leased assets and liabilities from the balance sheet. However, the result is that information relevant to the balance sheet isn't shown in the financial statements. This off-balance sheet status is what runs contrary to the principles of IFRS 16, and the IASB endeavors to prevent economically unjustified, off-balance sheet arrangements through appropriate accounting rules.

Thus, to achieve a true and fair view of leases, the IASB uses a risk-and-reward approach in lease accounting. A key factor in classifying finance leases or operating leases is the distribution of the rewards and risks associated with underlying assets.

**Example**

A car leasing company and a customer agree on a non-cancellable lease contract for one year. The useful life of the car is estimated to be five years, and ownership of the car will remain with the leasing company. No purchase, renewal, or early termination options exist in the leasing contract. The market fair value of the car is $80,000, and the present value of the lease payments is $40,000.

To determine the classification of the lease and the subsequent accounting rules, the car leasing company assesses the following:

- The car still belongs to the leasing company; hence, no ownership is transferred.
- No purchase option exists in the contract.
- The lease term is one-fifth of the useful life of the car and does not represent a majority of the asset's useful life.
- The present value of the lease annuities represents 50% of the fair market value of the car.

Based on these criteria, the leasing company concludes that the lease has no indicators of a finance lease. The risk and rewards and the ownership of the car stay with the leasing company; thus, the lease must be classified as an operating lease.

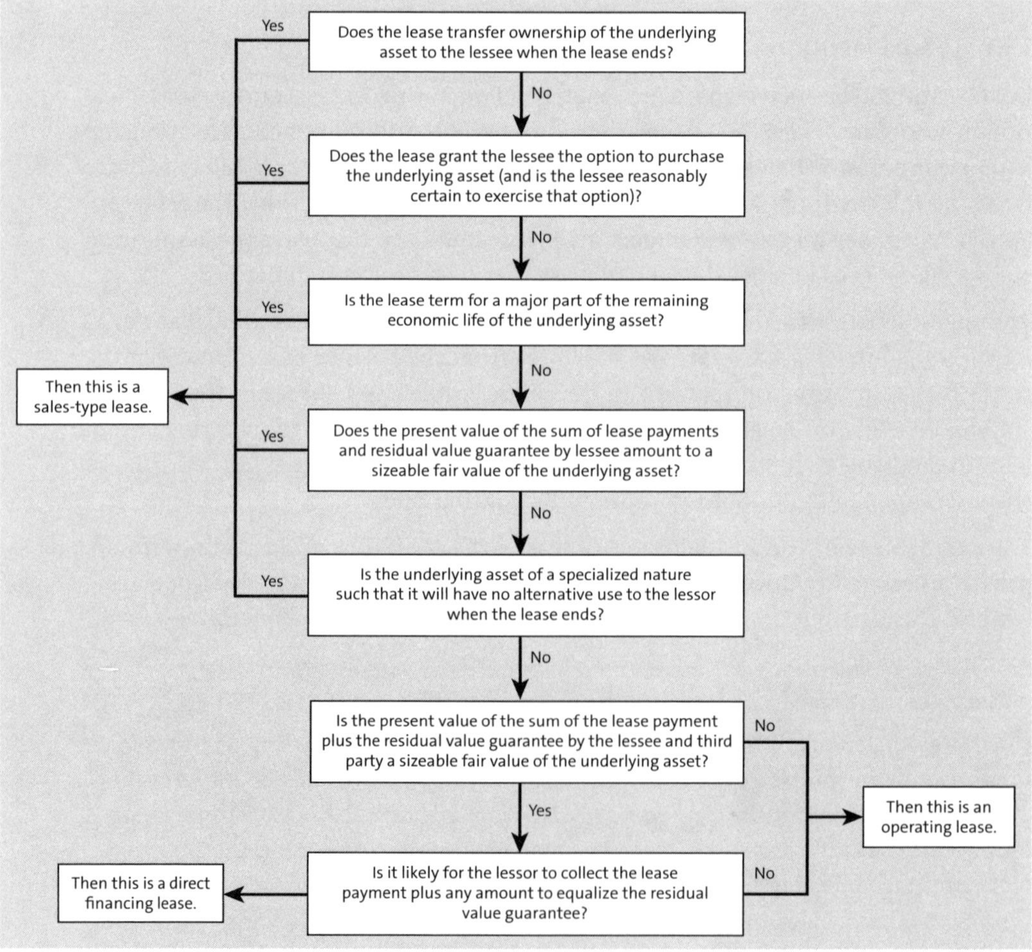


**Figure 1.11** Lease Classification Criteria for the Lessor

### 1.3.2 Lease Components versus Non-Lease Components

Regardless of their classification as operating or finance leases, many leasing contracts include non-lease components such as services, maintenance, insurance, and consumables. It's particularly common for leases in the healthcare industry to have such multielement arrangements to make their offerings more attractive to customers by reducing the equipment leasing portion to a minimum amount and letting the non-leasing components generate the bulk of the revenue.

Before IFRS 15 and IFRS 16, such multielement arrangements did not pose any challenge for accounting. IFRS 15 and IFRS 16 basically use similar criteria for separating lease and non-lease components, based on whether the goods and services are distinct. If both of the following statements are true, then the lessor must distinguish between lease components and non-lease components in their contracts:

- The lessee can benefit from use of the asset either on its own or together with other resources that are readily available to the lessee (IFRS 16, paragraph B32(a)). "Readily available" resources are goods or services that are sold or leased separately (by the lessor or other suppliers) or resources that the lessee has already obtained (from the lessor or from other transactions or events).
- The underlying asset is neither dependent on, nor highly interrelated with, the other underlying components in the contract.

Lessors should apply the guidance found in IFRS 15 (Revenue from Contracts with Customers) when allocating the transaction price to separate components. Allocation is based on the relative standalone selling prices (SSPs); if no observable information is available, then entities must estimate SSPs. IFRS 15 distinguishes among three methods of estimation: the adjusted market assessment approach, the expected cost plus margin approach, and the residual approach. Considering the interdependencies between the two standards, some companies have chosen to combine the adoption of the new lease standards with the new revenue recognition standard (effective January 1, 2018) to save costs.

The requirements under IFRS 16 for separating lease and non-lease components and allocating the consideration to separate components will require management judgment when identifying those components and applying estimates to determine the observable standalone selling prices. Lessees may not currently have the data required for separating lease and non-lease components. Hence, lessors might need to provide the information to separate lease and non-lease components to their customers. In the past, lessors may not have priced out these elements separately to customers.

**Example**

A hospital enters into a three-year contract for the right to use a specified, physically distinct CT scanner, including consumables for the scanner and maintenance services. Although the leasing contract stipulates that the scanner can only be used *in combination* with the consumables and the service, the service and the consumables for the scanner are readily available and can be purchased independently from the scanner without any restrictions. Thus, maintenance services and consumables must be separated in the leasing contract and must have their own standalone selling prices.

### 1.3.3 Revenue, Including Variable Consideration

Opposite to the lessee, the lessor must include variable payments for non-lease components into the contract consideration. The consideration of a contract is defined as total sum of the revenue from all components of a lease. Figure 1.12 shows how you can determine the correct allocated revenue per lease component. The key question is whether the agreement on variable payments is for the *provision* of non-lease components or for the *purchase* of additional non-lease components.

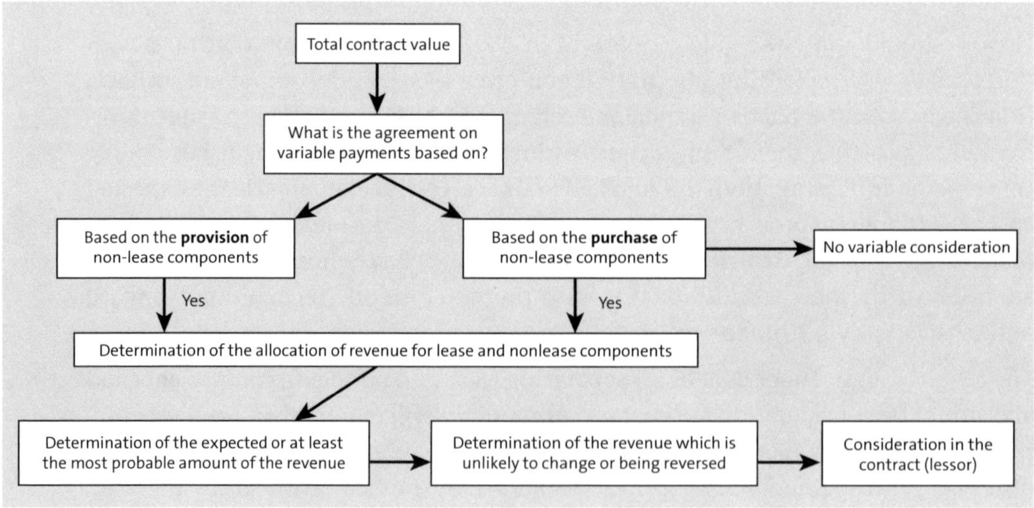


**Figure 1.12** Allocation of Revenue for Non-Lease Components

### 1.3.4 Collectability

When determining the correct accounting for a lease contract, another important factor is the *collectability* of the lease payments. Per ASC 842, paragraph 30-25-3, the lessor must consider whether lease payments are likely to be collected or not.

If lease payments are *unlikely* to be collected, then the received lease payments, including variable payments, must be recognized as a deposit liability until one of the following three things occurs:

- Collectability becomes likely.
- The contract is regular, late, or early terminated.
- The lessor triggers a repossession of the asset.

Note that, even if the payments are *not* likely to be collected, then the lessor *does not* automatically have the right to repossess the asset.

The consequences of uncertainty in collecting the lease payments leads to a significant accounting impact: Even if the lease was classified originally as a finance lease, the lessor must continue to keep the asset on its books, take care of depreciation, defer recognition of any initial direct cost (i.e., included in the net investment in the lease), and treat the lease payments as unearned revenue. Table 1.5 describes the various collectability scenarios that apply to the three lease types at commencement, at initial recognition, and during subsequent measurement (for example, during lease modifications).

| | Sales-Type Lease | Direct Finance Lease | Operating Lease |
|---|---|---|---|
| **Classification at Lease Start** | N/A | If collectability is probable and the other classification criteria are met, then this lease is a direct finance lease.<br>If collectability is not probable, then this lease is an operating lease, regardless of other classification criteria. | N/A |

**Table 1.5** Collectability Impact for Accounting

| | Sales-Type Lease | Direct Finance Lease | Operating Lease |
|---|---|---|---|
| **Initial Recognition and Measurement at Lease Start** | If collectability is probable, then the lessor must recognize any selling profit or loss.<br>If collectability is not probable, then the lessor does not recognize the underlying asset and instead accounts for the lease payments received as deposit liabilities. | N/A | N/A |
| **Subsequent Measurement** | If collectability is probable at least start, then the net investment is evaluated for impairment under ASC 310. | With a direct finance lease, the net investment is evaluated for impairment under ASC 310. | If collectability is probable, then the lessor must recognize income generally on a straight-line basis.<br>If collectability is not probable, then income recognition can be no greater than lease payments and variable lease payments received. |

**Table 1.5** Collectability Impact for Accounting (Cont.)

Once the lessor determines that lease payments are likely to happen, he must retire the asset from his books and remove the deposit liability recognizing the lease payments as revenue. Subsequently the lessor needs to record a net investment in the lease for the remaining payments (including any residual guarantees) plus any nonguaranteed portion of the residual value.

### 1.3.5 Initial Recognition and Measurement at Contract Lease Start Date

On the lease start date (i.e., the date on which the lessor makes an underlying asset available for use by a lessee), the lease liability and ROU asset need to be evaluated.

According to IFRS 16, paragraph 23-25, the initial evaluation of an ROU asset includes the amount of the discounted lease liability, other lease payments to be made before or with the conclusion of the lease, other directly attributable costs of the lessee, and any demolition or dismantling obligations. Payments by the lessor to the lessee, so-called *lease incentives*, must be deducted.

The initial valuation of a lease liability in accordance with IFRS 16 is made at the present value of the lease payments still outstanding at the time of initial recognition (IFRS 16, paragraph 27). Fixed lease payments include variable lease payments that depend on an index (e.g., consumer price index) or price (e.g., London Interbank Offered Rate, or Libor); any guaranteed residual value; the exercise price of a call option, provided that exercising the call option be sufficiently secure; and penalties resulting from lease termination if the duration of the lease requires such termination.

The subsequent valuation of the ROU asset is calculated at amortized cost in accordance with IFRS 16 minus accumulated depreciation and any other impairments (IFRS 16, paragraph 32). The principles of IAS 16 (Property, Plant and Equipment) apply to the updating of acquisition costs.

In accordance with IFRS 16, as with IAS 17, the depreciation period must be based on the shorter of the asset's useful life or the lease term. However, if ownership of the leased asset is transferred to the lessee at the end of its useful life, or if a purchase option exists, the end of the asset's useful life is the determining factor.

If the lessee uses the fair value model in accordance with IAS 40 (Investment Property), this procedure is also mandatory for corresponding leasing transactions. ROU assets that are assigned to an asset class subject to the revaluation method under IAS 16 (Fixed Assets) may also be measured using this method.

Lease liabilities are to accrue over the term of the contract; lease payments should be recognized at the same time as repayment. If the lease is modified, a revaluation is required so that the carrying amount of liability is in line with the changed circumstances reflected in the modified lease (IFRS 16, paragraph 36).

### 1.3.6 Recognition and Measurement Re-Assessment/Modification of the Lease

Changing lease contracts after the inception date will trigger a reassessment of the lease parameters, such as the lease liability and the ROU asset.

During the reassessment, the lessor must evaluate the lease receivables based on the changed input data at the revaluation date to make changes in the lease payments. The following events would trigger a reassessment:

- Changes occur in relevant factors, leading to a change in the terms of the lease, including the existence of significant economic incentives for the lessee.
- The lessee exercises an existing option to extend the lease term or to purchase the leased asset *or* deliberately decides *not* to exercise a termination option in the lease.
- Changes occur in the index or interest rate during the reporting period to determine the lease payments used, with reference to the end index or interest rate applicable during the reporting period.

Figure 1.13 describes in detail how to determine whether you need to reclassify a lease or create a new lease contract.

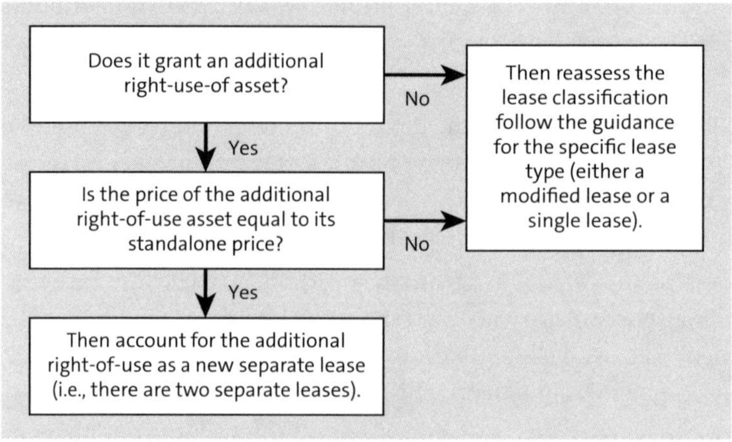


**Figure 1.13** Lessor Analysis of a Change in Lease

A reassessment of the lease term and the lessor's claim for leasing is also then required if the lessee decides to apply for an extension, although the lessor had previously determined that, for the lessee, no real economic incentive to exercise this option exists.

A reassessment of the lease term is required by the lessor if the lessee decides *not* to apply for an extension, even though the lessor had previously determined that a significant economic incentive for the lessee to exercise this option does exist.

Finally, the lessor must reassess the lease term and the lease liability if the lessee has an early termination option but decides not to exercise it because no economic benefits would be gained by terminating on schedule.

If the reassessment leads to a change in the lease term, then the lessor must determine how the change affects the lease payments (including amounts resulting from exercising renewal and termination options). At the revaluation of the lease, the lessor must check the interest rate *only if* one of the following aspects have changed (and only if the probability of such a change had not included in the previous interest rate):

- The term of the lease
- Relevant factors that let the lessee consider exercising a purchase option due to significant economic benefits or to decide not to exercise a purchase option due to the absence of such criteria.
- A reference interest rate on which variable lease payments are calculated.

If the leasing liability is reassessed, then the lessor must do two things:

- Adjust the book value of the ROU asset to reflect the value based on the new evaluation of the lease term, taking exercising or not exercising purchase options into consideration.
- Post, into the profit and loss account, before and after the reassessment, the difference between the amount of the lease liability and the book value of the ROU asset.

### 1.3.7 Impairment

In the event that an asset loses value—perhaps because it doesn't work properly or because the customer returns it damaged—then a lessor would recognize what is called a *lease impairment*.

If a *lease liability* must be impaired, the lessor must apply the guidance under IAS 39 (Financial Instruments: Recognition and Measurement). When determining the impairment amount for a lease liability, the lessor must also consider the related collateral. These collaterals represent cash flows that the lessor expects to recognize during the remaining term of the lease (excluding the cash flows the lessor is expected to obtain from the leased asset). Impairments of lease liabilities also fall under the new IFRS 9 policy released by the IASB.

In the event that an *ROU asset* must be impaired, the lessor must apply the guidance under IAS 36, which states that the lessor must first look for any indications for impairment in each reporting period. If so, the lessor must determine the recoverable amount of the concerned asset. If the recoverable amount is below the book value of the asset, then an impairment loss must be recognized.

After recognition of the impairment loss, the adjusted book value of the ROU asset also becomes the base for a new interest calculation. A lessor must perform a write-up if, after the last impairment loss, it is revealed that the asset has a higher recoverable amount. With a write-up, the adjusted book value may not exceed the book value that would have been determined (after depreciation), if no impairment loss had been recognized in previous periods.

When checking for impairment, the lessor must take into account amounts that he will expect from guaranteed residual values. Although such amounts are not included in the lease payments (and therefore not in the lease liability of the lessee), they must be included when assessing the ROU asset for impairment since these amounts can be part of future cash flows.

### 1.3.8 Sales-Type and Direct Financing Leases

A *sales-type lease* is a kind of finance lease, mostly provided by dealer and manufacturer lessors, often bundled together with additional non-lease components to make the equipment financing more attractive. The key differentiation to normal finance leases is that the lessor records operating profit equal to the difference between the discounted minimum lease payments and the cost of the leased asset at inception of the lease. This process is, of course, only the case when the lease receivables (i.e., the minimum lease payments) are higher than the cost of the leased asset. As for a finance lease, the lessor must record the interest portion of the lease payments as interest income for the duration of the lease.

**Example**

A healthcare company provides blood scanners to hospitals. Each scanner costs $4,000, and the company leases them over a term of three years for quarterly lease payments of $500. The present value of minimum lease payments is $5,000.

Because the present value of the minimum lease payments is higher than the cost of the leased asset, the lessor must record an operating income. In our example, the amount of the operating profit (i.e., $1,000) is the difference between $5,000 (minimum lease payment) and $4,000 (cost of the asset). On top of this one-time profit, which must be posted on the lease inception date, the lessor recognizes periodic interest income. For example, in the first quarter, the lessor earns an interest of $30.75 each quarter ($5,000 × 3% ÷ 4).

Contrary to the sales-type lease, a *direct finance lease* is a lease where the lessor purchases assets and leases them to customers. Income is created from the periodic interest portion of the lease installments.

In this lease type, lessors recognize the gross investment and the sum of all interest portions as unearned interest at the inception of the lease. Gross investment in the lease can be roughly calculated as the sum of lease installments minus cost plus unguaranteed residual value.

At least once a year, the lessor reviews the estimated residual value of the leased asset. If the residual value has declined and the decline is other than temporary, the lessor accounts for the decline as a loss in the current period. If the residual value has increased, no gain is recognized.

A direct financing lease is usually offered by financial services companies, such as fleet or equipment leasing companies.

## 1.4 Summary

In this chapter, we discussed fundamental lease basics, such as lease classifications, lease payments, asset identification, and rights of use. We also demonstrated how a lease impacts lessee and lessor accounting, including effects from lease modifications.

In the next chapter, we'll look at how to make sure that your organizational business processes, master data, and software application ecosystem are compliance ready for the new regulatory changes under ASC 842 and IFRS 16.

# Chapter 2
# Evaluating Compliance Readiness

*So far, we learned how the regulatory changes under Accounting Standards Codification 842 and International Financial Reporting Standards 16 could impact your business and system processes. Let's now evaluate and assess your master data, existing business, and current system in terms of your readiness to comply with regulatory changes.*

Before you implement SAP Lease Administration by Nakisa (hereafter, SAP Lease Administration) or SAP Flexible Real Estate Management (SAP RE-FX), you must consider how regulatory changes will impact your existing leases, master data, business processes, and IT systems.

In this chapter, we'll teach you how to assess your readiness for compliance with the upcoming leasing requirements. We'll walk you through answering the following questions:

- Which lease types you have (Section 2.1)?
- What kind of master data do you maintain, and where does the data live in your current system (Section 2.2)?
- What business processes are impacted by your leases (Section 2.3)?
- How will your software system change (Section 2.4)?

Let's begin by looking at different kinds of leases you may have.

## 2.1 Leasing Requirements

For most companies, the scope of lease administration involves two major areas:

- *Movable leases* are mainly equipment leases, software licenses, intellectual property rights, and vehicle (car/train) leases.
- *Non-movable leases* are mostly real estate leases such as land, buildings, farms, airports, corporate offices, power plants, and retail stores.

Note that any given company could be a lessor or a lessee (or both!) of both movable and non-movable leases. Table 2.1 shows movable and non-movable leases in several use cases:

- Lessor for non-movables (property)
- Lessor for movables (equipment)
- Lessee of non-movables (property)
- Lessee of movables (equipment)

| Entity | Non-Movable Lease | Movable Lease |
|---|---|---|
| Lessor | Landlords in real estate | Someone who rents out their cars, planes, mobile phones, or equipment to others |
| Lessee | Tenants of offices, facilities, land, or infrastructure | Someone who rents rather than owns their computer equipment, production machinery, cars, planes, software licenses, intellectual property rights, etc. |

**Table 2.1** Examples of Lease Administration Types

The biggest impact of ASC 842 and IFRS 16 will be on lessees for non-movable leases and movable leases (in other words, the bottom half of Table 2.1). Lessees in movable leases will be challenged the most in implementation because movable leases involve a wide range of lease contract scenarios.

Expanding on lease administration types and use cases, Table 2.2 shows recommended solutions for specific scenarios.

| Entity | Non-Movable Lease | Movable Lease |
|---|---|---|
| Lessor | SAP Flexible Real Estate Management (RE-FX) | SAP Lease Accounting (FI-LA) and Contract Management (FI-CA) |
| Lessee | SAP Flexible Real Estate Management (RE-FX) | SAP Lease Administration by Nakisa |

**Table 2.2** SAP's Lease Solutions for ASC 842 and IFRS 16

Let's look at each lease type in turn.

### 2.1.1 Non-Movable Leases

Whether you are a lessor or a lessee, the recommended lease software solution for non-movable leases is SAP RE-FX. SAP has completed a multiyear development effort to make this finance component compliant with the new leasing standards ASC 842 and IFRS 16.

SAP RE-FX enables you to manage your full lease contract lifecycle efficiently and effectively. Giving your lease administrator, your lease accountant, and your fixed asset accountant access the same lease record makes their collaboration and coordination easier. As a result, lease contracts can be properly classified and valuated. In most SAP product offerings, your employees can be assigned specific roles and authorizations of your employees to ensure a clear separation of duties.

Lease administrators manage and administer a lease portfolio, generate payment and reports, and perform the following real estate leasing processes:

- Attaching all leasing documents and notes to the lease contact
- Generating correspondence
- Managing critical dates
- Exercising renewal options
- Managing early terminations
- Managing rent escalations
- Managing sales-based rent
- Managing common area maintenance
- Settling service charges

Meanwhile, lease asset accountants can review lease contracts and evaluate the financial impact of each lease, classify assets, and perform the valuation postings required by the new leasing standards. SAP RE-FX generates postings for multiple lease accounting standards simultaneously and creates the required statutory reports.

Operating leases are currently reported off the balance sheet and disclosed in the notes of financial statements. However, due to the new leasing standards, organizations will now be required to capitalize many of these operating leases and record these leases in their balance sheets as assets and obligations.

Although a significant change in how businesses need to manage their leases, early adoption and planning can provide many benefits, including greater visibility on lease exposure and reduction in spending. Ultimately, to prepare for the new standards, your organization needs better, tighter integration. You'll need a framework that provides an efficient mechanism to collect the data required for meeting the new accounting standards.

### 2.1.2 Movable Leases

For movable leases, the recommended lease software solution is SAP Lease Administration, a certified solution extension developed by an SAP partner. SAP Lease Administration provides enterprise lease management and accounting functionality to accelerate your compliance with ASC 842 and IFRS 16 leasing standards. The key feature of SAP Lease Administration is that it provides a unified leasing contract data repository for all your leasing contracts. With SAP Lease Administration, you'll have all lease accounting capabilities, such as classification, accruals, contract status, payment obligations, and you'll be able to automatically generate disclosure reports that comply with ASC 842 and IFRS 16 and that can help you visualize the impact of the new standards on your financial statements over time. SAP Lease Administration's end-to-end lease management process improves the efficiency and accuracy of your business processes, lays the foundation of auditability for compliance, and most importantly provides big-picture clarity through comprehensive analytics and reporting mechanisms.

Now that you've reviewed your organization's own leasing requirements, let's look at the leasing data you have.

## 2.2 Master Data

In this section, we'll explore your company's existing master data, which plays a crucial role in your company's plan to implement SAP Lease Administration or SAP RE-FX. New regulatory changes in IFRS 16 and ASC 842 require you to create new asset classes, review accounting principles, and align your leases with your parallel ledgers.

### 2.2.1 What Kind of Data Do You Have?

As discussed in Section 2.1, leases can be divided into two lease types (movable and non-movable), each with their own set of master data.

If you're dealing with *non-movable* leases for managing buildings, office space, retail space, and residential units, then you'll likely use SAP RE-FX.

The business partner object in SAP has three technical aspects: the business partner role, business partner role categories, and business partner role views. Views define the sequence of screens and how they are processed, in this case, for the business partner role. The business partner role view forms the basis for all object-related information for representing real estate objects in the system. As shown in Table 2.3, master data is divided into two views that allow you to process real estate objects in different ways.

| Usage View | Architectural View |
|---|---|
| This commercial and accounting view includes the following fixed master data objects:<br>▪ Business entity<br>▪ Land<br>▪ Building<br>▪ Rental object<br>▪ Pooled space<br>▪ Rental space<br>▪ Rental unit | This technical view includes the following master data based on architectural object types that you can define in Customizing:<br>▪ Locality<br>▪ Land<br>▪ Building complex<br>▪ Building<br>▪ Floor<br>▪ Part of building<br>▪ Space (such as parking space, storage space, office space)<br>▪ Room of a space |

**Table 2.3** Master Data Views

If you are dealing with *movable* leases (i.e., for managing computer equipment, production machinery, cars, planes, mobile phones, or software licenses), then you'll likely use SAP Lease Administration. You must collect the following master data objects:

- **Master lease agreement**
  A master lease agreement (MLA) serves as the container for all contracts and is defined for a geographic area (or *lease area*). MLAs can be defined with or without a company code. Defining an MLA broadly without a company code allows you to merge lease contracts for all company codes in a specific geographic area under a single MLA.
- **Contract**
  This legal document contains the relevant information of the lease such as lease assets, terms and condition, financial information, and renewal options. All contracts should be created under an approved MLA so that contracts inherit the organizational elements already defined in the MLA.
- **Lease components**
  These components are the actual assets leased in the contract. A single contract can contain multiple lease components, but may not.

- **Activation group**
  An activation group is a group of units that have similar financial and accounting information within a lease component and are activated on the same date. The activation of an accounting group triggers the liability-related right-of-use asset (ROU asset) postings in SAP based on the generated amortization schedule.
- **Unit**
  Every lease asset is characterized as a unit in the system. Each unit has a corresponding fixed asset.

The master data we describe in this section can only provide high-level guidance; your master data may differ depending on how your company manages its leases.

### 2.2.2 Where Is Your Data Located and How Is It Stored?

Compiling all the necessary data may take considerable time and effort—especially in global organizations where lease information is spread around various jurisdictions. You'll need to identify where the defined master data is located (either onsite or offsite) and how the data is stored (in digital or paper format). As shown in Table 2.4, digital media can either be stored in the cloud or in some location that your IT team can access remotely. Give special consideration to off-premises data especially for paper media, since collecting and retrieving paper records requires more time and resources (see Table 2.5).

| File Type | Description |
|---|---|
| Databases | Databases store very complex information in tables. Data can be retrieved easily through Structured Query Language (SQL), and you can modify the table schema and table structures using Data Definition Language (DDL). SAP-supported database technologies include the following:<br>▪ Oracle database<br>▪ Microsoft SQL Server database<br>▪ IBM DB2<br>▪ SAP ASE database<br>▪ SAP HANA database<br>SAP HANA, SAP's newest database and application development platform, provides more efficient handling and processing of large data volumes in real time since it loads and retrieves data in-memory, instead of the traditional way of reading from disks. |

**Table 2.4** Digital Media File Types

| File Type | Description |
|---|---|
| Flat files | Flat files are text files stored in a computer file system, with information stored as strings. You can access and edit these files using any text editor, such as Notepad in the Windows operating system or using a visual editor in the UNIX/Linux operating system. |
| Spreadsheet files | In this file type, data is stored in cells, which are organized into rows and columns. A cell may contain text, number, or date data types. It can also be used for formulas that reference other cells. Common spreadsheet file extensions include *.xlsx*, *.ods*, and *.numbers*. Most leasing data resides in this type of file. |
| Digital image files | Digital image files are stored in *.tiff*, *.jpeg*, *.gif*, *.png*, and *.raw* image file formats. Data in these formats require a lot of time to extract, since you'll need to manually retrieve the required information. |
| Word document files | In this file type, your data is stored as Microsoft Word files (*.doc* and *.docx*) or OpenOffice Writer document files (*.odt*). |
| Portable document format | The portable document format (PDF) is a file format that can be viewed across different operating systems. PDF is an open standard maintained by the International Organization for Standardization (ISO). |

**Table 2.4** Digital Media File Types (Cont.)

| File Type | Description |
|---|---|
| Paper contracts | Hard copies of contracts that are printed out on paper and stored on or off your company's site. |

**Table 2.5** Paper Media File Types

### 2.2.3 How Do You Access Your Data for Lease Contracts?

Once you know where your data resides, you'll need to access it. As shown in Table 2.6, how you go about accessing your data can vary significantly.

| Media Type | Description |
|---|---|
| Digital media | Lease contracts stored in flat files, Word documents, PDFs, and spreadsheet files:<br>■ These files are stored in your company's network—meaning you'll need access privileges to view these files. Your IT department can grant you the privilege to access these files.<br>■ Once you are able to access the lease contract files, you'll browse through each document and retrieve important information such as contract amount, renewal options, lease commencement dates, lease terms, and more.<br>Lease contracts stored in databases:<br>■ You can access lease contract data through software applications or proprietary database management consoles. This requires an authorization role to access the database, which is given by your company's database administrator.<br>■ This may require you to have some technical knowledge of running SQL commands and an understanding of the data structure of your lease contracts. Often, you'll have to join multiple tables to retrieve the data that you need. |
| Paper media | The lease contract is printed out on paper, and all the pertinent information about the lease is stipulated in the contract. This media type can be accessed through filing cabinets used for storage—which presents an implementation challenge, since you need to be on-premises to collect the lease data information. |

**Table 2.6** Lease Contract Access through Different Media Types

### 2.2.4 How Do You Organize Contracts?

In this section, we'll explore how your company collects, combines, and classifies contracts. With this information, you'll be able to evaluate your company's practices against the new standards stipulated by ASC 842 and IFRS 16.

The new standards ensure that leases will be reflected as assets and liabilities in your financial statements and is consistent with the conceptual framework and new revenue recognition standard. Both of these standards record an ROU asset as property, plant, and equipment (PP&E) at present value, plus amortization over the lease life, and a lease liability that includes lease payments, terms, and interest rates.

Briefly, let's identify some of the notable differences between ASC 842 and IFRS 16, as shown in Table 2.7.

| Item | IFRS 16 | ASC 842 |
|---|---|---|
| Definition | ▪ Does not distinguish between finance and operating leases<br>▪ Land can be included in the lease<br>▪ Not necessarily a physical asset | ▪ Separate guidance for finance and operating leases<br>▪ Land is treated as a separate lease<br>▪ Generally a physical asset |
| Supersedes | ▪ IAS 17 | ▪ ASC 840 |
| Measurement | ▪ Assets valued under \$5,000 are exempt<br>▪ Allows alternative evaluation models<br>▪ Leases of shorter period, less than 12 months | ▪ No explicit low-value threshold<br>▪ Lease terms of 12 months or less can be exempted from recognizing lease assets and liabilities when the lessee opts to make an accounting policy election by underlying asset class |
| Statement of cash flow | ▪ Interest classed optionally as investing, financing, or operating activities | ▪ Interest classed as operating activity<br>▪ Amortization is a financing activity |
| Effectivity date | ▪ Accounting periods beginning on or after January 1, 2019 | ▪ Accounting periods beginning after December 15, 2018 |
| Transition | ▪ Early adoption allowed with the new revenue recognition standard | ▪ Early adoption allowed |

**Table 2.7** Comparison between ASC 842 and IFRS 16

The collection of a lease contract starts with identifying what comprises a compliant lease based on the new standards. Let's first discuss how to identify if a contract is a lease. If you have already mastered the leasing basics in Chapter 1, this will be a review.

### Lease Identification

A contract is, or contains, a lease if the contract conveys the right to control the use of an identified asset for a period of time in exchange for consideration. To determine whether a contract contains or is a lease, the following elements should be present:

- The identified asset
- The right to control the use of that asset
- The right to direct the use of that asset
- The right to obtain substantially all economic benefit from the use of that asset

#### Lease Classification

How you classify a lease depends on the substance of the transaction and is determined at the time of the commitment or signing of the lease, which may or may not match with the date on which the lessee actually receives the leased asset. This classification will be retained throughout the life of the lease, unless a contract modification is undertaken (i.e., a change to the lease terms, which will lead to a reassessment of the contract).

Leases can be classified in two ways:

- **Finance lease**
  This lease substantially transfers all risks and rewards incidental to the ownership of the underlying asset to the lessee. This type of lease recognizes depreciation and interest expense. As a result, a finance lease recognizes more expenses in the early part of the lease and fewer expenses later in the lease term.
- **Operating lease**
  This lease *does not* substantially transfer all the risks and rewards incidental to the ownership of the underlying asset. An operating lease recognizes a rent expense on a straight-line basis over the lease term.

How can you determine whether a lease is a finance or operating lease? Consider the following questions:

- Does the lease transfer ownership of an asset to the lessee?
- Does the lease grant the lessee a purchase option that is reasonably certain of being exercised?
- Is the lease term for a major part of the asset's remaining economic life?
- Is the present value of lease payments (including the lessee residual value guarantee) substantially all of the asset's fair value?
- Is the asset so specialized that it is expected to have no alternative use to the lessor?

If the answer to *any* of these questions is "yes," then the lease is a finance lease. If the answer to each question is "no," then the lease is an operating lease.

How leases are classified also differs between IFRS 16 and ASC 842, as shown in Table 2.8.



| Item | IFRS 16 | ASC 842 |
|---|---|---|
| Lease inception | No separate finance lease category:<br>■ Asset and liabilities are valued at *net* present value of lease payments over the lease terms<br>■ Right-of-user asset is depreciated<br>■ Lease liability is amortized | A lease is classified as operating or finance lease.<br>Operating leases:<br>■ Recognize one lease cost calculated as interest plus amortization<br>■ Allocated over the lease term on a straight-line basis<br>■ Classify cash payments within the operating activity cash flow<br>Finance leases:<br>■ Transfer of ownership of the asset at the end of the lease term or have used it for the majority of its economic life<br>■ Separate recognition on the amortization of the ROU asset and interest on the lease liability<br>■ Classify amortization in financing activities while interest payments in operating activity cash flow |

**Table 2.8** Lease Classification Comparison between IFRS 16 and ASC 842

### Lease Separation from Non-Lease Components

A given lease contract may contain a lease of an asset (lease component) and the provision of a maintenance service (non-lease component)—and you should account for these components separately.

For example, in a real estate lease, other required payments will be common, such as for common area maintenance. Typically, these payments would be considered non-lease components and are not included in the total lease payment. Another example is an equipment lease, where as part of the lease payment, the lessor provides periodic maintenance throughout the life of the lease.

Often a lease contract states one rent payment to cover both the lease components *and* the non-lease components. In those situations, you must allocate payments using the relative standalone selling price for each component. The accounting of non-lease components should be in accordance with other applicable standards, as shown in Table 2.9.

| Item | IFRS 16 | ASC 842 |
| --- | --- | --- |
| Lease inception | Separate leases from services | Separate lease and non-lease components |

**Table 2.9** Lease Separation Comparison between IFRS 16 and ASC 842

Both lessors and lessees are required to determine whether the right to use an underlying asset is a separate lease component in their contracts if both of the following criteria are met:

- If the lessee can benefit from use of the asset either on its own or together with other resources readily available to the lessee (ASC 842, paragraph 10-15-28, and IFRS 16, paragraph B32(a)). Readily available resources are goods or services that are sold or leased separately (by the lessor or other suppliers) or resources that the lessee has already obtained (from the lessor or from other transactions or events).
- If the underlying asset is neither dependent on, nor highly interrelated with, the other underlying assets in the contract.

### Contract Combination

In some cases, combining lease contracts may make sense. For example, an entity can combine two or more contracts entered into at or near the same time with the same counterparty (or related parties of the counterparty) and account for all the contracts as a single contract if *at least one* of the following criteria is met, as described in ASC 842, paragraph 10-25-19, and IFRS 16, paragraph B2:

- The contracts are negotiated as a package with an overall commercial objective that cannot be understood without considering the contracts together.
- The amount of consideration to be paid in one contract depends on the price or performance of the other contract.
- The rights to use underlying assets conveyed in the contracts (or some rights to use underlying assets conveyed in each of the contracts) form a single lease component.

**Example**

Lessee LA leases a retail space in a commercial building with a monthly rent of $2,000 and baking equipment of $10/day with a lease term of two years from Lessor SE in two separate contracts that are executed within the same time frame.

Lessor SE agrees to lower the rent for the retail space as an incentive to persuade Lessee LA to lease the baking equipment at higher than the market value. Since Lessee LA plans to open a pastry shop, the commercial objectives of both the retail space and the baking equipment can be understood as one, and both lease contracts can be combined as one as stated in the first and third criteria. Moreover, Lessor SE gave an amount of consideration to Lessee LA by offering an incentive: lower rent.

### 2.2.5 How Should You Prepare for Data Migration?

Data migration is a key phase in system implementation and involves master data like real estate objects, customers, vendor account information, and transactional data on leases. Your company may have the latest software solutions and the most efficient business processes, but if the data flowing through your IT ecosystem is corrupt, then the output will also be corrupt. To achieve the maximum value from your data, you should have best and latest version of your data to begin with, for which you'll need a firm understanding of the data migration process, including the data needed for the new system's master and transactional data.

The complexity of a data migration project depends on the source system's (or systems') configuration and state, data quality, existing data processes (when compared to the new data processes), and the way the system is used at the time of the migration as well as the configuration of the destination system. For example, migrating data from a number of Excel spreadsheets is different than migrating data from an internal legacy system. Migrating data into a system that is currently used and already contains data is even more complex. The logic you use for this type of a project depends on many parameters.

The data migration workflow shown in Figure 2.1 represents the process of converting your existing leases and migrating both financial and non-financial information from your existing system to either SAP Lease Administration or SAP RE-FX. The whole data migration process generally occurs in cycles or "mocks," which will serve as practice runs before the actual cutover and go-live schedules.

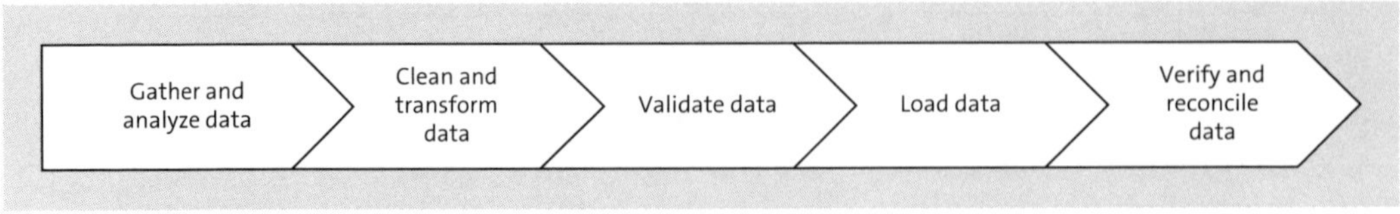


**Figure 2.1** Data Migration Process

Let's walk through each step in detail:

1. **Gather and analyze data.**
   The first step is to define and determine the lease data attributes you'll need. Working with functional and technical resources, your data team members will need to determine the source systems, file systems, applications, and paper media that are in scope for the lease data.

   We recommend that you include subject matter experts (SMEs) from the various departments in your company, such as accounting and finance, real estate and property, operations, procurement, IT, and business analytics, who are knowledgeable of your systems and business processes. Gathering all the data needed for ASC 842 and IFRS 16 compliance takes a lot of personnel and time, particularly in a global organization with lease information spread out around the world.

   One option would be to break down the implementation project into different roll-out phases based on regions, like Asia Pacific, Europe, and the US. As your company undertakes this first phase, you'll stumble through many errors. As you move along in the next phase of implementation, you'll learn from the previous phase and become more effective and efficient in future implementation projects.
2. **Clean and transform data.**
   Data migration specialists use the results from the previous step to aid in cleansing the data. This step requires you understand the data elements needed for the new system. The master data identified in the previous phase needs to be collected and converted to fit your new system (either SAP Lease Administration or SAP RE-FX). Cleansing the data includes matching data variables to the new system, merging business-leasing contracts and customers, and removing information that is not relevant. Your business analysts and data team members should develop source-to-target field mapping documents that include business rules and conversion logic to guide the development of cleansing transformations.
3. **Validate data.**
   Before data is transferred into the target system, functional team members and business users must review and validate the data to ensure accuracy, correctness,

and conformity to all business requirements. One best practice is to use a data migration template in spreadsheets (.odt or .xlsx) or comma-separated files (.csv) that have columns similar to the structure of the database tables in the destination system. In this way, you'll standardize your data preparation across your different geographic areas, and all team members can access, validate, and correct the data. With a single source file, keeping track of changes in real time is easier. When all the data is correct and accurate, a document should be signed off on to proceed with the next step of the data migration process.

4. **Load data.**

   After your business has signed off on the data validations, the data can now be transferred into your target system. We recommend migrating and validating a small subset of the data to the destination system first since a smaller subset is easier to manage and correct for data migration errors. Undertake adequate testing and perform a series of dry runs to ensure that the data will be properly migrated. Once everything is working as expected, you'll then proceed to migrate the entire dataset and validate whether all the data has been successfully migrated to the new system.

   You may involve business users and key users to help you validate the newly migrated data in your system. If you are using SAP, your SAP Basis team can use SAP Data Services, intermediate documents (IDocs), or the Legacy System Migration Workbench (LSMW).

   The data load process takes place during the cutover and go-live phases in your implementation project. Master data must be loaded into the system first before dependent downstream objects can be loaded because these objects reference the master data. Transactional data is usually loaded during a tight time window to ensure business operations are fully functional when the system goes live.

5. **Verify and reconcile data.**

   Once the data has been loaded into your target system, your data teams can then verify the migrated data to ensure that the data has been loaded successfully. Your team can log into the target system and execute test scripts to ensure the system has been configured properly, or your team can manually cross-verify the data with the shared spreadsheet file used during the data validation process. Your data team can generate post-load reports and compare these against pre-load reports. Your business end users are the ultimate owners of the data and must sign off on the post-load validations. If data errors and discrepancies arise, they should be reported immediately so that the data team can make the necessary corrections.

## 2.3 Business Processes

The new leasing standards will generate a high volume of new assets and require many present value calculations. Therefore, in light of the new regulations and depending on your company lease practices, you'll need to consider the overlap between your lease management practices and your peripheral business processes in financials and logistics.

In this section, we'll discuss the consequences of the new regulations (and their implementation in SAP RE-FX and SAP Lease Administration) on your organization's fixed assets, procure-to-pay (P2P) processes, materials management and plant maintenance, and general ledger accounting practices. We recommend that you take a cross-functional approach to implementation and involve subject matter experts from various departments, not just accounting and finance.

Figure 2.2 shows the integration of the different business processes of different components within the SAP ecosystem, such as Asset Accounting (AA), Investment Management (IM), Materials Management (MM), Production Planning (PP), and Plant Maintenance (PM), as well as Financial Accounting (FI) and Controlling (CO). Understanding how data flows to and from these various components will help you prepare and anticipate changes across business functions.

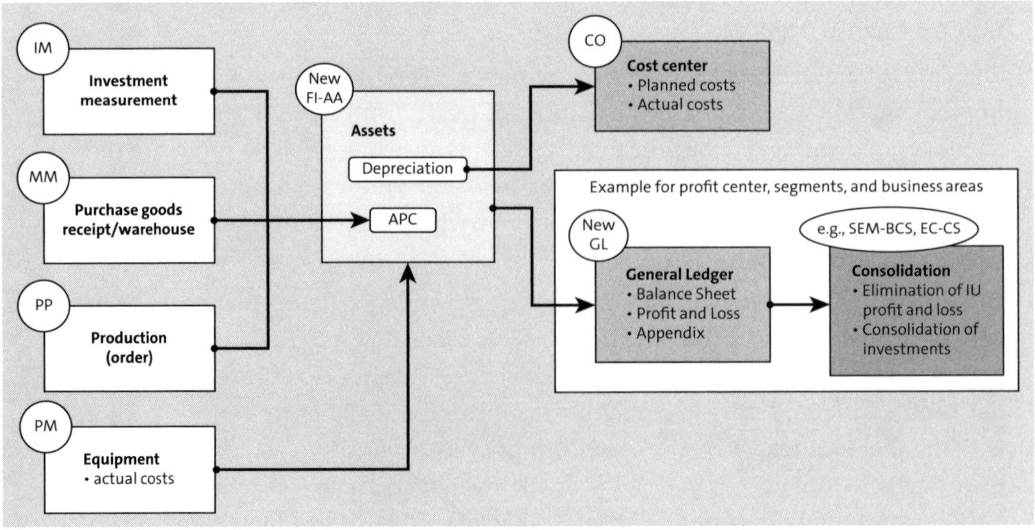


**Figure 2.2** Integration of Business Processes

For example, asset values can be determined either from an asset capitalization of an investment measure (IM) or from a direct purchase based on goods, invoices, or withdrawals of stocks from the warehouse (MM). Asset values can also result from settlements of production orders (PP) or can be maintenance costs that need be capitalized (PM). In turn, FI-AA sends acquisition and production cost (APC) values to Financial Accounting (FI) and depreciation costs to Controlling (CO).



### 2.3.1 Fixed Assets

Asset Accounting (FI-AA) in SAP is a subsidiary ledger to the general ledger and contains all relevant information pertaining to fixed assets and where fixed-asset processes (such as acquisitions, transfers, and retirements) can be performed. FI-AA is seamlessly integrated with the standard component of SAP ERP Financials and thus works well with SAP RE-FX for managing non-movable leases. Movable leases using SAP Lease Administration are also natively integrated and work well with SAP ERP Financials. For SAP S/4HANA, the new FI-AA is available together with the new SAP General Ledger (GL) accounting.

The new regulatory leasing standard emphasizes the management of assets and requires you to create new leased asset classes in FI-AA. As a result, you'll need to define an account determination key for new postings and assign this key to the newly created asset classes.

Remember that the new lessee accounting approach requires that a lessee recognize its leases on its balance sheet. This recognition involves recording:

- Right-of-use asset
- Lease liability

The lease liability is initially measured as the present value of future lease payments. The calculation of lease payments includes fixed payments for lease elements that are non-cancellable, for guaranteed residual value, or for inflation-linked payments when there is a change in the cash payment, and amounts to be paid in optional periods when renewal is reasonably certain. The lease liability is treated as a financial liability discounted at effective interest.

The initial measurement of the ROU asset is based on the lease liability and then adjusted for any prepaid rents, lease incentives received, and initial direct costs incurred. The ROU asset is treated like an acquired asset that is depreciated or amortized.

Lessors are mandated, under IFRS 16, to continue following the lessor accounting requirements found in IAS 17. Thus, a lessor will still classify his leases as either operating or finance leases and will have continue to account for these two types of leases differently.

The basic functions of asset accounting deal with the creation of asset master records; the recording of asset transactions (e.g., acquisitions, transfers, retirements); asset valuation; the calculation of depreciation; and the handling of closing operations. Asset accounting also handles assets that require special valuation adjustments and for special valuation purposes. Asset accounting can make special calculations, like reserves for special depreciation scenarios (e.g., tax depreciation), interest, and revaluation of fixed assets.

Reports used by management to monitor, analyze, and evaluate asset information, such as an asset history sheet and depreciation reports, are available in the information system. The system also allows the consolidation of asset values for companies with different currencies using parallel valuation. Both actual and parallel values are posted in the system simultaneously, but each has separate documents during posting.

You can use real estate objects to capture depreciation costs if these costs are manually maintained in the time-dependent tab of the asset master data as an account assignment object.

The integration of all pertinent asset accounting transactions (including asset acquisitions, additions, transfers, retirements, and depreciation postings) to the general ledger is automatic. The update occurs per depreciation area of accounting principle, which can either be in real time (i.e., for leading depreciation area) or periodically (i.e., depreciation area for special reserves).

The following are the key elements that determine which general ledger account the posting to an asset will be made:

- The chart of accounts assigned to the company code
- The automatic posting depreciation area
- The account determination key entered in the asset class

In the general master data, the asset class is assigned with an account determination key, which specifies the GL accounts to be used when posting the asset transactions, and the company code is mapped with a chart of accounts, which contains a group of general ledger accounts.



The account determination key is maintained for the chart of accounts linked to the company code as well as for the depreciation area in the chart of depreciation. The chart of accounts is mapped to each company code in a one-to-one relationship. For automatic depreciation posting to the general ledger, you can specify the relevant account in the account determination key.

### 2.3.2 Procure-to-Pay

Procure-to-pay (P2P) software solutions help you to manage your purchase orders (POs) and accounts payable (AP) more effectively and efficiently. From vendor planning and selection, to purchase order/service entry processing, to goods receipt and service completion, to invoice handling and vendor payments, P2P software helps your company fulfill its commitments and manage the operation and maintenance of your leases.

Both SAP Lease Administration and SAP RE-FX can be fully integrated with your current P2P solution handling the financial component of your ecosystem (either SAP Supplier Relationship Management [SRM] or SAP Ariba as well as SAP ERP). The key functionality of these solutions is to provide unified information management for all your lease contracts in all phases of the contract lifecycle, allowing you to streamline vendor sourcing and contract management processes. Thus, every lease contract will have full visibility for tracking asset maintenance and repair, from service vendor job orders up to the generation of vendor payments.

Figure 2.3 shows how a leasing solution can overlap with P2P solution to manage the purchase of a lease asset and handle its development, repair, and maintenance. Let's say, for example, you plan to buy a commercial space. You start by sourcing available units from a particular vendor or seller. You can then create a purchase order to complete the purchase of the unit, and the PO goes through the standard downstream process from goods receipt, to invoice handing, to vendor payments. The purchased lease asset's data can then be integrated with SAP Lease Administration and SAP RE-FX to create lease contracts.

IFRS 16 requires that the leasable asset be valued at $5,000 or more. For any purchased lease asset that meets this criterion, the data can be transferred and integrated to either SAP RE-FX or SAP Lease Administration.

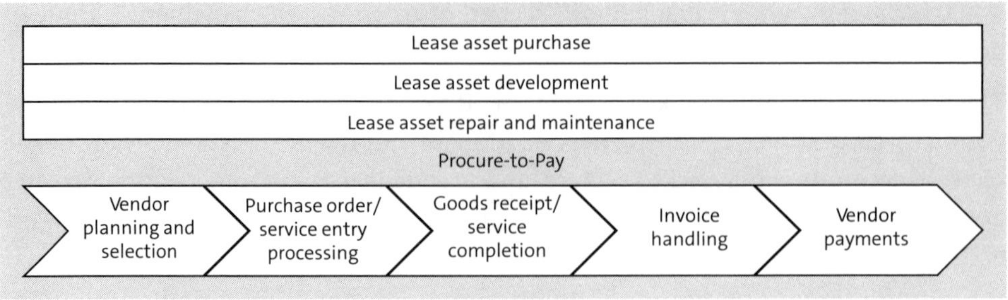


**Figure 2.3** Integration with Procure-to-Pay

### 2.3.3 Plant Maintenance and Materials Management

Plant Maintenance (PM) is one of the components that SAP offers to help you plan and manage all the work needed to maintain your real estate objects. From your leasing data, you'll need to identify the leased assets that must be maintained, repaired, or serviced. This functionality works also with Materials Management, but you'll need to first define material master data attributes and characteristics. Then, you can then plot maintenance plans, and based on the rules defined, generate a scheduled order. Since this business process is more focused on equipment (movable) and/or real estate (non-movable) maintenance, the new leasing standards do not directly apply.

To integrate SAP Lease Administration or SAP RE-FX with your material management and plant maintenance business processes, you'll need to use the Plant Maintenance (PM) and Customer Service (CS) components of SAP ERP. The PM component is use for managing the real estate objects of your own company, while the CS component is for the real estate objects of your customers or other companies within your group.

Integration begins with defining the fixed and non-movable parts of your real estate (e.g., maintenance rooms or business offices). In the initial definition, you can add classification characteristics and details about functional locations and equipment, such as the area of a room, date of construction, or the renovation costs. After the initial definition, you can assign the defined functional locations of PM and CS components to your real estate objects via the usage or architectural view. In this way, PM enables you to plan and manage the services needed for maintaining your real estate objects. An order is created in PM for tasks, such as business office renovation, preventive maintenance of building equipment, heater/air conditioner repair, and basic cleaning services. After the work is rendered, invoices coming from external service providers and workers costs will be posted against the order.

### 2.3.4 General Ledger Accounting

The accounting for SAP RE-FX can be set up in Customizing within the SAP RE-FX component, but the settings needs to be assigned to the Financial Accounting (FI) component in order for financial postings and transactions to be processed. You'll also need to install Financial Accounting (FI) and Controlling (CO) with the plug-in package for the integration between the two components to work.

The accounting in the Financial Accounting (FI) component can be both subledger and general ledger accounting. On one hand, posting to a reconciliation account is made in the subsidiary ledger, which contains the details of the transactions. On the other hand, the summary of the subledger transactions is posted to the general ledger, which contains the balance of the GL account. These postings will be the basis for financial statements preparation (e.g., balance sheets and profit and loss statements). For example, receivables and payables, or input and output taxes, from SAP RE-FX are posted to a subledger, which updates the balance of the GL account automatically.

As discussed earlier, SAP S/4HANA Finance is based on the new SAP General Ledger (GL) component. If you plan to use the new FI-GL, you'll need to migrate the application data from classic General Ledger Accounting to the new one. The impact of the new leasing standard in the general ledger will be substantial, considering that you need to recognize ROU assets and lease liability accounts in your financial statements. This recognition requires you evaluate and assess your existing lease data and ensure that these relevant accounts are posted in accordance with ASC 842 and IFRS 16 guidelines.

Several posting functions in accounting are relevant for SAP RE-FX. Let's look at some examples. One example is the use of special posting keys to record the payments made in advance for utility bills or operating expenses. These payments are posted to a special GL account instead of a customer or vendor reconciliation account. SAP RE-FX can post to multiple lease accounting standards at the same time even if the general ledger account or a parallel ledger is used.

Another example is the settlement of service charges, which can either be periodic or one-time postings. For periodic postings, receivables and payables to the contract partner are posted or reversed for every contract, or the expenses attributable to vacancy are posted to a vacancy cost object in a timely manner. In contrast, when using one-time posting, receivables are summarized in a single posting to a contract, passing the information directly to the customer account.

The final example is the accrual of operating costs and the deferral of rental income to recognize in the same period when the expense is incurred and when the revenue is earned—a classic example of the matching principle.

Another functionality posts incoming payments to contracts that are open for the period by using post with clearing and incoming payments fast entry. Using the electronic bank statement function, you can import electronic bank statements and automate the processing of debit or credit memos. Using the post process account statement function, you can match payments against the contract to which the payment belongs and to post documents.

Documents generated during periodic posting or during the settlement of service charges can be accessed in the posting log or in cash flows using the display of real estate-specific document function.

Similar to the dunning program used for accounts receivable in FI, SAP RE-FX has access to all dunning functions but also has special functions that are only applicable when, for example, setting the payment method for dunning, setting the separate dunning of each customer, and adding contractual partners as dunning recipients.

When you use SAP Lease Administration, posting functions are pushed to SAP ERP Financials and into the general ledger accounts. All leasing transactions performed in SAP Lease Administration are posted through the native integration technologies of SAP.

By using these integrated solutions, anything that may disrupt operations or affect business processes as a result of non-compliance can be addressed before the problem becomes expensive. Simulation and posting reports are available to assess the impact of both old and new accounting standards on a single lease or on the whole lease portfolio.

## 2.4 System Changes

Spreadsheets and paper media are commonly used to manage leases today, but these deficient mechanisms impede properly accounting for lease data.

Companies whose existing system is not fully integrated or is not fully compliant with the new standards should assess and evaluate the need to adopt a new system, since the new leasing standards bring intricacies and complexities to financial reports and since using spreadsheets, paper media, and your existing IT system may lead to errors feeding into financial reporting. Companies that have large and complex leases should look for software leasing solutions that handle the complexities brought about by the new leasing standards.

Most existing lease software solutions offered in the market are based on the current leasing standards, ASC 840 and IAS 17. And with the recent release of ASC 842 and IFRS 16, the functionalities offered by these solutions also need to adapt to comply with the requirements of the new leasing standards. So in this section, we'll discuss the ways in which ASC 842 and IFRS 16 will impact your current company's IT ecosystem. To start, we'll identify the required master data for the integration with your existing ERP. All lease contract data should be migrated to the new system, either SAP Lease Administration or SAP RE-FX. We will then discuss how these systems manage the lease lifecycle of the lease contracts and, finally, discuss the disclosure and reporting required by the new standards.

From our analysis on our current master data and business processes from the previous section, we will then need to identify system gaps and changes needed to fit our IT environments on the adoption of these new leasing standards. Thus, you can choose a lease software solution that can be integrated with your existing ERP systems and IT environment to best meet your needs in a cost-effective way.

The new standard will likely require enhancements to a company's existing IT infrastructure to accommodate the leasing data storage, valuation calculation, and statutory reporting requirements. Companies should consider whether to develop functionality within their current ERP system or to implement new modules or systems to help comply with the new standard. However, given the long lead times of system initiatives, more effective alternatives are available: SAP Lease Administration and SAP RE-FX enable compliance with current and new lease accounting standards and provide the necessary disclosure reports so you can avoid unwanted penalties from missed payments and evergreen fees (payments paid to the lessor when a lease contract is not formally terminated at the end of its lease term).

### 2.4.1 Integration with an Existing ERP System

In this section, we'll cover the integration of SAP RE-FX and SAP Lease Administration with your existing ERP. As shown in Figure 2.4, both systems are highly integrated (data is pushed out from SAP Lease Administration and SAP RE-FX and pulled into SAP systems), but for these systems to work with each other, you need to transfer the necessary leasing data information from your current ERP to/from SAP RE-FX or SAP Lease Administration. If you are presently using an SAP ERP system, then you can use

SAP's integration technologies such as remote function calls (RFCs) or intermediate documents (IDocs) to facilitate the data transfer. For non-SAP ERP systems, integration will depend on the communication interfaces that your current system supports. However, you can use web services, electronic data interchange (EDI) standards, OData/Excel/*.csv* files, or other commonly used standards.

For SAP RE-FX, integration with your existing SAP ERP Financials for real property leasing can be quickly implemented since SAP RE-FX is in fact a subcomponent of SAP ERP Financials. So within SAP ERP Financials, no integration project is needed to use modules such as Asset Accounting (AA), SAP General Ledger (GL), and Accounts Payable (AP). For other, non-financial modules such as Plant Maintenance (PM), you can use SAP's own integration technologies such as remote function calls (RFCs) or intermediate documents (IDocs) to transfer leasing data. SAP has released new accelerators designed to make adoption easier and to implement the leasing solution swiftly.

One key feature of SAP RE-FX is the close coordination and collaboration between your lease administrator and fixed asset accountant. This feature helps you properly classify and valuate your leases using a common platform; by accessing the same lease record, these employees can abstract existing lease agreements and lease terms and ensure that conditions are correct. As a result, your organization can quickly adopt the lease compliance project since the close collaboration provides accurate lease information and ensures that the accuracy of valuations posted to SAP ERP Financials.

If your company is currently using SAP RE-FX, we recommend that you implement the new leasing enhancements as soon as they are released so that you can begin loading your leases. With the leases in your system, you can analyze the financial report results for a better understanding of how the new standards impact your financial statements.

SAP Lease Administration delivers both compliance and smarter lease management that natively integrates with Asset Accounting (AA), SAP General Ledger (GL), Accounts Payable (AP), Plant Maintenance (PM), and SAP master data tables, meaning your business will see an overall reduction in implementation time, risk, and cost of ownership. SAP Lease Administration also leverages your investment in SAP ERP by meshing seamlessly with financial and materials management functions. You can integrate SAP Lease Administration with your existing SAP ERP Financials for equipment leasing or movable assets using RFCs, web services, or through OData/Excel/*.csv*.



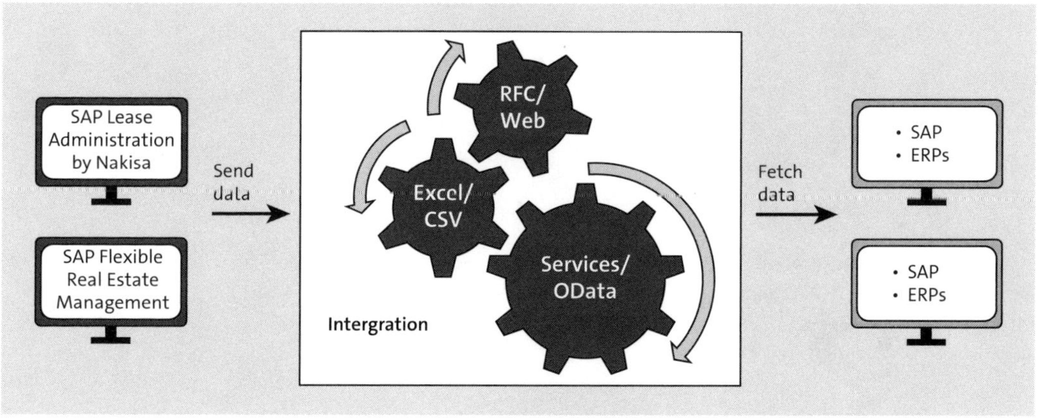


**Figure 2.4** SAP RE-FX and SAP Lease Administration Integration with SAP

### 2.4.2 Lease Lifecycle in the System

The new leasing standards affect more than your accounting practices. The new standards also affect how you abstract your master data and make you adopt new business processes. As a result of these changes, consequently, how you manage the entire lease lifecycle in your systems will be impacted. We'll spend a few pages on lease lifecycles in general, and then focus on SAP RE-FX and SAP Lease Administration.

In the era of IFRS 16 and ASC 842, the lifecycle of lease accounting takes on the following general steps shown in Figure 2.5: lease identification, lease classification, lease recognition and measurement, and lease assessment and remeasurement.

The first step is to identify a lease and its lease components. As we'll discuss in other chapters, whether a lease contract contains just one lease or multiple leases, the lease should mention both the identifiable asset and that the lessee has a right to control the use of this asset. (Exempt from the standard are short-term leases, which have a term of 12 months or less, and leases involving low-value assets.) Sometimes lease contracts contain non-lease components; you may choose not to separate lease and non-lease components by class of underlying assets and may account for each separate lease component along with the associated non-lease component as a single lease component.

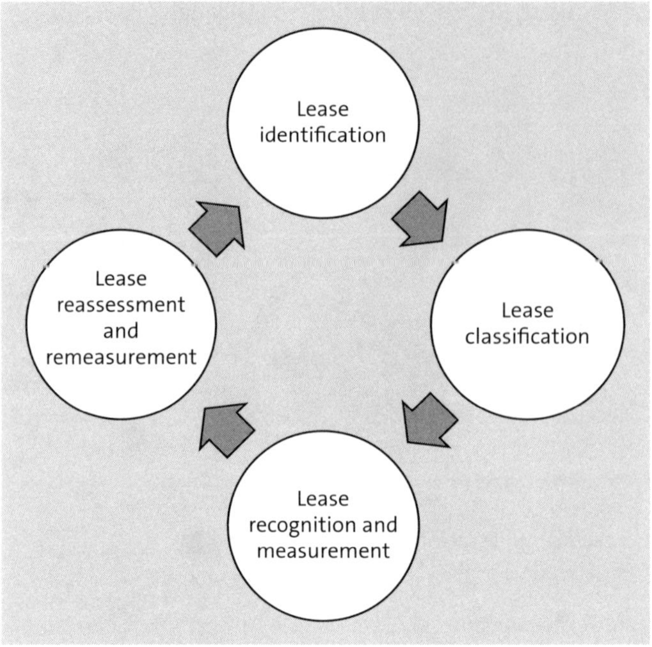


**Figure 2.5** Lease Lifecycle

The second step is lease classification. Basically, the classification of a lease as either a finance lease or an operating lease occurs at the inception date and is reassessed upon lease modification. Generally, a lease will be classified as a finance lease if the lease substantially transfers all the risks and rewards incidental to the ownership of an underlying asset to the lessee; otherwise, the lease is classified as an operating lease. Table 2.10 compares the different types of lease classification between ASC 842 and IFRS 16 standards; note that the classification criteria to classify a lease for ASC 842 are substantially similar to previous guidance.

| Accounting Model | ASC 842 | IFRS 16 |
|---|---|---|
| Lessee accounting | ▪ Finance lease<br>▪ Operating lease | ▪ Finance lease<br>▪ Operating lease |
| Lessor accounting | ▪ Sales-type lease<br>▪ Direct finance lease (operating lease) | ▪ Finance lease<br>▪ Operating lease |

**Table 2.10** Lease Classification

The third step is the recognition and measurement of the lease at its commencement date. The applicability of the standards also depends on what type of entity you are, as either:

- **Lessee**
  At the commencement date, a lessee shall recognize an ROU asset and a lease liability. The initial measurement of the ROU asset is at cost while lease liability is calculated at the present value for all lease payments that are yet to be paid. Apart from the fixed payment arising from the lease components, the following lease payments may need to be recognized or excluded, depending on the lease contract conditions:
  - Variable lease payments
    - Recognize lease payments that depend on an index or a rate and is measured at commencement date
    - Exclude lease payments that change due to factors after commencement other than passage of time
  - Purchase price or termination charge fees
    - Recognize lease payments for purchase of assets
    - Recognize lease payments for renewal or termination fees consistent with lease term
  - Guaranteed residual value
    - Recognize lease payments of the guaranteed residual value to be payable by the lessee
  - Lessor-provided incentives
    - Recognize lease payments made on behalf of the lessee
    - Recognize loss incurred by lessor resulting from assuming a lessee's preexisting lease from a third party
- **Lessor**
  A lessor shall classify each of its leases as either an operating lease (direct finance lease in ASC 842) or a finance lease (sales-type lease in ASC 842), and recognition and measurement will occur at the commencement date in the following ways:
  - A lessor shall recognize assets that are under a *finance lease* as accounts receivable in its statement of financial position. Subsequent measurement shall recognize finance income over the lease term, based on a pattern reflecting a constant periodic rate of return on the lessor's net investment in the lease.

- A lessor shall recognize lease payments from an *operating lease* as income generally on a straight-line basis. The lessor can apply another systematic basis if more representative of the pattern when the underlying asset depreciates.

The final stage of the lease lifecycle is the management of its ongoing requirements. For example, changes in the scope of a lease that were not part of the original terms and conditions of the lease contract will prompt a reassessment of the lease that considers the following:

- Whether the lease modification warrants a separate contract
- Whether the modified lease needs to be reclassified
- How initial direct costs, incentives, and any other payments should be accounted
- Whether the lease is being renewed or extended
- Whether the lease modification creates an additional ROU asset

Let's focus now on the SAP RE-FX and SAP Lease Administration solutions and how they align with this new lease lifecycle.

For all the processes in the lease lifecycle, SAP RE-FX facilitates close coordination between the lease accountant, lease administrator, and fixed asset accountant. SAP RE-FX is specifically designed to support majority of the real estate leasing processes like managing critical dates, building and equipment maintenance, early terminations or renewal option, rent escalations, valuation calculations and postings, and service charge settlement. Providing access to the same lease record, SAP RE-FX provides separate authorizations for the lease accountant, the lease administrator, and the fixed asset accountant. As a result, a clear separation of responsibilities and roles will help organize the entirety of the lease lifecycle. Figure 2.6 shows the lease lifecycle process in the context of SAP RE-FX.

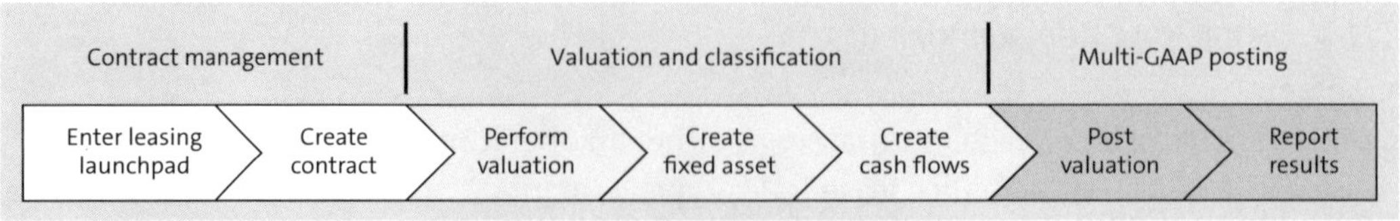


**Figure 2.6** SAP RE-FX Lease Lifecycle Process

- **Contract management**
  Contract management covers the lease identification. This process allows you to create and manage the lease contract information such as lease types, leasing

partners, terms and conditions of the lease, lease payments, and critical dates. You can also attach documents related to the lease contract.

- **Valuation and classification**
  This process covers lease classification and lease recognition and remeasurement; it allows you to define and customize the valuation rules from current or historic valuations and manages the creation or assignment of ROU asset. In addition, you can also perform classification and evaluation rules, create and link lease contracts to fixed assets, create cash flows, and reassess lease modifications. SAP RE-FX will automatically calculate and report on net present value of lease payments, asset depreciation, repayment, and interest rate.
- **Multi-GAAP posting**
  This process covers lease reassessment and remeasurement, wherein the calculation and posting of valuation cash flows will be based on multi-GAAP assignments, not only for IFRS and ASC, but for other accounting standards such as US GAAP or HGB in Germany. In this process, you'll manage your ROU assets, lease liabilities (lease payments) and accounting for customer and vendor accounts receivables and payables. The system will post depreciation and repayments and assign accounting entries to their respective controlling and profit centers.

SAP Lease Administration, too, manages the lease lifecycle starting from lease definition through lease termination. Figure 2.7 shows all the SAP Lease Administration processes in the lease lifecycle: lease definition, lease setup, and lease onboarding constitute lease identification and classification; lease operation and lease termination constitute lease reassessment and remeasurement.

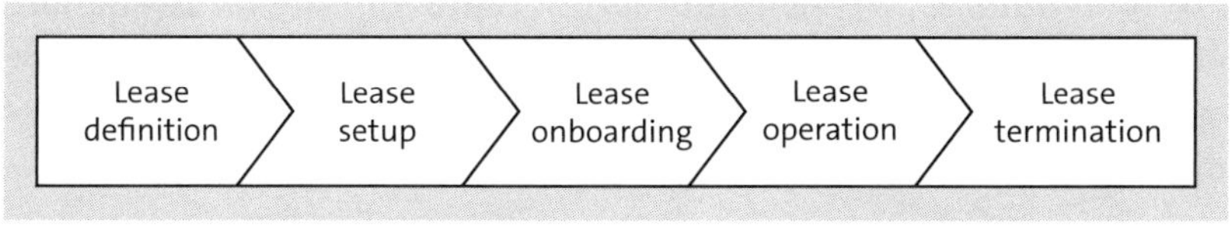


**Figure 2.7** SAP Lease Administration Lease Lifecycle Process

1. **Lease definition**
   The definition of a lease takes on a formal approach to determine the best outcome, support strategic decision-making, and optimize global assets. This process involves asking the "why" and "what" questions on every new lease proposal, which helps establish best practices for every leasing decision.

2. **Lease setup**
   This is the process wherein the contract details, activation, lease terms, and lease conditions are set up. With a unified and integrated solution, lease setup is simplified, and approvals processes are accelerated by enabling close collaboration between lease administrators and key stakeholders. New leases and lease renewals are communicated between authorized approvers to ensure that all legal, financial, and business implications are reviewed, validated, and addressed.
3. **Lease onboarding**
   Lease onboarding is when the lease asset is installed, accepted, and operational to the lessee. Data such as warranty start dates, lease types, sign-offs on operability, and other pertinent data attributes can be added and customized into the leased asset database when needed, which enables you to gather the most important and relevant information on the leased asset put into service.
4. **Lease operation**
   Lease operation is when a leased asset is in its operational term. SAP Lease Administration's intuitive dashboard provides real-time insight into leased asset information such as lease payments, business correspondence, servicing history, and maintenance of leased assets as well as the valuations of leased assets. The unified lease contract data also allows you to track key dates on renewals, maintenance, and expirations.
5. **Lease termination**
   Lease termination refers to the formal close-out of the contract. However, before the contract term ends, SAP Lease Administration automatically flags the lease for review and decision-making. Lease administrators and accountants will then evaluate whether to terminate or renew the lease contract, facilitate equipment returns, and calculate the residual value of the leased asset. This functionality enables companies to proactively collaborate among the various responsible managing units and determine the appropriate lease-end actions to avoid having leases move into an ambiguous state and eliminate evergreen leases that may increase costs significantly.

### 2.4.3 Disclosures and Reporting

This final section discusses the impact to your existing system of the new leasing standards ASC 842 and IFRS 16 on disclosure and reporting requirements.

From what we learned in the introduction to this book, these new standards will require the financial statements and notes to have qualitative and quantitative disclosures about leasing activities. As a result, the information that must be disclosed is increasing substantially, and companies embarking on a compliance project need to evaluate their current systems, business processes, and internal controls to capture the complete and accurate lease data required to formulate the financial statement notes.

However, you need to apply significant judgment in considering the level of detail to be disclosed in the financial notes. The report should not be so overly detailed that readers are overwhelmed with too much information; neither should the details be so high level that the information is not useful. Rather, you should provide enough information to supplement the financial statement values for users and stakeholders to comprehend more fully the nature of your leasing activities.

The disclosure and reporting requirements established by IFRS 16 and ASC 842 are not identical. Key areas of difference include the existing requirements for impairments and the accounting for investment properties. Some minor differences also exist in terms of the accounting for foreign exchange and embedded derivatives and in terms of the disclosure requirements for transitions, business combinations, and transfers/transitioning of secured lease receivables.

Let's look at disclosure and reporting requirements more closely. The disclosures objective of ASC 842 is to enable readers of financial statements to assess the amount, timing, and uncertainty of cash flows arising from leases, including qualitative and quantitative information; meanwhile, the objective of IFRS 16 is for lessees/lessors to disclose information in the notes, the financial position statement, the profit or loss statement, and the cash flow statement that would enable the readers of these financial statements to understand and assess the effect of the leases in their overall financial performance. The disclosure objective statement is the same for both lessee and lessor for these new leasing standards—the important difference relates to the notes that need to be disclosed.

We'll look at lessees first. Table 2.11 shows the information that the lessee needs to disclose whether adopting ASC 842 or IFRS 16. These disclosure requirements, described in ASC 842, paragraph 20-50-3 to 20-50-4 and IFRS 16, paragraphs 52–60, can help you evaluate your current business processes as this information will be readily available as you generate the notes to be included in the financial statements.

| IFRS 16 | ASC 842 |
|---|---|
| A lessee shall disclose information about the leases for which it is a lessee in a single note or as a separate section in its financial statements | A lessee shall consider the level of detail necessary to satisfy the disclosure requirements |

**Table 2.11** Lessee Disclosure Requirements for ASC 842 and IFRS 16

| IFRS 16 | ASC 842 |
|---|---|
| A lessee shall disclose qualitative and quantitative information about its leasing activities:<br>▪ The nature of the lessee's leasing activities<br>▪ Future cash outflows to which the lessee is potentially exposed that are not reflected in the measurement of lease liabilities<br>▪ Restrictions or covenants imposed by leases<br>▪ Sale-and-leaseback transactions | A lessee shall disclose all of the following:<br>▪ A general description of those leases<br>▪ The basis and terms and conditions on which variable lease payments are determined<br>▪ The existence and terms and conditions of options to extend or terminate the lease<br>▪ The existence and terms and conditions of the guaranteed residual value provided by the lessee<br>▪ The restrictions or covenants imposed by leases (e.g., those relating to dividends or incurring additional financial obligations) |
| A lessee shall disclose the following amounts:<br>▪ Depreciation charge from the ROU assets by class of underlying asset<br>▪ Interest expense coming from lease liabilities<br>▪ Expenses coming from short-term leases<br>▪ Expenses coming from leases of low-value assets<br>▪ Expenses coming from variable lease payments not are included in the measurement of lease liabilities<br>▪ Income from subleasing ROU assets<br>▪ Total cash outflow for leases<br>▪ Additions to ROU assets<br>▪ Gains or losses arising from sale-and-leaseback transactions<br>▪ Carrying amount of ROU assets by end of the reporting period and class of underlying asset | A lessee shall disclose the following amounts:<br>▪ Finance lease costs, separated between the amortization of the ROU assets and interest on the lease liabilities (lease payments)<br>▪ Operating lease cost<br>▪ Short-term lease cost with a lease term of 1 month or less, without expenses related to leases<br>▪ Variable lease cost<br>▪ Gross income coming from subleases that are separate from the operating or finance lease expense<br>▪ Net gains or losses arising from sale-and-leaseback transactions |

**Table 2.11** Lessee Disclosure Requirements for ASC 842 and IFRS 16 (Cont.)

In contrast, Table 2.12 shows the information that the lessor needs to disclose whether adopting ASC 842 or IFRS 16 as described in ASC 842, paragraph 30-50-2 to 30-50-13, and IFRS 16, paragraphs 90–97.

| IFRS 16 | ASC 842 |
|---|---|
| A lessor shall disclose these amounts within the reporting period:<br>■ Finance leases—selling profit or loss, finance income on the net investment in the lease, income from variable lease payments not included in the measurement of the net investment in the lease.<br>■ Operating leases—lease income, separately disclosing income involving to variable lease payments that do not depend on an index or a rate. | A lessor shall disclose lease income recognized in the specified report format which includes the following information:<br>■ For sales-type leases (finance leases) and direct financing leases (operating leases)—a profit or loss should be recognized at the commencement date together with the interest income that is either in combined or separated by components of the net investment.<br>■ For operating leases—lease income coming from lease payments.<br>■ Lease income involving to variable lease payments not included in the measurement of the lease receivable |
| A lessor shall disclose these information:<br>■ The nature of the lessor's leasing activities<br>■ How the lessor manages the risk associated with any rights it retains in underlying assets. In particular, a lessor shall disclose its risk management strategy for the rights it retains in underlying assets | A lessor shall disclose both of the following:<br>■ Information about the nature of its leases such as general description of the lease, terms and conditions on which variable lease payments are determined<br>■ Information about significant assumptions and judgments made in applying the requirements<br>A lessor shall disclose information about how it manages its risk associated with the residual value of its leased assets. In particular, a lessor should disclose all of the following:<br>■ Its risk management strategy for residual assets<br>■ The carrying amount of residual assets covered by guaranteed residual value<br>■ Any other means by which the lessor reduces its residual asset risk |

**Table 2.12** Lessor Disclosure Requirements for ASC 842 and IFRS 16

As shown in this section, the new ASC 842 and IFRS 16 disclosure requirements for lessees and lessors involve numerous notes and calculations. SAP Lease Administration and SAP RE-FX can automatically generate the disclosure reports you need to comply with these leasing standards and can help you adopt the new standards quickly and effectively.

## 2.5 Summary

This chapter discussed the impact of new leasing standards and provided you with important information on how to assess your current business processes, your master data, and your software application ecosystem to determine compliance readiness and your ability to adopt the new regulatory changes ASC 842 and IFRS 16.

In the next chapter, we focus on project management for your SAP RE-FX and SAP Lease Administration implementations.

# Chapter 3
# Managing Your Leasing Project



*Good project management and governance are key to sizing up challenges that may lie ahead and to determining which aspects of implementation require the most resources and time. Apart from establishing competent project teams and timelines, you must thoroughly evaluate system and process readiness when planning for an International Financial Reporting Standards 16 or Accounting Standards Codification 842 compliance project.*

Project management and delivery activities are closely tied to the techniques and concepts of using resources effectively. The aim of this chapter is to present an overview of approaches used in project management that have been integrated with established, structured strategies and best practices in SAP. We will cover how several risks associated with delivering large, complex projects can be mitigated by defining the scope of the leasing project (Section 3.1), establishing timelines and deliverables (Section 3.2), choosing your team (Section 3.3), setting your budget (Section 3.4), and holding an effective project kick-off meeting (Section 3.5). Note that much of this information can be applied to non-leasing software projects as well.

## 3.1 Defining the Scope

In this section, we'll delve into how managing project scope can help a leasing project team and its stakeholders appropriately evaluate the amount of effort required to complete a project. This evaluation includes steps to be taken to maintain constant communication between the parties, which will in turn create shared perceptions and a common vision.

### 3.1.1 Choosing Business Processes and Functions

Defining what business processes and functions will be supported by the new system provides both business process experts and end users visibility and awareness of additional SAP functionality they would like to have. Solution experts should have a keen eye for identifying potential technical roadblocks and challenges that might arise, even during conceptualization of requirements.

Any changes in scope must be documented, preferable in a change request. Scenarios where processes are inadvertently overlooked during the business blueprint phase are no exception. Where additional functionality is required, relevant parties (such as the project manager, steering committee, and executive stakeholders) must agree, and this agreement must be recorded before the functionality is added.

One way to prevent unwelcome surprises with changes in project scope is to clearly separate core functionalities and "nice-to-have" functionalities. The latter can be considered after the most crucial issues have been closed. Be sure to also provide for a contingency strategy because changes in scope will usually require more funding and resources.

### 3.1.2 Determining Project Duration

Accurately assessing a project's timeline is a critical factor of SAP project management, as the timeline can serve as a framework for organizing, planning, budgeting, and executing a project to achieve target and goals. For leasing projects, the IFRS 16 and ASC 842 compliance deadlines will influence your implementation timelines.

The responsibility of building best practices guidelines and standards, as well as ensuring that a project is on track lies with the *project management officer* (PMO). The PMO should also have a good understanding of customer requirements as well as knowledge of the SAP software ecosystem. Key factors to be considered while creating an estimate of the project timeline include the project scope (what must be done), the budget (what will it cost), and the schedule (how long you will need to implement the project).

The duration of a project's implementation is influenced by a myriad of factors. Navigating timelines with complex landscapes, cost constraints, and the logistical constraints of large teams can be challenging. Project duration overruns are common pitfalls in failed implementations, often due to shortfalls in change management and a lack of cross-cultural integration. As a result, timelines, budgets, and logistic plans can suffer.

SAP project managers have several tools at their disposal to monitor, assess, and administer projects from start to finish. Evaluating which tools to use and determining how these tools can aid in mitigating risks can be difficult tasks. Proper risk management is therefore essential to ensure that a project is kept within its stipulated timeline.

### 3.1.3 Managing Risks

Identifying all risks as early as possible, preferably at the beginning of your project, will enable you to manage the project effectively. Documenting, monitoring, and measuring risks according to their level of urgency (high, medium, or low) can help team members visualize and understand the impact of potential issues. These risk scenarios may arise due to the lack of resources, the complexity of business requirements, or time constraints, to name a few. Contingency action plans should be built around these issues with a consideration for additional effort and cost that might ensue.

Table 3.1 provides a non-exhaustive list of potential risks that might occur during the implementation of an SAP project. (Remember, we're talking about project risks, not non-compliance risks!) Some risks might be the main cause of delay in project timeline or may be the consequence of the project schedule's prolongation altogether.

| Risk | Cause | Priority | Contingency Plan |
|---|---|---|---|
| Project duration | Wrong time estimation, failure of resource allocation, scope creep | High | Reassessment and reevaluation of timeline required |
| Budget overrun | Inadequate scope management, wrong cost estimation, lack of expenses monitoring | High | Use a more appropriate model to estimate budgets, implement new controls for expense reporting |
| Quality risks | Inadequate solution validations and testing, inadequate project quality standards, insufficient guidelines available | High | Establish new procedures, ensure that adequate quality management processes are implemented |
| Development risks | Misunderstanding of business requirements, unclear expectations of the business, technical difficulties, lack of resources and experienced talent | High | Make use of project management tools to boost communication and collaboration, eliminate ambiguity to facilitate a better understanding of requirements |
| Change management risks | Lack of formal methodology in handling change orders | High | Define criteria for accepting change requests and adjustments made to requirements |

**Table 3.1** Potential Risks in a Project

Should these scenarios arise, be sure to consider factors that are unique to each circumstance and create a detailed plan of the responsible parties involved. For example, some entities may be more prepared than others in consolidating lease data for transition to the new lease standard. While they might have crucial data such as lease terms and payments on hand, they could still encounter gaps in information. Discount rates are unlikely to have been determined for operating leases under IAS 17, and estimating these will demand a great deal of time and resources from teams. Scenarios like these need to be considered while defining and evaluating risks to a leasing project.

Projects running overtime will likely go over budget and fail to create business value and optimal business processes if necessary changes are not executed.

While failing to meet IFRS 16 and ASC 842 compliance timelines may not result in overt consequences, adhering to the new standards is an important demonstration of an entity's professionalism. If stakeholders wish to assess a company's financials, balance sheet numbers will be telling. Furthermore, debt covenants, investment agreements, or the ability to source for credit lines may be affected if an entity is noncompliant.

Delaying IFRS 16 compliance may also impact an entity's choice in determining which transition accounting approach to undertake. Late adopters may find the full retrospective approach to be an unfeasible, time-consuming process, leaving them with the modified retrospective approach (which may not be the more beneficial judgment for the business).

## 3.2 Establishing Timelines and Deliverables

A robust implementation plan is key to realizing a successful project. SAP's standard practice follows the Accelerated SAP (ASAP) implementation methodology. The latest ASAP 8 methodology provides prescriptive, step-by-step frameworks and structures that enable organizations to efficiently and rapidly implement SAP solutions. This methodology charts the key phases of a project from its inception to post-project solution management. Built around each phase is a list of deliverables and supporting activities, where templates, accelerators, and samples that support best practices in SAP are accessible to users.

In this section, we'll discuss how ASAP 8 moves beyond the traditional ASAP methodology to deliver a comprehensive approach to streamlining project management and planning and describe ways in which ASAP 8 can be combined with Agile and Scrum industry standards to prepare organizations for complex customer requirements.



### 3.2.1 Choosing a Project Management Strategy

Both ASAP and ASAP 8 methodologies optimize time, resources, and project teams through six established, consecutive phases. As shown in Figure 3.1 and outlined in Table 3.2, this roadmap provides a rudimentary framework for managing the project, irrespective of the work and activities involved.

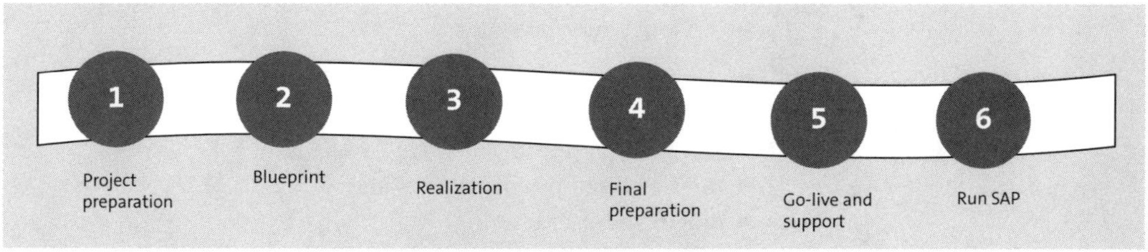


**Figure 3.1** Roadmap of the SAP ASAP 8 Methodology

| Phase | Description |
|---|---|
| 1. Project preparation | ■ Plan project and set up project platform<br>■ Establish implementation standards and procedures<br>■ Identify key stakeholders and determine project requirements<br>■ Kick off the project<br>■ Set up development and quality systems<br>■ Install production hardware<br>■ Run quality check for project preparation |
| 2. Blueprint | ■ Outline detailed documents of the business requirements<br>■ Gather information pooled from meetings and workshops and develop a thorough description of the expected processes and outcomes<br>■ Define the system environment<br>■ Collect configuration requirements<br>■ Generate lists of open issues and change logs<br>■ Develop training and testing plans |

**Table 3.2** ASAP and ASAP 8 Project Implementation Cycle

| Phase | Description |
|---|---|
| 3. Realization | ■ Execute implementation per the business blueprint<br>■ Create technical specifications based on previously defined functional specifications<br>■ Validate organizational configuration<br>■ Validate business processes<br>■ Run organizational change management<br>■ Do production support planning and cutover planning<br>■ Run integration and user acceptance tests<br>■ Plan end-user training<br>■ Conduct internal reviews |
| 4. Final preparation | ■ Transport deliverables to the preproduction system and begin user acceptance testing<br>■ Map out long-term support plans<br>■ Address high-priority open issues<br>■ Begin end-user training<br>■ Fine-tune and polish cutover plans<br>■ Execute cutover<br>■ Perform quality check for the final preparation<br>■ Start production |
| 5. Go-live and support | ■ Monitor live environment<br>■ Resolve any remaining open issues<br>■ Perform quality check for go-live |
| 6. Run SAP | ■ Follow up from go-live and ensure that solution is operable<br>■ Execute previously established long-term support plans<br>■ Refine, optimize, and automate the solution implemented |

**Table 3.2** ASAP and ASAP 8 Project Implementation Cycle (Cont.)

Some differences between ASAP and ASAP 8 exist that make the latter the recommended implementation methodology for SAP RE-FX and SAP Lease Administration projects. ASAP 8 incorporates Agile and Scrum industry standards, using iterative development, which allows for greater flexibility when managing requirements that frequently change.

### Agile Development

The Agile development strategy emphasizes creating business value, seamless integration of systems, and a user-centric design while the project is in its initial stages. Both pragmatic and creative, Agile design helps teams quickly identify gaps in requirements. So instead of following a strictly sequential process before finally achieving a project's goal, Agile design seeks to put the goal first and subsequently build solutions on the problems encountered.

However, combining ASAP with Agile methodology is not without its challenges. While its benefits include the simplification of software delivery through an iterative framework, certain conditions may threaten the stability of the Agile method during project implementation, such as the following:

- Projects with applications that are dependent on one another or that have complicated system landscapes
- Frequent changes in business requirements
- Lack of cultural transition or the existence of organizational dependencies
- Narrow communication bandwidth in large teams

In these instances, deploying ASAP and Agile in combination with a Scrum approach is necessary for navigating these notoriously complex landscapes.

### Scrum Framework

*Scrum* is a popular Agile framework revolving around short iterations of work. These iterations, where products are built and implemented rapidly, and which are fixed in length, are called *sprints*.

The Scrum framework contrasts with the traditional sequential approach of the waterfall methodology shown in Figure 3.2, in which established phases can be easily derailed by changes in project requirements. End users might come to realize that a product is poorly fitted to their needs only during the user acceptance test phase. Where integration points are not met, the project ultimately does not pass muster.

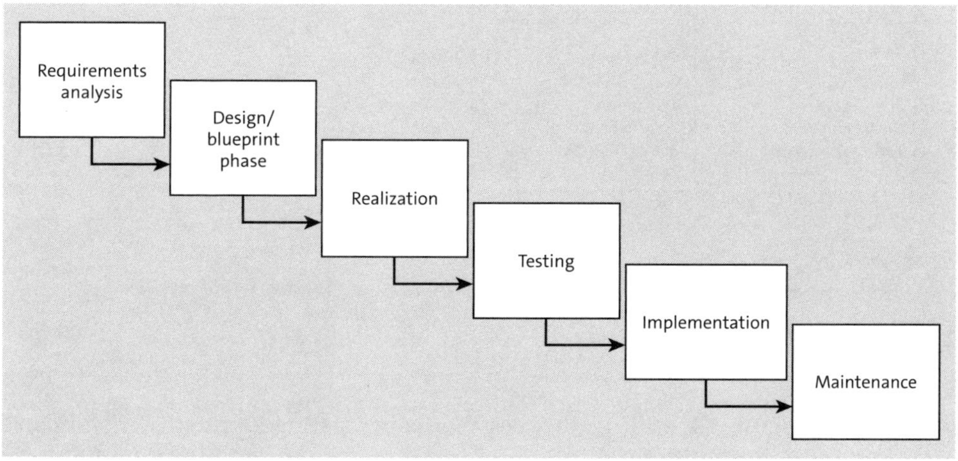


**Figure 3.2** The Waterfall Methodology

As shown in Figure 3.3, an Agile Scrum sprint sees the Scrum team taking small, digestible sets of requirements and transforming them into shippable software. Once coded and tested, these features are integrated into an evolving product.

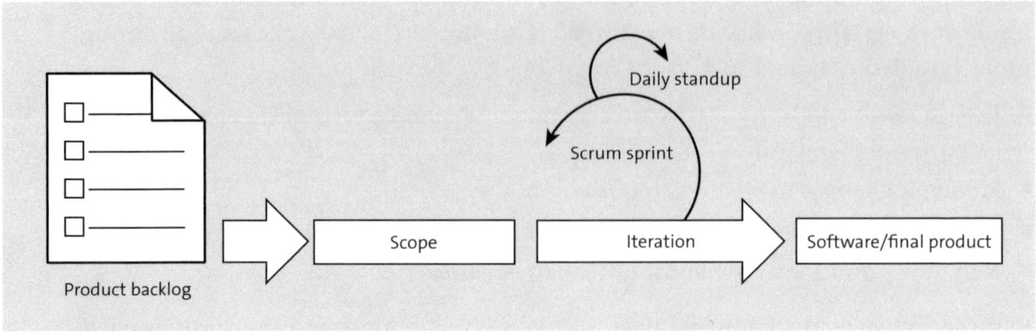


**Figure 3.3** The Scrum Methodology

The Scrum process is broken down into several subprocesses, which is a big advantage over traditional waterfall. The latter requires an extended period of developing, testing, and reviewing before the actual product is delivered. There is a substantial risk that the final software shipped does not meet the requirements and expectations of the customer; this risk is side-stepped with Scrum where a smaller process is developed and deployed in a shorter time frame and the customer can immediately give their feedback on the acceptability of the software.

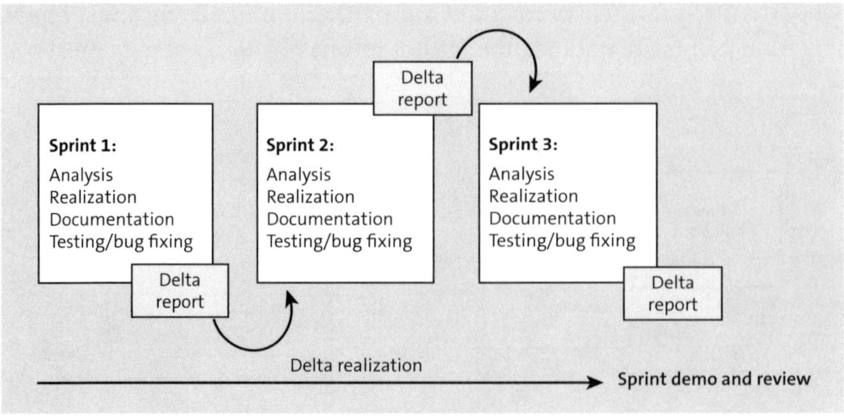


**Figure 3.4** Agile Sprint Plan

As shown in Figure 3.4, each sprint sees the team creating a potentially shippable product increment within an accelerated timeframe. The aim is typically to build the most important functionality or feature of a release; therefore, each sprint is likely to be oriented around a short-term goal. The customer will then be able to gain an empirically based understanding of the software and its development progress.

Scrum teams are often self-organizing and cross-functional (their skills span development, testing, and a good understanding of business requirements) and synchronize their work through daily scrums. A scrum team consists of the project members, the scrum master, and the product owner. The scrum master takes ownership of the project management, schedule, and delivery. This individual also takes on the responsibility of resolving issues that may arise. The product owner, on the other hand, oversees the end-user experience of the product and its acceptance. Together, the scrum team will primarily focus on clearing Scrum backlogs, which lists of requirements generated by the customer.

Scrum teams may also use a burndown chart like the one shown in Figure 3.5, which is a graphical representation of the remaining tasks (or scrum backlog) versus time. The chart is helpful in tracking whether project tasks are on schedule and is an iterative process that depicts functionalities that have been agreed upon with the customer. With every release, features are bundled, and eventually the final product will constitute all the required functionalities that meet customer expectations.

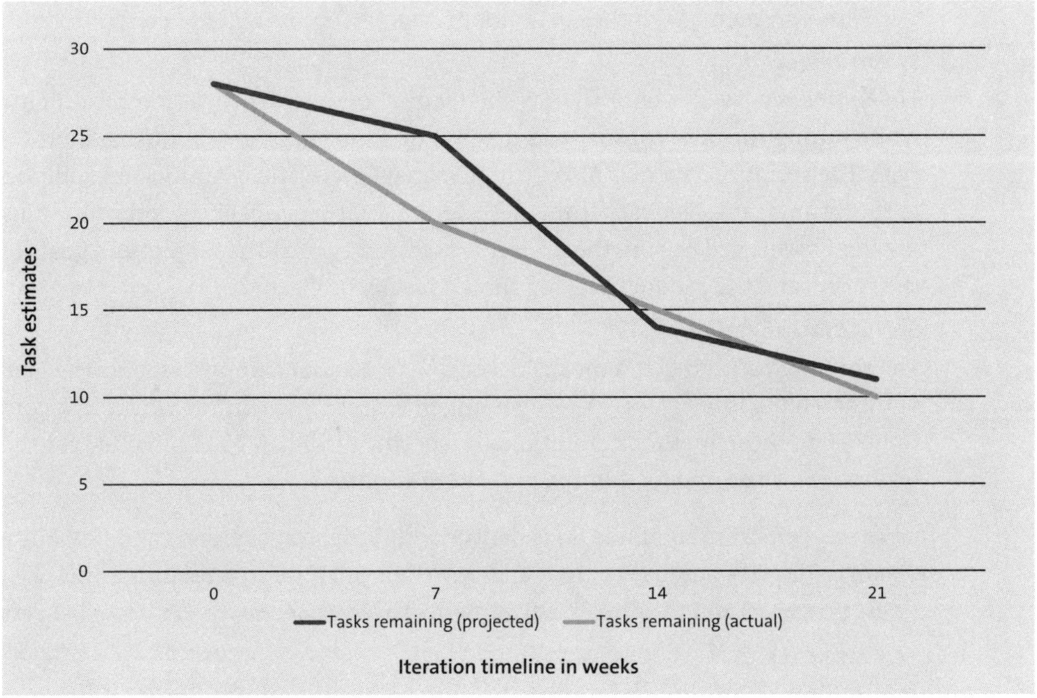


**Figure 3.5** Sample Burndown Chart

A sprint has four crucial factors:

1. **Sprint planning**
   During *sprint planning*, the product owner and the scrum master discuss the product backlog items that will be moved into the sprint backlog. Although the work for the team to do is determined, the team will have the autonomy to decide how the work will be done.

   While the sprint is ongoing, code is developed and tested simultaneously using *test-driven development* (TDD) techniques, continuous integration, and pair programming. Scrum teams are usually cross-functional as well as self-organizing.

2. **Daily scrum**
   Also known as the "daily stand-up," the *daily scrum* is a meeting for the software team get into sync on the tasks to be completed in the coming days. The meeting, which is typically brief and succinct, is attended by the team members, the scrum master, and the product owner. During the daily scrum, team members will review the tasks that have been completed the day before and the tasks to do for the current day and examine if any obstacles complicate the remaining work. Obstacles brought to light during the stand-up are the scrum master's responsibility to rectify. The scrum master may need to help team members debug a program or to clarify requirements with the customer.

3. **Sprint review**
   The *sprint review* is where the Scrum team showcases their accomplishments made during the sprint, usually as a demo of a new functionality using a prototype. The sprint review may also include management and customers in addition to the scrum team. Feedback from these demonstrations will likely determine how the next sprint will be run; the project is assessed against the targets and goals of the sprint, and the product backlog should ideally be cleared.

4. **Sprint retrospective**
   The *sprint retrospective* is a means of seeking continuous improvement. The goal of this meeting is to evaluate methods and practices to determine whether to continue using those methods. Additionally, specific tasks can be highlighted for the team to prioritize and focus on in upcoming sprints.

What the Agile/Scrum methods do is deliver additional transparency and flexibility for changes directly because of their ability to demonstrate to a customer their key business processes and to perform adjustments based on feedback. With smaller sets of features that the development team can work on and refine in incremental cycles, the risk of failure is diminished. The end product built by the development team will be one that is comprehensible and coherent to the customer. Instead of expending teams' energy and resources on developing software that is rejected by other stakeholders, the customer can receive a product that adds value to their critical business processes.

The summary of the ASAP Agile/Scrum methodology's benefits are as follows:

1. **Reduced implementation costs**
   The prescriptive, streamlined ASAP roadmap has the added benefit of advanced delivery management principles that help achieve efficient implementation.
2. **Risk mitigation**
   Identifying risks in every step throughout the process make can help you side-step potential pitfalls. Increased flexibility is afforded as changes are made in increments that can be subsequently released, easing the change management process.
3. **Valuable guidelines from strategy to operations**
   Content is robust, providing implementation accelerators, templates, and guides for projects.
4. **Clear and transparent value delivery**
   Bilateral commitment exists with both the development team and the customer coming to a consensus on deliverables. Regular reflection on the business case also allows parties to monitor changes made.
5. **Enhanced customer engagement**
   By engaging with the customer early in the project, clear communication patterns can be established. Poor communication becomes a less probable cause in project pitfalls.
6. **Business process management guides**
   The tenets of a successful project are broken down into guidelines for good project governance, quality management, and change management.
7. **A sound approach**
   The Agile/Scrum methodology offers a strategy that is mindful of the IT architecture, business processes, and end users.
8. **The entire project lifecycle**
   Comprehensive coverage of each project stage, from evaluation to go-live to post-project solution management is offered.

9. **Provision of content that is consistent in quality and with best practices in SAP**
   Content is provided in value maps, solutions, configuration, and business process monitoring.
10. **Available Solution Explorer**
    The Solution Explorer enables users to search for the most ideal software solutions for their business model and operations.
11. **A proven scalable methodology**
    Solution operations can be set up by guiding teams through use of the methodology.
12. **Ability to integrate with the SAP Solution Manager in both solution operations and implementation**
    The methodology offers simplification of the implementation project and can yield a more seamless implementation process.

The SAP ASAP 8 methodology also serves as a tool for programmers to create software for multiple releases through object-oriented coding, avoiding scenarios where several change requests may arise during a later stage in the project. The methodology features accelerators and rapid deployment tools that truly lay the foundation for a fast and efficient SAP implementation. In defining requirements clearly and allowing room for change requests, the Agile/Scrum framework helps to manage expectations and create greater visibility of the project evolution.

### 3.2.2 Planning Project Phases

Utilizing the correct methodology for your organization is crucial to exercising control over project timelines. A project may have any number of phases depending on its complexity. A single phase is the grouping of logically related activities that result in the completion of one or more deliverables. While multiple phases can exist in a project, they are typically part of sequential processes that have been made to guarantee control over the project and its desired outcomes.

So, the Agile/Scrum methodology can reduce total cost of ownership with preconfigured use cases and test scenarios, which help to accelerate an implementation. As previously discussed, transparent development and delivery methods help the team consistently reflect on the business case. By breaking the implementation down into straightforward and manageable processes, business scenarios can be easily measured against defined best practices. The framework of the SAP ASAP 8 methodology can also be applied using the methods of the Scrum framework, with the sprint cycle beginning during the blueprint phase shown in Figure 3.6.

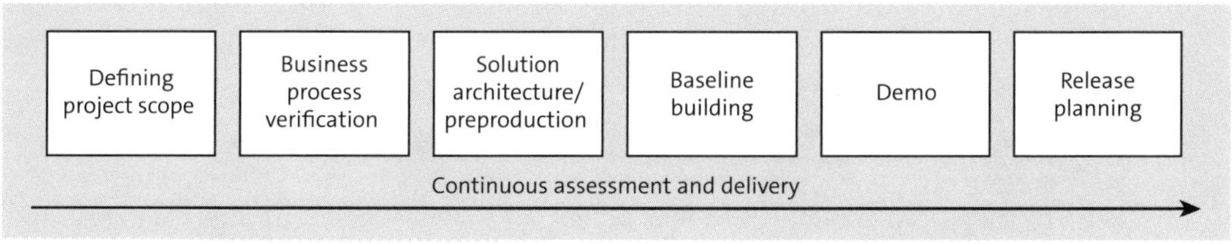


**Figure 3.6** Agile Business Blueprint

### Project Preparation

The project preparation phase is where scrum roles and responsibilities are set in stone and documentation standards alongside hardware requirements are examined by the team. Master data, conversions, security, authorizations, and interfaces are thoroughly discussed during this phase.

### Blueprint Phase

Preconfigured scenarios that the team will map to business processes during this phase will serve as the established baseline for the sprint cycle. The core objective is to dissect complex requirements into tangible sprint release cycles that allow manageable features for every release. During this phase, the product backlog, which details the list of custom developments and priorities (the *delta list*), will be established with the standards SAP configuration.

The product owner's focus will be on the experience of the end user, and the product owner should also be mindful to difference between "need-to-have" and "nice-to-have" functionalities. The project team will evaluate the amount of effort required for the developments by distinguishing crucial processes that can be achieved using standard SAP software with the delta list requirements.

After blueprint workshops have been conducted, teams ought to come to a consensus on the set of features that will be implemented as the baseline and the features that will be part of future sprint cycle releases. The baseline configuration will constitute:

- System configuration
- Planned number of release cycles based on delta customization requirements

Teams can scope out projects based on their business' unique priorities before deciding how to map business processes in the SAP solution. An effective way to determine scope is to define key activities and deliverables when analyzing project goals and objectives. Table 3.3 shows an example of how activities might be examined during the blueprint phase.

| Activity | Key Milestones | Deliverable |
|---|---|---|
| Map business processes to preconfigured SAP models | Customer signing off on process design | Envisioning processes and creating the solution design |
| Documentation of the to-be processes | Customer signing off on solution design | Designing the to-be business processes |
| Gap analysis of functionalities and features | Delta list/product backlog | Effort estimation and evaluation of processes |
| Final business sign-off | Resolution of identified gaps in functionality | Approval of design documents by the product owner and the business |
| Sprint and release cycle planning | Evaluation of scope and of scrum backlog | Sprint realization and definition |

**Table 3.3** Sample ASAP Agile Blueprint Plan

#### Realization Phase

Recall from Figure 3.3 that the sprint cycle is implemented after initial analysis, based on the product backlog requirements that were collected and defined in the blueprint. These two phases are already accelerated where the preconfigured scenarios (such as order-to-cash) are deployed. The subsequent sprint releases will see the team implementing backlogs, which are additional requirements otherwise known as features. With each incremental release, a set of features is introduced to the customer, although releases may change per the requirements of the business. Documentation and testing typically follow the realization phase, and these two activities are primarily automated.

#### Final Preparation

During the final preparation phase, the sprint backlogs (which are vetted by the product owner) should have been cleared and all required releases completed.

In this phase, teams will complete system readiness checks prior to go-live. Preparation and plans for cutover activities is crucial; the latter must also be approved by management, team leads, and the steering committee. Be sure to allocate time for knowledge transfers between consultants, technical teams, and end users to ensure that every team member understands the functionalities of the new system. Finally, the entire system should be tested and fine-tuned until new processes are running smoothly.



#### Go-Live and Support

The final product release will be the final go-live of the project; the frequency and number of go-lives and release durations will depend on the complexity of the project.

This phase will see teams move to a live system environment, monitoring system performance and testing extensively. Post go-live support must be set up to ensure that system behavior is optimized, and all open issues must be resolved as soon as possible.

#### Run SAP

This phase is important to ensure that, once implemented, the solution functions as expected. Additional support from external teams may be required in monitoring and supporting systems over the course of the following quarter. Teams must be well prepared for various scenarios and ensure that all functionalities are optimized and fully operable.

The methodology that SAP ASAP 8 provides offers several guides and project templates that can navigate project implementations in accordance to best practices.

### 3.2.3 Setting Project Timelines

The success of an SAP project is strongly influenced by the duration of its implementation; in other words, the longer a project takes, the more likely the project will experience a budget overrun and impinge on actual benefits derived. Leasing projects are no different.

Organizations hope to implement new software in the fastest, most cost-effective manner possible while creating value for their business. However, specific tasks and deliverables vary drastically from project to project, and poor planning, the misalignment of expectations, and the lack of solution validation are impediments to setting the right implementation timeline and completing key project tasks and deliverables on time. While any number of factors might influence a project's time horizon, proper process management and the deployment of a good project management methodology can help to overcome both business-related and project-related pitfalls.

Let's go through some tips for setting a realistic implementation timeline.

Comparing your business to similar organizations (or to those in the same industry) can provide valuable insight into the amount of time to expect when implementing initiatives.

The size and nature of a company's business will greatly influence the resources required for a leasing project. The implementation timeframes for SAP Lease Administration and SAP RE-FX projects may range from one up to two years. Activities in this cycle include impact assessment, lease data collection and evaluation, business process verification, and disclosure optimization in addition to the ASAP phases described. Naturally, effort estimation will also depend on existing gaps in your current IT system. Entities must also consider if current processes and controls are robust enough to tackle reporting and compliance risks.

The difficulties faced during implementation may be unique to the industry, and deployment may take longer if requirements are complex, but you can get a reasonable idea of how long your project should take by observing your peers' projects and undertaking these activities:

- **Creating a comprehensive implementation plan**
  Determining precisely which business processes will be improved and what the expected outcome should be is helpful. Don't try to tackle everything all at once; limiting the scope of the processes to be implemented during each phase or sprint can provide clarity and help teams within your organization prioritize accordingly.
- **Building and training teams**
  Establishing team structures and setting goals along with roles and responsibilities will streamline the setup of solution operations and eliminate confusion.
- **Prioritizing governance and control**
  It is crucial for project teams to leverage controls to ensure that change requests, scope increases, and other pitfalls do not derail the project timeline. Clearly defining decision-making processes and instituting a chain of command will aid in communication among stakeholders and mitigate the risks of project overruns.

### 3.2.4 Leveraging Accelerators

The accelerators used in the ASAP methodology provides structured, prescriptive, and scalable methods or powerful workarounds to implementing SAP software.

For example, sprint planning revolves around creating shippable software through incremental release cycles. Templates and guidelines available for the custom code lifecycle are therefore primarily focused on the realization phase of development. When beginning custom code development, good change control plays a crucial part in ensuring that all project phases run smoothly. Unidentified gaps may surface only during the realization phase, resulting in defects; therefore, utilizing a software requirements specification template is important to aid in the tracking of these gaps in requirements that were not established in the scrum baseline.

The team can also make use of custom code developed for similar projects, eliminating the need to build code from the ground up. However, when writing code from scratch, adherence to coding standards and best practices is essential.

### SAP Eclipse

During the sprint release cycle (which coincides with the realization phase), teams should trace changes in business requirements and constantly refer to the original technical and functional specification. This technique is used by the team to avoid having to make any design overhauls, and progress is measured against tangible product releases and delivered features. Technical documentation, which usually is heavily focused on the implementation of code in relation to the development language used, is cumbersome to integrate into operational manuals.

In recent years, the documentation process has been streamlined and standardized by an integrated development environment software suite known as Eclipse, which consolidates the basic tools and workspace needed by developers to code and test their software. Most specifically, SAP Eclipse encompasses documentation that has been introduced in the code itself, which delivers a sustainable and scalable means of documenting technical specifications that can be combined with an operational handbook. This feature addresses the challenges faced when technical documentation quickly becomes obsolete each time a change request is implemented.

Two *integrated development environments* (IDEs) are offered by SAP: the SAP NetWeaver IDE Workbench and the ABAP in Eclipse Workbench. The latter offers the essential features for an ABAP development project and has several advantages over the SAP NetWeaver IDE, such as:

- Integrated documentation
- Flexible and customizable Eclipse user interface for ABAP development tools
- Ability to develop virtual database models and create Core Data Service (CDS) views

### The Switch Framework

The Switch Framework simplifies system landscapes by adopting industry solutions as part of a standard system. The framework allows the user to manage the visibility of repository objects or their components using "switches." These solutions are delivered with the system but are in an inactive state—where required, one does not need to install the solution but simply activates it. The switch controls whether the code within its framework is executed at run time or otherwise. All reports, includes, classes, function modules, and Web Dynpro ABAP user interface may be changed or enhanced.

The Switch Framework shown in Figure 3.7 consists of three components:

- **A business function set**
  Can refer to an industry solution and is part of a group of business functions
- **A business function**
  An independent function comprising a set of switches
- **A switch**
  A repository object that controls the visibility of other repository objects

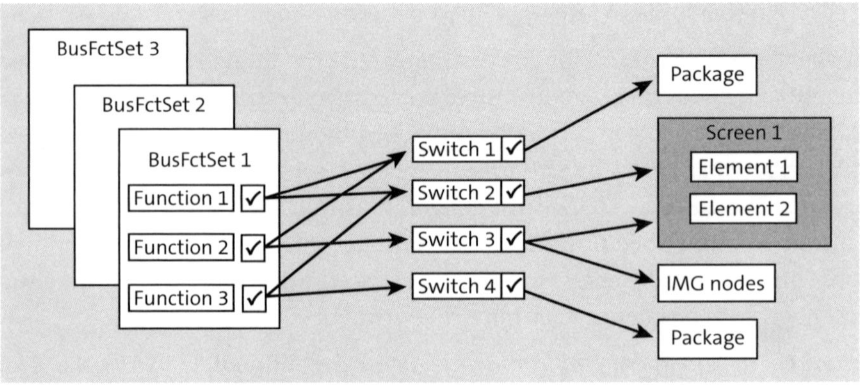


**Figure 3.7** The Switch Framework Architecture

Enhancements in code may also be added to standard SAP software, utilizing enhancement points within the tenets of the Switch Framework. These enhancements can be easily added or retired per their usage or as required by the business. They help to eliminate redundancies and maintenance that ensues with substantial amounts of custom code.

### RACI Matrix

Another extremely helpful tool in custom code development is the *Responsible Accountable Consulted Informed* (RACI) matrix. RACI is often used in project management as a framework to determine and document project roles and responsibilities. Miscommunication between teams can often be avoided by deploying this matrix to ensure successful change management.

The key activities of the RACI matrix are as follows:

- During the project planning phase, identify and list all tasks in the scrum backlog as well as additional features. These tasks should be documented chronologically and in order of priority. During this phase, project teams may also incorporate ASAP methodology-derived deliverables.
- Project stakeholders should be identified and recorded in the chart.
- As shown in Table 3.4, for each task, the model will be used to determine who will be responsible (R), accountable (A), consulted (C), and informed (I).
- For every task, whether a work package or deliverable, only one stakeholder is held accountable.
- Conflict resolution and collaboration are essential activities in creating the RACI model with all project stakeholders, which should occur before the deployment of the SAP software.

| Activity/Deliverable/ Work Package | Deployment Team | Project Manager | Core Team | Process Owner | PMO |
|---|---|---|---|---|---|
| Bug fixing/defect approval | C | A | R | I | I |
| Integration test script writing | R | A | C | C | I |
| User acceptance test execution | C | A | I | R | I |

**Table 3.4** Sample RACI Test Deliverables Matrix

### SAP Solution Manager

SAP Solution Manager is a centralized application management solution designed to support complete project lifecycles. This environment offers project management tools, process modeling, change management, and solution documentation templates among other accelerators. SAP Solution Manager is content rich in preconfigured methods that can be deployed immediately for evaluation and operational processing of systems.

SAP Solution Manager acts as a knowledge repository of accelerators to guide teams along each phase of the project and:

- Offers project and process best practices in the form of plans and templates
- Provides end-to-end functionality for application management, providing project plans and process models to help with process mapping and solution design
- Provides full lifecycle support
- Delivers tools that are centered around the implementation, operational and optimization aspects of an SAP project

Tools available include the following:

- Project Estimator
- Concept Check Tool
- SAP Implementation Assistant
- ASAP 8 Implementation Roadmap
- Question and Answer Database
- Business Process Master List
- Implementation Guide
- Continuous Business Process Engineering

SAP Solution Manager can be used to support all project stages of your leasing implementation:

1. **Preparation/blueprint phase**
   Methodology definition, system landscape setup, and the establishment of documentation processes can be seamlessly executed, thanks to the process-driven approach provided by SAP Solution Manager. Business scenarios, configurations, and testing processes can be extracted from the central repository. Subsequently, process steps can be structured into the project using readily available blueprint documents and functional processes.

   Document templates have change histories and can also be customized based on the needs of the project—examples of customization include business hierarchies and process-level customization. From managing functional specifications to handling development and testing of custom code, SAP Solution Manager is a powerful platform for project administration.

2. **Realization phase**

   This phase will govern the actual system configuration, and SAP Solution Manager helps ensure the quality of deliverables by allowing traceability of all changes that have been made and status updates of developments that have been released. These change management processes include the approval of process for change requests, as well as the deployment and analysis of changes.

   The Change Request Management (ChaRM) functionality may also be used to address certain challenges faced, such as:

   - Unknown dependencies may exist in SAP components.
   - Changes successfully tested in the source system (e.g., quality) may have unprecedented results in the target system (e.g., production) because of missing transports or configuration.
   - Development and quality systems might become out of sync when imports occur out of sequence or if transports are left out.

   The ChaRM functionality provides the project team with the ability to trace requirements, individual change requests, and overall project progress. Through workflows, team members can communicate activities that need to be completed for each change request. Measures and safeguards are also in place to determine where transports can be applied based on the project phase—if a project, while in its testing phase, is met with an attempt to apply a transport to production, an error message will be triggered.

3. **Final preparation**

   SAP Solution Manager acts as a centralized repository of testing materials and results that supports cross-component testing. This capability accelerates the preparation of test scripts as well as execution. Included in the software is a service desk that can help users handle incidents efficiently with centralized managing of support messages. All phases of the project are given technical support, from planning to deployment, operations, and optimization.

   You can also set up real-time monitoring of systems with SAP Solution Manager, thus easing administrative workload.

As demonstrated, the SAP Solution Manager is a powerful tool in project management and administration. Adept in handling activities and tasks related to the entire project implementation, SAP Solution Manager is also equipped with functions to help avoid common pitfalls in projects by isolating performance bottlenecks; increasing transparency of activities, users, and processes; and efficiently identify and map changes made to the project landscape. The software behaves like a central administration interface for all kinds of transports and system landscapes, integrating development workbenches into a change control system.

Altogether, SAP Solution Manager is an excellent platform to consider in supporting document management, implementation monitoring, and change control management during the project roadmap stages. The solution is immensely useful in bolstering good project management and avoiding common issues that plague implementation projects such as scope creep, budget overruns, and unrealistic schedules.

## 3.3 Choosing Your Team

Past SAP projects have shown that people are the decisive factor in a project's success or failure. The more elaborate the project landscape and environment, the greater the need to detail what resources will be required, how they will be deployed, and when they will be involved.

In our experience with leasing projects, each organization will require both internal and external personnel.

### 3.3.1 Internal Personnel

Your organization has limited internal resources, which makes it particularly important that you plan ahead.

#### Manpower Planning

Strategic resource planning begins with determining your internal team members' actual availability—including accounting for time used for trainings, public holidays, and vacation times. It is also important to ensure that the appropriately qualified employees are present for the entire project duration. Furthermore, as shown in Figure 3.8, different manpower requirements may arise during distinct phases; for example, the blueprint phase will require persons with skills in strategy and business process analysis. In the realization phase, individuals with strong technical skills and the ability to analyze user and business needs are essential.

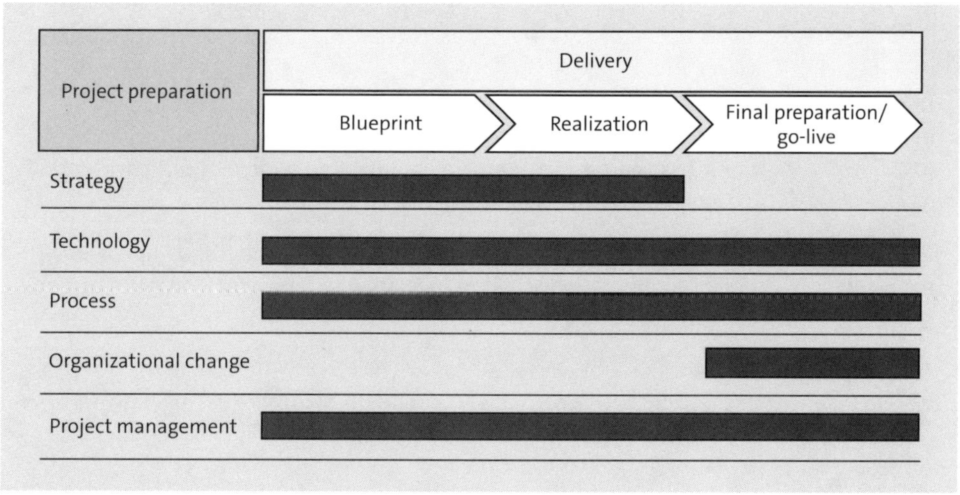


**Figure 3.8** Manpower Planning for Project Implementations

Therefore, capacity requirements should be consolidated based on the required skill levels and mapped against key project roles. These key project roles will then in turn be outlined to provide an idea of the skill sets required throughout the project lifecycle. Specific roles and functions of personnel may vary depending on the type of project and its complexity, some of which are listed in Table 3.5.

| Role | Description |
| --- | --- |
| Project manager | The project manager will assume responsibility for planning and executing all aspects of the project. He or she will oversee all project teams and deliverables; perform quality assurance checks and change management; budget for the project; and deliver methods, standard, and guidelines. |
| Integration manager | This individual will oversee supervision and training of technical personnel, as well as execute project management procedures to ensure the successful integration of business and technical design. The project and integration managers will work closely together to define the standards for solution design, testing, deploying, and cutover approaches for the project. |
| Team lead | The team lead will manage the project team staff while directly supporting the project manager in planning, solution monitoring, and general control over project management. |

**Table 3.5** Personnel Roles and Functions

| Role | Description |
|---|---|
| Organizational change management (OCM) lead | The OCM lead is responsible for spearheading and integrating activities centered around organizational change management with established project deliverables. This individual will oversee human and organizational risks posed to the implementation and set in motion activities that can help to avoid or minimize these risks. |
| Configuration manager | This configuration manager will oversee the planning and implementation of configuration activities in relation to the system infrastructure and environment. |
| Test manager | The test manager will take charge of all activities related to the test phase of the project. This person will coordinate, plan, and manage the testing of IT solutions that were developed or acquired during the development phase. |
| Training lead | The training lead will have a system-specific set of capabilities and strong knowledge and understanding of areas like development and solution design in addition to the business requirements. He or she will impart system knowledge to stakeholders where required and take ownership of trainings and workshops that may be held. |

**Table 3.5** Personnel Roles and Functions (Cont.)

The benefits of having an in-house team will be that these individuals typically have a deeper understanding of the business and its unique processes and challenges. Familiarity with company standards and best practices, naming and terminology are factors that can greatly ease the implementation process—as internal advisors to the project, in-house team members have an advantage in the areas of strategic change trajectories or culture transformations. Their commitment to realizing their own designs will run deep as they will continue to play a crucial role post-implementation. Moreover, internal persons' existing relationships shared with their colleagues and other departments provide them with stronger, more efficient channels of communication.

#### Balancing Project Work and Daily Activities

However, maintaining a comprehensive in-house leasing project team can be costlier when compared to outsourcing, as in-house teams need training and employee turnover scenarios may need to be managed.

Furthermore, organizations operate in dynamic corporate landscapes that are subject to change. Restructuring, mergers and acquisitions, and other changes that may occur will demand the time and attention of internal project employees, preventing them from being fully engaged in the project.



In preparing for a leasing project, you should involve departments such as accounting, real estate, operations, procurement, IT, and tax in planning. The daily responsibilities of employees can also hinder a project from being executed quickly and efficiently. The deployment of the qualified employees at the right time in the project can become an even more daunting task.

### 3.3.2 External Consulting

External consultants help to facilitate requirement definitions, and aid the project in navigating through standardization and change management processes. They bring the following benefits to the project:

- Established project methodologies and procedures
- Sufficient manpower on the project team
- Relevant system expertise
- Industry knowledge

However, if the leasing project team is made up of solely external personnel, company culture and organizational change management may hinder information flow. Information deficits can consequently arise where discussions of key aspects of the business processes and requirements are kept within internal departments. Despite efforts for coordination and communication, the separation between externals and internals can serve as a weak point in the project. If these gaps in information flow escalate, developments made by the external team may miss the mark entirely and not suit the business' requirements at all.

The disadvantages posed by strictly internal or external teams can be avoided by having both in-house and external consultants on the project team. From a project management perspective, involving external consultants can give the project team greater awareness of best practices in the realization of to-dos and established deliverables. These external persons will be free from bias and will be able to evaluate organization standards, processes, and structures objectively. Flaws in the organization's operations and patterns of behavior are more likely to be quickly identified and resolved.

Engaging external consultants also means that companies can leverage the wealth of resources and collective knowledge that a team of specialized professionals can provide. Consultants can ease the load on your internal departments and can be sources of vital information about the project implementation. With their hands-on leasing project experience, they are well equipped to train your employees and promote knowledge transfer within the company.

The formation of functioning teams made up of both internal and external personnel creates a platform for high degrees of information exchange. Striking a good balance between having access to information and understanding of the business requirements and adhering to project implementation best practices is an important, even critical, success factor in spreading system-specific knowledge within the company and bolstering the expertise of both parties.

## 3.4 Setting Your Budget

Budgeting is a cost estimation process that leverages estimating tools, past project experience, and a detailed work breakdown structure (WBS) for cost allocation. Estimating costs at the initial stages of a project is crucial to obtaining a complete and accurate quote on the total cost of a project to continue the process of project evaluation. Quantifying all factors that go into a budget plan can be challenging and time consuming, particularly for large organizations executing projects of high degrees of complexity. While estimating your leasing project budget and costs, consider the following five key elements, regardless of scope, timelines, or required functions.

### 3.4.1 Implementation Teams

Costs associated with implementation teams may constitute education, training, project management, and external consultancy support to name a few. This implementation cost is indicative of the scale of work and overall size of project teams. While implementation team costs may be comprised by myriad factors, we can break them down into key components to determine the estimated level of effort, which in turn provides a platform for a more accurate estimation of the budget. The components to be considered when aligning resources may include:

- Project management
- Business process analyses
- Quality assurance management

- Organizational change management
- Solution design and deployment
- Configuration
- Documentation
- Training
- Testing

### Internal Teams

Internal teams may gather the heads of divisions such as operations, real estate, controlling, treasury, and information technology. Where their expertise is required for the IFRS 16 or ASC 842 project, they will be contacted to aid in data gathering and performing readiness assessment checks. These tasks may include determining which of the entities' contracts contain leases and determining whether existing systems and processes will be adequate for ongoing audit assessments. These heads of divisions will inform the project management team of the number of billable hours their division will require.

### Blended Rates

This pricing model uses a single rate for all resources, regardless of their level of skill, expertise, or location. This method of skill-pool pricing would, for example, see a $200/hour charge for all developer resources irrespective of their years of experience. Blended rates are typically the average rate charged based on hourly rates billed.

### External Teams

Vendors or external consulting firms may charge a fixed cost for services or charge on a time and material (T&M) basis. Table 3.6 breaks down an example of a T&M engagement card that charts the hourly rates for external consultants, architects, and developers on a project.

| Experience | Consultant | | Technical Architect | | ABAP Developer | |
|---|---|---|---|---|---|---|
| Onsite | Offsite | Onsite | Offsite | Onsite | Offsite | |
| 3–4 years | $250 | $150 | $275 | $200 | $250 | $150 |
| 5–7 years | $300 | $250 | $350 | $275 | $300 | $250 |
| 8–10 years | $400 | $350 | $425 | $325 | $400 | $350 |

**Table 3.6** Sample T&M Engagement Card

Separate phases of the project will entail different implementation resource demands; therefore, project expenditures will vary throughout the implementation if a T&M contract is used. Unlike a blended rate, different grades of consultants will command different charges.

At the tail end of a project, before go-live, it is paramount that you plan for hours dedicated to knowledge transfer to the application management support (AMS) team. In budgeting for teams, don't forget to consider travel expenses, including airfare, accommodation, and allowances.

### 3.4.2 Software and License Fees

Determining the total software cost begins by reviewing your business's existing licenses, as well as the potential products in the market that could be purchased to leverage the project implementation. The team can identify additional licenses for the SAP system by evaluating and documenting existing gaps in capabilities and project scope.

Costs are also incurred during the course of the project for key services. Table 3.7 gives an example of service fees estimated by the number of hours and skills required.

| Service | Description | Hours | Estimation |
|---|---|---|---|
| Installation of server | Installation may include subsystems, operating systems, databases, and specific SAP components | 8 | $1,100.00 |
| Conversion of legacy software | Conversion of data from the firm's legacy software maybe required. Tasks that may be included in this service include importing the chart of accounts, summarizing the general ledger accounts, and converting your master data | 30 | $4,250.00 |
| Application setup | The implementation of SAP RE-FX, for example, will entail the integration of the solution with SAP Finance, eliminating several applications from the system landscape. | 28 | $3,500.00 |
| Forms and report modifications | Document types may need to be created to differentiate transactions posted (e.g., for SAP Lease Administration). Reports may also need to be modified to accommodate reporting on the ledger. | 6 | $500.00 |

**Table 3.7** Example of Service Fees

Some assumptions also must be made while budgeting for software costs, including initial costs, service fees, timing that the cost is incurred (usually at project inception), support from SAP, and subscription timeframes.



### 3.4.3 Hardware Costs

"Hardware costs" is a broad term that may constitute personal computer costs and overhead associated with using facilities for workshops and meetings. The nature of this type of cost is largely dependent on team sizes and peak headcounts over the course of the project.

For example, facility costs may be calculated by square foot per resource, which may fluctuate depending on rents on the space, or the number of reserved workstations required for onsite activity. PC costs, on the other hand, will likely arise from the need to provide company laptops to new external members on the project team, while the existing headcount can leverage existing PC resources. Having the entire project team operate through laptops owned by the business can facilitate information flow and reduce security risks.

### 3.4.4 Maintenance Costs

Ongoing maintenance of installed SAP software refers to the essential resources required to support the application software and delivered modules post implementation and in production. A business may choose to continue existing maintenance procedures and contracts or leverage its own internal resources and human capital instead. This support may be divided into three areas:

- **Functional application support**
  Support in this area requires personnel with both technical and functional skills. Moreover, these individuals should possess knowledge and expertise of business processes and configuration know-how. They will support the project post-implementation by performing root cause analysis where needed. Functional support teams usually directly liaise with the business to identify bugs and other problems and to facilitate issue resolution.
- **Technical application support**
  Persons providing technical application support should be equipped with the skills to debug programs and address problems by identifying the root causes in the code. These individuals may also liaise directly with SAP as a vendor or by reporting incidents in the support portal. These teams may also be involved in the application of patches as well as solution monitoring.

- **Infrastructure support**
  This support includes support from SAP Basis teams, as well as the monitoring of operating systems and servers. Technical hardware support encompasses both the physical architecture of servers and the core technical software components. Floor costs should also be accounted for, where floor space, electricity, and handling expenses that are associated with the architecture.

### 3.4.5 Contingencies

Changes in project scope and additional requirements from the business may arise over the course of the project implementation. Budgeting for these scenarios is key to project risk management and to avoiding common pitfalls like unexpected budget overruns. Incidents that can contribute to a change in scope include the following:

- **New requirements**
  Requirements may be overlooked during the business blueprint and design phase, only to arise later in the project.
- **New product capabilities**
  New releases of software modules may enter the market. These new products may have capabilities that the business would want to leverage in their implementation, extending the project's time horizon.
- **Changes in implementation timelines**
  Many reasons exist for a shift in timelines, such as resource constraints or organizational changes. A change in timelines would significantly impact implementation costs.

#### Work Breakdown Structure for Costing and Resource Allocation

Complex projects can be made more manageable by breaking activities down into individual components following a hierarchical structure—also known as a *work breakdown structure* (WBS). Tasks that can be performed independently of others are defined, easing the process of resource allocation and allowing tasks to be more easily monitored. Using a WBS, actual and planned utilization can be easily compared.

Task planning begins with the WBS, and the project schedule should list projected deadlines, specifying dependencies among tasks to aid the project team in exerting greater control over project progress. Listed below are the steps that can be defined in the project schedule:

1. Identify and document tasks to be completed in a WBS.
2. Define dependencies between WBS elements.
3. Perform effort estimation for every activity and task listed.
4. Allocate resources for each task.
5. Provide a well-informed estimate of the project start and end dates, as well as the resources to be allocated for each component and phase of the project.

The WBS tool can also define a sequence of tasks and a clear hierarchy of elements. As shown in Figure 3.9, each WBS generates a hierarchy level, which is then broken down into layers of component parts.

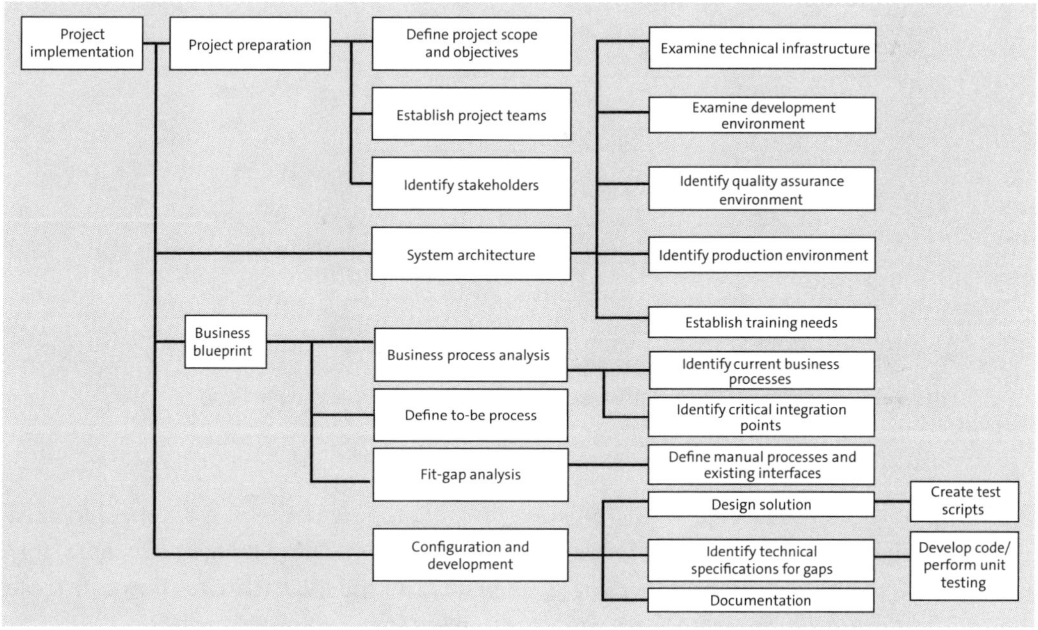


**Figure 3.9** Using a WBS for Project Planning

The WBS, when combined with a project methodology like ASAP, can help mitigate poor project planning and can successfully guide organizations in forecasting and planning realistic budgets by decomposing SAP project phases into defined deliverables. The WBS equips the PMO to recognize how budgets can skyrocket the longer a task is worked on.

While most projects follow the S-curve graph of estimated cumulative expenditure over time shown in Figure 3.10, exerting control over the timing of these expenditures can aid in proper budget planning. This pattern of expenditure is typical of many projects where resources are slowly expended before increasing exponentially, and then tapering off as the project ends.

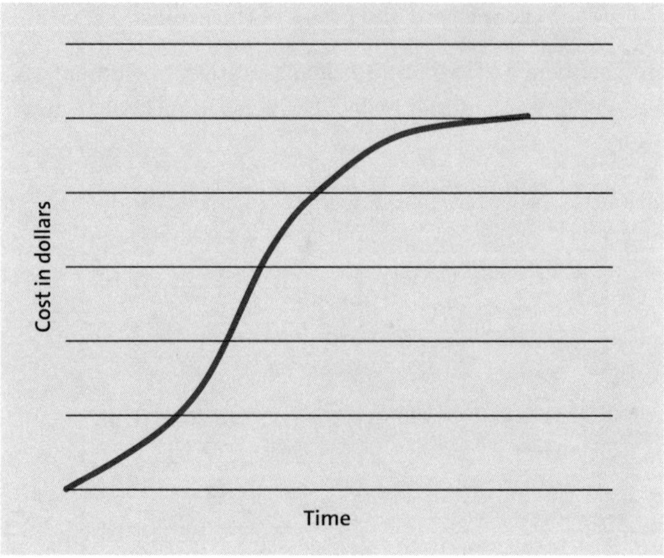


**Figure 3.10** Estimated Cumulative Expenditures of the Project over Time

### Earned Value Management

Upon agreement of the scope of work, budgets for elements of work are allocated through the *earned value management* (EVM) process. These budgets are invariably tied to baseline-approved work package plans, and the EVM metrics shown in Table 3.8 can help you evaluate these work parameters for a successful project.

| Metric Name | Description | Formula |
|---|---|---|
| Budget at completion (BAC) | Total amount budgeted for the task | Value |
| Planned value (PV) | The approved budget for the work schedule with a deadline | Planned % complete × BAC |

**Table 3.8** EVM Metrics

| Metric Name | Description | Formula |
|---|---|---|
| Earned value (EV) | The approved budget of work that was completed within a deadline | % complete × BAC |
| Actual cost (AC) | The actual costs incurred for the work completed by the specified date | Value of actual cost |
| Cost performance index (CPI) | The ratio of the approved budget for work performed to what was spent for work | EV/AC |
| Cost variance (CV) | Earned value less actual cost: The difference between the budgeted amount and the amount spend for work performed | EV – AC |
| Schedule variance (SV) | Earned value less planned value: The difference between the budgeted amount for actual work done and work planned | EV – PV |
| Schedule project index (SPI) | The ratio of the budget for work completed to the budget for work planned | EV/PV |
| Estimate at completion (EAC) | Estimate of total cost of a task | BAC/CPI |
| Variance at completion (VAC) | Estimate of the amount of budget required to complete outstanding work for the task | BAC – EAC |

**Table 3.8** EVM Metrics (Cont.)

The EVM process is comprised of three key components:

- The planned value (PV) is the approved budget for the work schedule with a deadline and is equal to a task's budget at completion (BAC), which is the total budgeted amount for the task.
- The earned value (EV) is the approved budget of work that was completed within a deadline.

- Actual cost (AC) is the actual costs incurred for the work completed by the specified date.

The premise of EVM is that the value that a task holds is equivalent to the resources that have been allocated to it—in this instance, the funds that have been budgeted for its completion. Each task defined through the WBS is assigned a planned value and an earned value. Once the project is run, the real earned value can be obtained.

As shown in Table 3.8, the EVM method provides a wealth of metrics against which to measure a project. As shown in Table 3.9, EVM can also be used as a report tool to identify patterns such as overspending and to identify deviations between actual and planned.

| Plan Type | Planned Value | Earned Value | Actual Cost | Cost Variance | Schedule Variance |
|---|---|---|---|---|---|
| Initial | 200 | 195 | 200 | -5 | -5 |
| Final | 350 | 240 | 250 | −10 | −110 |

**Table 3.9** Reporting with EVM Metrics

The EVM concept can link a time-phased budget into specific tasks, providing a platform for the team to track work progress against a baseline plan. EVM provides timely data and information that can bolster analysis of the project and trigger calls to action.

Overall, remaining flexible when budgeting for projects is important; you should accept that frequent changes to business requirements and plans occur. Utilizing prior project experience, accelerators, and metrics such as EVM can yield impressive results when budgeting and forecasting for a project.

## 3.5 Kicking Off Your Project

Once you've defined the scope, set up your project leadership and steering committees, received proposals from systems integrators, and prepared your statement of work, it's time to kick off the leasing project.

The kick-off meeting is instrumental to setting a tone that can last all the way to the project go-live, which is important especially if the implementation entails an onslaught of changes for the business. This event will be the project team's and other stakeholders' first acquaintance with the project overview and vision. During this event, you'll set the project scope and objectives, along with stakeholder expectations; discussing the project purpose, expected outcomes, and schedules are often part of the agenda.



### 3.5.1 Setting the Stage

Introductions from team members on the customer side (project manager, steering committee, and key users) as well as your own participants (project manager, project lead, and consultants) will facilitate the exchange of vital information such as names, contract details, and the tasks and functions each person is responsible for. A round of introductions is also good for building credibility and enthusiasm within the team.

Preparing a meeting agenda to be distributed and shared with attendees will ensure that all teams are aware of what the project will entail, communicating both the impact on the business (e.g., changes to leasing KPIs and financial statements) and on IT system strategies. With attendees from various levels and positions within the organization, presenting the agenda in a big-picture, high-level manner will yield greater engagement from the audience. Delivering an explanation of the goals and the vision is also a means for you to communicate the project's purpose and importance to adding value to the organization's business processes. Throughout the meeting, be inclusive of all individuals and allocate time for feedback from the audience.

### 3.5.2 Establishing Project Management Tools

Introduce your collaborative project management tools during the kick-off meeting. These tools may include project management software and platforms, so teams can easily visualize the project deliverables and timelines. Consider also real-time collaboration tools such as WebEx and Skype that can support the kick-off event; these allow project teams to conduct multiple meetings and accommodate colleagues that work in different geographical locations and time zones. You may also choose to record the project kick-off if there are team members who are absent from live meetings.

### 3.5.3 Defining Standards and Procedures

Defining standards and procedures for activities such as status reporting, time tracking, approval, expense reporting, and giving instructions on how to use forms and templates as well as document uploading to the shared database repository is essential.

Be sure to establish implementation standards that are in line with best practices, guidelines, and procedures in SAP for the following objects:

- Business blueprint document
- Configuration documentation
- Business process design
- Business use cases and scenarios
- Test scripts
- Requirements traceability matrix
- Acceptance criteria of deliverables

For each of the project phases (e.g., preparation, implementation, realization, final preparation, and go-live), identify the nature and structure of information that has been documented, the activities, and the sequence of steps that are involved. Document the tasks that are to be performed, how to customize business process activity in IMG for every scenario, and how to document the customizing activity for each scenario's business process.

**Tip**

If your SAP RE-FX or SAP Lease Administration implementation involves third-party consultants and specialists, remember to provide access of relevant shared databases to these external teams, so that information can be made readily available for all who are involved. This also ensures that all teams can obtain the same working papers and view or extract data from an up-to-date knowledge repository.

### 3.5.4 Distributing Responsibilities

Having a solid project plan and a well-defined work breakdown structure is key to delivering visibility of essential activities. While defining the WBS can be done in greater detail in the blueprint phase, at the kick-off meeting, starting a discourse about the responsibilities that teams and individual members will assume is important. You'll want to convey a sense of how teams are expected to collaborate. Providing the "why" in addition to the "what" regarding the activities to be completed will pave the way for a clearer ownership of tasks and create a proper frame of mind for team members to be in so they can plan their work accordingly.

### 3.5.5 Communicating Project Milestones

Leverage this meeting to establish the thresholds of performance that the project is expected to deliver within the given time frame and their respective compliance deadlines. Clarify any milestones to be achieved during the various phases, alongside the post-implemented business processes that are to be measured against the objectives of the project. This is an appropriate time to emphasize that targets can only be met through a concerted effort of the parties involved.



### 3.5.6 Managing Business Expectations

Managing expectations includes monitoring stakeholder communications regularly, because the attitudes and actions of the business can greatly impact the success of a project. Creating a dialogue with the customer and maintaining a good working relationship are vitally important. Managing business expectations begins with addressing key concerns of the business efficiently and clearly. These matters may include:

- How the project implementation will transform the way end users such as lease accountants interact with the system
- Whether the business' internal employees have been adequately trained and prepared to use SAP RE-FX and SAP Lease Administration
- The steps to be taken if the new system does not meet expectations

Appropriately and effectively communicating with stakeholders ensures that they acquire the information relevant to their concerns, building up positive attitudes about the new system and the leasing project.

## 3.6 Summary

In this chapter, we examined how project implementations can be complex, costly, and difficult to navigate. Common pitfalls that result in failed implementations are often a consequence of poor planning in areas such as the project scope, schedule, timeline, and budget amongst others. We explored how best practices, methodologies, and accelerators can help SAP RE-FX and SAP Lease Administration projects begin and end well while at the same time minimize risks. With robust project planning and the utilization of the right approaches in evaluating key phases of the project, organizations are placed in good stead for implementation success.

In the next chapter, we dive into an implementation project for SAP Lease Administration by Nakisa.

# Chapter 4
# Implementing SAP Lease Administration by Nakisa



*Now that we've discussed project management, let's take a closer look at administering leases in SAP Lease Administration by Nakisa specifically.*

The purpose of this chapter is to provide guidance on the steps for configuring SAP Lease Administration. Because complete configuration instructions are available from Nakisa for all SAP Lease Administration projects (to the tune of several hundred pages!), we have chosen to focus on the best practices—the tips and tricks that will "unlock" existing documentation and streamline your SAP Lease Administration project. Of course, we can't cover everything, so we'll focus providing some insights that will keep your project on schedule, under budget, and trouble free.

To this end, we'll start with the steps and choices required at the start of your SAP Lease Administration implementation project: selecting the implementation tool, running through your system prerequisites and customer-specific requirements, familiarizing yourself with the AdminConsole, and reviewing the recommended implementation sequence. All of these topics will be covered in Section 4.1.

Next, we'll dive into the specifics of the implementation project, adhering to the tabs found in the AdminConsole: **Settings** (Section 4.2), **Master Data Configuration** (Section 4.3), **Data Management** (Section 4.4), **Build Management** (Section 4.5), **Schedule Jobs and Thresholds** (Section 4.6), **Field Management** (Section 4.7), **Caption Editor** (Section 4.8), and **Logs and RFC Traces** (Section 4.9).

## 4.1 Before You Begin

Before we get started, this section will guide you through choosing the SAP Lease Administration implementation tool that best meets your project needs.

### 4.1.1 Choosing an Implementation Tool

You can deploy SAP Lease Administration on-premises or in the cloud. On-premise deployment gives you more freedom to customize features but requires a longer deployment cycle, whereas cloud deployment is faster and features existing, but rich, preconfigured capabilities. The solution is a web-based application installed on the company's server; its full capabilities can be accessed through two web browsers:

- Microsoft Internet Explorer 11
- Google Chrome

This section describes the overall implementation sequence for the three SAP Lease Administration deployment tools (assuming that the pre-deployment scoping and system setup prerequisites have been met; we'll cover these shortly!).

**Resources**

For the remainder of this section, we'll suggest a few helpful resources at particular moments during your SAP Lease Administration implementation project:

- **Environment Checklist**
  The Environment Checklist lists the software, hardware, and SAP requirements and lists the supported RDBMS databases.
- **Deployment Guide**
  This document is intended for Nakisa developers, consultants, and administrators who are familiar with deploying and configuring Nakisa applications.
- **Administrator Guide**
  The Administrator Guide provides instructions for securing and administering SAP Lease Administration applications.
- **User Guide**
  The User Guide includes information on features and functions available in the User Console. This document provides end-to-end instructions on lease accounting within the application.

#### On-Premise Deployment with Tomcat

SAP Lease Administration can be installed onto a Tomcat server. When using Tomcat, each system software requirement is installed in a separate container. Although this configuration increases the complexity of implementation and can be time consuming, this architecture enhances system security because each component exists in a separate location.

Table 4.1 outlines the steps to take when using Tomcat to implement SAP Lease Administration.

| Step | Action | Activities | Server | Reference |
|---|---|---|---|---|
| 1 | Configure the SAP ERP system | Ensure that the SAP ERP system meets the master data and configuration prerequisites. Note that the master data required by SAP Lease Administration must exist in the SAP ERP system before the two solutions can be integrated. To operate the application, new SAP General Ledger (GL) accounts, new asset classes to manage right-of-use assets (ROU assets), and new transaction types are recommended. The backend accounting system (Financial Accounting and Controlling) must be already configured to support the new lease accounting standards. See Section 4.1.2 for further details. | SAP backend | Deployment Guide |
| 2 | Set up the RDBMS database | An RDBMS database is required to store all application data, such as contract data, accounting profiles, and user/role information. | Database server | For a list of supported RDBMS databases, refer to the Environment Checklist and the Compatibility Matrix. |
| 3 | Deploy SAP Lease Administration components | Before deploying the software in Tomcat, specific files must be configured within the server. Thereafter, the Web Archive (WAR) must be installed and deployed with Tomcat. In addition, the *conf.properties* file and the *nakisa.jaas* configuration file must be configured. | Application server | Deployment Guide |

**Table 4.1** Tomcat Deployment Guidance

| Step | Action | Activities | Server | Reference |
|---|---|---|---|---|
| 4 | Install and configure Elasticsearch | Elasticsearch must be installed and configured individually on each server and separately from SAP Lease Administration and Tomcat (i.e., to embed Elasticsearch in the application). | Application server | Deployment Guide |
| 5 | Set up the queue | The application has a job scheduler feature for which queue configuration is required. | Application server | Deployment Guide |
| 6 | Configure the system and application | Configure the software components that sync the data and enable live postings between SAP Lease Administration and SAP. | Application server | Administrator Guide |

**Table 4.1** Tomcat Deployment Guidance (Cont.)

### On-Premise Deployment with Docker

Docker is another on-premise deployment tool, preconfigured by Nakisa to deploy SAP Lease Administration. These containers have Tomcat, Elasticsearch, and queue components preinstalled. As result, Docker can really expedite the implementation process. Currently, a Nakisa ID is required for deployment with Docker. The requirements for deploying with Docker are similar to those required for Tomcat deployment with the exception of files for Linux, 32-bit Windows, and 64-bit Windows. Be sure that you are using the correct files.

Table 4.2 outlines the steps to take when using Docker to implement SAP Lease Administration.

| Step | Action | Activities | Server | Reference |
|---|---|---|---|---|
| 1 | Configure the SAP ERP system. | Ensure that the SAP ERP system meets master data and configuration prerequisites. Before integrating the solution, the master data used by SAP Lease Administration must exist in the SAP ERP system. To operate the application, new SAP GL accounts are required as well new asset classes to manage ROU assets. See Section 4.1.2 for further details. | SAP backend | Deployment Guide |

**Table 4.2** Docker Deployment Guidance

| Step | Action | Activities | Server | Reference |
|---|---|---|---|---|
| 2 | Use Docker to install Tomcat and deploy the Nakisa application, Elasticsearch, and the queue | | Application server | Deployment Guide |
| 3 | System and application configuration | Configure the software components that sync the data and enable live postings between SAP Lease Administration and SAP. | Application server | Administrator Guide |

**Table 4.2** Docker Deployment Guidance (Cont.)

### Cloud Deployment with SAP Cloud Platform

SAP Lease Administration is available on the cloud following the software-as-a-service (SaaS) model, using SAP Cloud Platform (SCP). Cloud deployments allow for virtual private network (VPN) connections to an on-premise ERP system via a secure VPN tunnel or an SSH connection or as a standalone system. The benefits of deploying in the cloud include reduced maintenance and infrastructure management.

Table 4.3 outlines the steps to take when implementing SAP Lease Administration in the cloud.

| Step | Action | Activities | Server | Reference |
|---|---|---|---|---|
| 1 | Configure the SAP ERP system | Ensure that the SAP ERP system meets master data and configuration prerequisites. Before integrating the solution, the master data used by SAP Lease Administration must exist in the SAP ERP system. To operate the application, new SAP GL accounts are required as well new asset classes to manage the ROU assets. See Section 4.1.2 for further details. | SAP backend | Deployment Guide |

**Table 4.3** SCP Deployment Guidance

| Step | Action | Activities | Server | Reference |
|---|---|---|---|---|
| 2 | Secure VPN or SSH connections | A secure connection to ERP is available. | N/A | Deployment Guide |
| 3 | Configure ERP connections | In case of connected system ERP, connections will be required. | Admin-Console | Deployment Guide |

**Table 4.3** SCP Deployment Guidance (Cont.)

### 4.1.2 Checking General Prerequisites

In all three scenarios (implementation via Tomcat, Docker, or SAP Cloud Platform), several prerequisites must be met prior to configuration. Configuring the application is the last step in software implementation.

Begin by checking your ERP system for the following prerequisites:

- Fully functional SAP ERP 6.0 EHP 5 (or later) system or SAP S/4HANA 1503, 1610, or 1709 system
- Customized and functional FI-AA and CO solutions in accordance with your business requirements
- Business role customization to suit your business requirements

Similarly, before you can install and implement SAP Lease Administration, several system requirements must be in place. For detailed step-by-step instructions, refer to the Deployment Guide:

- SAP ERP master data and configuration prerequisites:
  - The master data used by SAP Lease Administration must exist in the SAP ERP system.
  - For entities with dual reporting (governed by International Financial Reporting Standards 16 and Accounting Standards Codification 842), the new SAP GL account is enabled and ready for use.
  - FI-AA must be enabled and ready for use.
- WEB GUI prerequisites: WEB GUI service is available via SAP ITS and is used to execute specific SAP reporting transactions from SAP Lease Administration. Because of browser limitations in Google Chrome, additional configuration is required in the SAP ERP system to utilize SAP WEB GUI with Google Chrome. See SAP Note 1655306 (Google Chrome for End Users and Administrators) for more information.
- SAP ERP validations: Validation rules must be created in the SAP ERP system to ensure SAP users are warned when generating manual postings directly in a gen-

eral ledger used by SAP Lease Administration. On the document header level, you might see a message like "Document type is reserved only for SLAN postings," while, on the line item level, a message like "G/L Accounts used are reserved only for SLAN postings" can appear.



### 4.1.3 Outlining Customer-Specific Requirements

Other than the general and system installation prerequisites, we have to discuss additional customer-specific requirements, which will have to be finalized with key stakeholders prior to deploying the application.

#### Lease Organizational Structure

Every company has its own organizational structure. Your company's structure can be represented in SAP Lease Administration to replicate current controls and facilitate business reporting in the system. To establish your company's structure in SAP Lease Administration, you'll use the fields listed in Table 4.4.

| Field | Description |
|---|---|
| **Lease Area** | This field represents different regional areas or legal responsibilities (e.g., America, Europe, and Asia). |
| **Lease Business Units** | This field represents a grouping of companies or responsibilities (e.g., production, distribution, transportation). |
| **Company Code** | This field represents a legal entity used for accounting purposes. |
| **Lease Department** | This field represents a department or line of business (e.g., marketing, finance, rail, water). |
| **Lease Group** | This field represents a team or product line (e.g., Group A, Group B). |

**Table 4.4** Organizational Structure Fields

Let's start by looking at asset classes. Since lease accounting disclosure reports must include a lease asset type, you should create a new asset class to segregate ROU assets from fixed assets that you own. Additionally, asset classes inherit the defined useful life in SAP, which is used to classify the lease (i.e., as either a finance lease or an operating lease under ASC 842) and, in specific circumstances defined under the lease new accounting standards, may be used to amortize the ROU asset. For instance, when a lease contains a transfer of ownership or a purchase option, the ROU asset is amortized over the asset's useful life as opposed to over the lease term. Therefore, you must create appropriate asset classes for each type of lease property and for each expected useful life duration.

Next, let's consider general ledger accounts. The Administrator Guide provides a list of general ledger accounts used by the application. Although certain accounts may already exist in your chart of accounts (e.g., "Interest Expense") we recommend you create new sets of general ledger accounts to facilitate reconciliation and disclosure reporting. Moreover, other general ledger accounts may no longer be useful (e.g., operating expense accounts).

Since specific number ranges are commonly used to classify each type of account for consolidated reporting purposes, you must thoroughly discuss and review the new general ledger accounts against the existing chart of accounts before deploying the application.

### 4.1.4 Exploring the AdminConsole

The AdminConsole consists of sixteen pages for monitoring and configuration tasks. Figure 4.1 shows a full list of the pages available in the AdminConsole.

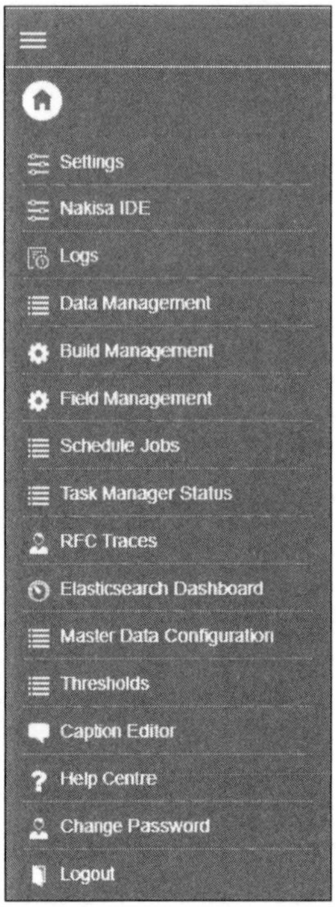


**Figure 4.1** AdminConsole Pages

While "configuration" consists of using the available resources from the published product, "customization" is defined as performing core modifications to the product. Functional administrators can configure the application to preferred settings within the AdminConsole, including, but not limited to, the following settings:



- Turning features on or off for use
- Tailoring the experience of available SAP Lease Administration functionalities to increase relevance to your clients' business needs (e.g., managing available fields and captions)
- Application and system master data configuration

### 4.1.5 Reviewing Best Practices

Although all SAP Lease Administration projects are a little different, Nakisa recommends a particular workflow to help make sure you address all possible options. Table 4.5 describes the recommended system setup for SAP Lease Administration and for integration with an SAP ERP system using an Excel template.

| Step | Configuration Steps Using Excel for a Connected SAP Environment | Notes |
|---|---|---|
| Analysis | Data volume sizing for SAP synced tables | Any table with large record volumes (of which only a fraction relate to lease accounting) needs to be identified and removed from the online sync process. SAP tables that may contain such large amounts of data include tables for assets, vendors, equipment, projects, work breakdown structures (WBS), cost centers, profit centers, and internal orders. |
| Analysis | Frequency of syncing for each SAP table | After the initial syncing with SAP is performed, you need to determine the frequency of subsequent sync operations for each table. |
| Analysis | Application configuration analysis: customer-specific requirements | The usage and configuration of the following tables needs to be discussed with the business and set up accordingly: number range, asset classes, lease area, business unit, and authorization profiles. Additionally, customer-configurable fields available for grouping and reporting (**Document Category**, **Agreement Group**, **Contract Category**, **Form of Lease**, **Contract Group 1**, and **Contract Group 2**) must be configured. |

**Table 4.5** SAP Lease Administration System Setup and Integration

| Step | Configuration Steps Using Excel for a Connected SAP Environment | Notes |
|---|---|---|
| Pre-Step | Settings menu/data connections have been created | Verify data that connections are working; test that the connection is successful. |
| Pre-Step | Data management/ recreate data base | Re-create an empty database to remove demo data. Note that this step is required for the initial setup only. |
| 1 | Master data configuration: Upload application configuration in Excel | Insert and update Excel file *Application_Config.xls* and then validate all data loaded correctly in the AdminConsole.<br>Note that this step is required for the initial setup only or if changes to the application configuration are required to support an additional system. |
| 2 | Settings menu/data connections | Verify data that connections are working; test that the connection is successful. |
| 3 | Master data configuration: Add system | Add the system for the required data connection. |
| 4 | Master data configuration: Add companies | Manually add companies (only company codes are required). If you need to add a large number of companies, you can also load them into the system using an Excel file with only the **CT_Company** tab. |
| 5 | Configure SAP sync settings based on table volumes | Turn on/off online sync settings for specific SAP tables with large data volumes. Set the **SAP Sync Setting** to **False** using Config Editor. These tables can then be synced in batch, using the Job Scheduler. |
| 6 | SAP system sync | Verify all SAP tables loaded with expected values and record counts. |
| 7 | Master data configuration: Upload system configuration via Excel | Upload the Excel file *System_Config-XXX.xls* and then validate all the data in the AdminConsole. Make sure you have a separate Excel file for each connected system. |

**Table 4.5** SAP Lease Administration System Setup and Integration (Cont.)

| Step | Configuration Steps Using Excel for a Connected SAP Environment | Notes |
|---|---|---|
| 8 | Run batch jobs for tables excluded from online SAP Sync | Ensure that all batch jobs have been completed successfully by reviewing the batch history and ensure that the required data has been loaded into the corresponding SAP tables by reviewing record counts. |
| 9 | SAP system sync | Verify *all* SAP tables have been loaded with expected values and record counts. |
| 10 | Frontend configuration validation | Undertake functional testing of various lease scenarios to ensure configuration is complete and working. Scenarios will vary depending on number of accounting standards, asset classes, lease areas, business units, company codes, number ranges, authorization profiles, and more. |

**Table 4.5** SAP Lease Administration System Setup and Integration (Cont.)

Now that your SAP Lease Administration implementation project has been planned, let's dig into the AdminConsole, beginning with the **Settings** tab.

## 4.2 Settings Tab

The **Settings** tab, shown in Figure 4.2, allows administrators to configure global settings, manage role types and relationship options, and establish connections to ERP systems.

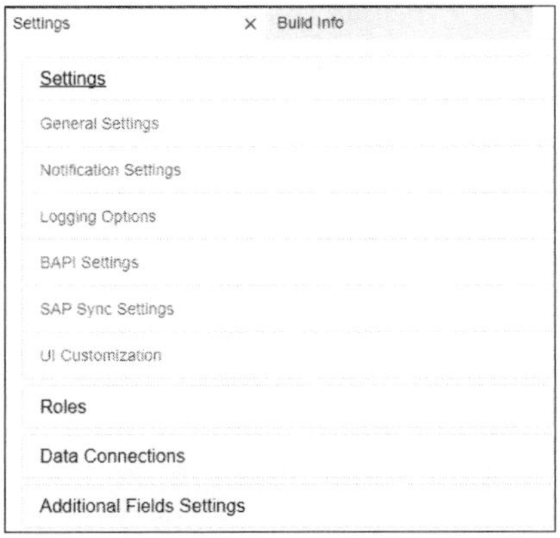


**Figure 4.2** The Settings Tab in the AdminConsole

### 4.2.1 Settings

The **Settings** section of **Settings** tab, as shown in Figure 4.2, is where you'll set general application settings.

The **General Settings** subsection is used to set the language options available in the user interface (UI), including the default language for the application as well the required date format in both short and long formats. In this subsection, you can also configure the automatic updating of the analytics index and audit logging.

The **Notification Settings** subsection is used to enable or disable email notification features available in SAP Lease Administration. Notifications are sent to selected users for approvals throughout the lease onboarding process and when a lease contract is coming to an end. If enabled, email configuration is required to ensure notifications are properly transmitted.

The **Logging Options** subsection is used to configure what error logs report. The logs help diagnoses issues for troubleshooting and can be configured in the following ways:

- **Errors Only**: Provides a log on the errors produced by the application.
- **Error and Warnings**: Provides system warnings and the errors produced by the application.
- **Maximum Logging**: Provides info logs, database tracing, and authentication logs as well as system warnings and a breakdown of the errors produced by the application.

The **BAPI Settings** subsection provides a complete list of all the business application programming interfaces (BAPIs) used by the application to execute specific business functions in the SAP ERP system. To create a custom BAPI or replace an existing BAPI, update the name of the BAPI used and click **Save**.

The **SAP Sync Settings** subsection is used to enable or disable the SAP tables from online synchronization with the SAP ERP system. These tables can be then updated routinely in the backend via scheduled sync jobs for each synced table.

To enhance the sync time or to support the scenario where entities wish to only sync a portion of the data within a given table, such tables with large record volumes can be disabled and synced separately via the Job Scheduler or uploaded using the Excel system configuration template. Typically, such tables include assets, vendors, equipment, projects, WBSs, cost centers, and internal orders.

The **UI Customization** subsection is used to customize optional aspects available in the application frontend. This setting is company specific and therefore should be discussed with key stakeholders prior to deployment. The steps for customizing the available UI aspects can be found in the Administrator Guide. The following are the most commonly enabled UI customizations:

- Changes to the default application icons in both the AdminConsole and SAP Lease Administration.
- Enable/disable the lease determination step in the contract onboarding process. If disabled, the user will have to set the lease type.
- Enable/disable the charge list page in the activation group.
- Enable/disable carry-over balance fields for lease components and activation groups, which are required to support transition accounting.
- Enable/disable the option to update units via Excel files. If enabled, users can exports units to an Excel, apply modifications to the file, and then upload the changes back into the application.
- Enable/disable the automatically selected tax jurisdictions. A tax jurisdiction can be prepopulated based on the cost center entered, which is configured in the cost center master data.
- Show/hide additional fields in the **Unit** window such as **Room**, **Location***, **Evaluation Group 1**, **Type Name**, **Responsible Cost Center**, **Plant***. (*The fields can be set at the contract level or at the activation group level and can then be overridden at the unit level.)
- Modify the hierarchy options in the master lease agreement (MLA), including displaying/hiding lease business unit and company code and enabling/disabling the prepopulated lease area and lease business unit, which would be based on the company code selected.
- Prevent multiple postings (payments, interest accruals, and asset depreciation) simultaneously. If enabled, when a user posts a selected entry, the other posting buttons are disabled until the action is complete.
- Set the default size for smart searches.
- Enable/disable Excel imports or exports from the application frontend.

### 4.2.2 Roles

The **Roles** section of the **Settings** tab of the AdminConsole is used to map user roles to the role types available in SAP Lease Administration and to determine from the source of user role data.

#### Authentication Methods

Several authentication methods are available:

- **Logon Screen**: Prompts users to enter a user name and password to access the application. Login credentials are transmitted to the server over the HTTP connection using HTTP POST.
- **Single Sign-on with User ID**: Authenticates users based on their SAP credentials.
- **Single Sign-on with Logon Tickets**: Utilizes SSO2 logon tickets to authenticate users based on their SAP credentials.
- **Non-SAP SSO Setup**: Leverages the SSO configuration set up on the container (e.g., Tomcat) as long as the container populates either the user principal object or request header with the proper user name.
- **Active Directory Integration**: Automatically authenticates users based on their Windows login credentials. Users must be on the same domain as the authentication server.
- **Active Directory Form**: Prompts users to enter a user name and password to access the application. Users are authenticated through the Active Directory and are not required to be on the same domain as the server.

User information (such as the display name and email) is not fetched from the SAP ERP system. This information must be added by the system administrator. The source of user roles is fetched, and the authentication method can be amended with additional customizations. To make such changes, contact your implementation partner to customize the *nakisa.jaas.config* file.

By default, the application uses the Active Directory first to authenticate users. If the user is not found, the application authenticates the user with the SAP ERP system.

### Role Mapping

Once a user has been authenticated, the default setting for the user's role will be the user's Active Directory role or SAP role.

As shown in Figure 4.3, the default setting of the **Role Mapping Source** field is **Integrated with Authentication**. As a result, the application will fetch the user's role right after authentication (from wherever the user is authenticated). The source can be changed to any of the following options: **Database**, **SAP**, or **SuccessFactors**.

Roles have a many-to-one relationship, meaning that multiple user role types can be mapped to the same SAP Lease Administration role. As shown in Figure 4.4, if one user has multiple roles (i.e., both an Active Directory role and an SAP role), then only the first matched role will be retrieved and used for role mapping in SAP Lease Administration.

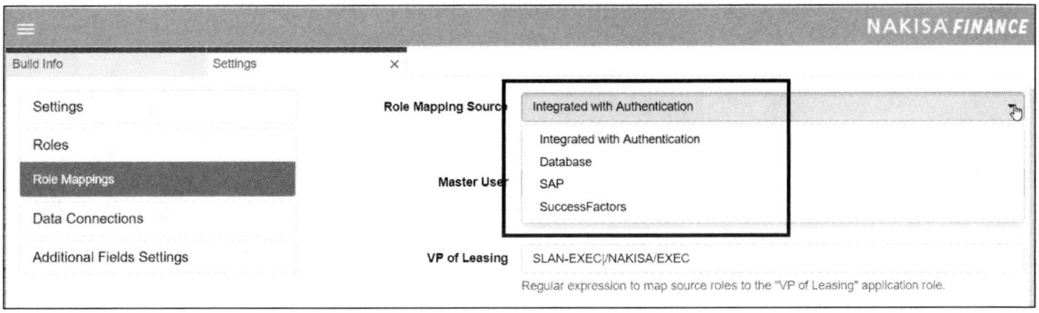


**Figure 4.3** Role Mapping Source

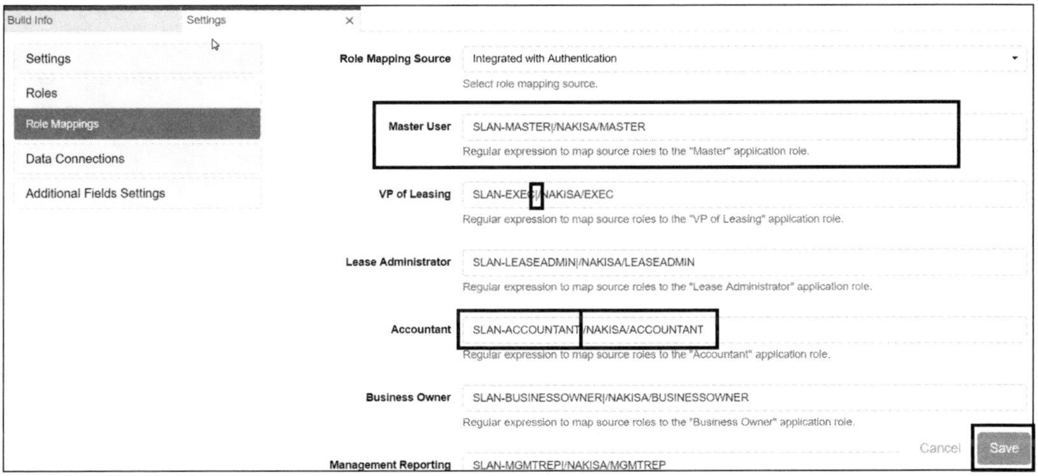


**Figure 4.4** Role Mappings Section

Note that you'll need to enter a pipe (a "|" character) between each role without spaces to separate multiple roles (e.g., SLANACCOUNTANT|/NAKISA/ACCOUNTANT).

Table 4.6 lists the available default roles in SAP Lease Administration.

| Role | Description |
|---|---|
| Master user (NAKISA_MASTER) | Users can do all actions allowed by the other roles. |
| VP of leasing (NAKISA_EXEC) | Users can approve MLAs and contracts.<br>Users have access to disclosure reports, management reports, and transaction reports. |

**Table 4.6** SAP Lease Administration Roles

| Role | Description |
|---|---|
| Lease administrator (NAKISA_LEASEADMIN) | Users can:<br>■ Create and define MLAs, contracts, lease components, and activation groups.<br>■ Activate activation groups.<br>■ Modify contracts and reassess activation groups.<br>■ Request approvals for the different objects.<br>Users have access to management reports and transaction reports. |
| Accountant (NAKISA_ACCOUNTANT) | Users can approve MLAs; define lease components and activation groups; and maintain, activate, classify, and reassess activation groups.<br>Users have access to disclosure reports, management reports, and transaction reports. |
| Business owner (NAKISA_BUSINESSOWNER) | Users can assess and approve activation groups.<br>Users have access to management reports and transaction reports. |
| Management reporting (NAKISA_MGMTREP) | Users can view management reports and transaction reports. |
| Financial disclosure reporting (NAKISA_FINDISCREP) | Users can view management reports, disclosure reports, and transaction reports. |
| Power user (NAKISA_POWER) | The only role that provides access to both the frontend and backend of the application.<br>Users have the same rights as master users combined with technical administrators and functional administrators.<br>Note that this role is not affected by authorization profiles (i.e., data scoping). |
| Technical administrator (NAKISA_ADMIN_TECH) | Users have complete access to the AdminConsole with the exception of the master data configuration. Users do not have access to configure the frontend of the application. |
| Functional administrator (NAKISA_ADMIN_FUNC) | Users have access to the AdminConsole with the exception of selected pages (Nakisa IDE, Logs, Build Management Elasticsearch Dashboard). Users do not have access to configure the frontend of the application. |

**Table 4.6** SAP Lease Administration Roles (Cont.)

Note that you would set up data scoping (i.e., determining which MLAs and contracts each user can see, via authorization profiles) by navigating to **Master Data Configuration • Application Configuration • User Management Node**.



#### SAP Service Users and Authorization Objects

The SAP *service user* is required so that the application can integrate with SAP to perform data syncs and document/asset transaction postings using remote function calls (RFCs) and BAPI calls. That service user must first be created in SAP using the authorization objects table listed in the Administrator Guide.

The authorization object for *system users* (i.e., the users logging in to the application) must be `S_RFC` when using SAP authentication. However, when using single sign-ons with logon tickets as the authentication method, system users post the transactions initiated from SAP Lease Administration in the SAP ERP system and therefore require the same authorization objects as service users.

### 4.2.3 Data Connections

The third section of the **Settings** tab of the AdminConsole is the **Data Connections** section. In this section, you'll define the connection string(s) required to connect to external SAP system(s). SAP Lease Administration supports up to four SAP connections out of the box and has native functionality to test connections once set up.

To add additional connection strings, contact your implementation partner. However, you should know that increasing the number of connected ERP systems will impact the performance of the application during authentication.

To establish a connection to an SAP ERP system, follow these steps in your SAP Lease Administration system:

1. In the **Data Connections** panel, shown on the left side of Figure 4.5, select the SAP connection you wish to configure.
2. In the **SAP Authentication without Any Credentials** field at the top, enter the first connection string *without* the user.
3. In the **SAP Connection** field, enter the same connection string but this time, include the system user. If your connection string contains a password element, enter the characters {password} in the connection string.
4. Click the **Test Connection** button.

5. In the **Connection for Role Mapping if Using SAP** field, enter the appropriate connection string. Again, if your connection string contains a password element, enter the characters {password} in the connection string.
6. Click **Test Connection** again and then click **Save**.

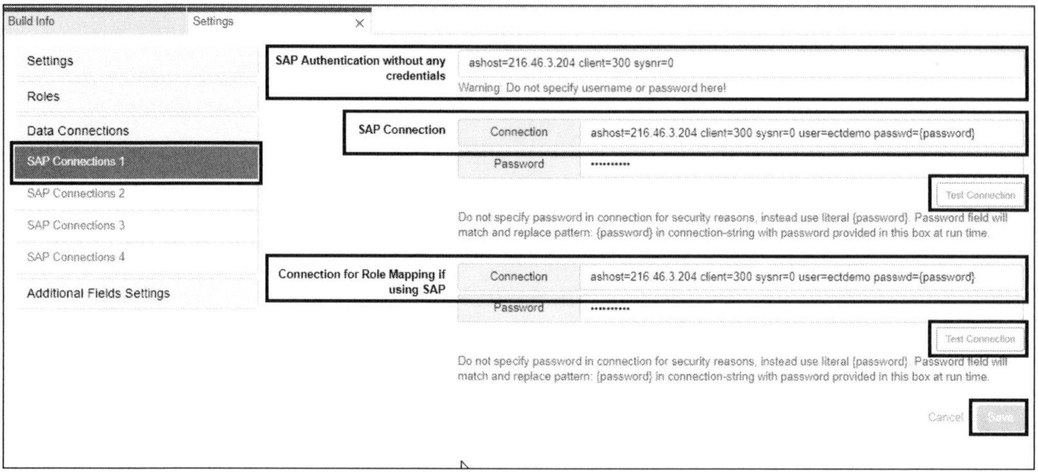


**Figure 4.5** Connecting SAP Lease Administration to SAP ERP

Note that the **User** field specified in the **Connection String** area defines the service user that will post to the SAP ERP system. Thus, this service user must *not* be set up as a dialog user in SAP and *must* have the appropriate credentials in SAP to:

- Post documents in the FI-GL, FI-AP, and FI-AA modules.
- View and create master data in FI-AA.

### 4.2.4 Additional Field Settings

The last section of the **Settings** tab in the AdminConsole is the **Additional Field Settings** section. In this section, you'll enable/disable additional pages (or steps) for MLAs, contracts, lease components, and activation groups, which will appear on the left of these objects. These pages can be used to store additional information and may each contain up to five sections with six fields each that are fully customizable.

However, these pages do not have any embedded logic attached. Each section can house specific field types as follows:

- Section 1: Up to 6 text fields
- Section 2: Up to 6 number fields
- Section 3: Up to 6 true/false fields
- Section 4: Up to 6 date fields
- Section 5: Up to 4 text areas (descriptions)

For units, the additional sections are available in the **Edit Form** for the unit.

To add a page and fields in SAP Lease Administration to any of the four predelivered levels of a lease contract, follow these steps:

1. First, click **Settings • Additional Field Settings**.
2. In the **Additional Field Settings** section, select the object you wish to work in, either **MLA Additional**, **Contract Additional**, **Lease Component Additional**, **Activation Group Additional**, or **Unit Additional**, as shown on the left side of Figure 4.6.

**Figure 4.6** Adding Fields for Additional Information in SAP Lease Administration (I)

3. Ensure **Show Step "Additional" in MLA Wizard** is enabled by sliding the gray bar to the right or clicking the bar to turn it blue (activated). By default, the bar will have been disabled.
4. Review the next set of options (**Show Section X on "Additional" Step** options) to enable or disable *specific sections* on the page. Then, review the next set of options (**Show Text X in Section 1** options) to enable or disable *individual fields* on the page. Don't forget that you can scroll down to view more options!
5. Repeat these steps for each object that requires an additional page of information. When you're done, click the **Save** button at the bottom right of Figure 4.7.

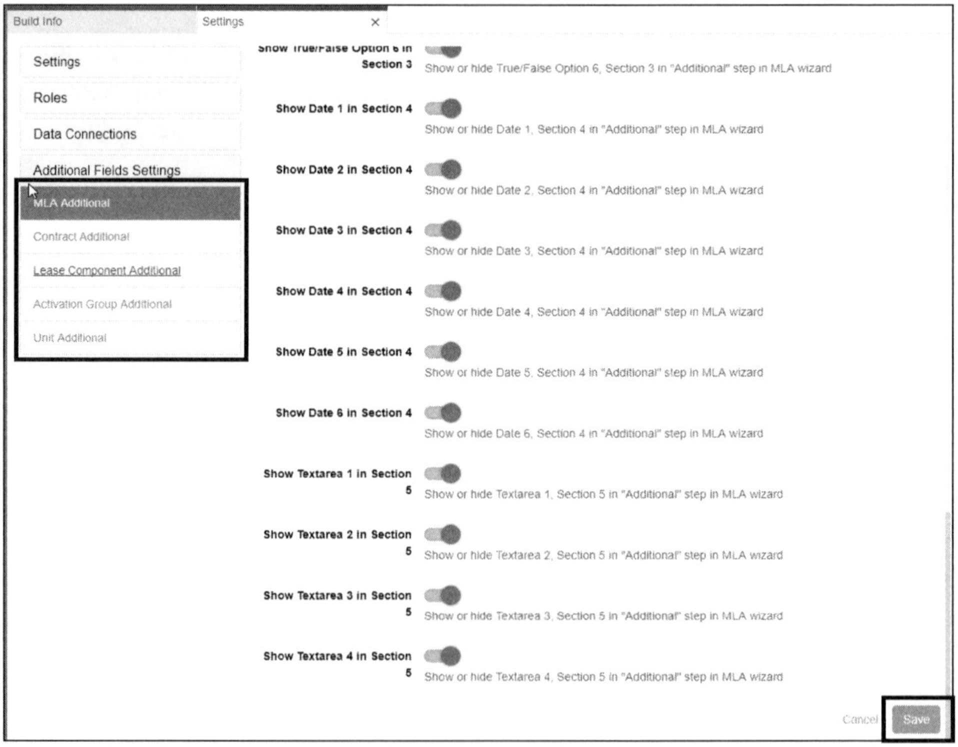


**Figure 4.7** Adding Fields for Additional Information in SAP Lease Administration (II)

When you finish, you should cross-check your work in the frontend of the application, as shown in Figure 4.8. To perform this cross-check, log into the application from the frontend. Ensure that the additional step (activated by **Show Step "Additional" in MLA**

**Wizard**) is visible for the object(s) you configured and then verify that the appropriate sections and fields appear on the page.

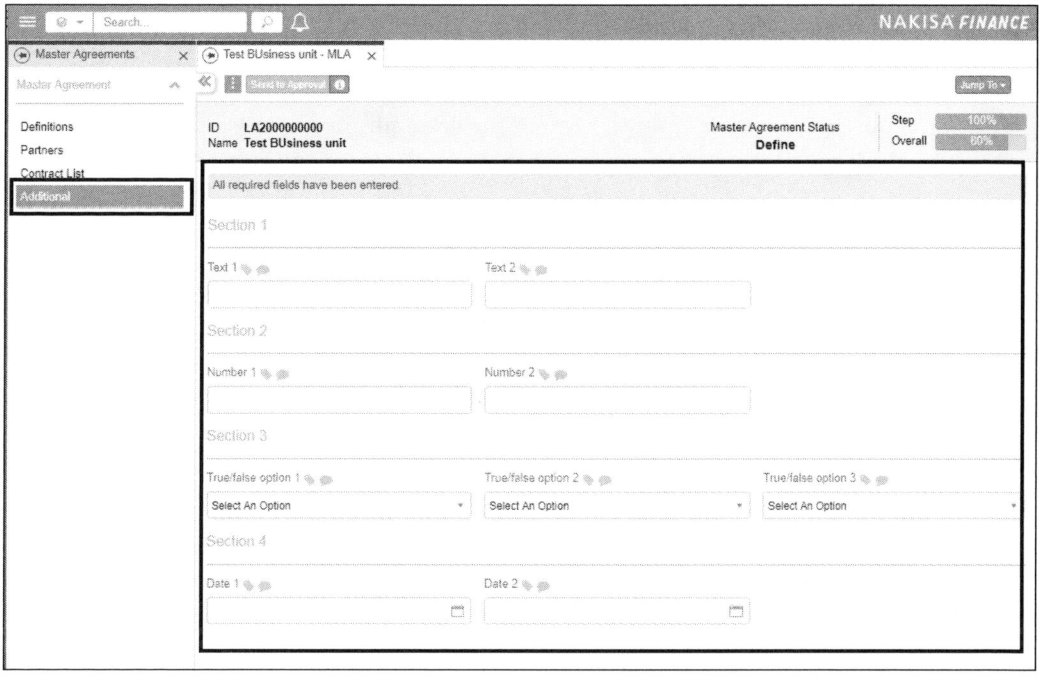


**Figure 4.8** Cross-Checking Added Fields in SAP Lease Administration

So far, we've been focusing on the **Settings** tab of the AdminConsole. Let's turn our attention next to master data configuration.

## 4.3 Master Data Configuration

The **Master Data Configuration** page is an important central area that requires configuration. You can expand the navigation tree on the left and select a specific page within that area to configure.

Master data configuration requires you to review and modify two components before the solution is available for use:

- **Application configuration**
  Review and modify the system settings and internal configuration tables used in

the frontend of the application. The application configuration is not system specific (i.e., the configuration is applicable to all systems).

- **System configuration**
  Establish the solution's settings to successfully integrate with SAP ERP. Separate system configurations are required for each connected system/data connection.

By choosing an option from the top of the configuration tree (see Figure 4.9), functional administrators can work in either **View** mode or **Configure** mode:

- To modify configuration settings, users must enter **Configure** mode.
- The **View** mode allows users to view the configurations for all systems at the same time.

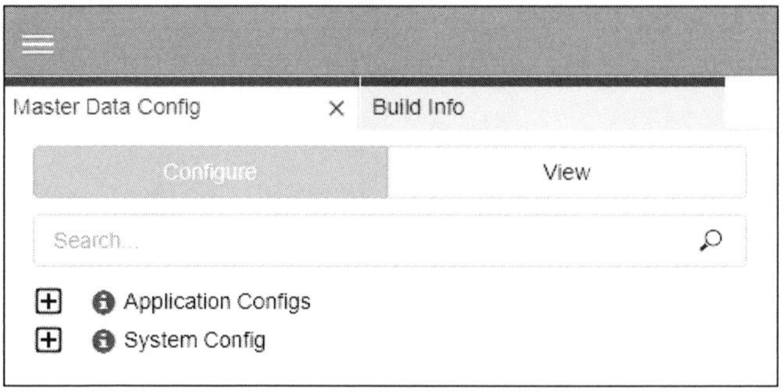


**Figure 4.9** Master Data Configuration

Before we look at system configuration, let's first dig into application configuration.

### 4.3.1 Application Configuration

The **Application Configs** section, shown in Figure 4.10, contains all the data that is specific to SAP Lease Administration. In this section, you'll define the lease areas and business units—all the fields proprietary to the SAP Lease Administration application and *not* passed on to SAP. These internal objects in the database are often referred to as *config tables* or *CT tables*.

As shown in Figure 4.10 and Table 4.7, five SAP Lease Administration areas require configuration: **Application Settings**, **Lease General Setup**, **Lease Area**, **Lease Financial Setup**, and **User Management**. Note that most of these areas are groupings for informational purposes only (notice the "i" icon in Figure 4.10), but the **Lease Area** section is in fact a node unto itself (notice the gear icon). Table 4.7 reflects the hierarchical nature of groupings and nodes; for example, there are several layers of tables underneath the **Users** node.

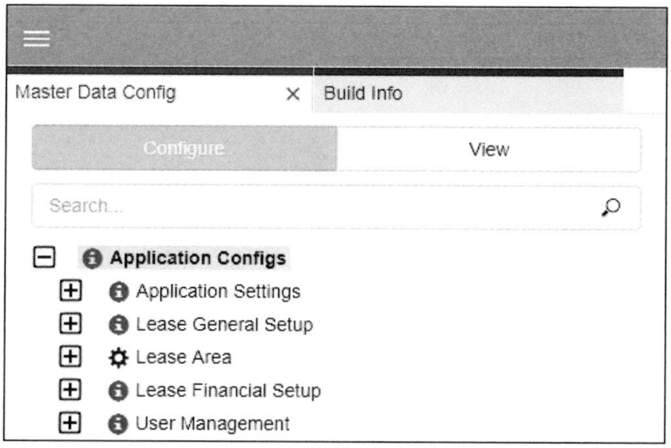


**Figure 4.10** Application Configuration

| SAP Lease Administration Area | Nodes |
|---|---|
| **Application Settings** | Number Range |
| | Questionnaire |
| | Lease Type |
| | Asset Class Mapping |
| | Reason Code |
| | Remeasurement Reason |
| | Notification |
| | Unit Status |
| | Internal Language |
| | Internal Currency |
| | Uploaded Document Type |

**Table 4.7** Application Configuration Hierarchy

| SAP Lease Administration Area | Nodes | | |
|---|---|---|---|
| **Lease General Setup** | Document Category | | |
| | Agreement Group | | |
| | Contract Category Group | | |
| | Partner Roles | | |
| | User Responsibility | | |
| | Form of Lease | | |
| | Principal Position | | |
| | Contract Group 1 | | |
| | Contract Group 2 | | |
| **Lease Area** | Business Unit | | |
| | Business Unit to Company | | |
| **Lease Financial Setup** | Non-Lease Amount Category | | |
| | Term Category | Types | |
| | Modality | | |
| | Payment Frequency | | |
| | Consumer Price Index | | |
| | Compounding Frequency | | |
| | Conversion | | |
| | Interest Expense Method | | |
| **User Management** | Users | Authorization Profile | Authorization Profile Item |

**Table 4.7** Application Configuration Hierarchy (Cont.)

**Hint**

The Application Config template downloaded from the AdminConsole is a sample file but also contains all the required SAP Lease Administration configuration settings. During initial deployment only, you must first update this file with your entity's configuration requirements and then upload this file into SAP Lease Administration.

Make sure you only update the tabs that are customer specific. Refer to the **Introduction** tab of the template for a list of the customer-configurable tables.



Most tables in the **Application Configs** section are required, standard values that the application needs and should not be modified. However, for certain configuration tables, setup and configuration are entity specific, which means that you'll need discuss with your end users how best to configure the application. As shown in Table 4.8, of these customer-specific tables, some are mandatory, and others are optional. (Be sure to cross-check with the Administrator Guide, User Guide, and/or the Application Config Excel template to know which objects can and cannot be modified!)

| Mandatory Tables | Optional Tables |
|---|---|
| ▪ Number Range<br>▪ Asset Class Mapping<br>▪ Lease Area<br>▪ Business Unit<br>▪ User Authorization Profiles | ▪ Document Category (MLA)<br>▪ Agreement Group<br>▪ Contract Category<br>▪ Contract Group 1 and Contract Group 2 |

**Table 4.8** Customer-Specific Application Configuration Tables

For training and demo purposes, the **Default** authorization profile is set to have access to *all* data. To use authorization profiles, the **Default** will need to be changed to a restrictive configuration. Therefore, in the initial setup, the user will need to be assigned to the correct the authorization profile in SAP Lease Administration because this information does not get pulled when SAP performs the authorization check.

Be careful here. By default, the first time a user logs into SAP Lease Administration, a record is created in the **Users** table, and the user is assigned the authorization profile **Default**. Do not delete this profile!

Now that we've finished with application configuration, let's move on to system configuration.

### 4.3.2 System Configuration

The system configuration takes place in Step 7 under the recommended implementation approach shown in Table 4.5. Table 4.9 details the required system setup during configuration.

| Step | Activity |
|---|---|
| 7.01 | Maintain the Module Management table |
| 7.02 | Update the Accounting Standard table with the depreciation area and account standard type |
| 7.03 | Create a classification and attach to the accounting standard |
| 7.04 | Create a transaction type and attach to the accounting standard |
| 7.05 | Update the company with main and secondary accounting standards |
| 7.06 | Attach the company code to business units |
| 7.07 | Create lease departments and attach to the company |
| 7.08 | Create lease groups and attach to the lease departments |
| 7.09 | Attach a unit of measure to the company |
| 7.10 | Maintain IBR data and attach to the company |
| 7.11 | Attach internal order type to the company |
| 7.12 | Attach the asset transfer variant to the company |
| 7.13 | Attach asset classes to the company |
| 7.14 | Attach the depreciation area to the asset class |
| 7.15 | Enter external asset class mappings and attach to the company |
| 7.16 | Attach exchange rate type to the company |
| 7.17 | Attach document types to the company |
| 7.18 | Enter account determination mappings and attach to the company |
| 7.19 | Enter NonLeaseAccountDetermination mappings and attach to the company |
| 7.20 | Attach payment terms to the Company |
| 7.21 | Attach the payment method to the Company |
| 7.22 | Attach the payment block to the company |
| 7.23 | Attach reversal reasons to the company |
| 7.24 | Attach the purchasing organization to the company |

**Table 4.9** Detailed System Configuration in Step 7

In this section, we'll walk through each of these steps.

### System Setup, Company Code, and SAP Sync

Setting up the system and adding a company code are performed in Steps 1 through 4 under the SAP Lease Administration best practice integration approach described in Section 4.1.5. These steps are executed within the **System Config** section.

To add a system, follow these steps:

1. Click the **System** node in Figure 4.11.
2. Click the task menu icon (three bars) on the right and then click **Add**.
3. In the **CT_System** window that pops up, maintain the required fields: **System ID**, **Name**, **Type**, **System Date Format**, **Connection Type**, **ConnectionConfig**, and **ConnectionDesc**. Note that, in the **System Date Format** field, you should enter the date format as set in the SAP ERP system, which must follow standard Java date formats.
4. Click **Submit**.

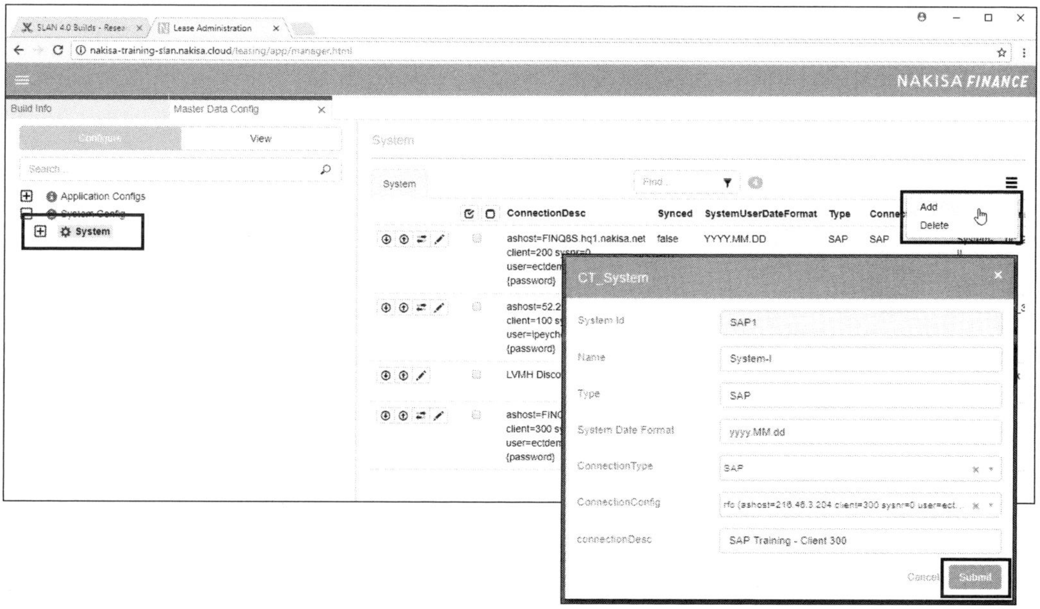


**Figure 4.11** Adding a System in Setup

To add a company code, follow these steps:

1. Select the system you wish to work with from the list.
2. Click the **Company** node shown on the left side of Figure 4.12.
3. Click the task menu icon (three bars) and then click **Add**.

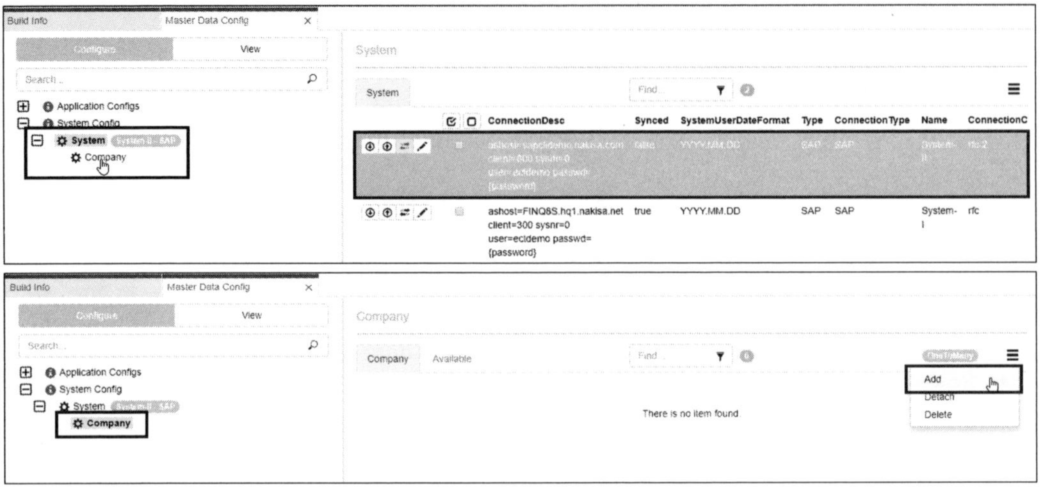


Figure 4.12 Adding a Company Code (I)

4. Enter the company code into the **Company Code** field shown in Figure 4.13. You can leave the **Description**, **Country**, **FyVariant**, and **Currency** fields blank, as SAP Lease Administration will sync these fields from the connected SAP system.

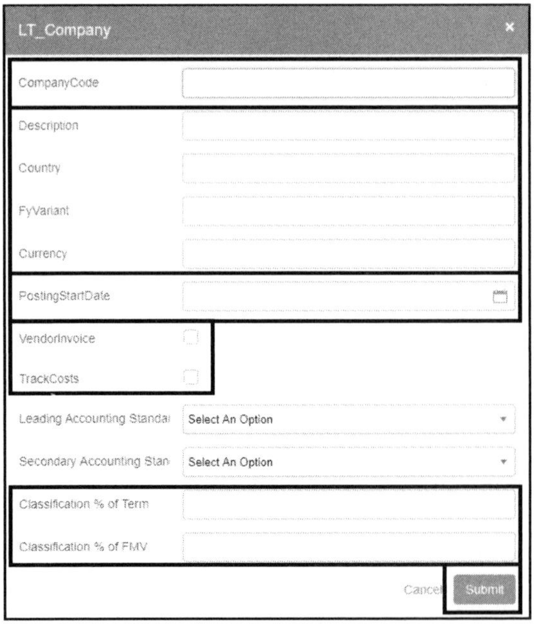


Figure 4.13 Adding a Company Code (II)

5. Manually enter ## into the **Classification % of Term**, and **Classification % of FMV** fields, which are required for classification of operating and finance leases under ASC 842.
6. In the **Posting Date** field, enter the start date on you wish to start posting to SAP.
7. Select the **Vendor Invoice** and/or **Track Costs** (internal order) checkboxes, if you wish to have these options enabled by default for end users.
8. Click **Submit** and repeat these steps for each company code.

Once the company codes have been added, the next step is to sync the SAP tables to the application. To execute the synchronization process, follow these steps:

1. Click the **System** node shown in Figure 4.14.

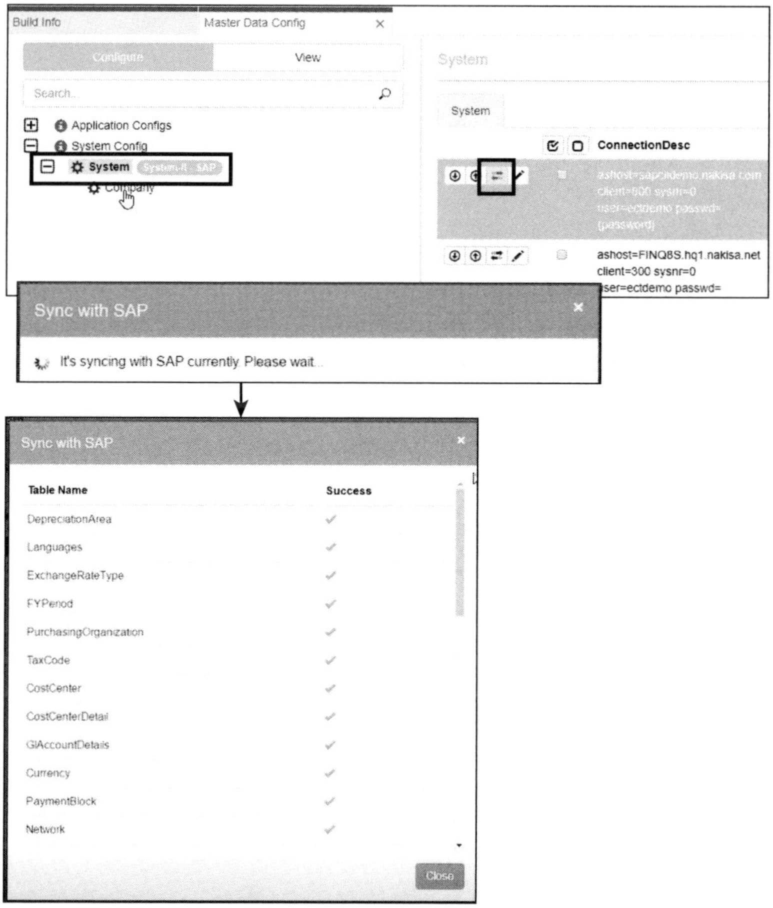


Figure 4.14 Syncing with SAP

2. Click the **Sync** button.
3. Wait until the syncing process is finished. As the system syncs up with SAP, various pieces of information will be pulled in, even at low levels like projects, WBSs, and cost centers. Therefore, sync times for the initial SAP sync can vary greatly, depending on the size of data in each entity's SAP system. Note that you should disable large tables from online sync in **General Settings • SAP Sync** settings and do them in batches using jobs scheduling.

Once the sync process has completed, the data retrieved will now appear in the tree structure for that system. Some data relationships are established automatically and attached to the company code; others you'll need to attach manually. The available records will be shown in the **Available** tab.

### Module Management

The **Module Management** window is where the SAP modules are enabled for integration with the application. By default, the application integrates with the following SAP modules: SAP GL, FI-AA, FI-AP, and SAP ERP CO; of these, integration with SAP GL and FI-AA are mandatory.

Note that the Module Management table will not ensure that general ledger postings or asset entries are posted and mapped correctly; it simply tells SAP Lease Administration how many, which fields to use, and which types of postings are required. You then need to perform some configuration to support the enabled modules.

Activating the modules prompts a specific program logic. For instance, the new SAP GL allows for parallel accounting with parallel ledgers or accounts, while the classic general ledger in SAP does not support parallel accounting.

To determine how SAP Lease Administration will integrate with the modules in the **Module Management** configuration page, follow these steps:

1. Select the **Module Management** section shown in Figure 4.15.
2. Click the task menu icon (three bars) on the right and then select **Add**.
3. Place a checkmark next to the module(s) that are used for the selected system.
   - **NewGeneralLedger**: Posts the documents in accordance to the general ledger grouping previously set in the SAP ERP system.

- **NewAssetAccounting**: Ensures that asset-related entries are correctly posted and mapped between SAP ERP and SAP Lease Administration. This setting is only required for SAP S/4HANA systems and should be disabled for SAP ERP 6 systems.
- **EnableQuantityUpdate**: Updates the unit quantity in the SAP asset master data. This setting is mandatory for SAP S/4HANA systems.
- **MaterialManagement** and **PlantMaintenance**: These options are reserved for future use.

In our example, for ModuleID **01**, we selected **Enable** and **NewGeneralLedger**.

4. Click **Submit**.

**Figure 4.15** Integrating with Modules

### Cross-Company Code Configuration

The next step is cross-company code configuration. The **Cross Company Code Configuration** section, shown in Figure 4.16, contains the configuration tables valid for all company codes in the SAP ERP system.

**Figure 4.16** Tables within the Cross Company Code Configuration Section

The SAP sync process updates most configuration tables within the cross-company code configuration, but you must configure some tables manually. Table 4.10 provides a list of the configuration tables within the **Cross Company Code Configuration** section and lists any required manual steps.

| Table | Tasks |
|---|---|
| Currency | Synced from the SAP ERP system and automatically attached to the system. This table is matched to the internal currency (application configuration) based on the ISO codes. |
| Language | Synced from the SAP ERP system and automatically attached to the system. |
| FY Period and FY Period Date | Both tables are synced from the SAP ERP system and automatically attached to the system. |
| External URL | Contains the links from the application to the SAP WEBGUI and must be maintained manually (see Figure 4.17). The following URL names must be used:<br>▪ **sapDocument**: To view documents<br>▪ **sapAsset**: To view assets |

**Table 4.10** Cross Company Code Configuration Tables

| Table | Tasks |
|---|---|
| Accounting Standard | Synced from the accounting principles in the SAP ERP system only if New GL is present. Otherwise, you must establish a link between the SAP accounting standard and SAP Lease Administration accounting treatment. Additional configuration is required after the initial syncing, as we'll describe in the next section on accounting standards:<br>▪ **Classification**: This table must be maintained manually.<br>▪ **Transaction Type**: This table must be maintained manually. |
| Exchange Rate | Synced from the SAP ERP system and automatically attached to the system. |
| Trading Partner | A legally independent company belonging to the group. Synced from the SAP ERP system and automatically attached to the system. |

**Table 4.10** Cross Company Code Configuration Tables (Cont.)

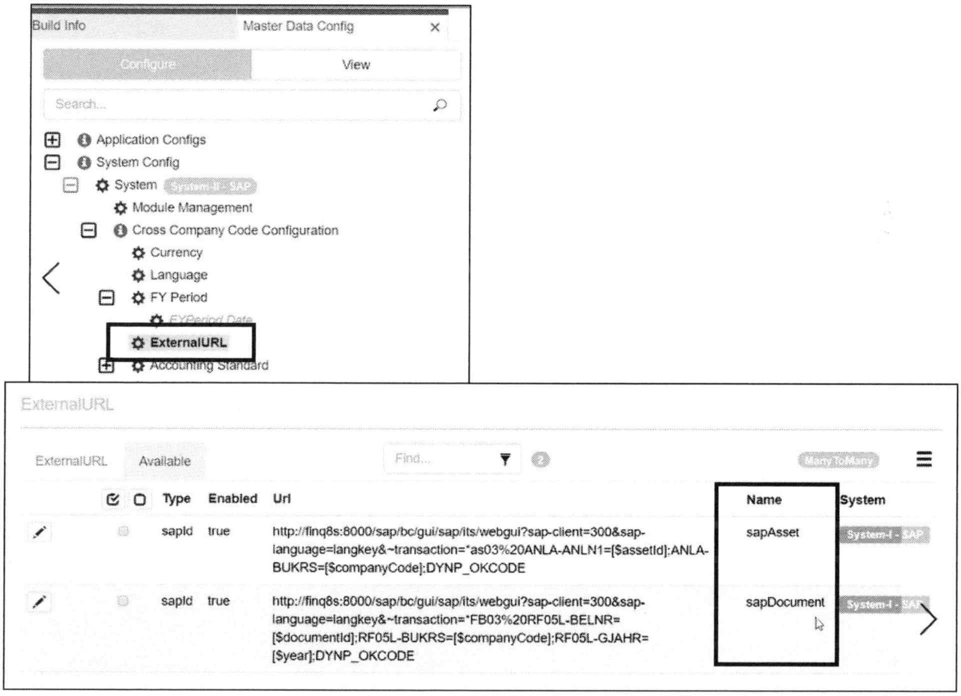


**Figure 4.17** External URL Table

### Accounting Standard

This step consists of completing the configuration of the **Account Standard** table by adding the depreciation area and standard lease type to each accounting standard.

To configure this table, follow these steps:

1. Click the **Edit** button next to the standard you wish to update. Note that by default the **Depreciation Area** and **Type** columns are blank. In our example shown in Figure 4.18, we've selected **GAAP**.
2. Select the appropriate depreciation area and standard type from the **Depreciation Area** and **Type** dropdowns.
3. Click **Submit** and then repeat for other accounting standards.

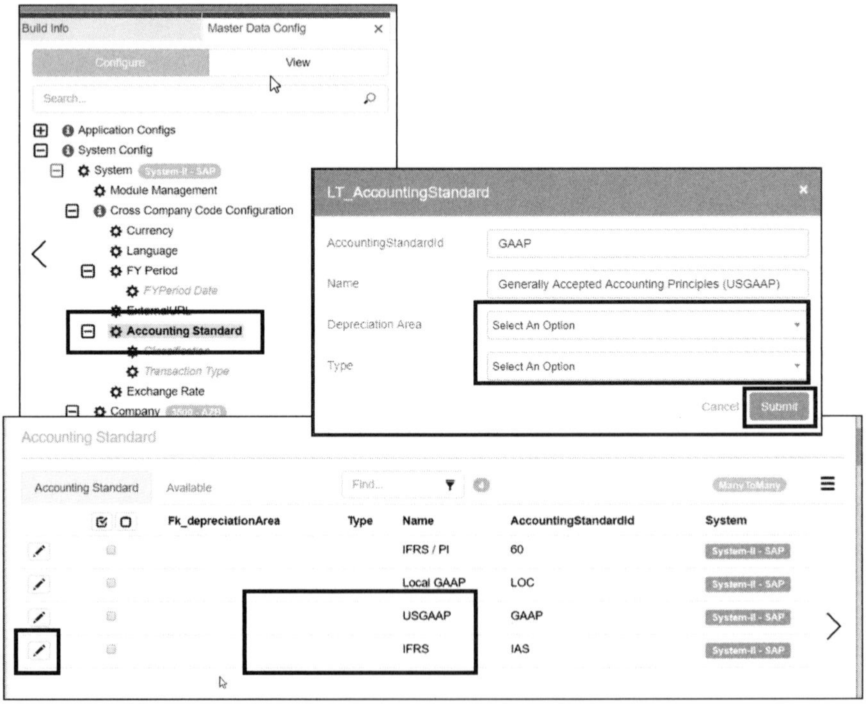


**Figure 4.18** Configuring the Accounting Standard Table

### Classification

Configuring the **Classification** table means attaching the lease classification to each accounting standard configured in the application. Follow these steps while referring to Figure 4.19:

1. Make sure you have selected a standard before you set up the classification.
2. Click the **Classification** node.
3. Select the **Available** tab and select the classifications you wish to attach. In our example, we selected the **Finance** and **Operating** classifications.
4. Click the task menu icon (three bars) and then click **Attach**. Repeat these steps for other standards.

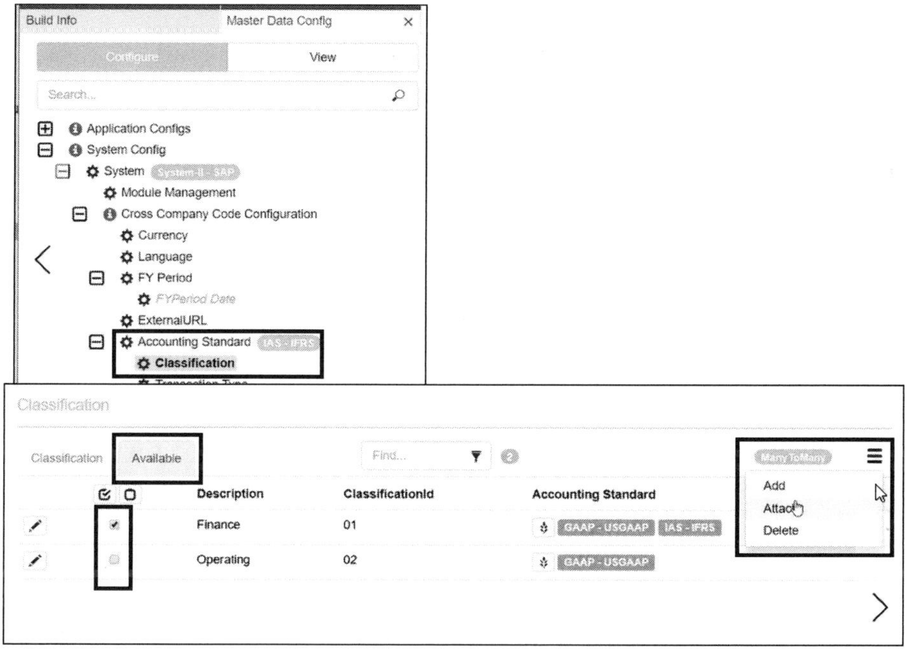


**Figure 4.19** Attaching Classifications to Accounting Standards

### Transaction Type

Transaction types in SAP must be created and attached to the accounting standards in the **Transaction Type** configuration table. Note that these must be valid SAP transaction types; we recommend that you create new transaction types specifically for SAP Lease Administration.

To create transaction types, follow these steps:

1. Make sure you have selected standard before you set up the transaction type.
2. Click the **Transaction Type** node, as shown Figure 4.20.
3. Click the task menu icon (three bars) and then click **Attach**.

4. Complete the fields according to your business requirements.
5. Click **Submit**.

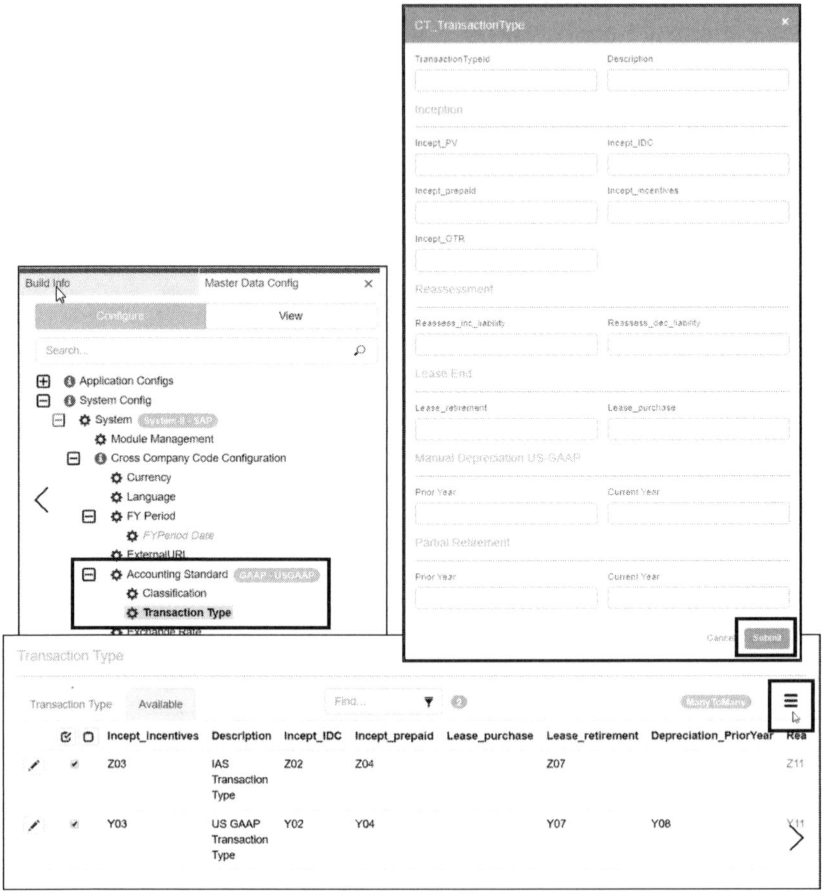


**Figure 4.20** Attaching Transaction Types to Accounting Standards

## Company Code

Company codes must be updated and added to the main and secondary accounting standards in the **Company** table. To update company codes, follow these steps:

1. Select the **Company** node, as shown in Figure 4.21.
2. Click **Edit** next to the company you wish to update.
3. Specify the posting start date, as required, in the **PostingStartDate** field. Enable the defaulted **Vendor Invoice** and **Track Cost** options, which are required.

4. Update the **Leading Accounting Standards**, **Secondary Accounting Standard**, **Classification % of Term**, and **Classification % of FMV** fields for this company code.
5. Click **Submit** and repeat these steps for all other required companies.

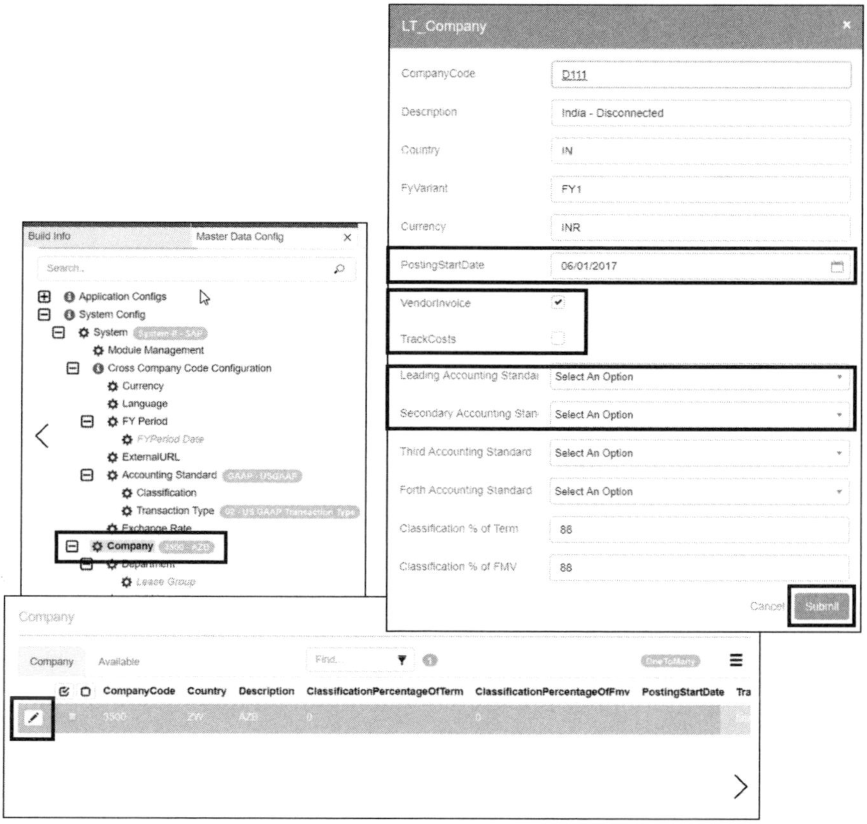


**Figure 4.21** Updating the Company Codes

## Business Unit

Now that you've configured the company codes, you'll need to map the relevant business units to their related company codes in the **Business Unit** table found in the **Application Configuration** section of the AdminConsole.

To establish links between business units and company codes, follow these steps:

1. Click the **Business Unit to Company** node, as shown in Figure 4.22.
2. Select all the desired business units in the list on the left and select the desired company code in the list on the right.

3. Click the **Add** button. The linked relationship will be displayed in the **Linked** list below.

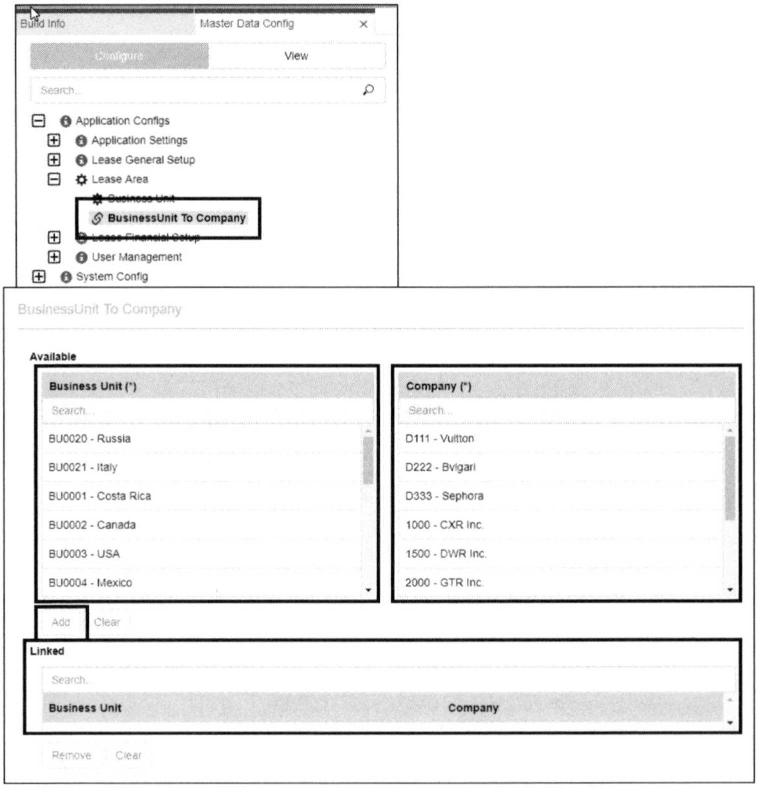


Figure 4.22 Configuring the Business Unit

### Lease Department

Lease departments are the fourth level of the organizational hierarchy and can represent a grouping of responsibilities, functions, products, or teams. A department can be attached to more than one company.

You'll have to manually maintain the **Lease Department** table, since it does not sync with SAP. Follow these steps to create a lease department and attach it to an SAP company:

1. Make sure that you have selected the company you wish to work in from the pane on the left.
2. Click the **Department** node, as shown in Figure 4.23.

3. Click the task menu icon (three bars) and then select **Add**.
4. In the **CT_LeaseDepartment** window, enter a description and a description ID in the corresponding fields. Note that you can also attach existing departments to the company, if required.
5. Click **Submit**.

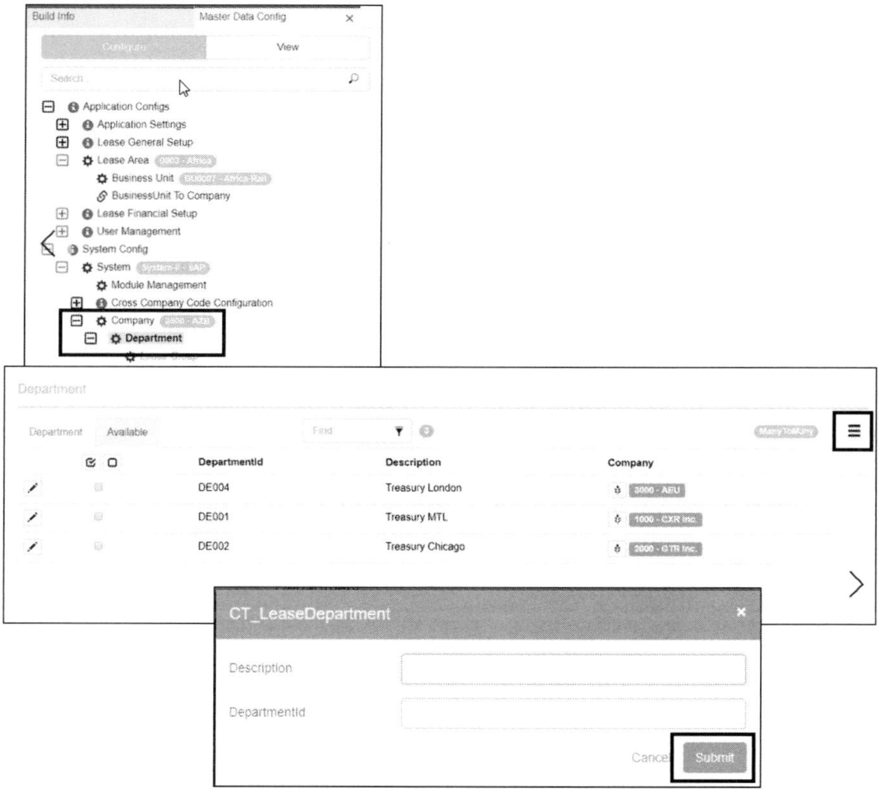


**Figure 4.23** Creating and Attaching a Lease Department to a Company

### Lease Group

Lease groups are the fifth level of the organizational hierarchy, which can also represent a grouping of responsibilities, functions, products, or teams. A lease group can be attached to more than one department.

Similar to the lease departments, the **Lease Group** table is maintained and its values attached to the related lease department manually. Follow these steps to create a lease group and attach it to an associated lease department:

1. Make sure that you have selected the department you wish to work in from the pane on the left.
2. Click the **Lease Group** node, as shown in Figure 4.24.
3. Click the task menu icon (three bars) and then select **Add**.
4. In the **CT_LeaseGroup** window, enter a description and a description ID in the corresponding fields. Note that you can also attach existing lease groups to the department, if required.
5. Click **Submit**.

**Figure 4.24** Creating and Attaching a Lease Group and to a Lease Department

### Unit of Measure

The **Unit of Measure** table is synced from SAP, but you'll have to manually attach the appropriate unit of measures that will be used for each company.

To add or modify a unit of measurement table, follow these steps:

1. Make sure that you have selected the company you wish to work in from the pane on the left.
2. Click the **Unit of Measure** node, as shown in Figure 4.25.
3. Click the task menu icon (three bars) and then select **Attach**.
4. From the **Available** tab, locate and select the **EA** (each) checkbox.

**Figure 4.25** Attaching a Unit of Measure Table to a Company

### Incremental Borrowing Rate

You'll manually maintain and define per company the incremental borrowing rate (IBR). The application selects the IBR value at the activation group level if the contract rate is not entered based on the following parameters:

- Company code
- Valid standard term start date
- Valid standard term end date
- Creation date of the activation group

To maintain and attach IBR data to a company, follow these steps:

1. Make sure that you have selected the company you wish to work in from the pane on the left.
2. Click the **Incremental Borrowing Rate** node, as shown in Figure 4.26.

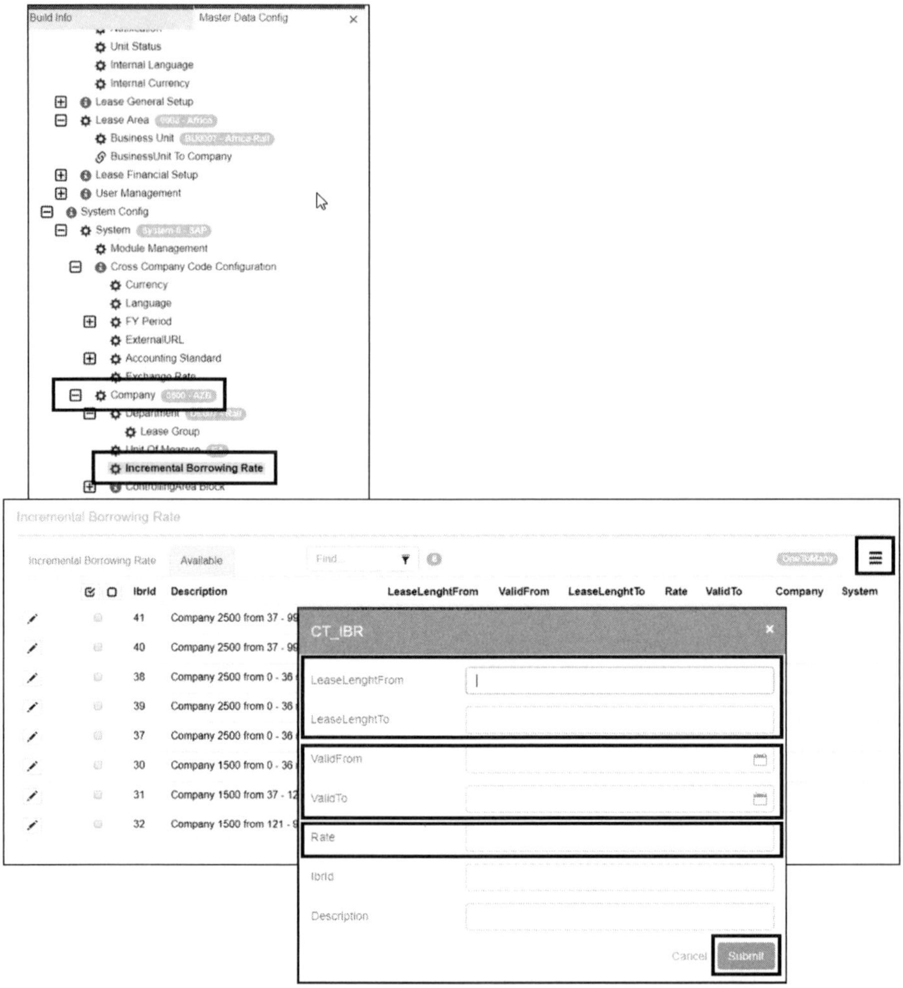


**Figure 4.26** Maintaining and Attaching IBR Data to a Company (I)

3. To add a new IBR, select **Attach** from the task menu icon (three bars).
4. From the **CT_IBR** window, complete the following fields:
   - **LeaseLengthFrom** and **LeaseLengthTo** (duration in months)
   - **ValidFrom** and **ValidTo** (effective time frame)

- **Rate** (borrowing rate)
- **IBRID** (generated based on the various parameters)
- **Description**

5. Click **Submit**.
6. From the **Available** tab shown in Figure 4.27, select the checkboxes for the IBR options you wish to associate to the active company.
7. Click the task menu icon (three bars) and then select **Attach**.

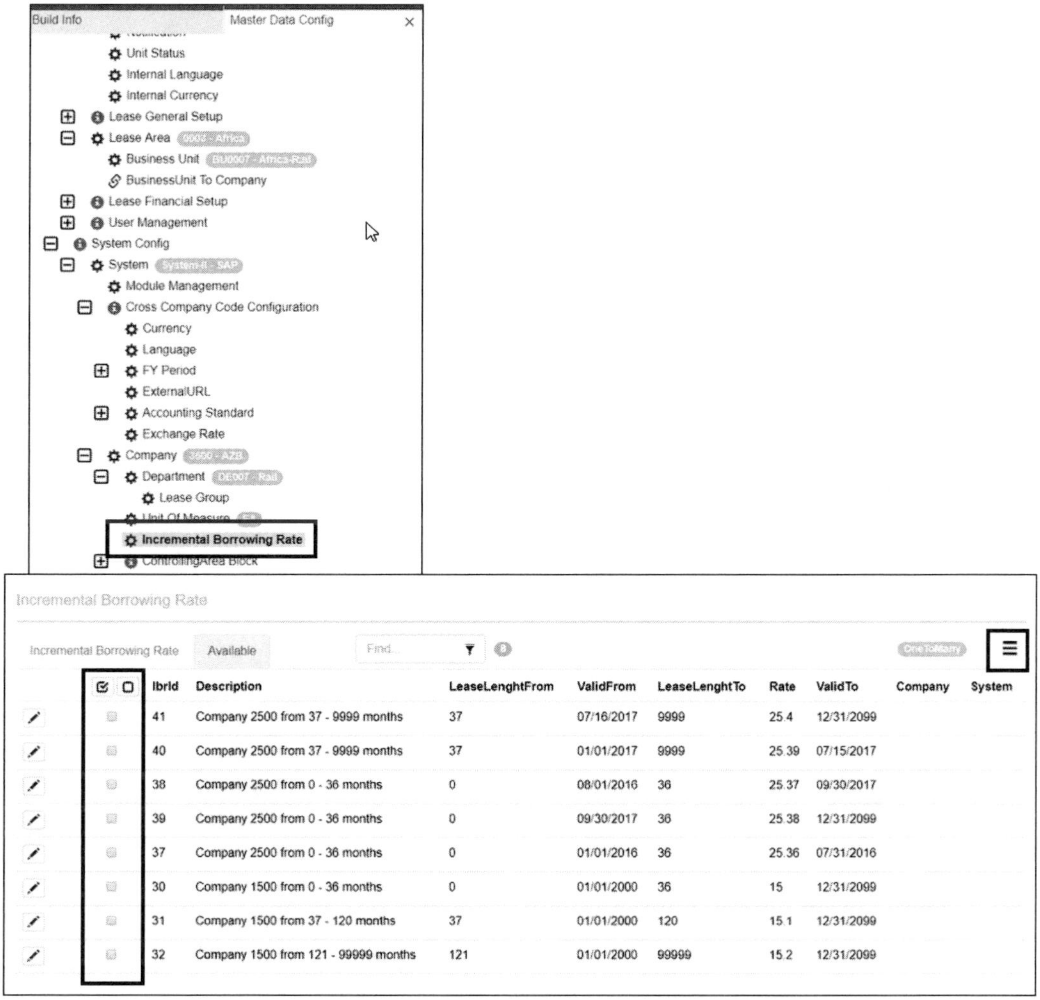


**Figure 4.27** Maintaining and Attaching IBR Data to a Company (II)

### Internal Order Type

An internal order is used to track costs of an organization but needs to be assigned to an internal order type. If cost tracking is activated in the contract, then either an internal order will be created, or the user may select an existing internal order. The **Internal Order** table is defined by company and therefore must attached to a company. Follow these steps:

1. Make sure that you have selected the appropriate company from the pane on the left.
2. Click the **Internal Order Type** node, as shown in Figure 4.28.
3. Click the task menu icon (three bars) and then select **Attach**.

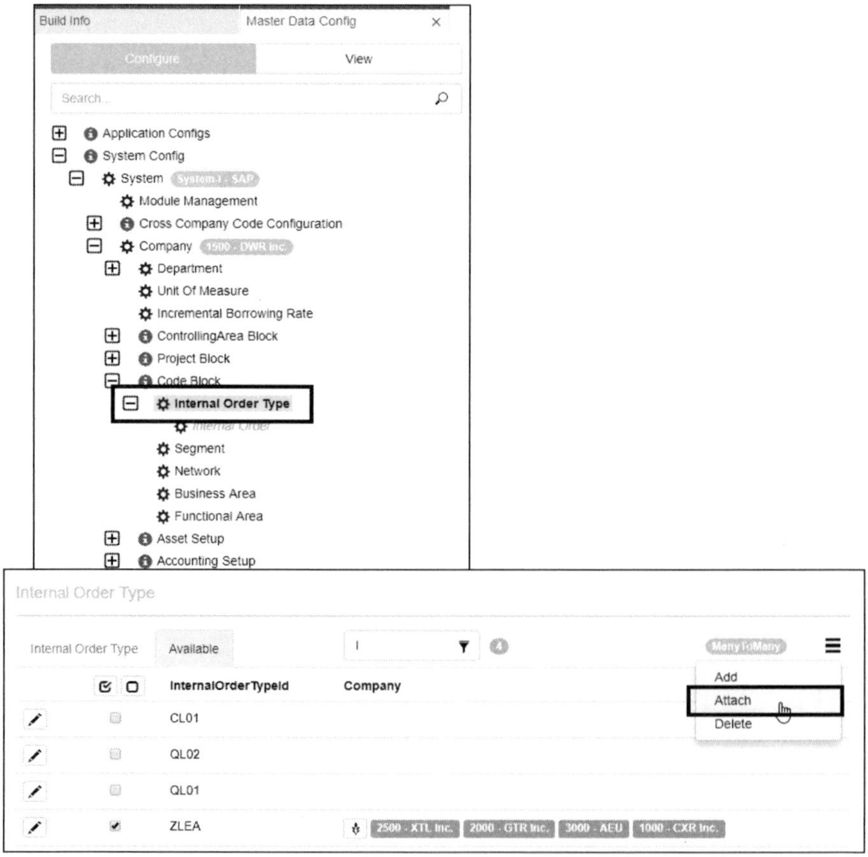


**Figure 4.28** Attaching an Internal Order Type to a Company

### Asset Transfer Variant

The **Asset Transfer Variant** table consists of SAP-specific configuration that is activated when a purchase option is exercised at the end of a lease. Asset transfer variants must be defined per accounting standard.

To attach a company to a transfer variant, follow these steps:

1. Make sure that you have selected the appropriate company from the pane on the left.
2. Click the **Asset Transfer Variant** node, as shown in Figure 4.29.
3. From the **Available** tab, select the checkboxes for the variants you wish to attach.
4. Click the task menu icon (three bars) and then select **Attach**.

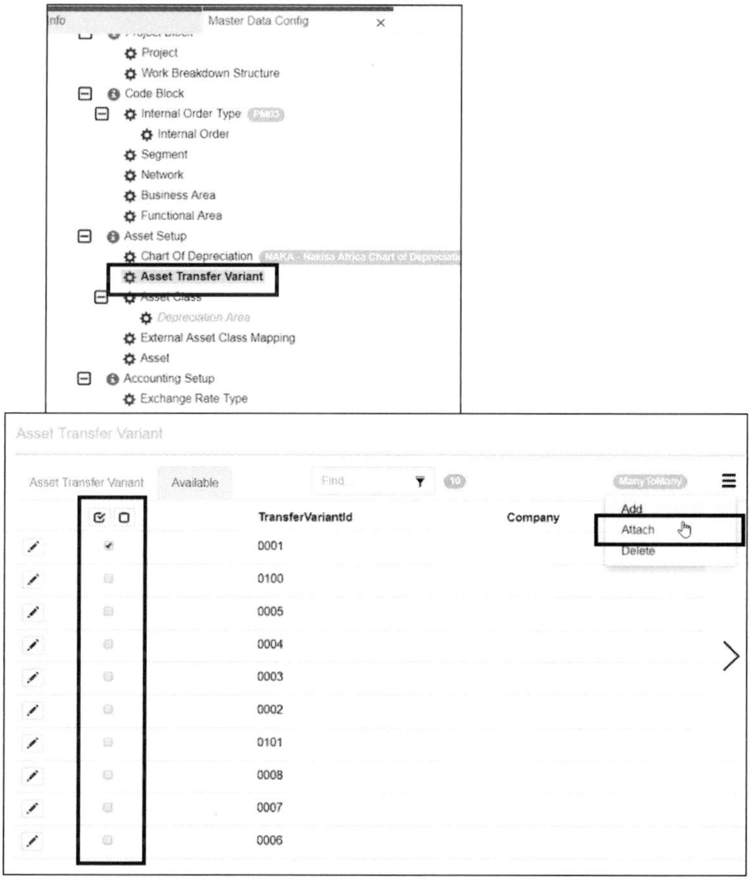


**Figure 4.29** Attaching an Asset Transfer Variant to a Company

### Asset Class

To manually attach an asset classes to a company, follow these steps:

1. Make sure that you have selected the appropriate company the pane on the left, as well as the appropriate asset class, as shown in Figure 4.30.
2. In the **Available** tab, select the checkboxes for the classes you wish to attach.
3. Click the task menu icon (three bars) and then select **Attach**.

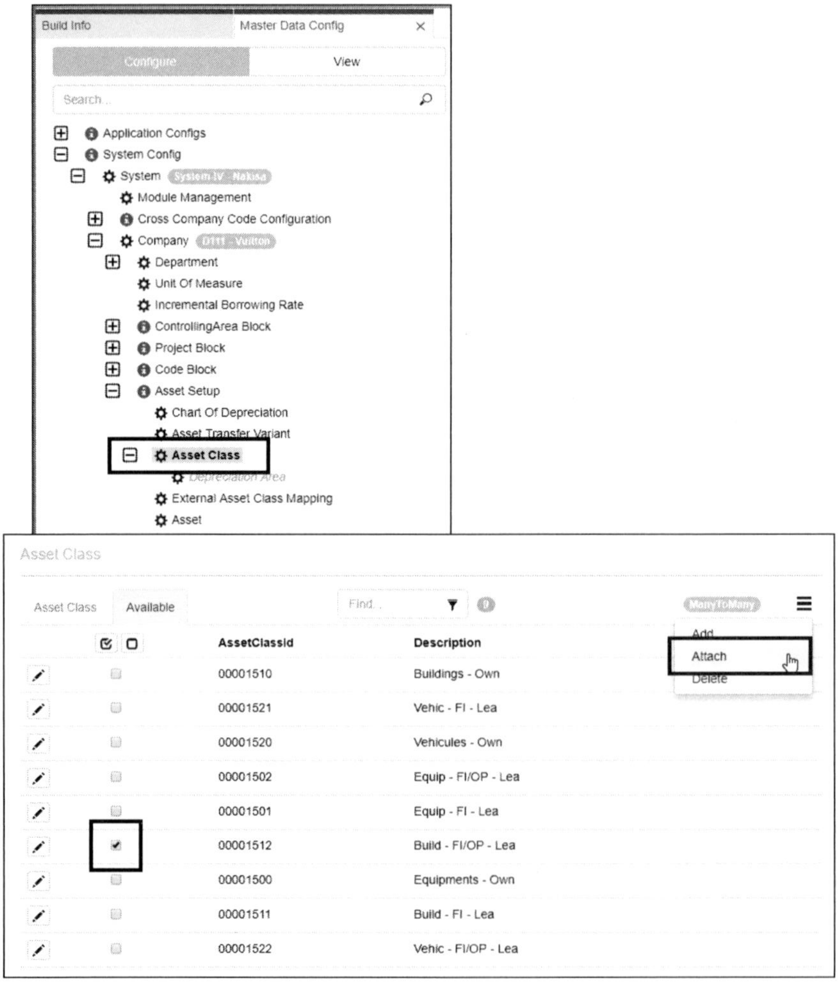


**Figure 4.30** Attaching an Asset Class to a Company

### Depreciation Area

The depreciation area defines the valuation method of an asset. In SAP Lease Administration, the **Depreciation Area** table is maintained by company and by asset class.

To attach a depreciation area to an asset class, follow these steps:

1. Make sure that you have selected the appropriate company from the pane on the left.
2. Click the **Depreciation Area** node, as shown in Figure 4.31.
3. On the **Available** tab, select the checkboxes for the depreciation areas you wish to attach.
4. Click the task menu icon (three bars) and then select **Attach**.

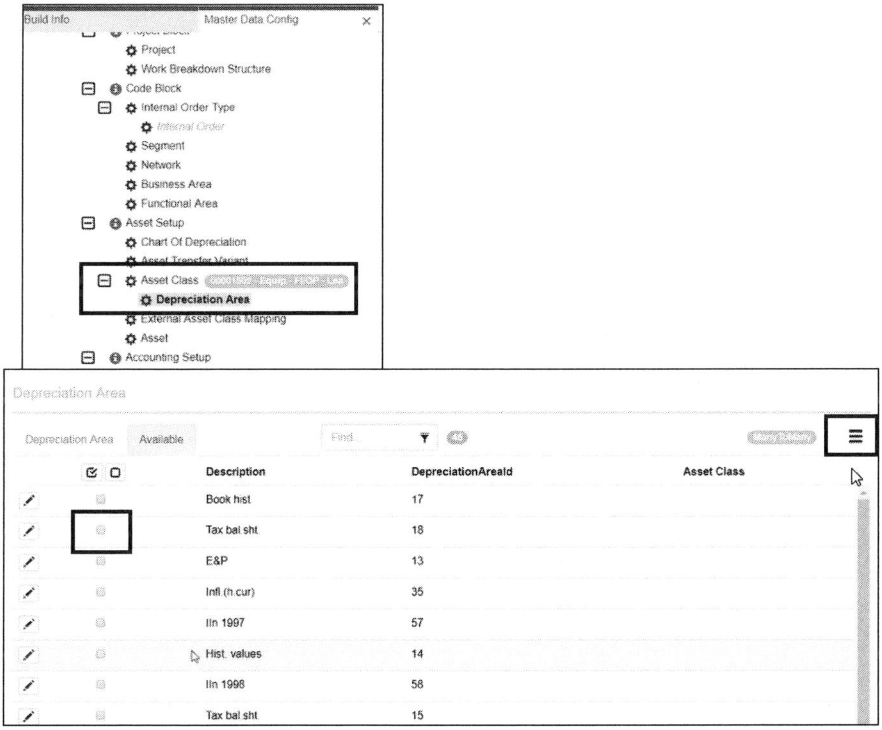


**Figure 4.31** Attaching a Depreciation Area to an Asset Class

### External Asset Class Mapping

External asset class mapping links the asset classes defined in the application configuration tables and the SAP ERP system, as shown in Figure 4.32.

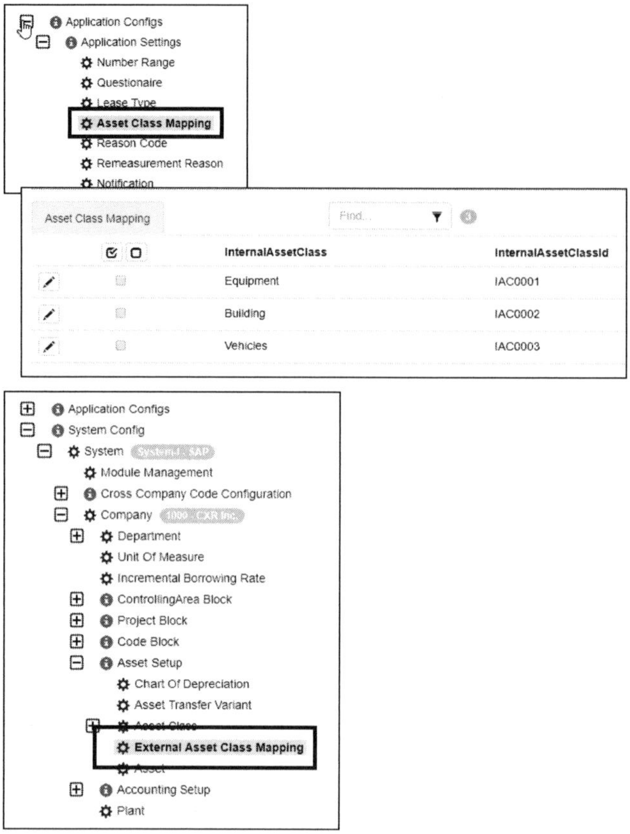


**Figure 4.32** Asset Classes versus External Asset Classes in the AdminConsole

The **External Asset Class** table in the system configuration includes the useful life of each asset class, which is defined in the SAP ERP system and used by SAP Lease Administration for lease classification. The classification threshold (percentage of useful life) used to classify a lease as either a finance lease or an operating lease under ASC 842 is set in the company defaults. Asset classes are mapped by company code and by accounting standard.

To map external asset classes and attach them to associated companies, follow these steps:

1. Make sure that you have selected the appropriate company from the pane on the left.
2. Click the **External Asset Class Mapping** node, as shown in Figure 4.33.
3. Click the task menu icon (three bars) and then select **Add**.

4. In the **CE_ExternalAssetClassMapping** window, enter the required information in each field.
5. Click **Submit**.

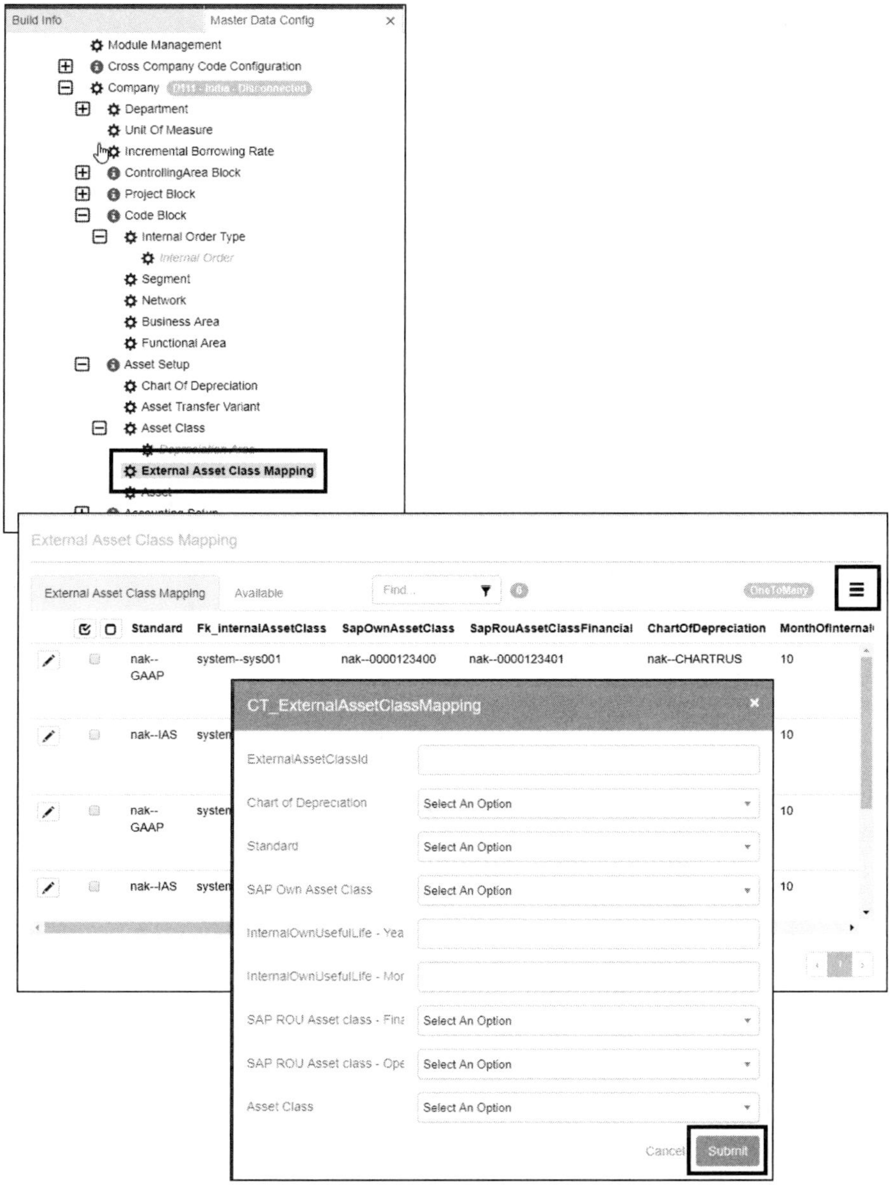


Figure 4.33 Mapping External Asset Classes and Attaching Associated Companies

Each internal (SAP Lease Administration) asset class should be mapped to three external ERP asset classes, as shown in Figure 4.34:

- Asset Class 1: finance/finance
- Asset Class 2: finance/operating (depreciation key = MANU)
- Asset Class 3: purchased (OWNED)

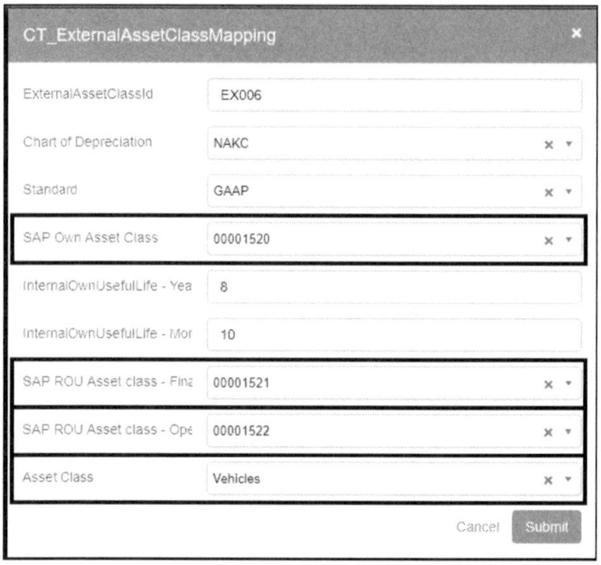


**Figure 4.34** SAP Lease Administration Asset Class Mapped to Three SAP Asset Classes

## Exchange Rate Type

The **Exchange Rate Type** table is used for currency translation. Therefore, the related companies must be attached to the exchange rate type table. Most entities use the "M" for transaction translation; this is a monthly average foreign exchange conversion rate.

To attach a company to the exchange rate type, follow these steps:

1. Make sure that you have selected the appropriate company from the pane on the left.
2. Under **Accounting Setup**, click the **Exchange Rate Type** node, as shown in Figure 4.35.

3. Click the task menu icon (three bars) and then select **Attach**.
4. On the **Available** tab, select the checkboxes for the exchange rate types you wish to attach.

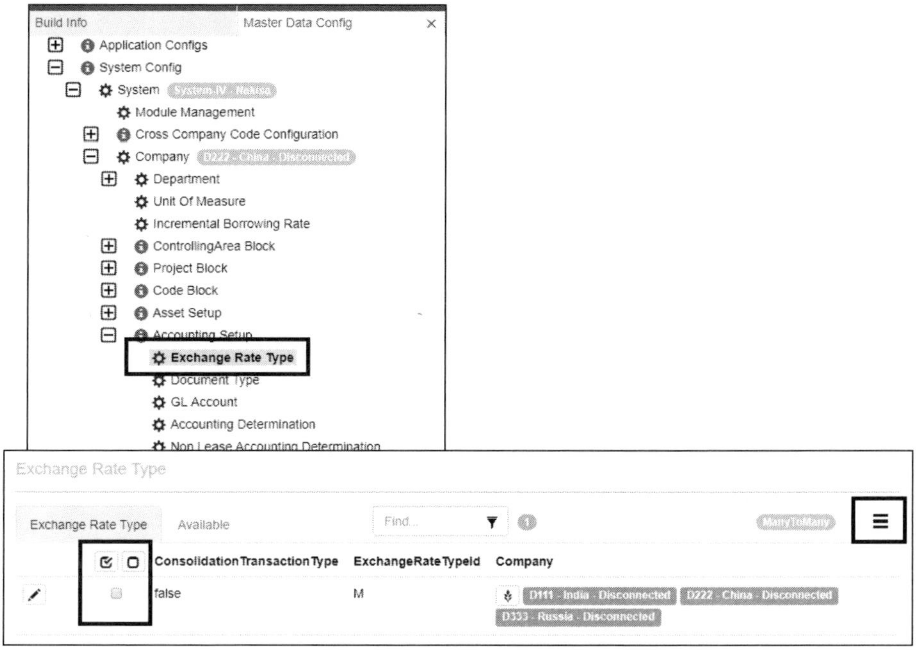

Figure 4.35 Attaching an Exchange Rate Type to a Company

### Document Type

You'll need to assign to each company an appropriate SAP document type, which is used to classify postings to each company.

To attach a document type to a company, follow these steps:

1. Make sure that you have selected the appropriate company from the pane on the left.
2. Under **Accounting Setup**, click the **Document Type** node, as shown in Figure 4.36.
3. Click the task menu icon (three bars) and then select **Attach**.
4. On the **Available** tab, select the checkboxes for the document types you wish to attach.

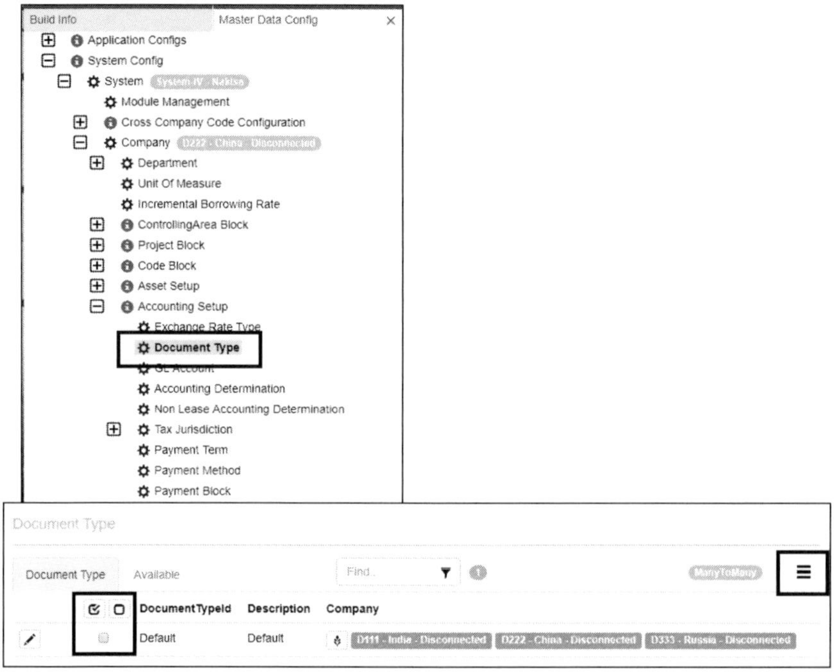


Figure 4.36 Attaching a Document Type to a Company

## Accounting Determination Mapping

The **Accounting Determination** table is used to map SAP accounts to lease contracts that are in active company codes. Note that you should already have set up the document types and general ledger accounts in SAP ERP before proceeding with this step.

To configure the accounting determination mapping, follow these steps:

1. Make sure that you have selected the appropriate company code from the pane on the left, next to the **Company** node, as shown in Figure 4.37.
2. Select the **Accounting Determination** node.
3. Click the task menu icon (three bars) and then select **Add**.
4. On the **Available** tab, select the checkboxes for the accounts you wish to attach.
5. Input the appropriate data in the section defining the standard, lease type, and classification. Then, input the appropriate data to define the mapping to the different document types in SAP. Finally, input the appropriate data to define the mapping to the different general ledger accounts.
6. Click **Submit** to save your changes, as shown in Figure 4.38.

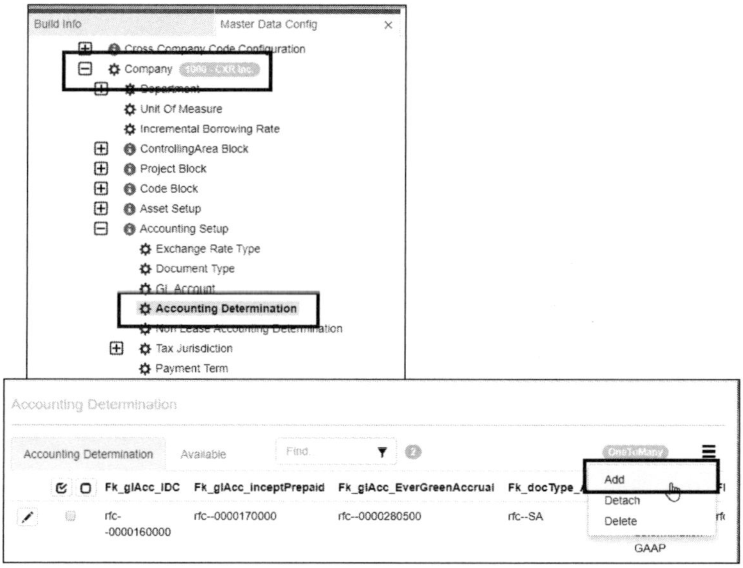


**Figure 4.37** Configuring the Accounting Determination Mapping (I)

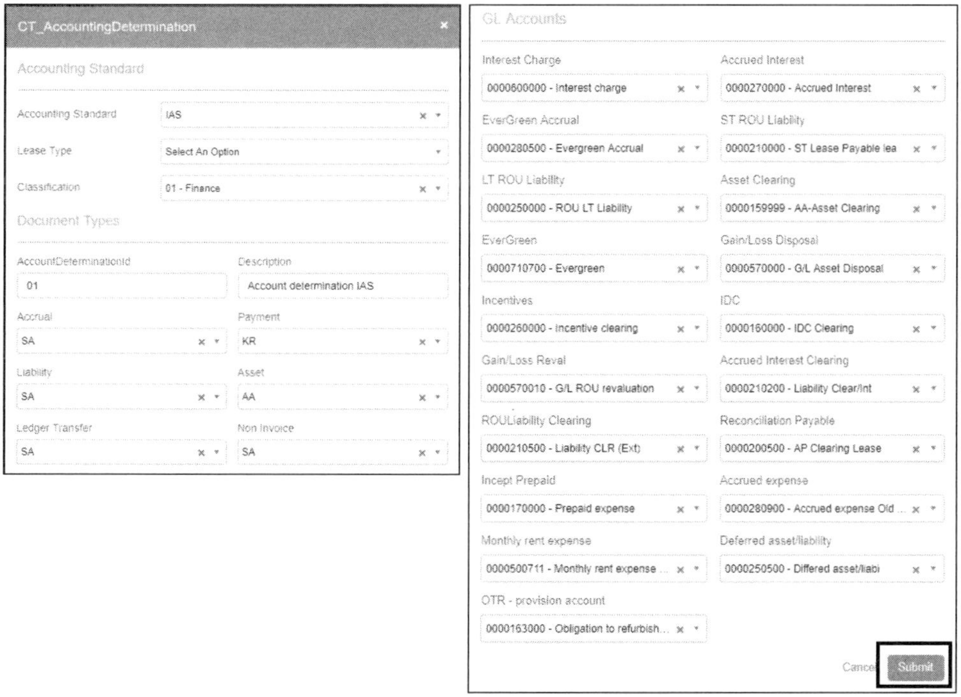


**Figure 4.38** Configuring the Accounting Determination Mapping (II)

## Non-Lease Account Determination

To add and map a non-lease account determination, follow these steps:

1. Make sure that you have selected the appropriate company code.
2. Under **Accounting Setup**, click the **Non-Lease Accounting Determination** node, as shown in Figure 4.39.
3. Click the task menu icon (three bars) and then select **Add**.
4. In the **CT_NonLeaseAccountingDetermination** window, complete the fields per your business requirements.
5. Click **Submit**.

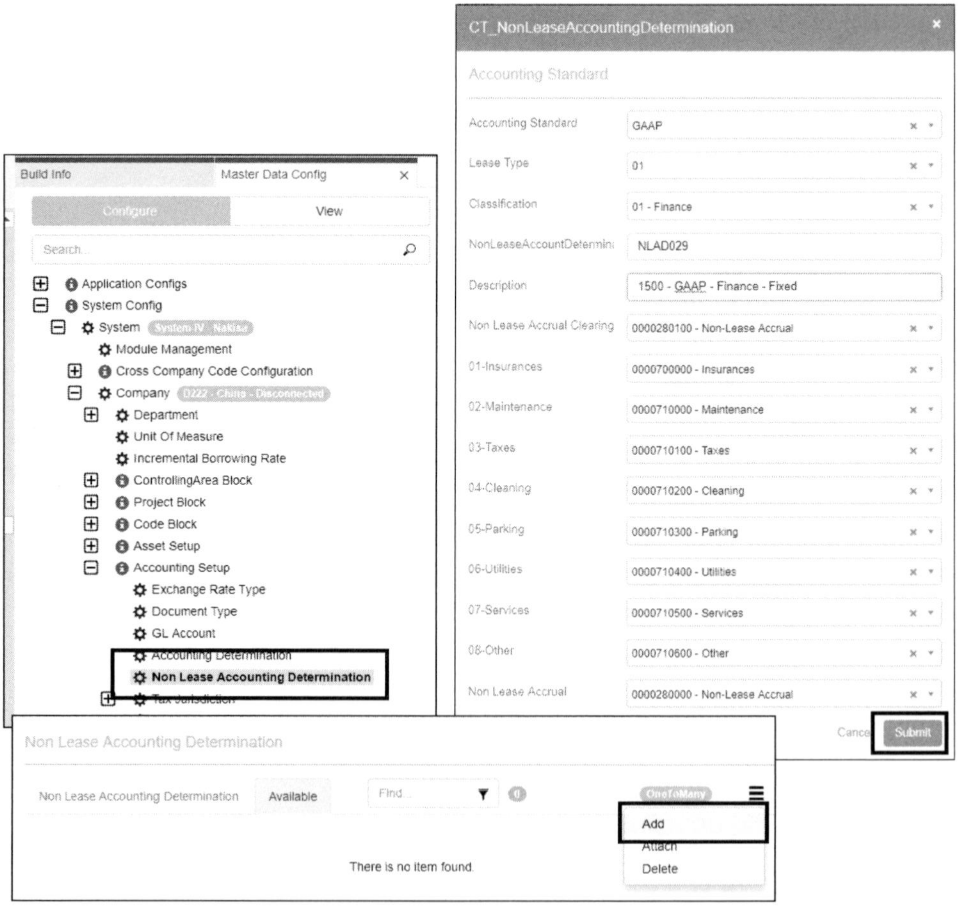


**Figure 4.39** Adding a Non-Lease Account Determination to a Company

### Payment Terms, Payment Method, Payment Block, Reversal Reasons, and Purchasing Organization

To modify payment terms, payment method, payment block, reversal reasons, and/or purchasing organization, follow these steps:

1. Make sure that you have selected the appropriate company code. Then, under **Accounting Setup**, click the appropriate node; in our example in Figure 4.40, we've chosen **Payment Term**.
2. Click the task menu icon (three bars) and then select **Attach**.
3. On the **Available** tab, select the checkboxes for the payment options you wish to activate.

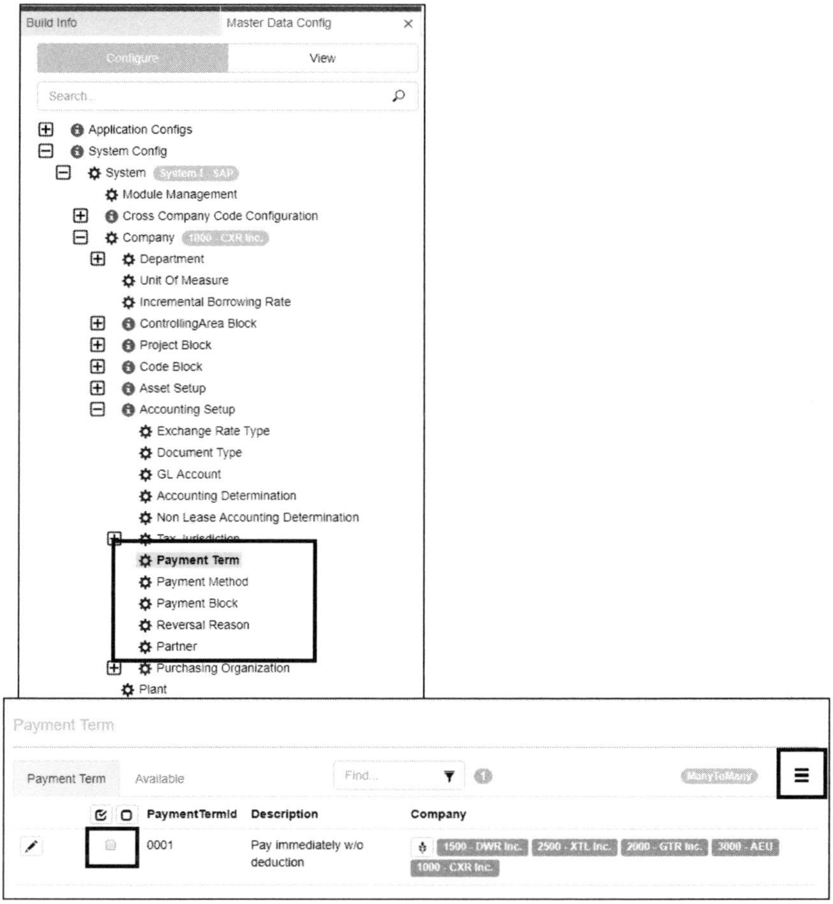


**Figure 4.40** Modifying the Corresponding Sections

Figure 4.41 shows how SAP Lease Administration integrates with SAP once you've configured the master data. SAP Lease Administration syncs the listed configuration tables directly from the SAP master data, and uses BAPI and RFC calls to generate live postings in SAP FI and AA and to retrieve and store the SAP document number as confirmation. Note that additional information such as GL mappings and IBR tables are manually configured in SAP Lease Administration using Excel data upload templates.

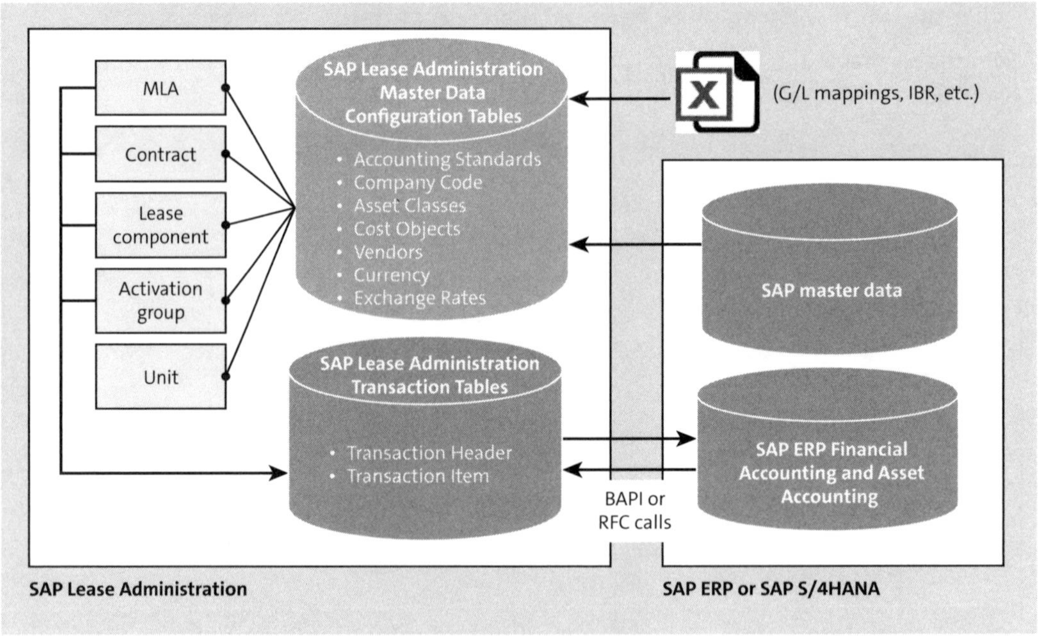


**Figure 4.41** SAP Lease Administration Integration and Configuration

Table 4.11 provides a complete list of the tables that sync with SAP and the mandatory tables that require additional manual configuration.

| SAP-Synced Tables | |
|---|---|
| ■ Depreciation Area<br>■ Asset Class<br>■ Chart of Depreciation<br>■ Controlling Area<br>■ Cost Center<br>■ Currency<br>■ Exchange Rate Type<br>■ FY Period<br>■ GL Account<br>■ Language<br>■ Partner<br>■ Unit of Measure<br>■ Internal Order<br>■ Profit Center<br>■ Purchase Order<br>■ Tax Code | ■ Asset<br>■ Asset Transfer Variant<br>■ Business Type<br>■ Exchange Rate<br>■ Functional Area<br>■ Internal Order Type<br>■ Payment Block<br>■ Payment Method<br>■ Payment Term<br>■ Project<br>■ Purchasing Organization<br>■ Reversal Reason<br>■ Tax Jurisdiction<br>■ Trading Partner<br>■ Work Breakdown Structure |
| **Mandatory Tables to Configure** | |
| ■ Module Management<br>■ Company<br>■ Accounting Standard<br>■ Classification<br>■ Account Determination | ■ External Asset Class Mapping<br>■ Non-Lease Account Determination<br>■ Incremental Borrowing Rate<br>■ Lease Department/Lease Group (optional) |

**Table 4.11** Mandatory and Synced Tables

At this point, you've completed the initial system configuration for your SAP Lease Administration implementation. Let's look next at data management.

## 4.4 Data Management

The **Data Management** tab is used to administer the data within SAP Lease Administration. Figure 4.42 shows the various buttons available, which are described in Table 4.12.

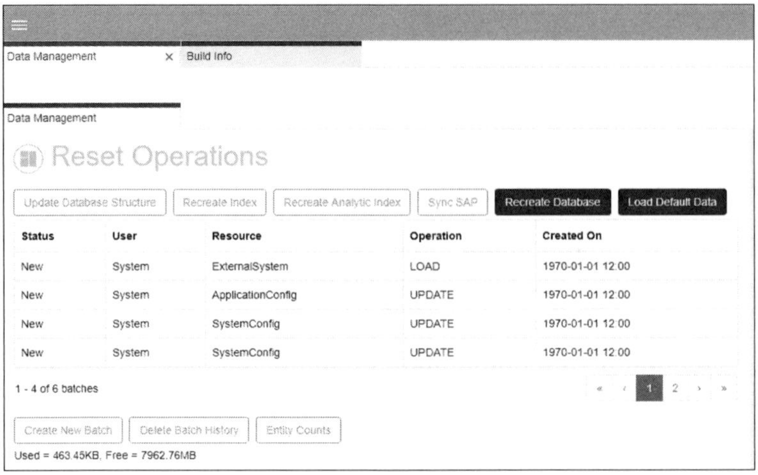


**Figure 4.42** Data Management Tab

| Operation | Description |
|---|---|
| **Update Database Structure** | Updates the database schema by adding (empty) fields and relations but does not delete any existing data. |
| **Recreate Index** | Autoindexing is enabled by default in the application, but clicking this button manually triggers the reindexing of tables. |
| **Recreate Analytics Index** | If analytic indexing is not automatic, click this button to update the weighted average graphs in the disclosure reports. |
| **Sync SAP** (will be deprecated) | Syncs with SAP ERP connected system(s). Note that *all* systems will be synced when this button is pressed, which could take a significant amount of time. |
| **Recreate Database** | Deletes the current database and re-creates ALL tables in your database to give you a new, empty schema for your data. Use with caution! |
| **Load Default Data** | Assuming you have re-created the database beforehand, this operation will load default startup data. |

**Table 4.12** Operations Available on the Data Management Tab

| Operation | Description |
| --- | --- |
| **Delete Batch History** | Removes the batch import history records that are generated in the **Reset Operations** section. |
| **Entity Count** | When clicked, compiles then displays a window with a count of all the entities in system. |

**Table 4.12** Operations Available on the Data Management Tab (Cont.)

This module is most often used to upload data. As shown in Figure 4.43, the data can be uploaded into the module either through the **Data Management** page (i.e., from the backend) or from the frontend of the application during the contract onboarding process.

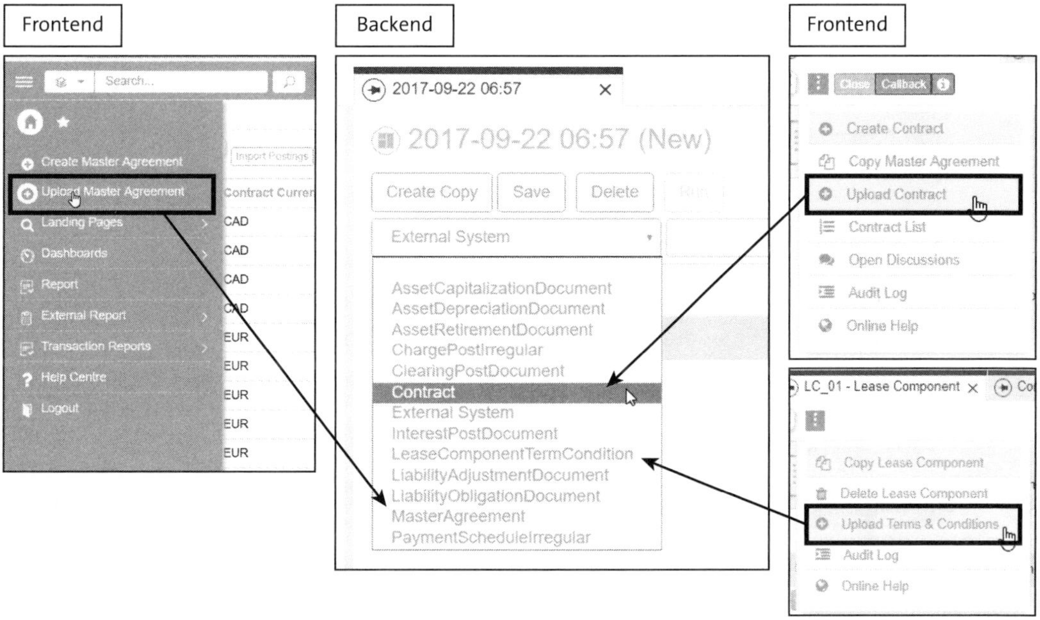


**Figure 4.43** Uploading Data in SAP Lease Administration

To upload data from the **Data Management** page, follow these basic steps:

1. Navigate to the **Data Management** tab in the AdminConsole.
2. Click **Create New Batch**, as shown in Figure 4.44. Data update options will be available on the right side of the screen.

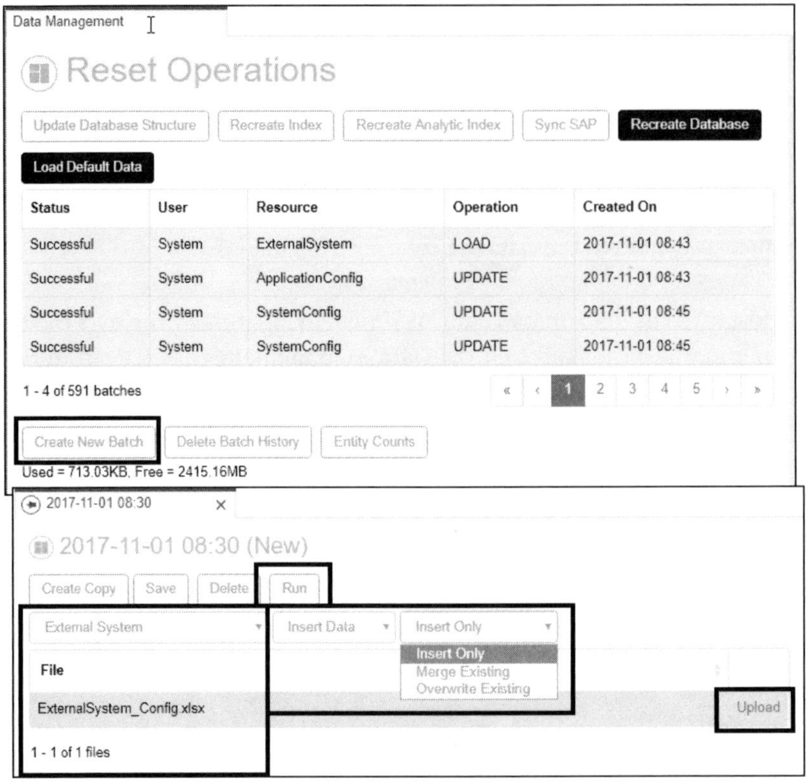


**Figure 4.44** Uploading Data in the Data Management Tab

3. From the **External System** dropdown menu, select "what" is to be uploaded. Table 4.13 describes the available options found in this dropdown menu.

| Upload Option | Description | Frontend |
|---|---|---|
| **AssetCapitalizationDocument** | Uploads asset capitalization transactions in a disconnected system | ✓ |
| **AssetDepreciationDocument** | Uploads asset depreciation transactions in a disconnected system | ✓ |
| **AssetRetirementDocument** | Uploads asset retirement transactions in a disconnected system | ✓ |
| **Contract** | Uploads contracts to the application | ✓ |

**Table 4.13** Upload Options: The "What"

| Upload Option | Description | Frontend |
|---|---|---|
| **External System** | Uploads multiple CT_System records into the master data configuration | |
| **LeaseComponentTermCondition** | Uploads irregular payments to the application | ✓ |
| **LiabilityAdjustmentDocument** | Uploads liability adjustment transactions in a disconnected system | ✓ |
| **LiabilityObligationDocument** | Uploads liability obligation transactions in a disconnected system | ✓ |
| **Master Agreement** | Uploads MLAs to the application | ✓ |

**Table 4.13** Upload Options: The "What" (Cont.)

4. From the **Insert Data** and **Inset Only** dropdown menus, select "how" to upload the data. Table 4.14 describes the available options in these dropdown menus.

| Method | Definition |
|---|---|
| **Load Data** | Deletes all existing records and loads the new data (overwrites) |
| **Insert Data** | Offers the following options:<br>▪ **Insert Only**: Inserts new records and ignores the existing ones (based on ID)<br>▪ **Merge Existing**: Inserts new records; merges records that already exist<br>▪ **Overwrite Existing**: Inserts new records; overwrites existing records with new values |
| **Update Data** | Offers the following options:<br>▪ **Update Only**: Only imports records that already exist and updates them<br>▪ **Update & Insert**: Updates existing records and inserts the new ones |
| **Delete Data** | Deletes all records in the system with matching IDs regardless of the object's status (i.e., active) |
| **Apply Delta** | Currently not used |

**Table 4.14** Upload Options: The "How"

5. Click **Upload**, then select the Excel file that contains the data to be uploaded. The Excel templates are downloaded from the frontend of the application and contain various tabs that represent different areas within the master lease agreement object. See Figure 4.45 and Figure 4.46.

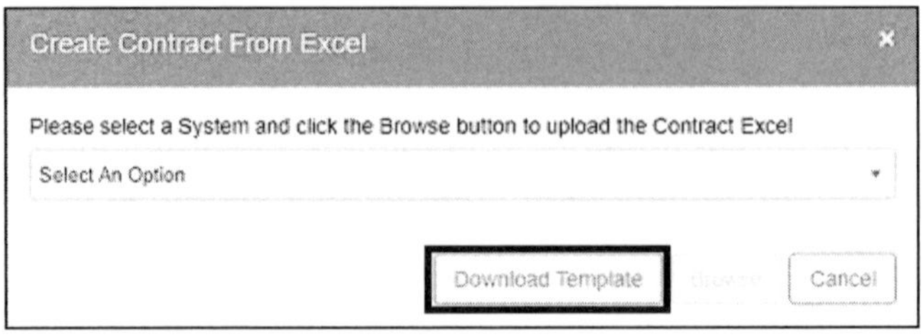


**Figure 4.45** Excel Template to Upload Data

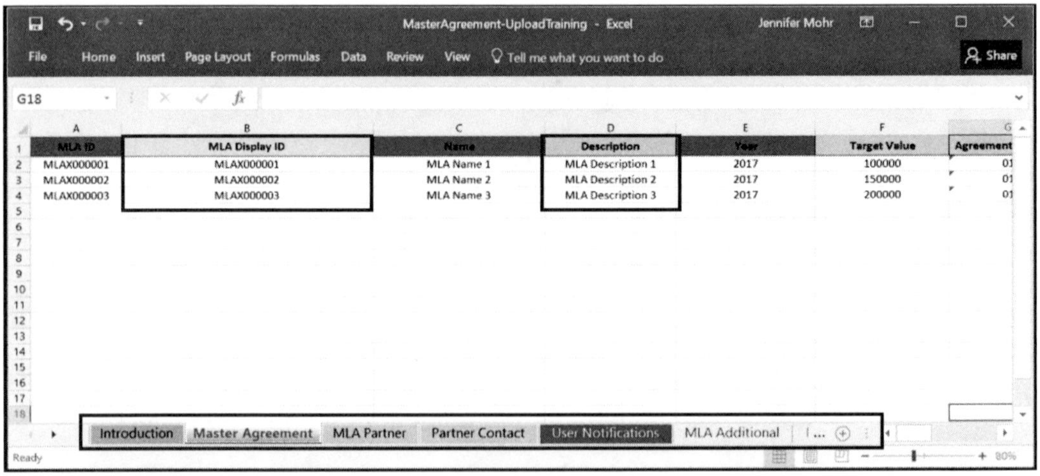


**Figure 4.46** Master Agreement Template

6. Click **Run** to launch the upload process.

## 4.5 Build Management

The **Build Management** tab allows users to download the original out-of-the-box build along with any future changes made to the build and master data configuration. Users can upload any customized configuration and reset the build configuration to the original out of the box configuration.

Note that the **Build Management** module does not affect any existing MLA and contract data in the application.

Figure 4.47 displays the **Build Management** landing page.

The configuration for the original, out of the box build is executed through the **Export Foundation** button. The configuration and language files of the original build must be exported (downloaded), which will generate a ZIP file (which will be called *foundation[date][hour]_[identifier].zip*). This package does not include the master data configuration.

When changes have been made the current active build, users may download a package that contains the changes to the build configuration and language files as well as the master data configuration by executing the **Export Changes** button. The package will be a ZIP file (which will be called *customizations [data] [hour]_[identifier].zip*). The package includes build configuration files, such as:

- User modifications via AdminConsole and uploaded customization packages
- Language files that have been modified
- All master data configuration (i.e., database entities and relations)

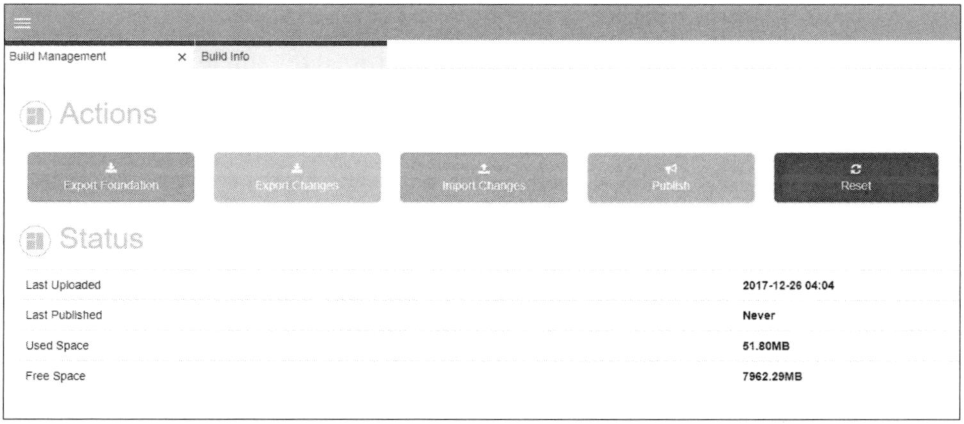


**Figure 4.47** Build Management Tab

To upgrade the current build to the requested customization, the **Import Changes** and **Publish** buttons are used. Click **Import Changes** to upload customization and/or master data configuration and click **Publish** to merge the changes into the effective build.

This feature can be used in various types of scenarios, such as for applying custom features; for updating configuration files that cannot be modified via the AdminConsole; for upgrading to a new build (which may require you to export and send the configuration changes to Nakisa, who will then merge these changes into the build); and for migrating to new environments (e.g., from quality assurance to production).

When migrating to a new environment, you must take a few additional steps:

- If both environments require different build configurations, you must download and send the customizations to Nakisa.
- If both environments have the same build configuration but different master data configurations, you must remove the **Data** folder from the customization package before executing **Import Changes** and **Publish** in the new environment.
- If both environments have identical builds and master data configurations, you must export the customizations before executing **Import Changes** then **Publish** in the new environment.

If the foundation package is uploaded instead of the customization package, the system will essentially revert the current build to its original, out-of-the-box configuration.

Uploading the foundation package does not override the master data configuration. If overriding master data configuration is required, load the original default master data configuration in the **Data Management** tab.

Once the customization package has been uploaded and published, the most recently uploaded and published information is updated in the **Status** section. This section also provides information about the used and free space available to the application on the server.

Be sure to verify the configuration for the new build. For example, the **Number Range** must be maintained to ensure that the same **ID**s are not reused.

To upgrade to a new build, follow these steps:

1. Navigate in AdminConsole to **Build Management** and click **Export Changes**.
2. Save the exported package.
3. Navigate in the AdminConsole to **Build Management** and click **Export Foundation**.
4. Save the foundation package.
5. Send both packages to the Nakisa Technical Consultant Prime.
6. Once the new build has been received from Nakisa, uninstall the current version of SAP Lease Administration and deploy the latest build received.

7. Navigate in the AdminConsole to the **Build Management** page, click **Import Changes**, and import the package from step 6.
8. Once the package has been imported, click **Publish**.
9. Navigate in the AdminConsole to **Data Management** and click **Update Database Structure • Recreate Index**.
10. To reset the current build to its original, out-of-the-box state, click **Reset**. All customizations uploaded and merged to the build will be cleared, but master data configuration and application data will not be erased. To replace the master data configuration, navigate to the **Data Management** page of the AdminConsole and load the default master data configuration.

## 4.6 Schedule Jobs and Thresholds

Scheduled jobs are used to automate the execution of tasks, the synchronization of operations, and the postings to the application.

The **Schedule Jobs** tab in the AdminConsole lists all of the available jobs, which can be enabled or disabled individually.

Let's take a closer look at this tab. As shown in Figure 4.48, the **Status** column indicates the status of the job (i.e., "Scheduled," "Not Scheduled," or "Paused"). "Paused" is defined as the job was once scheduled but has since been disabled.

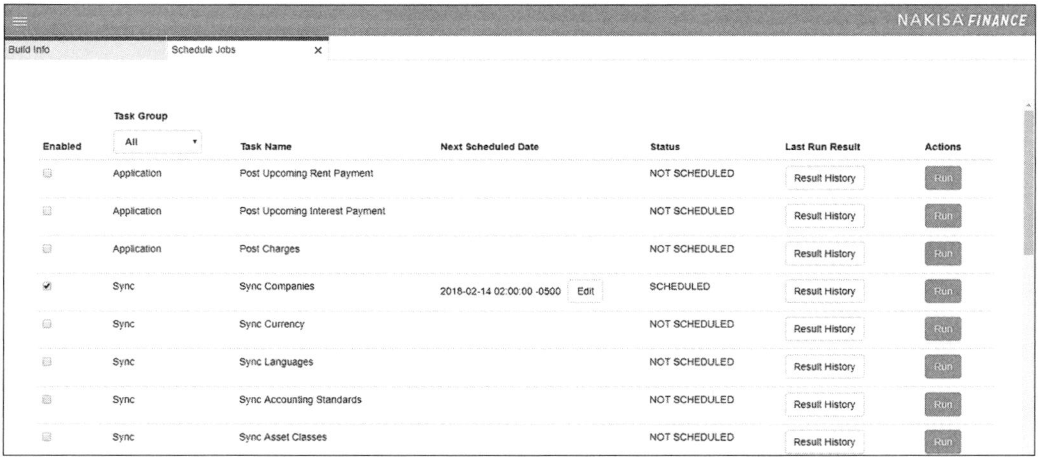


**Figure 4.48** Schedule Job Landing Page in the AdminConsole

If a functional administrator wants to run a job immediately, that person would click **Run** to trigger and execute the task.

The **Task Group** column segregates scheduled jobs into two categories:

- The scheduled jobs under **Application** are tasks that generate postings, such as:
  - The **Post Upcoming Rent Payment** job will post all rent payments that are due today or earlier as defined in the payment schedule of contract, under its terms and conditions.
  - The **Post Upcoming Interest Payment** job will post the accrued interest that is due today or earlier as defined in the payment schedule of contract, under terms and conditions.
  - The **Post Charges** job will post individual charge items defined at the **Activation Group** level under **Charge List**.
- The scheduled jobs under **Sync** perform data synchronization with the SAP ERP system. The frequency for syncing each SAP table needs to be discussed with key stakeholders as this configuration must fulfill the user's needs. **Sync** schedule jobs can be edited according to the requested frequency.

To edit a job's schedule, follow these steps:

1. Ensure the job is enabled.
2. Under the **Next Scheduled Date** column, click **Edit**.
3. Select the preferred time frame tab (**Hourly**, **Daily**, **Weekly**, or **Monthly**).
4. Adjust the related scheduling parameters of the job in question.
5. Click **Submit** to commit this new job schedule.

To view a job's history, follow these steps:

1. Click **Run History** next to the job that is being reviewed.
2. The **Result History** window displays the start and end time, the result, and the run mode (**Manual** or **Automated**).

Under the **Thresholds** tab in the AdminConsole, you'll define the criteria and conditions that trigger system tasks and alert notifications. For instance, a task threshold may be used to post periodic accruals for all existing units, thus saving a user from having to enter the application and click **Post** for each individual unit, one by one.

By default, the system provides two different sets of thresholds—task thresholds and notification thresholds—as listed in Table 4.15. You might use a notification threshold to inform the relevant parties to a contract that the contract end date is approaching so that negotiations can start earlier, instead of after the lease ends.

| Task Thresholds | Notification Thresholds |
|---|---|
| ▪ Interest/accruals activation group<br>▪ Interest/accruals unit<br>▪ Depreciation (main)<br>▪ Inactive user management<br>▪ Close MLA<br>▪ Lease end (active contracts)<br>▪ Payable activation group<br>▪ Payable unit level<br>▪ SAP reversal notification | ▪ Contracts approaching end date<br>▪ Contracts to be closed (with no payments)<br>▪ Standard terms notifications<br>▪ Evergreen notification<br>▪ Casualty notification<br>▪ Lease end—units to be closed<br>▪ Lease closed—units are not retired (exception report) |

**Table 4.15** Task and Notification Thresholds

## 4.7 Field Management

The **Field Management** page allows you to disable and hide specific fields within the application that are not required by your users. Fields are grouped by category so that you can see the total number of visible and hidden fields for any single category. Note that this area shows *all* the fields that exist in the database tables; some of these fields may not be used in the application but will still be indicated as visible fields.

To show/hide fields in the application, follow these steps:

1. From the **Main** menu, click the **Field Management** option, as shown in Figure 4.49.
2. Select the category you wish to work with from the left panel. In the table of fields for each category, the **Used In** column indicates where the field is used:
   - **Form**: The field is used in a page or popup.
   - **AggsPanel**: The field is used in the filters in the left panel.
   - **Form - AggsPanel**: The field is used in both the page or popup and in the filters.
3. From the **My Profile** menu, select **Show** or **Hide** from the list. Make sure you don't hide any mandatory fields; users will not be able to progress to the next step in their SAP Lease Administration workflow if a mandatory field is hidden.
4. Use the scroll bar to view all fields you wish to enable/disable in this list.
5. Click **Save** to commit to your changes.

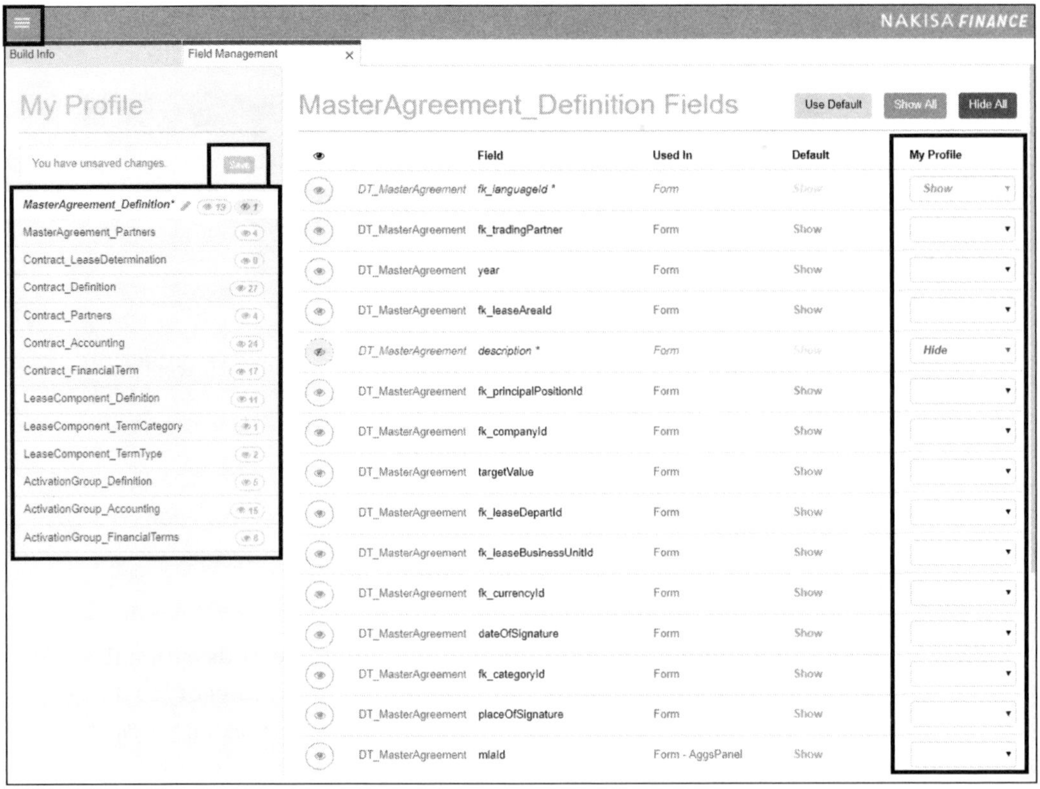


**Figure 4.49** Showing and Hiding Fields

## 4.8 Caption Editor

Captions are defined as text items that appear on the SAP Lease Administration frontend. A caption could be the name of a button, a message that pops up after a user performs an action, the content of menus, and more.

The **Caption Editor** module allows you to change the text within the application, including changes to captions that have been translated into a language other than English.

To change a caption, follow these steps:

1. Navigate to the **Logs** tab.
2. Select the appropriate option from the **Search Option** dropdown menu.

3. Search for the caption by entering the text from the caption in the **Search** field shown in Figure 4.50. A list of captions that match the search criteria will be shown. To filter the results to show only the captions that have been modified, select the **Modified Only** checkbox.
4. Mouse over the caption you want to change and click the **Edit**. This opens fields for the caption in each of the active pages in the application.
5. Enter the new caption into the appropriate field, then click **Save**.

**Figure 4.50** Caption Editor Tab

## 4.9 Logs and RFC Traces

The **Logs** tab within the AdminConsole houses two kinds of logs: engine logs and CDS logs. Figure 4.51 shows a portion of the **Logs** tab:

- The engine log is used to troubleshoot the values and calculations displayed in the contract amortization schedules. The log displays the inputs and outputs to the business and accounting engine (per asset group). A new log entry is saved every time a schedule is generated and is identified by its timestamp. Note that the engine log is disabled by default; to enable it, contact your implementation partner.
- The CDS log records application and database errors. A new log is created once the current log reaches 20 MB in size, and the application keeps up to 1000 MB (i.e., 50 logs). Whenever a new log file is created, the previous one is renamed to cds.log.x where "x" is a number (the oldest log is numbered 1).

The information captured in the error log could have three levels of severity:

- **Info**: Informational messages related to regular activity (e.g., when a user logs in).
- **Warning**: Signals a condition that does not prevent the completion of the task but requires action from the administrator.
- **Error**: Signals an incomplete task depending on the setting of other parameters. As a result, this error requires immediate administrative action.

To view a log, follow these steps:

1. Navigate to the **Logs** tab, as shown in Figure 4.51.
2. Select the type of log (either **Engine Log** or **CDS Log**).
3. Click **View Log**. The page then displays the information such as log inputs, payments, casualties, and outputs of the business and accounting engine. Use the navigation arrows if a selected log extends multiple pages.
4. To view the full error message, select a log under the **Message** column, and the full error message will be displayed under the **Details** section below in blue, as shown in Figure 4.51.

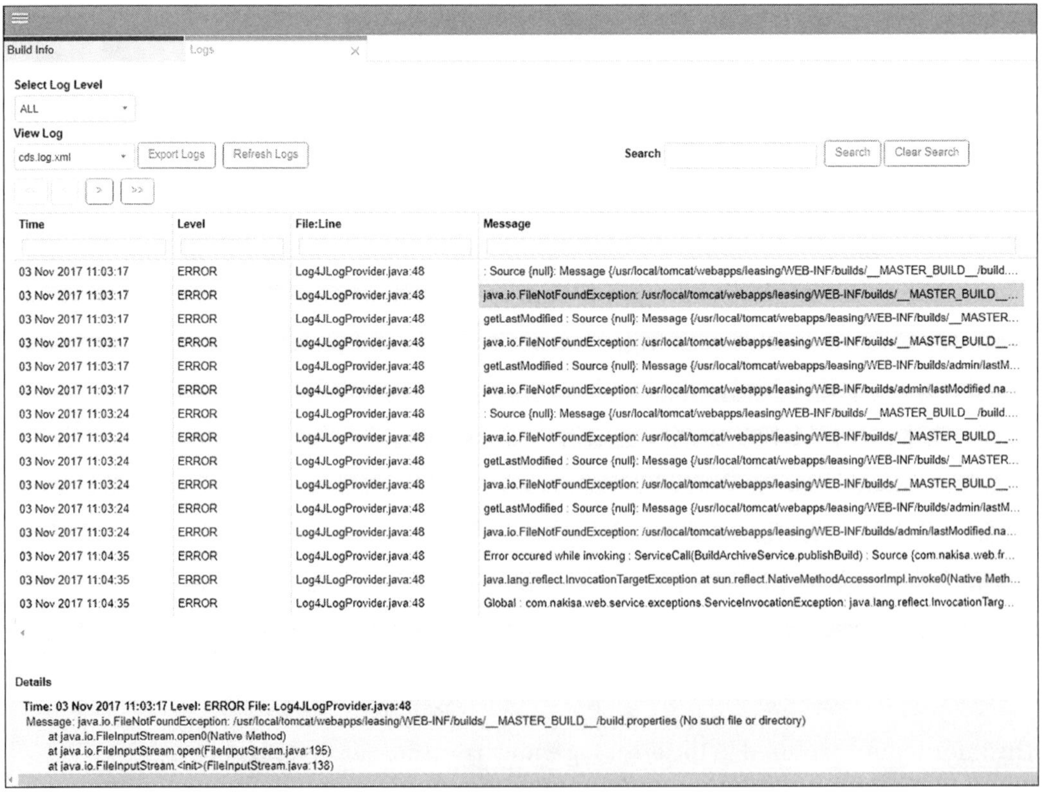


**Figure 4.51** Logs Tab

The **RFC Trace** tab is used to monitor the interaction between the solution and the SAP ERP system. The logs on this tab consist of the transactions sent to and from your SAP ERP systems (e.g., when creating and capitalizing assets or posting accruals).

As shown in Figure 4.52, the **On** button in the top right corner must be green to ensure the trace feature is enabled. To view details about the function (such as input and output information and errors), click on a selected row to open the **Trace Details** window, as shown in Figure 4.53.

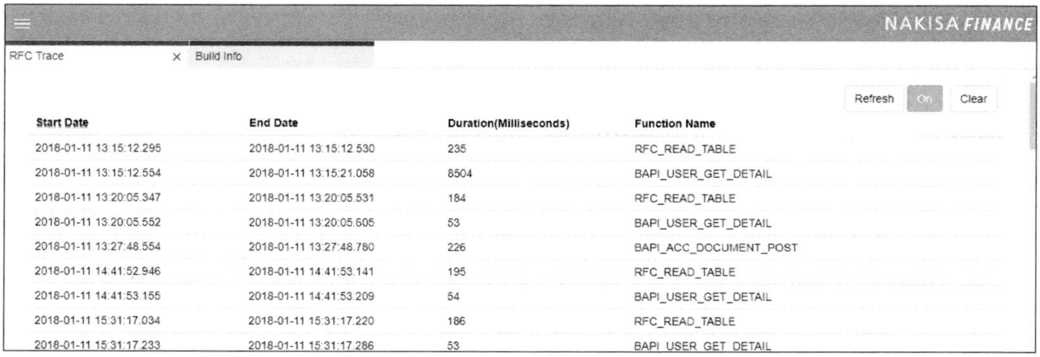


**Figure 4.52** RFC Traces Tab

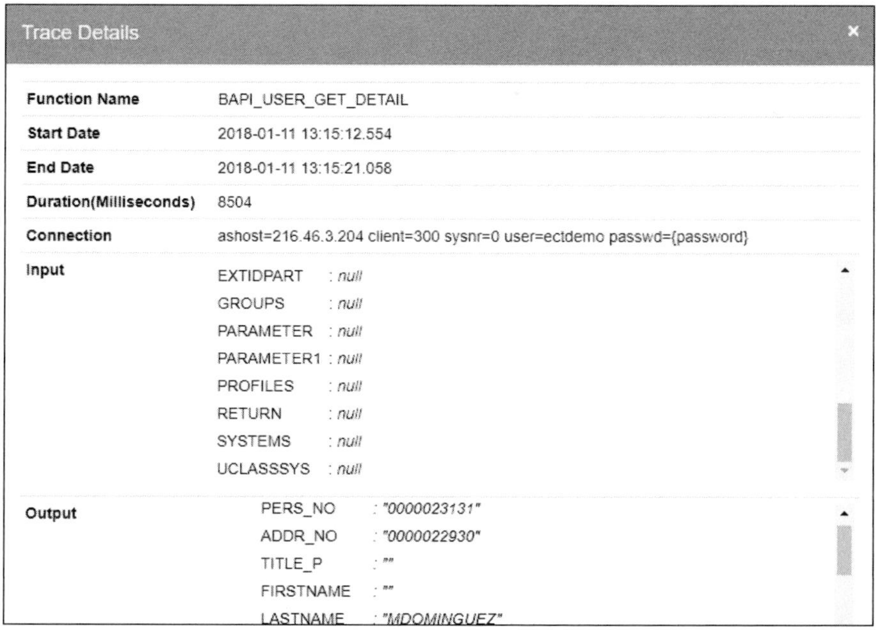


**Figure 4.53** Trace Details Window

## 4.10 Summary

In this chapter, we distilled the best practices for implementing SAP Lease Administration by Nakisa to help comply with IFRS 16 and ASC 842 leasing requirements. Be sure to make use of all available documentation as you undertake your project and to consult with your implementation team.

# Chapter 5
# Configuring SAP Flexible Real Estate Management for Lease Valuations

*Let's dig into the system configuration for lease valuations with SAP Flexible Real Estate Management.*



For more transparency in a company's financial position, the International Accounting Standards Board (IASB) and the Financial Accounting Standards Board (FASB), as specified under International Financial Reporting Standards 16 and Accounting Standards Codification 842, respectively, have changed their rules on how leases must be presented in financial statements.

To enable compliance with these new rules, SAP has extended the capabilities of SAP Flexible Real Estate Management (SAP RE-FX) with new functionalities for valuating lease contracts under the new rules. This chapter only covers the additional configuration in the IMG required for SAP RE-FX to execute lease valuations compliant with IFRS 16 and ASC 842; we won't instruct you on how to set up the rest of the SAP RE-FX solution, which would be outside the scope of a leasing project.

We'll start in Section 5.1 by describing the basic settings for lease valuations in SAP RE-FX. Once the basic settings have been set, we'll configure the balance sheet valuation of contracts in Section 5.2. Then, in Section 5.3, we'll walk you through the steps to set up the account determination, which is needed to create postings in the new SAP General Ledger and the FI-AA subledger for the right-of-use asset (ROU asset) and for the lease liability. We'll also explain the postings for the profit and loss account, which will periodically change the balances for the ROU asset and lease liability. In Section 5.4, we'll deal with several special topics related to the balance sheet valuation of contracts.

The first step, of course, is to access the relevant parts of the IMG via one of three SAP transaction codes. As shown in Figure 5.1, Transaction SPRO will send you to the full IMG, of which the **Flexible Real Estate Management (RE-FX)** section contains the possible entry options.

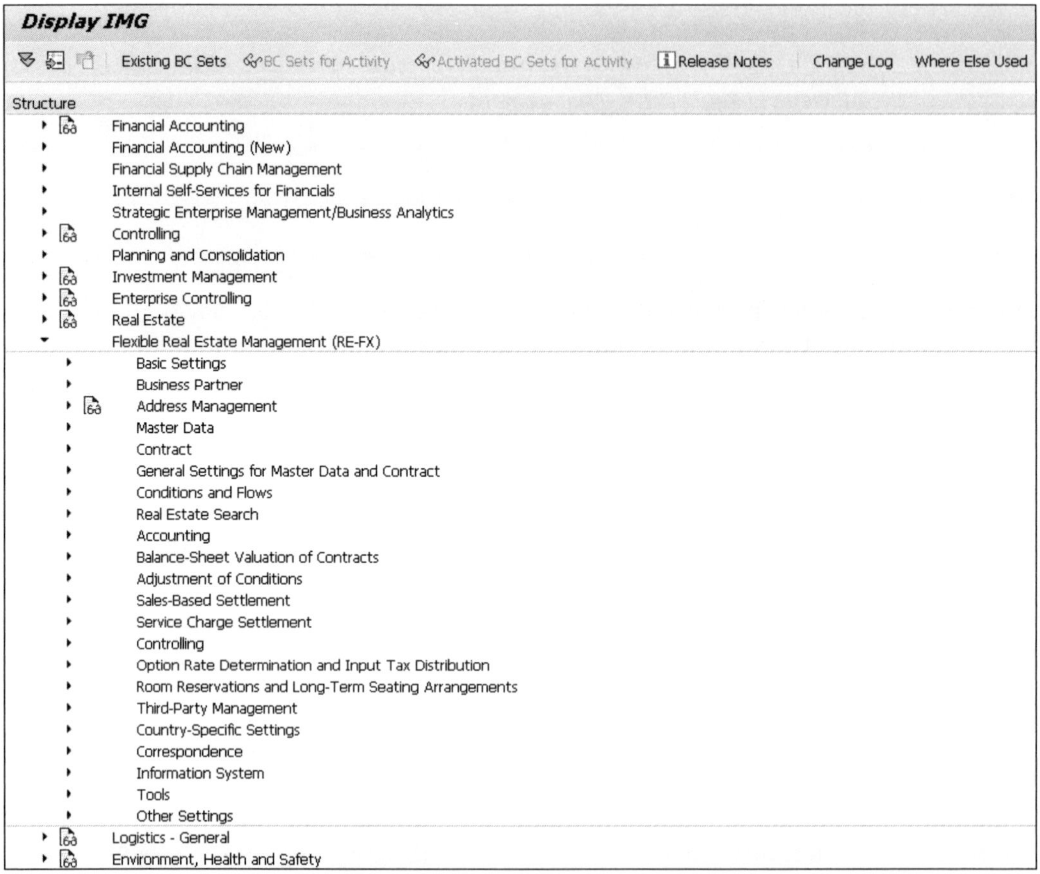


**Figure 5.1** Transaction SPRO

Transaction RECACUST brings you directly to the SAP RE-FX part of the IMG, as shown in Figure 5.2.

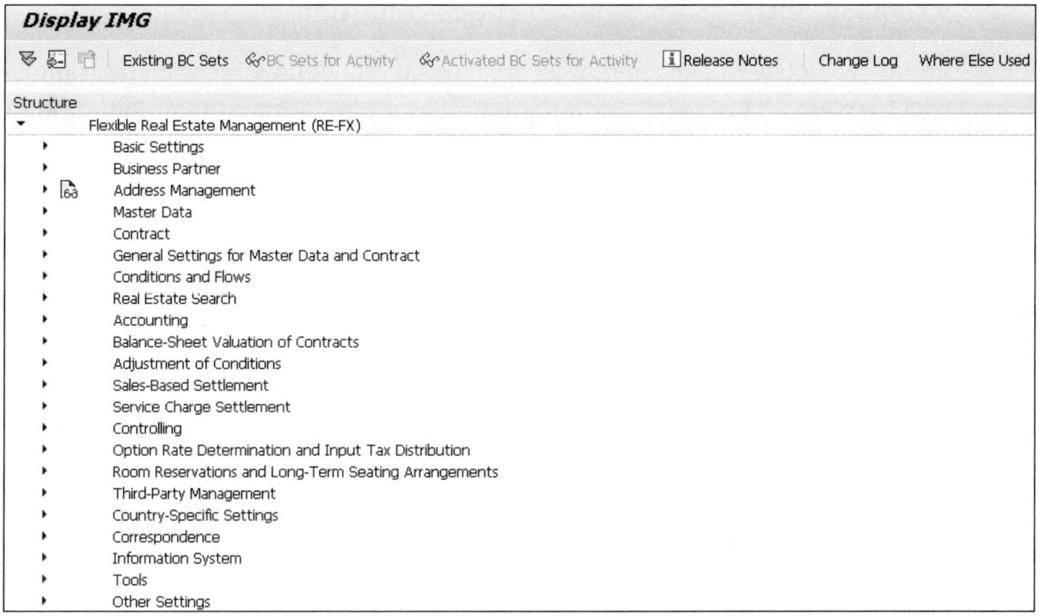


**Figure 5.2** Transaction RECACUST

Finally, Transaction RECECUST accesses just the balance sheet valuation part of the IMG, as shown in Figure 5.3.

**Figure 5.3** Transaction RECECUST

## 5.1 Basic Settings for Balance Sheet Valuation

In this section, we'll explain how to prepare SAP RE-FX for lease valuations under IFRS 16 and ASC 842.

For the sake of simplicity, we'll assume that you're not currently using SAP RE-FX—that you're undertaking a brand new SAP RE-FX project prompted by the need to comply with IFRS 16 and ASC 842, which begins with lease valuation. For customers currently using SAP RE-FX for processing incoming and/or outgoing payments for lease contracts, the first step can be skipped.

First, the Real Estate Extension has to be activated in your SAP ERP system. We recommend that you read the documentation provided by SAP before activating the Real Estate Extension.

To activate the Real Estate Extension, follow the IMG menu path: **Flexible Real Estate Management (RE-FX) • Basic Settings • Activate Real Estate Extension**. Select the **Extension Active** checkbox in the **Activate Real Estate Extension** part of the screen, as shown in Figure 5.4.

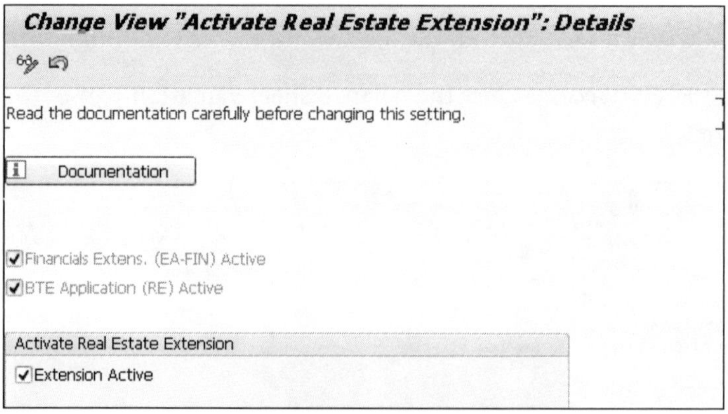


**Figure 5.4** Activating the Real Estate Extension

Next, activate the subfunction for contract valuation by following the IMG menu path: **Flexible Real Estate Management (RE-FX) • Basic Settings • Activate Subfunction**. Click the **Actv.** checkbox for **CE01 – Contract Valuation**, as shown in Figure 5.5. (Note that the other subfunctions shown on this screen are options in SAP RE-FX for after valuation capabilities have gone live.)

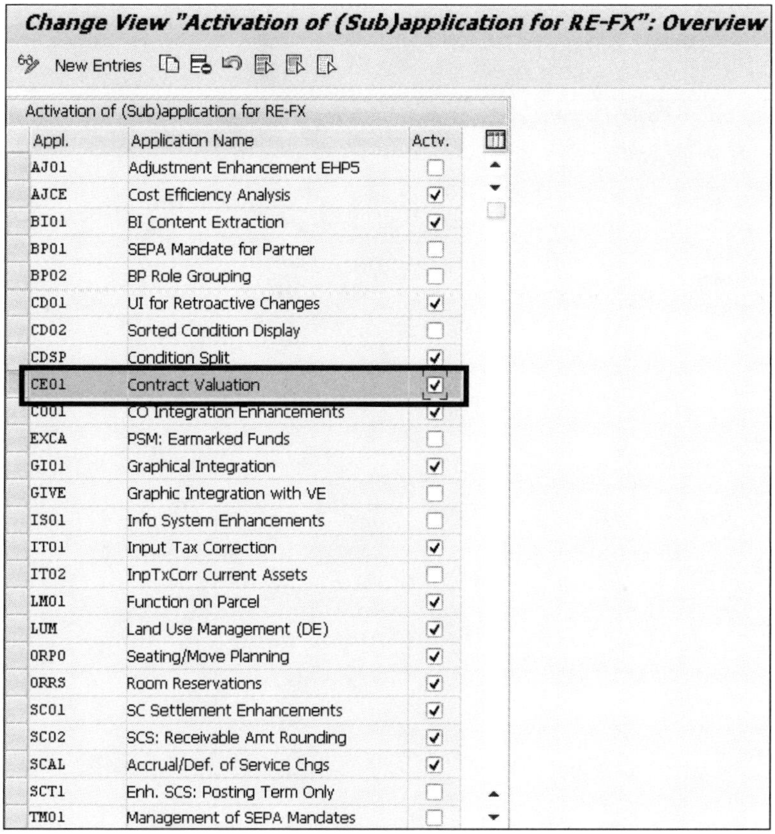


**Figure 5.5** Activating the Contract Valuation Subfunction

Next, you'll need to take some configuration steps for the company code that manages your lease contracts, by following the IMG menu path: **Flexible Real Estate Management (RE-FX) • Basic Settings • Make Basic Settings in Company Code**.

Three important columns are displayed on this screen, as shown in Figure 5.6:

- **CCTp**: If the company code is also used to manage real estate that belongs to that company code, then select **Manager Company Code** from the dropdown list.
- **Accounting Syst**: The fields in the accounting system column are normally blank or contain the value **FI** (for SAP ERP Financial Accounting). You can enter a different accounting system in this field only if you've already activated the Public Sector Contract Accounting (PS-CD) component in the client.

- **Company Code Opts**: The last column contains checkboxes that specify whether the company code opts to pay input tax.

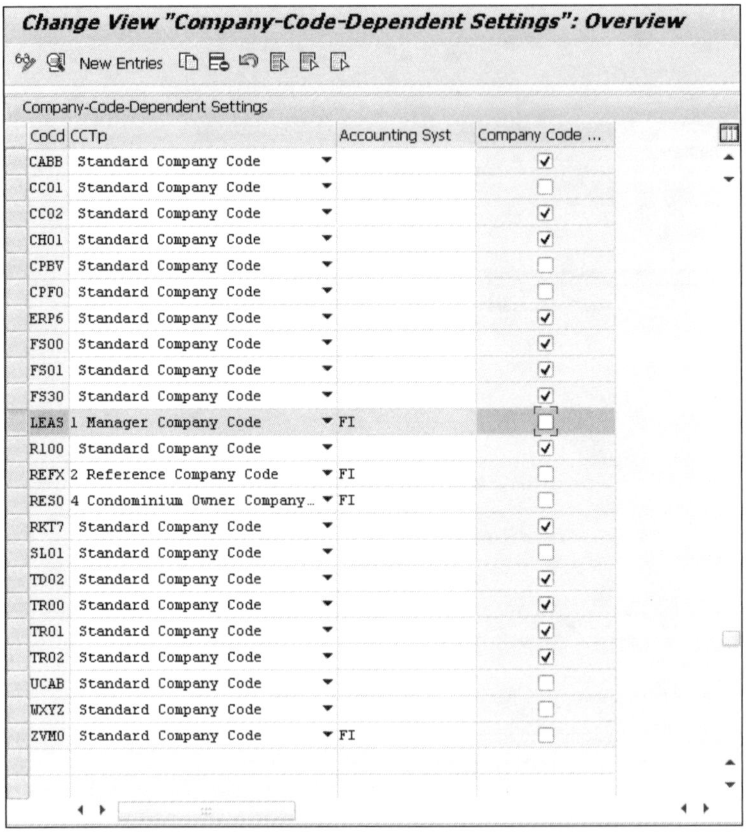


**Figure 5.6** Making Company Code-Dependent Settings

For the final two steps in the basic settings area, follow the IMG menu path: **Flexible Real Estate Management (RE-FX) • Basic Settings • Activate Real Estate Management in Controlling Area**. (Note that we're assuming that you're using CO and have already set up the standard CO configuration.)

To activate SAP RE-FX in the active controlling area (in the **Activate Components/ Control Indicators** folder shown in Figure 5.7), select or input the following data:

- **Cost Centers**: Select **1 Component Active** from the dropdown menu.
- **AA: Activity Type**: Select this checkbox if you want the system to assign actual primary costs directly to the activity type of a cost center.

- **Order Management**: Select **1 Component Active** from the dropdown menu.
- **Commit. Management**: Select **1 Component Active** from the dropdown menu.
- **Acty-Based Costing**: Select **2 Component Active for Parallel and Integrated Calculation** from the dropdown menu.



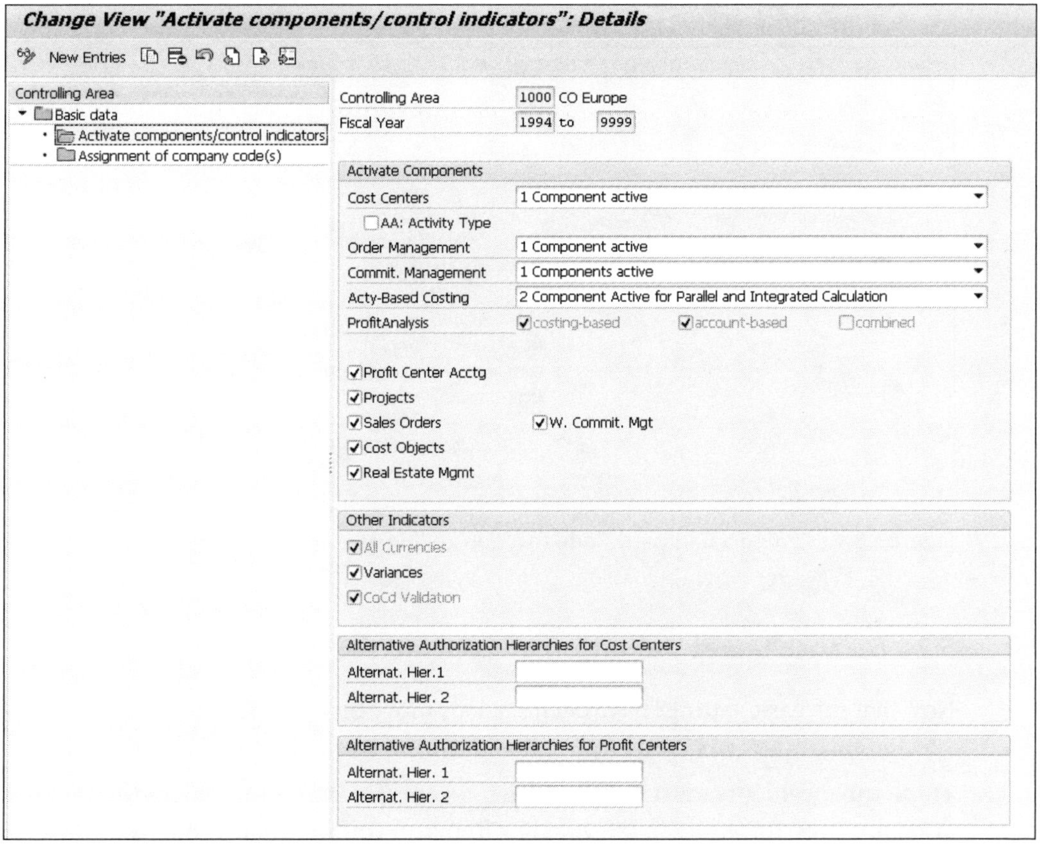


**Figure 5.7** Activating SAP RE-FX in the Active Controlling Area

Activate the following checkboxes:

- **Profit Center Acctg**
- **Projects**
- **Sales Orders**
- **Cost Objects**

- **Real Estate Mgmt**
- **W. Commit. Mgt**
- **Variances**

To assign a company code to the controlling area (in the **Assignment of Company Codes** folder shown in Figure 5.8), select the company code LEAS.

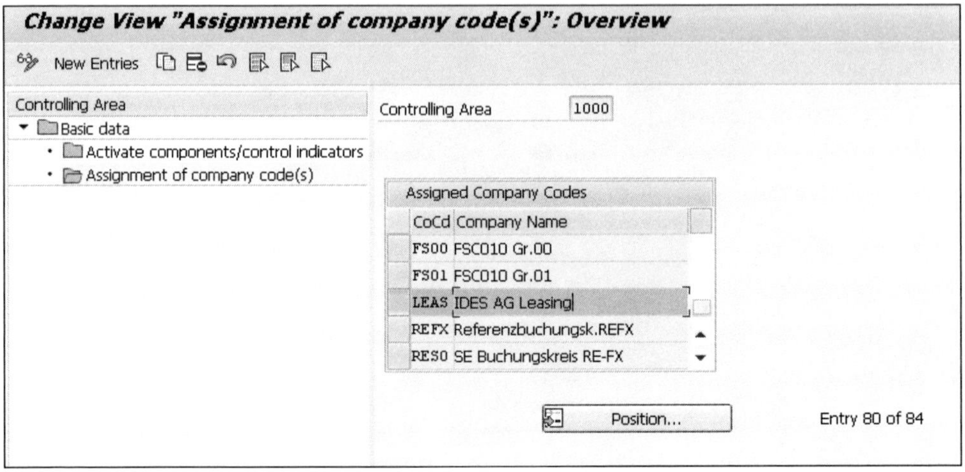


**Figure 5.8** Assigning a Company Code to a Controlling Area

## 5.2 Balance Sheet Valuation of Contracts

Now that the basic settings have been set, let's move on to configuring the valuation-specific enhancements found in SAP RE-FX.

These enhancements must be configured to generate the correct values (in the valuation postings) for the lease-relevant line items on your company's quarterly balance sheet and profit and loss statement.

### 5.2.1 Control Settings for Each Contract Type in a Company Code

Follow the IMG menu path: **Flexible Real Estate Management (RE-FX) • Balance-Sheet Valuation of Contracts • Control Settings for Each Contract Type in Company Code**.

On this screen, you can configure settings for the company code (the **CoCd** column) and contract type (the **Contract Type** column) with regard to three elements:

- The screen sequence (**ScnSeq** field) of contract entry screens, which we'll explain in Section 5.2.2.
- The type of integration (**IntegrType** field) for the creation of an ROU asset. Select one of the two options from the dropdown menu:
  - **Asset Accounting**: Full integration with FI-AA is the default setting, as shown in Figure 5.9.
  - **Direct Balance-Sheet Postings**: Postings for the creation and depreciation of an ROU asset are made directly on the designated general ledger account.
- A reference interest rate (**RefIntRate** field). For example, if you enter "LIBOR + 0.6%" in this field, this interest rate is then transferred to the valuation rule and used for the valuation calculation of the ROU asset in a lease contract valuation.

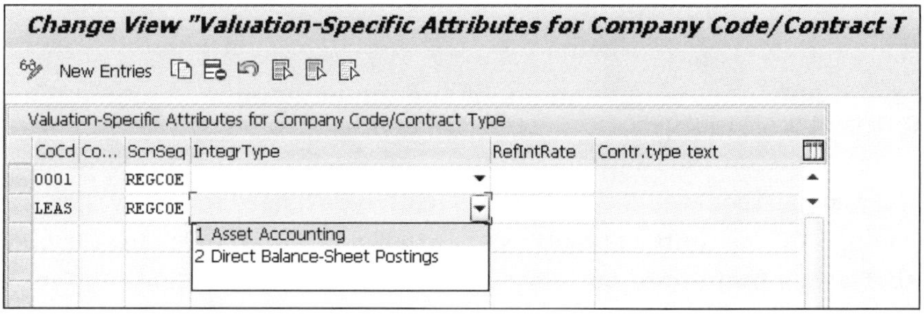


**Figure 5.9** Company Code Settings

## 5.2.2 Screen Sequence for Entering Contracts in SAP RE-FX

You'll have to enter contract details into the system for them to be valuated. Multiple options are available for entering such data.

The entry screen is divided into tabs for the different groups of data to be entered (e.g., tabs for general data, terms, objects, conditions, valuation parameters, etc.). The sequence of tabs is called a *screen sequence*.

Transaction RECN (shown in Figure 5.10) contains a default screen sequence for entering contracts for balance sheet valuation.

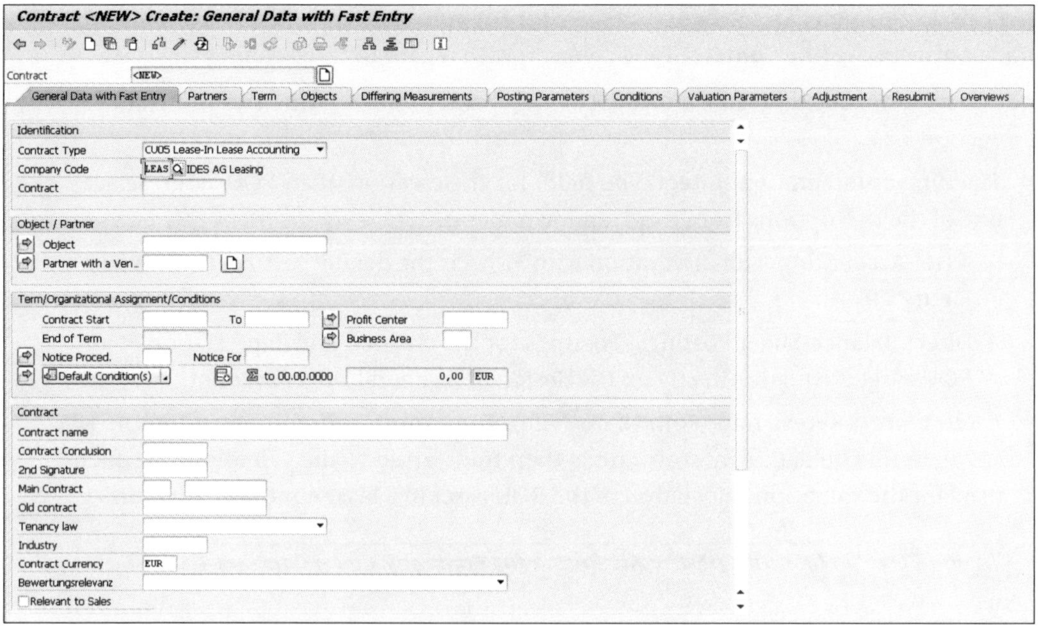


**Figure 5.10** Default Screen Sequence for Entering Contracts

To change the screen sequence for Transaction RECN, you'll need to review the Customizing settings for the contract type, as shown in Figure 5.11, by following the IMG menu path: **Flexible Real Estate Management (RE-FX) • Contracts • Contract Type • Define Contract Types**.

The content of a screen sequence can be defined in the Business Data Toolset (BDT), which is an easy-to-use tool for enhancing screens. BDT is based on the concept of *module pool programming*. First, we'll define field groups (groups that contain fields), and then we'll assign those field groups to views. These views may be further assigned to sections, and sections may be assigned to screens.

To create an alternative screen sequence exclusively for contract valuations, you can use Transaction RECECN (shown in Figure 5.12). This alternative entry screen allows you to separate duties, with different roles for employees entering valuation-relevant data versus employees executing the valuation posting with this data.

The screen sequence used in this transaction can be found in the Customizing settings for valuation-specific attributes for contract type in company code (return to Figure 5.9 and check the **ScnSeq** column).

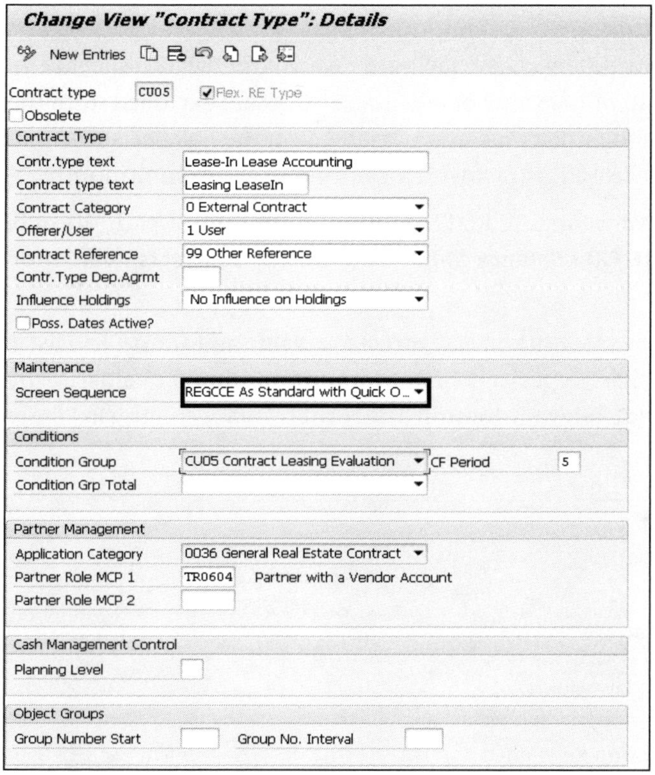


**Figure 5.11** Transaction RECN

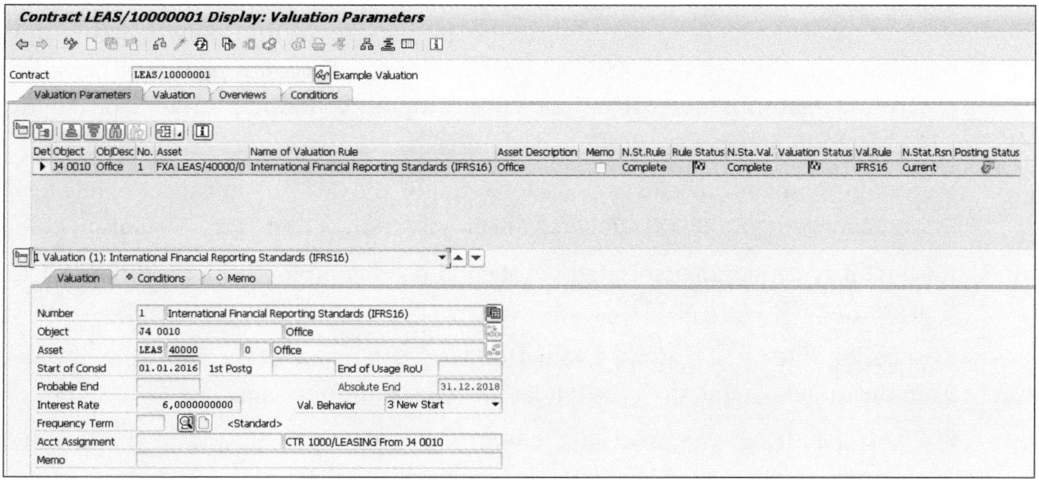


**Figure 5.12** Transaction RECECN

### 5.2.3 Valuation Relevance

Under IFRS 16 and ASC 842, not all lease contracts are relevant for balance sheet valuation. Lease contracts with an initial value of less than $5,000 are excluded from the rule that an ROU asset must be calculated and presented on the balance sheet. The same exception applies for a lease contract with a duration of less than 12 months.

To configure valuation relevance in SAP RE-FX, follow the IMG menu path: **Flexible Real Estate Management (RE-FX) • Balance-Sheet Valuation of Contracts • Valuation Relevance**.

In the screen shown in Figure 5.13, you can categorize low-value and short-term lease contracts and indicate that these types of contracts are not relevant for valuation by placing a checkmark in the **Not Relevant** column (the **Nicht relevant** column in Figure 5.13).

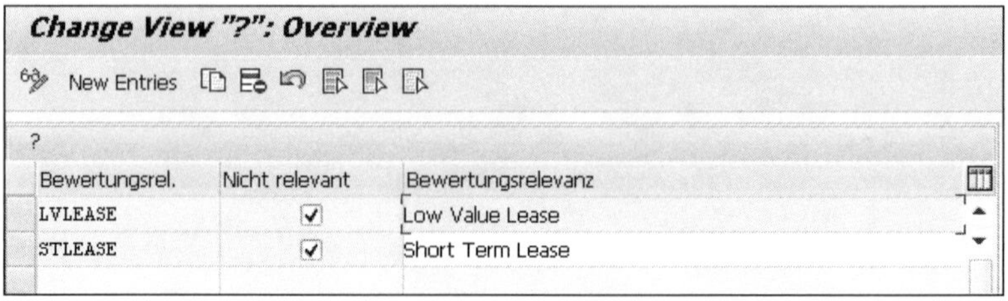


**Figure 5.13** Determining Valuation Relevance

### 5.2.4 Valuation Rules

Valuation rules are defined according to the specifications outlined in the accounting principles, such as IFRS 16 or ASC 842, or in a local set of accounting rules. The valuation rule is then subsequently assigned to a company code and contract type (Figure 5.14, Figure 5.15, and Figure 5.16).

To configure valuation rules in SAP RE-FX, follow the IMG menu path: **Flexible Real Estate Management (RE-FX) • Balance-Sheet Valuation of Contracts • Valuation Rule**.

A valuation rule has an associated set of conditions combined in a condition valuation group.

A valuation rule must contain a valuation type. Select one of the following options from the dropdown menu in the **Valuation Type** column, as shown in Figure 5.14:

- **Transfer Posting**: The associated conditions are transfer-posted to the account assignment object specified in the valuation rule (e.g., HGB).

- **Linearization**: The associated conditions are linearized over the contract term (e.g., FASB 13).
- **Balance-Sheet Capitalization**: Balance-sheet capitalization is carried out with creation of the ROU asset and lease liability (e.g., IFRS or US GAAP).

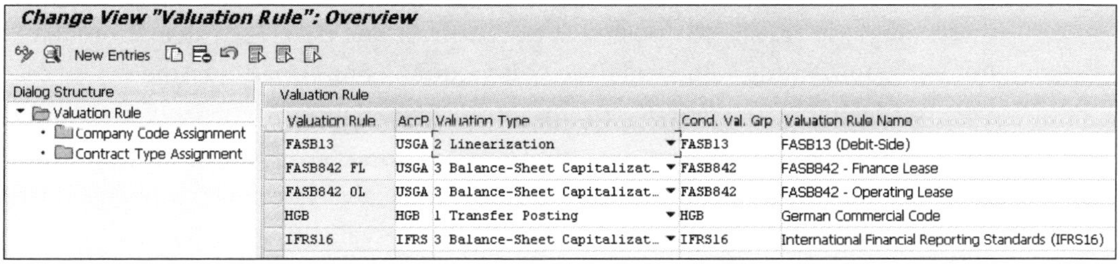


**Figure 5.14** Selecting a Valuation Type

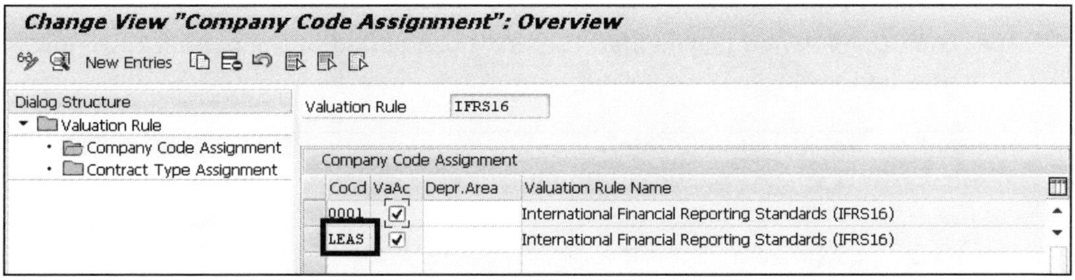


**Figure 5.15** Assigning a Company Code

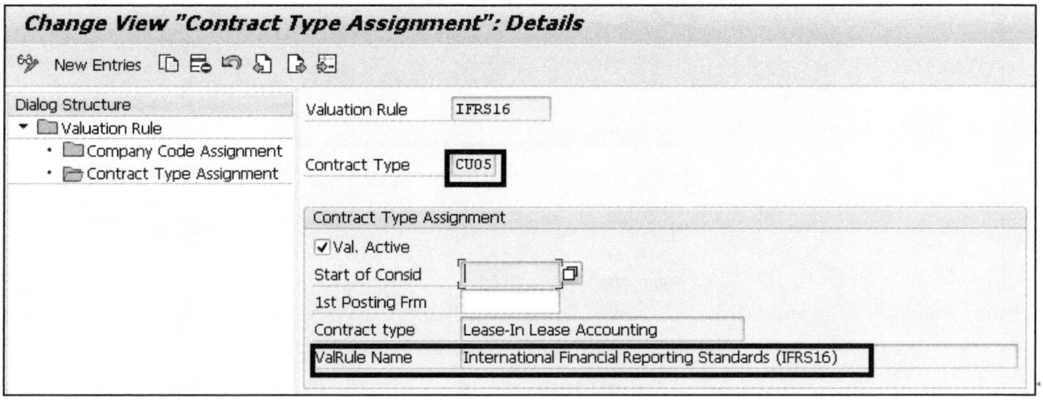


**Figure 5.16** Giving the Valuation Rule a Name

For linearization over time, select one of the following options in the **Linearization Type** dropdown menu, shown in Figure 5.17:

- **From Open Period (Linearization)**: The date of the first open period of the linearization cash flow is used as the new start date. As a rule, linearization is not changed retroactively. However, if a contract is terminated or conditions are changed so that all periods are already posted at the contract end date, the calculation determines the remaining value and posts this value as a one-time adjustment, if necessary, retroactively to the period of the contract end date.
- **From Start**: The original start date of the calculation is always used as the calculation start date. Any linearization rates posted are always corrected retroactively and distributed over the complete calculation interval.
- **From Start of Analysis Period**: The consideration start date (which could be a future date) is used as the new start date. Any retroactive changes to relevant conditions can also lead to retroactive corrections to the linearization.
- **From Open Period (Payments)**: The first open period of the partner cash flow is used here.

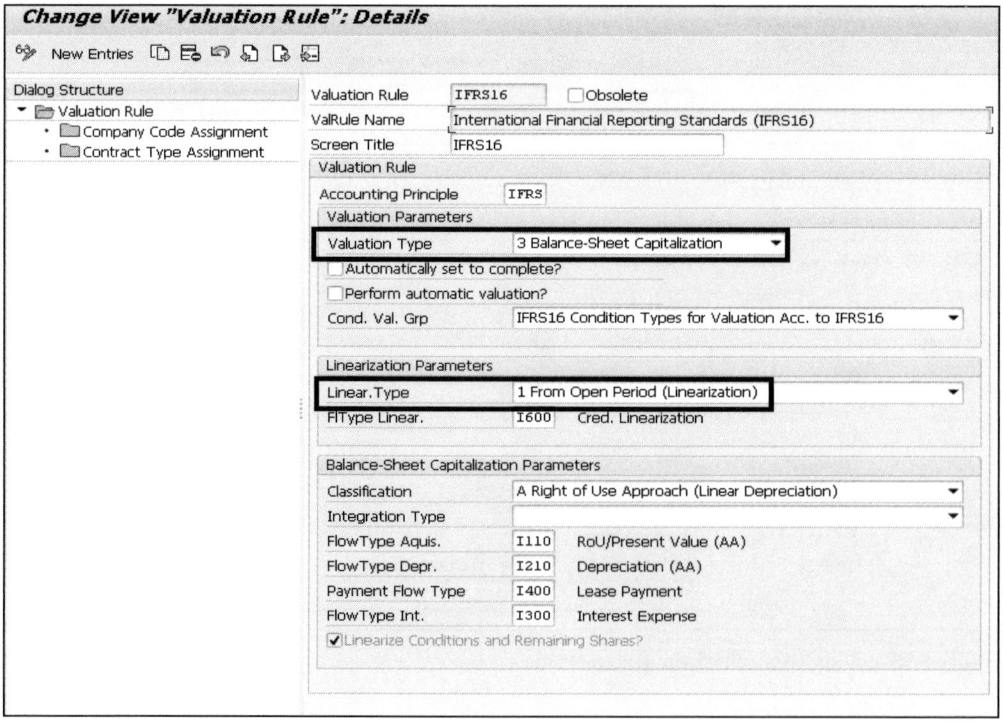


**Figure 5.17** Configuring Linearization Settings

In the **Balance-Sheet Capitalization Parameters** area, you'll have to specify a classification, which controls how the depreciation values are calculated, from one of the following options:

- <empty> = not relevant: Select this option of the valuation rule is not used to carry out a balance sheet capitalization. As a result, no acquisition, depreciation, interest, or payment schedules are created.
- **A = Right of Use Approach (Linear Depreciation)**: Select this option if depreciation is linear.
- **B = Straight-Line Lease (Linearized Commitment)**: Select this option if depreciation values should be calculated as the linearized commitment minus the interest.
- **C = Finance Lease without Depreciation**: Select this option if the finance lease amount is to be calculated without depreciation.

In this screen, you can also define whether to use **Integration with Asset Accounting** (default setting) or **Direct Balance Sheet Postings**. If you choose **Integration with Asset Accounting**, then a separate subledger asset is created for the ROU asset, and the periodic depreciation for this ROU asset is managed through FI-AA. If you choose **Direct Balance Sheet Postings**, then postings for the creation and the depreciation of the ROU asset are made directly on the designated general ledger account.

Finally, a number of flow types must be entered for the valuation rule, as shown at the bottom of Figure 5.18. Flow types are used to control all automatically generated postings into the general ledger. Flow types are freely definable through a 4-character key; you'll assign certain properties to a flow type to determine how the system will act during automatic postings:

- **Flow Type Acquisition**: This flow type is transferred to the cash flow for asset transactions (acquisitions and retirements) in FI-AA. The general ledger accounts used for postings are derived from this flow type. Note that reference flow types for delta changes must also be defined in the Customizing for these flow types.
- **Flow Type Depreciation**: This flow type is transferred to the cash flow for depreciation transactions (depreciation and write-up) in FI-AA. The general ledger accounts used for postings are derived from this flow type. Note that reference flow types for delta changes must also be defined in Customizing.
- **Payment Flow Type**: This flow type is transferred to the cash flow for payment flows on the lease liability. The general ledger accounts to be used for postings are derived from this flow type. Note that reference flow types for delta changes must also be defined in Customizing.

- **Flow Type Interest**: This flow type is transferred to the cash flow for interest transactions on the lease liability. The accounts to be used for postings are derived from this flow type. Note that reference flow types must also be defined for delta changes in Customizing.

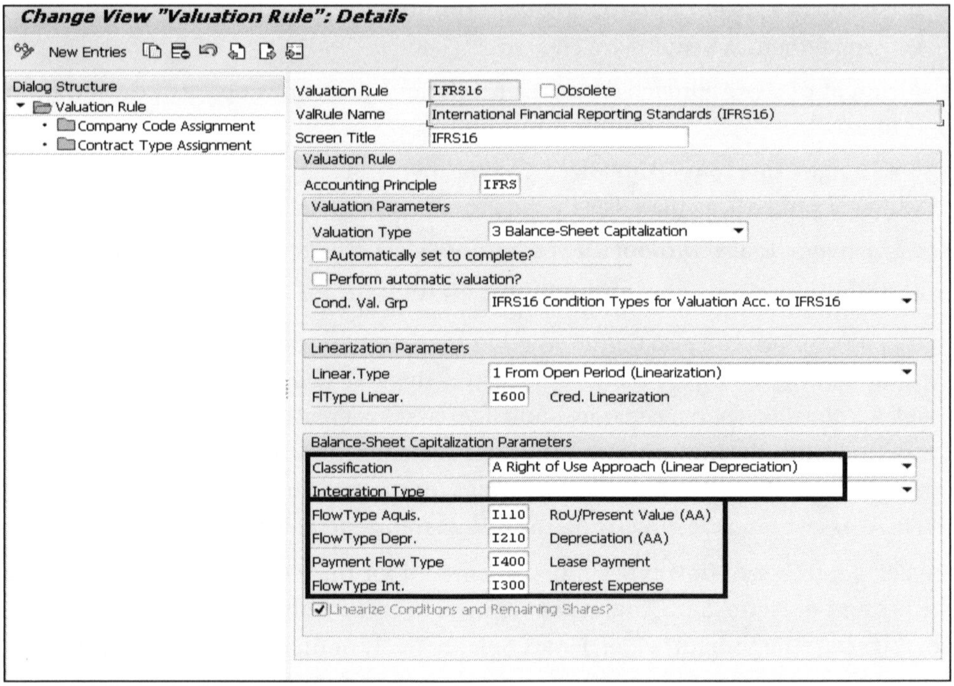


**Figure 5.18** Configuring Flow Types

### 5.2.5 Condition Valuation Groups

Contract conditions are included in lease valuations in different ways. To control contract conditions, you'll create condition valuation groups and assign condition types to them. Using the assignment to the valuation rules, you'll define how the conditions are used in the respective valuation calculations.

Contract conditions are typically conditions that model rent, lease payments, or one-time payments and are posted during the periodic posting for the payment cash flows. For proper valuation, these actual rents are not always sufficient. Additional conditions play a role in valuation but are not relevant for the periodic lease payment cash flows mentioned. Therefore, you should also use *statistical* conditions if additional conditions may have an impact on valuation cash flows (e.g., initial costs, rent incentives, guaranteed residual values, asset retirement obligations, etc.).

To configure condition valuation groups, follow the IMG menu path: **Flexible Real Estate Management (RE-FX) • Balance-Sheet Valuation of Contracts • Condition Valuation Groups**.

For each condition type, you'll define the external purpose in the **ExPp** column, as shown in Figure 5.19, using the following options:

- A = Actual Rent
- B = One-Time Actual Rent
- C = Cost Rent
- D = One-Time Cost Rent
- E = Market Rent
- F = One-Time Market Rent
- G = Vacancy Rent
- H = One-Time Vacancy Rent
- I = Statistical
- J = Waiver
- K = One-time Statistical Posting
- V = Comparative Rent

We want to call your attention to a few of these options. "Actual rent" represents a real rent value that a customer has to pay. "Market rent" represents a rent that "the market" would ask a customer to pay, but the lessor probably charges a lower actual rent to keep a customer happy or if a customer has temporary financial difficulties. Finally, one-time statistical postings represent amounts needed for the valuation calculation but that are not charged to a customer.

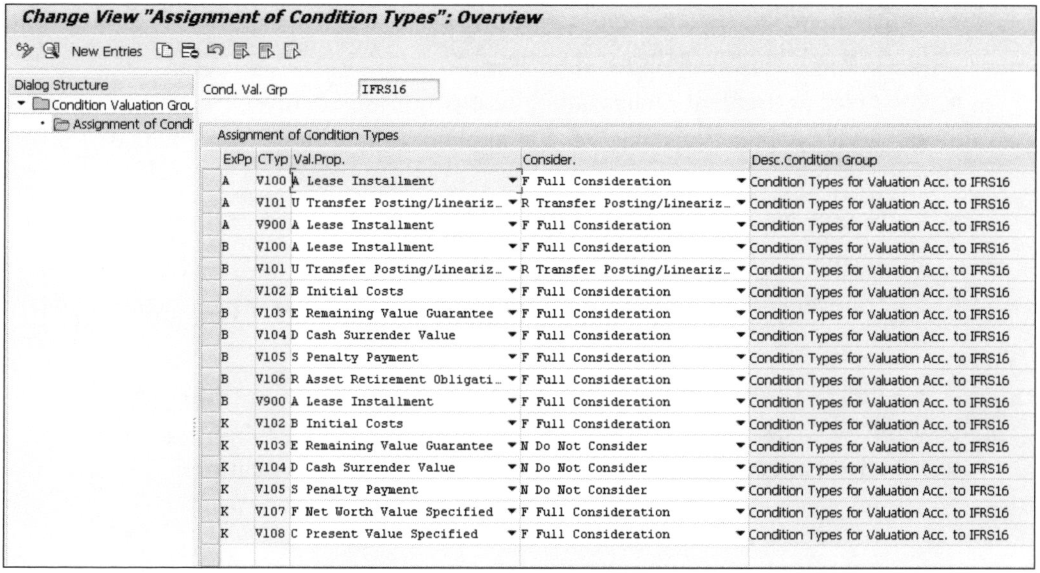


**Figure 5.19** Assigning Condition Types

Condition types require a condition valuation property. Choose from among the following options in the **ValProp** column, shown in Figure 5.19:

- **A = Lease Installment**: Such conditions are included in the calculation of the present value.
- **B = Initial Costs**: The amounts of the related one-time conditions (irrespective of their validity) form, in total, the initial costs that increase the asset's initial value. Note that all initial costs must have either the **One-Time Statistical Posting** condition purpose or the **One-Time Posting** purpose. For initial costs, a valuation cash flow item is generated depending on the purpose and transfer-posts the costs for specific accounting principles.
- **C = Present Value Specified**: These conditions specify the present value.
- **D = Cash Surrender Value**: These conditions define (irrespective of their validity) the cash surrender value at the end of the term.
- **E = Remaining Value Guarantee**: These conditions define (irrespective of their validity) the remaining value guarantee at the end of the term.
- **F = Net Worth Value Specified**: Such conditions specify the net worth value.
- **G = Depreciation**: These conditions define (irrespective of their validity) extraordinary depreciation or write-up (depending on the flow type for the condition) at the start of consideration.
- **I = Incentive**: These conditions define (irrespective of their validity) the initial rent incentives that reduce the asset value.
- **R = Asset Retirement Obligation**: These conditions define (irrespective of their validity) the obligations that are to be applied for a retirement and increase the net worth value.
- **S = Penalty Payment**: These conditions define (irrespective of their validity) penalty payments at the end of the term (e.g., due to early termination).
- **U = Transfer Posting/Linearization**: These conditions are transfer-posted or linearized.
- **V = Sublet**: These conditions are included in the calculation of the present value of the head lease.
- **X = Miscellaneous**: These conditions are not used in the valuation.

Sometimes a rent is not a pure rent but instead includes a portion for services. However, for the valuation calculation, only the pure rent is relevant, so the service portion has to be separated out by defining a consideration for the condition type.

For each condition type, you also specify for which consideration (portion) the related flow type should be included in calculations in the **Consider.** column:

- **F = Full Consideration**: 100% of the condition is used in the valuation. The **Percentage Share of Condition** and **Absolute Share of Condition** fields are not ready for input.
- **N = Do Not Consider**: The condition is not used in the valuation. The **Percentage Share of Condition** and **Absolute Share of Condition** fields are not ready for input.
- **R = Transfer Posting/Linearization**: The condition is not used in the valuation. The **Percentage Share of Condition** and **Absolute Share of Condition** fields are not ready for input.
- **O = As Specified**: The **Percentage Share of Condition** (%) and **Absolute Share of Condition** (e.g., EUR 300) fields are ready for input.

Note that consideration of a condition type specifies how the related flow type is used in the valuation calculation, in combination with its condition valuation property. Table 5.1 lists the allowable combinations of condition valuation property and consideration.

| Condition Valuation Property | Condition Consideration |
|---|---|
| A = Lease Installment | F = Full Consideration and O = As Specified |
| B = Initial Costs | F = Full Consideration |
| C = Present Value Specified | F = Full Consideration |
| F = Net Worth Value Specified | F = Full Consideration |
| G = Depreciation | F = Full Consideration |
| D = Cash Surrender Value | F = Full Consideration |
| E = Remaining Value | F = Full Consideration |
| R = Asset Retirement Obligation | F = Full Consideration |

**Table 5.1** Condition Valuation Properties and Condition Considerations

| Condition Valuation Property | Condition Consideration |
|---|---|
| S = Penalty Payment | F = Full Consideration |
| U = Transfer Posting/Linearization | R = Transfer Posting/Linearization |
| X = Miscellaneous | N = Do Not Consider |

**Table 5.1** Condition Valuation Properties and Condition Considerations (Cont.)

In our example in Figure 5.20, the description for the condition groups is **Condition Types for Valuation Acc. to IFRS 16**.

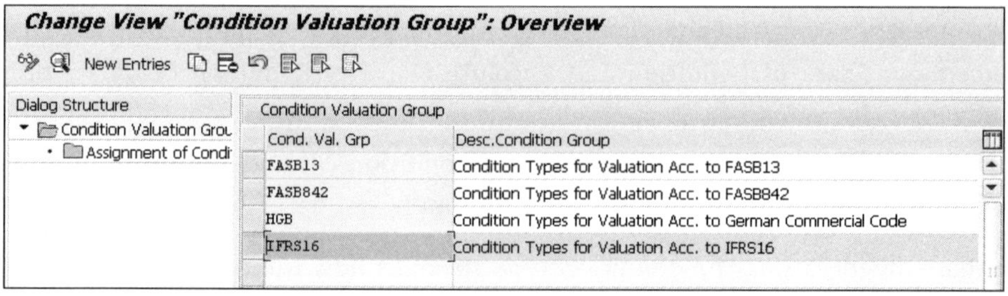


**Figure 5.20** Condition Valuation Groups

### 5.2.6 Valuation Object-Dependent Control Parameters

The valuation object-dependent control parameters specify the asset class in FI-AA in which the ROU asset will be created for the leased object.

To configure valuation object-dependent control parameters, follow the IMG menu path: **Flexible Real Estate Management (RE-FX) • Balance-Sheet Valuation of Contracts • Valuation Object-Dependent Control Parameters**.

You can specify a number of (combinations of) control parameters, as shown in Figure 5.21:

- Company code (**CoCd** field)
- Object type (**Type** and **Object Type Name** fields), for example, a parcel of land, a building, a piece of equipment, or a contract object
- Differentiation criteria (**DifCrt** and **Diff. Criterion Name** fields), for example, property, machinery, or vehicles

- Contract type (**CType** and **Contr. Type Text** fields), for example, a commercial, residential, or internal lease
- Account determination value (**AcctDeter** field), for example, facility management, SAP RE-FX leasing

Not all combinations of control parameters are possible/allowed.

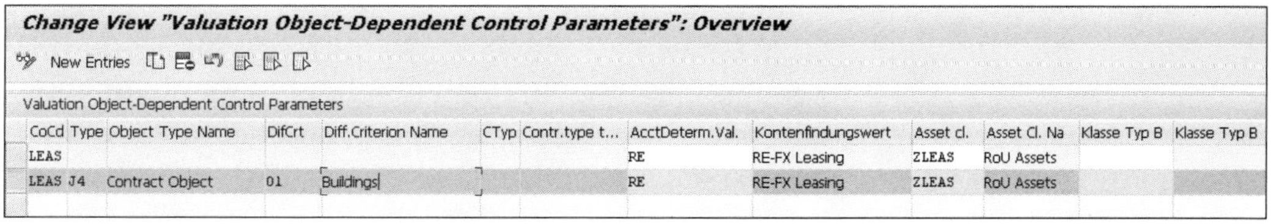


**Figure 5.21** Setting Valuation Object-Dependent Control Parameters

### 5.2.7 Assignment of Asset Transaction Type to Real Estate Flow Type

The transaction type in asset accounting classifies the business transaction; in other words, the transaction type controls various system activities when business transactions are posted.

To configure a transaction type, follow the IMG menu path: **Flexible Real Estate Management (RE-FX) • Balance-Sheet Valuation of Contracts • Assign Asset Transaction Types**.

As shown in Figure 5.22, first choose a process from the **Process** dropdown menu:

- **A = Acquisition**
- **B = Credit Memo in Acquisition Year**
- **C = Credit Memo in Following Year**
- **D = Depreciation (on Current-Year Acquisitions)**
- **E = Depreciation (on Prior-Year Acquisitions)**
- **N = Retirement (from Current-Year Acquisitions)**
- **P = Reactivation**
- **R = Retirement (from Prior-Year Acquisitions)**

The real estate flow types for the individual lease contracts must be assigned to the corresponding asset transaction types in FI-AA that you want to use for posting to

ROU assets. In our example shown in Figure 5.22, we selected flow type **I110** from our earlier valuation rule linked with asset transaction type **ZI0**.

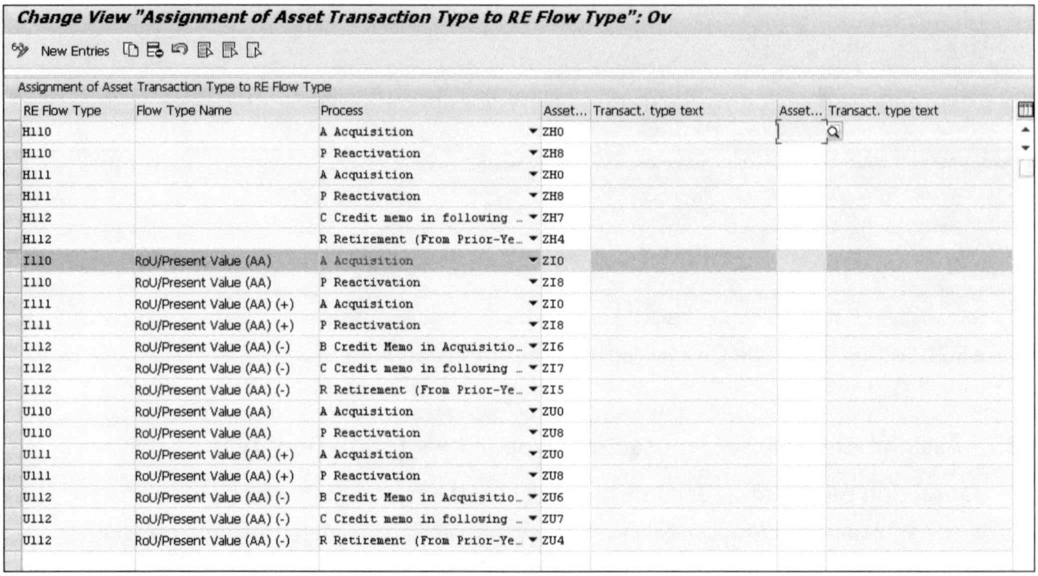

Change View "Assignment of Asset Transaction Type to RE Flow Type": Ov

New Entries

Assignment of Asset Transaction Type to RE Flow Type

| RE Flow Type | Flow Type Name | Process | Asset... | Transact. type text | Asset... | Transact. type text |
|---|---|---|---|---|---|---|
| H110 | | A Acquisition | ZH0 | | | |
| H110 | | P Reactivation | ZH8 | | | |
| H111 | | A Acquisition | ZH0 | | | |
| H111 | | P Reactivation | ZH8 | | | |
| H112 | | C Credit memo in following ... | ZH7 | | | |
| H112 | | R Retirement (From Prior-Ye... | ZH4 | | | |
| I110 | RoU/Present Value (AA) | A Acquisition | ZI0 | | | |
| I110 | RoU/Present Value (AA) | P Reactivation | ZI8 | | | |
| I111 | RoU/Present Value (AA) (+) | A Acquisition | ZI0 | | | |
| I111 | RoU/Present Value (AA) (+) | P Reactivation | ZI8 | | | |
| I112 | RoU/Present Value (AA) (-) | B Credit Memo in Acquisitio... | ZI6 | | | |
| I112 | RoU/Present Value (AA) (-) | C Credit memo in following ... | ZI7 | | | |
| I112 | RoU/Present Value (AA) (-) | R Retirement (From Prior-Ye... | ZI5 | | | |
| U110 | RoU/Present Value (AA) | A Acquisition | ZU0 | | | |
| U110 | RoU/Present Value (AA) | P Reactivation | ZU8 | | | |
| U111 | RoU/Present Value (AA) (+) | A Acquisition | ZU0 | | | |
| U111 | RoU/Present Value (AA) (+) | P Reactivation | ZU8 | | | |
| U112 | RoU/Present Value (AA) (-) | B Credit Memo in Acquisitio... | ZU6 | | | |
| U112 | RoU/Present Value (AA) (-) | C Credit memo in following ... | ZU7 | | | |
| U112 | RoU/Present Value (AA) (-) | R Retirement (From Prior-Ye... | ZU4 | | | |

**Figure 5.22** Assigning Asset Transaction Types

## 5.3 Account Determination

To ensure that the required postings for IFRS 16 and ASC 842 compliance are booked on the correct general ledger accounts and the appropriate subledger accounts for a company code, you'll need to configure account determination next. We'll explain this process in this section.

The account determination for balance sheet valuation postings is carried out based on the flow types specified in the valuation rule. To configure postings for balance sheet valuation, follow the IMG menu path: **Flexible Real Estate Management (RE-FX) • Balance-Sheet Valuation of Contracts • Valuation Rule** (as shown in Figure 5.23).

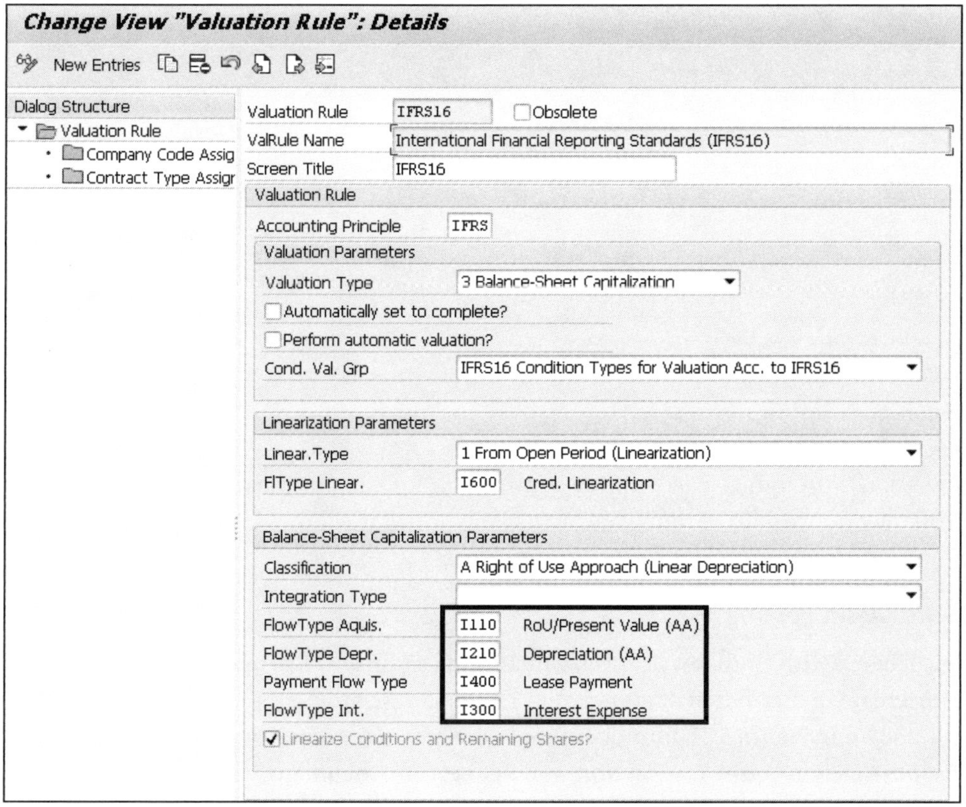


**Figure 5.23** Valuation Rules

The following postings are created when the valuation of a standard lease contract is executed:

- The first posting (**Asset Posting**) and the last posting (**Transfer**), shown in Figure 5.24, are made on the balance sheet to create the ROU asset and the lease liability. We'll examine these topics more closely in Section 5.3.1 and Section 5.3.4.
- The second posting (**Clearing Posting**) refers to the reduction of the lease liability due to the payment of the periodic lease rate. We'll examine this topic more closely in Section 5.3.2.
- The third posting (**Interest Posting**) is the result of the posting made on the profit and loss statement for the interest expense and increases the lease liability. We'll examine this topic more closely in Section 5.3.3.

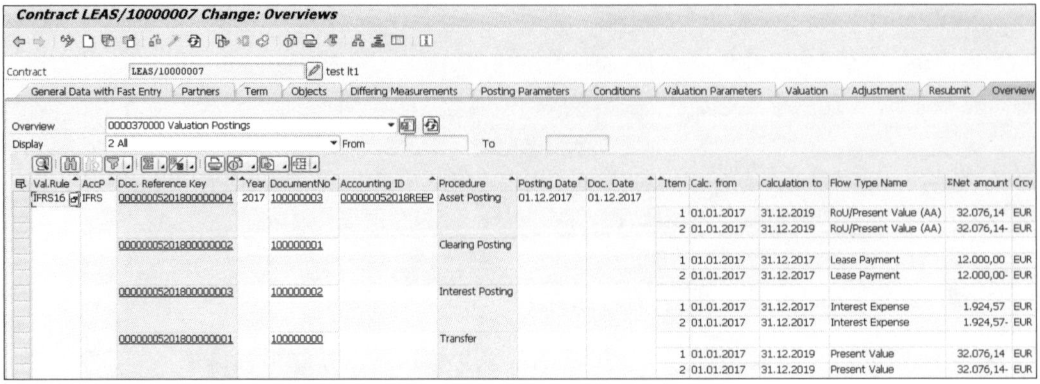

Figure 5.24 Postings

Let's walk through the account determination for each of these four postings next. You may notice a lot of repetition across the postings.

## 5.3.1 Asset Posting

We'll begin with the asset posting, which posts against a clearing account. The valuation creates a number of documents in accounting for the asset posting. In our example shown in Figure 5.25, four documents are created: **Accounting Document**, **Special Purpose Ledger**, **Asset Transaction**, and **Real Estate Document**.

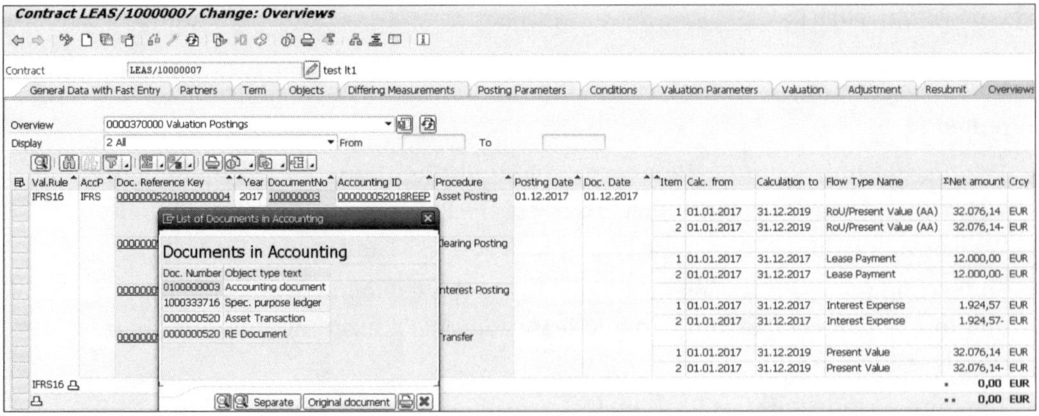

Figure 5.25 Asset Posting Accounting Documents

In Figure 5.26, we can see that SAP RE-FX is posting the accounting document as a regular general ledger posting.

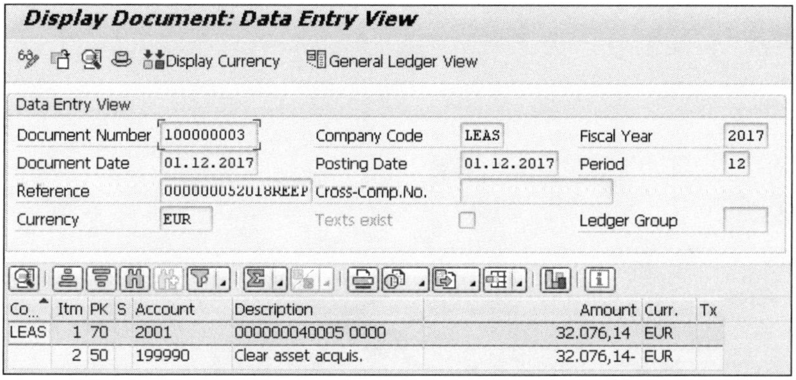


Figure 5.26 General Ledger Posting

The fourth document is the **Real Estate Document**, which shows the relevant flow type from the valuation rule. In our example shown in Figure 5.27, the flow types are both **I110**.

Figure 5.27 Real Estate Flow Types

The flow types from the **Real Estate Document** have account symbols assigned to them, which are shown in Figure 5.28 in the **Debit Account Symbol** and **Credit Account Symbols** columns. To assign account symbols to flow types, follow the IMG menu path: **Flexible Real Estate Management (RE-FX) • Accounting • Automatically Generated Accounting Documents • Account Determination • Assign Account Symbol to Flow Type**.

SAP delivers some standard account symbols, but you can also create and define your own. The following standard, predelivered symbols can be listed as both credit and debit account symbols:

- **LEASREVENUE**
- **TREV**
- **ROUASSET**
- **LEASLIABILITY**
- **CLEARING_ASSET**
- **DEPRECIATION**
- **INTERESTEXPENSE**

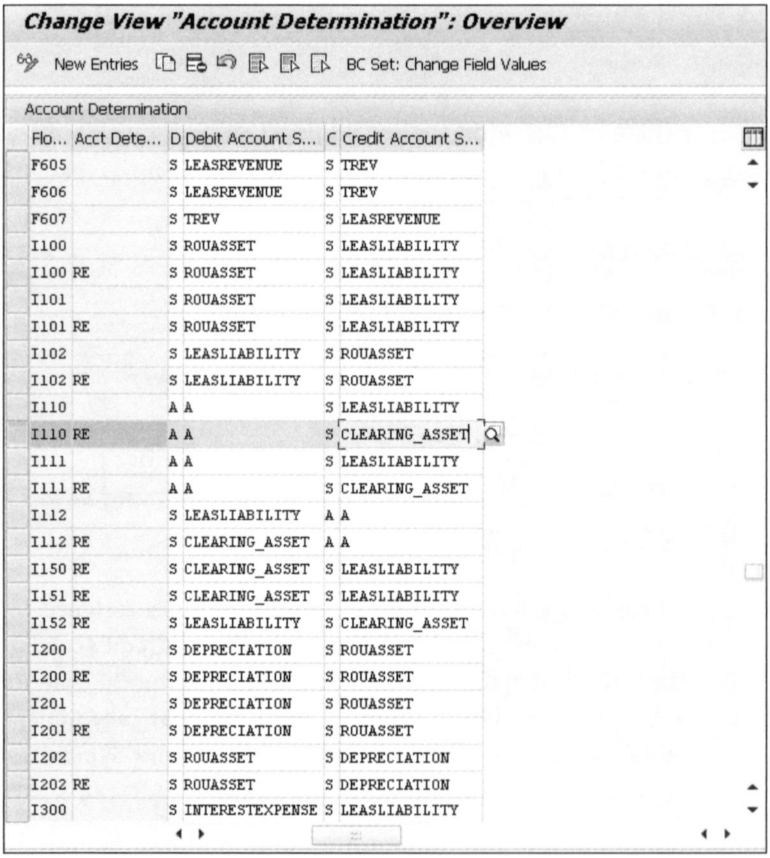


| Flo... | Acct Dete... | D | Debit Account S... | C | Credit Account S... |
|---|---|---|---|---|---|
| F605 | | S | LEASREVENUE | S | TREV |
| F606 | | S | LEASREVENUE | S | TREV |
| F607 | | S | TREV | S | LEASREVENUE |
| I100 | | S | ROUASSET | S | LEASLIABILITY |
| I100 | RE | S | ROUASSET | S | LEASLIABILITY |
| I101 | | S | ROUASSET | S | LEASLIABILITY |
| I101 | RE | S | ROUASSET | S | LEASLIABILITY |
| I102 | | S | LEASLIABILITY | S | ROUASSET |
| I102 | RE | S | LEASLIABILITY | S | ROUASSET |
| I110 | | A | A | S | LEASLIABILITY |
| I110 | RE | A | A | S | CLEARING_ASSET |
| I111 | | A | A | S | LEASLIABILITY |
| I111 | RE | A | A | S | CLEARING_ASSET |
| I112 | | S | LEASLIABILITY | A | A |
| I112 | RE | S | CLEARING_ASSET | A | A |
| I150 | RE | S | CLEARING_ASSET | S | LEASLIABILITY |
| I151 | RE | S | CLEARING_ASSET | S | LEASLIABILITY |
| I152 | RE | S | LEASLIABILITY | S | CLEARING_ASSET |
| I200 | | S | DEPRECIATION | S | ROUASSET |
| I200 | RE | S | DEPRECIATION | S | ROUASSET |
| I201 | | S | DEPRECIATION | S | ROUASSET |
| I201 | RE | S | DEPRECIATION | S | ROUASSET |
| I202 | | S | ROUASSET | S | DEPRECIATION |
| I202 | RE | S | ROUASSET | S | DEPRECIATION |
| I300 | | S | INTERESTEXPENSE | S | LEASLIABILITY |

**Figure 5.28** Assigning Account Symbols

You can differentiate between the account symbols for a given flow type by specifying an additional account determination value. To configure these additional values, follow the IMG menu path: **Flexible Real Estate Management (RE-FX) • Accounting • Automatically Generated Accounting Documents • Account Determination Values**.

In our example shown in Figure 5.29, we've added **Building** (value **01**).

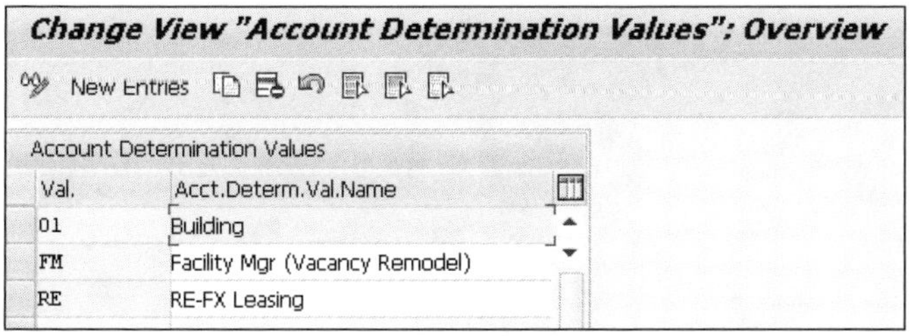


**Figure 5.29** Assigning Account Determination Values

This differentiation can be used, for example, if you want postings for this flow type to be posted to one set of general ledger accounts for lease contracts on buildings and also to another set of general ledger accounts for generic lease contracts, as shown in Figure 5.30.

To configure these postings, follow the IMG menu path: **Flexible Real Estate Management (RE-FX) • Balance-Sheet Valuation of Contracts • Valuation Object-Dependent Control Parameters**.

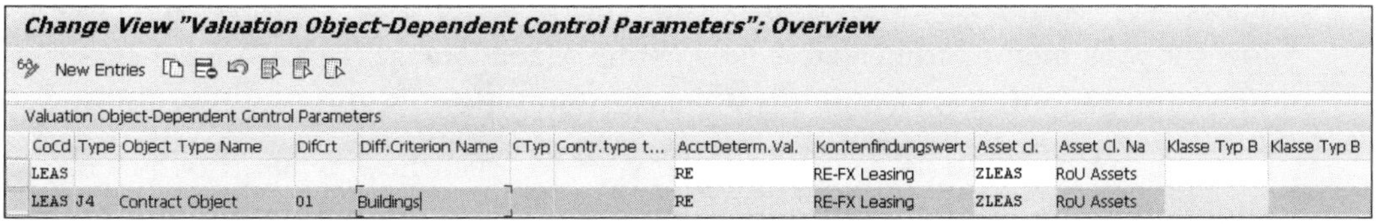


**Figure 5.30** Account Symbol Differentiation

When the posting process is executed, then the account symbols are replaced by real general ledger accounts. To replace the account symbols, follow the IMG menu path: **Flexible Real Estate Management (RE-FX • Accounting • Integration FI-GL, FI-AR, FI-AP • Account Determination • Replace Account Symbols**.

In our example shown in Figure 5.31, the account symbol **CLEARING_ASSET** has now been replaced by the general ledger account **199990** in the **G/L Account** column.

Change View "Substitute Account Symbols": Overview

New Entries BC Set: Change Field Values

Substitute Account Symbols

| Ch... | Account Symbol | Account Symbol Name | Spe... | G/L account | Short Text | AtAltFiscY | Acct Valuation | AcctVal.DiffYr |
|---|---|---|---|---|---|---|---|---|
| INT | 208 | SCS:Writeoff AP OC Own/Vacancy | | 470590 | Breakdown DC costs | | | |
| INT | 209 | SCS: Clearing AP Vacancy OC | | 470750 | Clg vcy op.cst adv.p | | | |
| INT | 215 | COA Settlement: Revenue | | 841500 | Rev.3-prty usg op.cs | | | |
| INT | 240 | Expected AP Earnings RO | | 841070 | Rev.op.cst flat rate | | | |
| INT | 241 | Credit Entry Revenue AP Contr. | | 841070 | Rev.op.cst flat rate | | | |
| INT | 250 | COCP: Write-Off AP OC | | 470590 | Breakdown DC costs | | | |
| INT | 252 | COCP: Clearing AP OC | | 470750 | Clg vcy op.cst adv.p | | | |
| INT | 301 | | | 470000 | Occupancy costs | | | |
| INT | 302 | | | 470850 | Clg RE rntl mgnt exp | | | |
| INT | 311 | | | 841050 | Other rental rev. | | | |
| INT | 312 | | | 841850 | Clg RE rntl mgnt rev | | | |
| INT | 500 | Bank | | 841800 | Rev. mgnt rntl obj. | | | |
| INT | 700 | Irrecoverable Debt | | 481200 | Writeoff - unc.recvs | | | |
| INT | 999 | Legacy Data Transfer | | 841070 | Rev.op.cst flat rate | | | |
| INT | A | Assets Reconciliation Account | | | | | | |
| INT | ACSCS | Accr/Def. Apportionable Costs | | 211000 | Accrued Expenses | | | |
| INT | ACSCSCEXT | Accr/Def. Ext. Apport. Costs | | 431010 | Account Adjustment | | | |
| INT | ACSCSPREP | Accr/Def. AP Posted as Revenue | | 431010 | Account Adjustment | | | |
| INT | CLEARING | Leasing Clearing Account | | 990047 | Clearing Leasing | | | |
| INT | CLEARING_ASSET | Clearing Asset | | 199990 | Clear asset acquis. | | | |
| INT | CLEARING_PAYED | Offsetting Costs Already Paid | | 470098 | Offsett. Paid Costs | | | |
| INT | CUEXT01 | Reservation Expense | | 470000 | Occupancy costs | | | |
| INT | CUEXT02 | Reservation Revenue | | 841050 | Other rental rev. | | | |
| INT | CUEXT03 | Cont. Occupancy Expense | | 470000 | Occupancy costs | | | |
| INT | CUEXT04 | Cont. Occupancy Revenue | | 841050 | Other rental rev. | | | |

**Figure 5.31** Replacing Account Symbols

The account determination for the general ledger account for an ROU asset is found via the account determination for FI-AA. The flow type from the valuation rule is linked with the relevant asset transaction type. To assign asset transaction types, follow the IMG menu path: **Flexible Real Estate Management (RE-FX) • Balance-Sheet Valuation of Contracts • Assign Asset Transaction Types**.

You can set multiple asset transaction types for each flow type. In our example shown in Figure 5.32, the flow type **I110** has both **Z10** and **Z18** asset transaction types.

Asset transactions are linked with the execution of postings in FI-AA. Figure 5.33 shows the customizing view for asset transaction types. Note that SAP delivers some types with standard content, but if you want to add additional types, we recommend that you use the Z or Y namespace for your custom types. Once you've created additional types, you can configure the depreciation area specifications, as shown in Figure 5.34.

To configure the transaction types, follow the IMG menu path: **Financial Accounting (New) • Asset Accounting • Transactions • Acquisitions • Define Transaction Types for Acquisitions**.

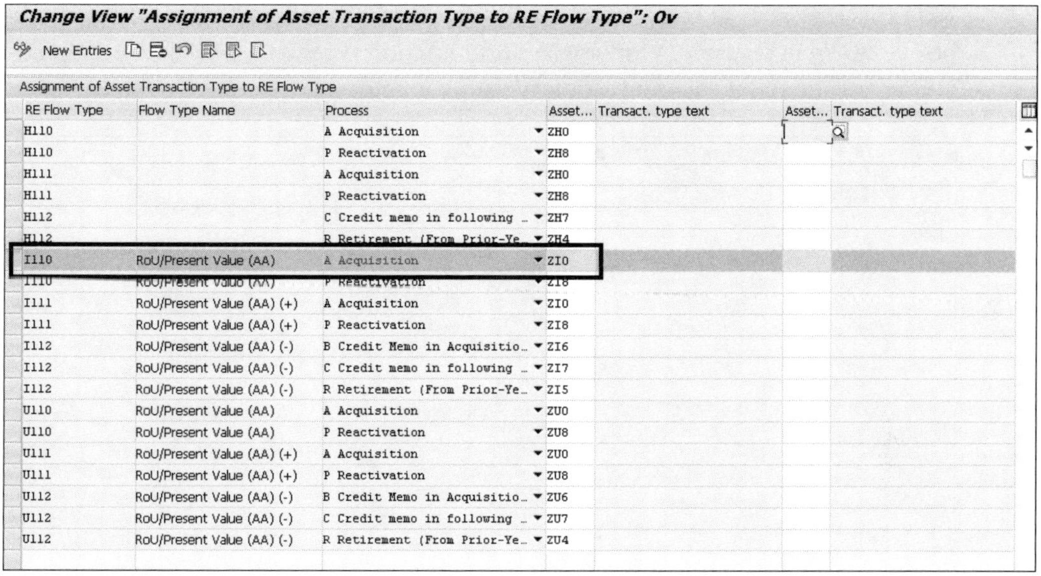


**Figure 5.32** Assigning Asset Transaction Types

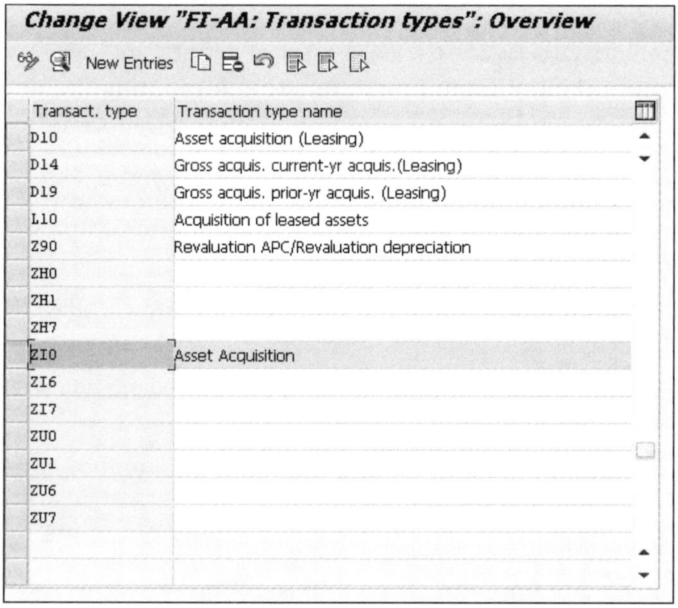


**Figure 5.33** Defining Transaction Types

Note that you should select both the **Display for Selection** and **Always Post** checkboxes shown in Figure 5.34 for your new transaction type to be available for depreciation runs and to set the transaction type up for automatic postings.

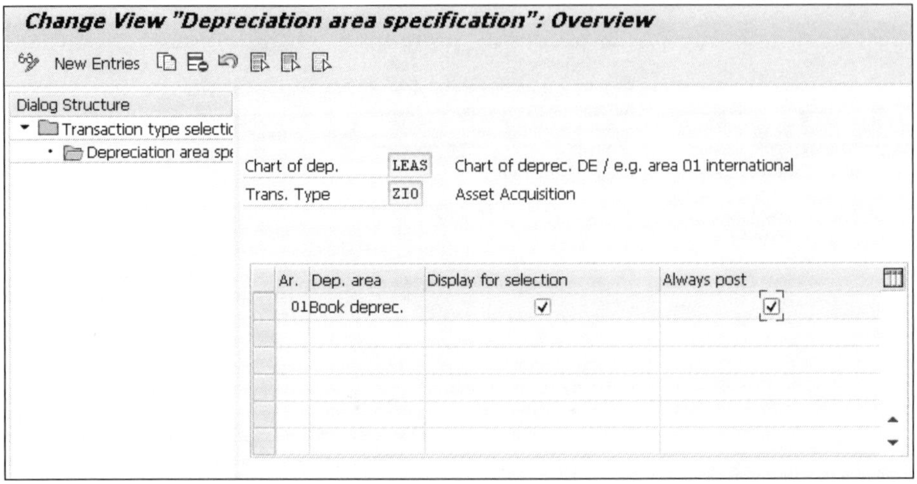


**Figure 5.34** Specifying Depreciation Areas

For the valuation, a separate asset class for the ROU asset is defined in FI-AA. To define the asset classes, follow the IMG menu path: **Financial Accounting (New) • Asset Accounting • Organizational Structures • Asset Classes • Define Asset Classes**.

The input data into fields shown in Figure 5.35:

- **Asset Class**: Input a description for your new asset class.
- **Short text**: Insert a short version of the description here.
- **Account Determination**: If you created a special account determination for IFRS 16 compliance, you can fill it in here.
- **Screen Layout Rule**: Screen layouts define which fields are suppressed, mandatory, and optional.
- **Base Unit**: Leave this field blank unless you want to define a special unit of measurement.
- **Number Range**: Define your own number range for the asset master data.
- **External Sub-Number**: If you don't need to create subassets, leave this checkbox empty.
- **Status of AUC**: Choose from the following radio buttons:

- Select **No AUC or Summary Management of AUC** if dealing with fixed assets (compared to assets under construction).
- Select **Line Item Settlement** to receiving assets or cost centers if you have assets under construction.
- Select **Investment Measure** if an asset under construction can be created solely in relation to capital investment measures (internal orders or WBS elements).



- **Asset Class is Blocked**: Select this checkbox to prevent new assets from being created in this asset class.
- **Real Estate Indicator for Asset Class**: Select **0 Other Asset without Real Estate Management** if the assets in this class should also be managed in SAP RE-FX as real estate or buildings.

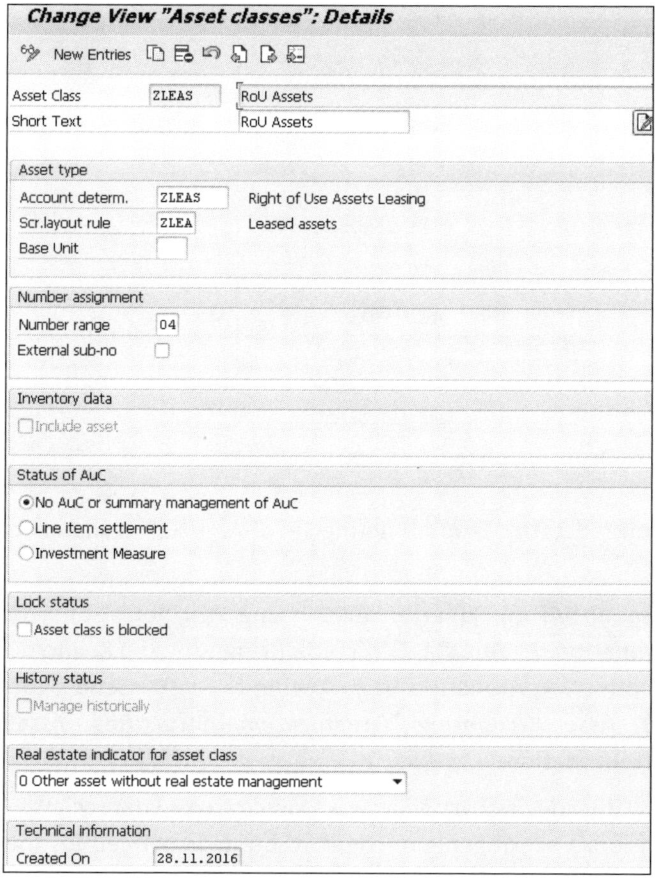


**Figure 5.35** Defining Asset Classes

Additionally a separate chart of depreciation for ROU assets is assigned by company code. To configure these charts of depreciation, follow the IMG menu path: **Financial Accounting (New) • Asset Accounting • Organizational Structures • Assign Chart of Depreciation to Company Code**.

In our example shown in Figure 5.36, we entered "LEAS" (a company code) into the **Chart Deprecation** column.

**Change View "Maintain company code in Asset Accounting": Overvi**

| CoCd | Company Name | Chrt dep | Description |
|---|---|---|---|
| ID01 | Template ID | | |
| IN01 | India Model Company, IN | | |
| LEAS | IDES AG Leasing | LEAS | Chart of deprec. DE / e.g. area 01 international |
| R100 | IDES Retail GmbH | | |
| R300 | IDES Retail INC US | | |
| REFX | Referenzbuchungsk.REFX | 1DE | Chart of deprec. DE / e.g. area 01 international |
| RESO | SE Buchungskreis RE-FX | 1DE | Chart of deprec. DE / e.g. area 01 international |
| RKT7 | RKT7 | RKT | RKT-Training |
| S300 | IDES Services | | |
| S330 | SP POST | | |
| SL01 | Services Logistics SP | 1US | Sample chart of depreciation: USA |
| TD02 | Company 02 | | |
| TR00 | Company 00 | | |
| TR01 | Company 01 | | |
| TR02 | Company 02 | | |
| UCAB | IDES US INC | 1US | Sample chart of depreciation: USA |
| WXYZ | IDES US INC | 1US | Sample chart of depreciation: USA |
| ZA01 | IDES South Africa | 1GB | Sample chart of depreciation: Great Britain |
| ZVMO | IDES AG (ZVMO) | 1DE | Chart of deprec. DE / e.g. area 01 international |

**Figure 5.36** Assigning a Chart of Depreciation to a Company Code

Finally, a separate FI-AA account determination is defined in FI-AA itself, as shown in Figure 5.37.

Note that, if you've already set up SAP ERP Financial Accounting, then you've already set up your account determination. At this stage in configuring SAP RE-FX, all you need to do is select the account determination by following the IMG menu path: **Financial Accounting (New) • Asset Accounting • Organizational Structures • Asset Classes • Specify Account Determination**.

For a combination of a company code's chart of accounts and chart of depreciation plus the account determination, a set of general ledger accounts is defined for the acquisition of the right of use.

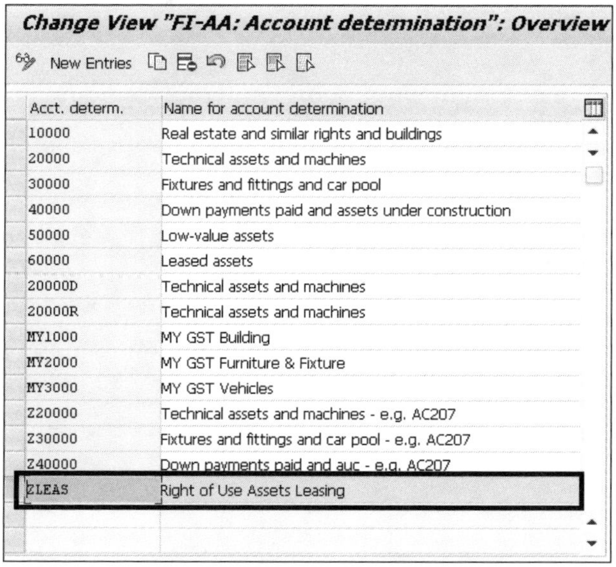


**Figure 5.37** Selecting the Account Determination

To configure the acquisition accounts, follow the IMG menu path: **Financial Accounting (New) • Asset Accounting • Transactions • Acquisitions • Assign Accounts**.

In our example shown in Figure 5.38, we have selected the **ZLEAS** account determination. Thus, in Figure 5.39, we'll see the value **ZLEAS** in the **Account Determination** field; next, we'll input the corresponding account numbers in the **Balance Sheet Account APC**, **Contra Account: Acquisition Value**, **Acquisition from Affiliated Company**, and **Revenue from Post-Capitalization** fields.

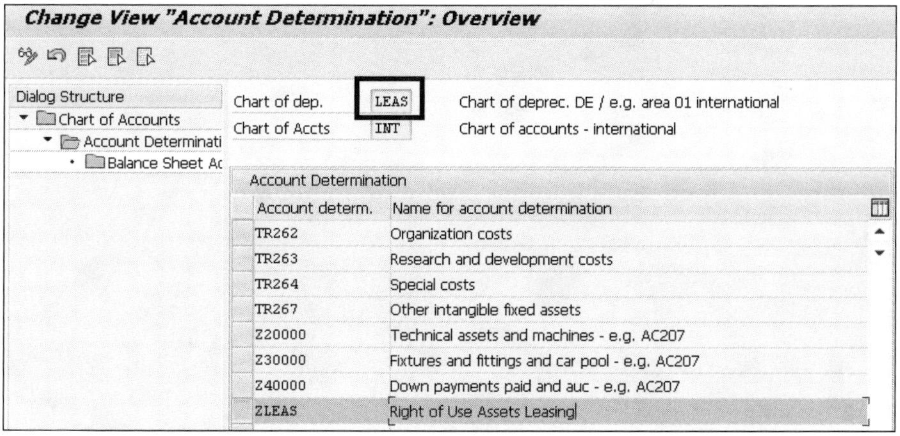


**Figure 5.38** Selecting the Account Determination

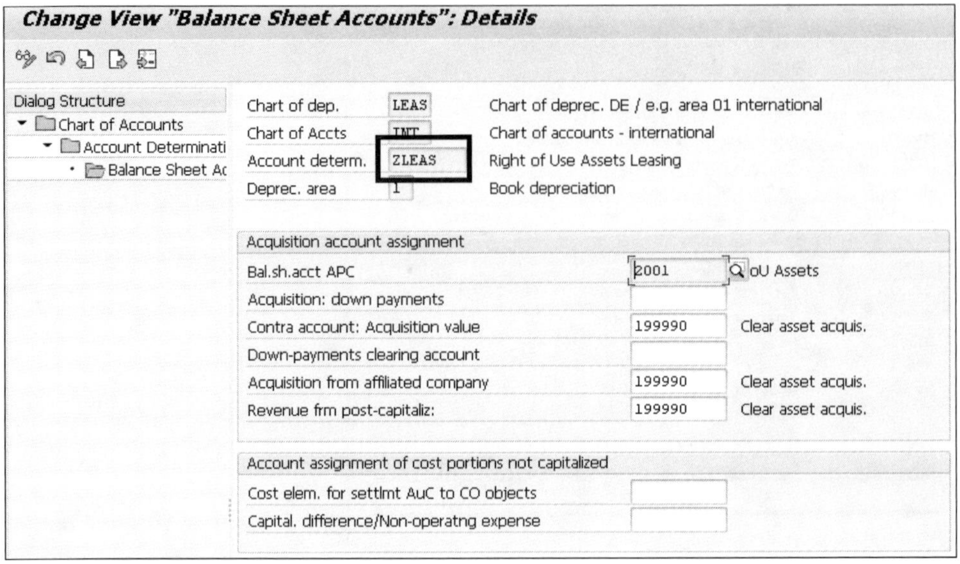


**Figure 5.39** Adding Balance Sheet Accounts

## 5.3.2 Clearing Posting

The clearing post was the second posting in our example, shown in Figure 5.24, in Figure 5.40, and later in the chapter. A clearing posting represents a periodic lease payment and reduces the total lease liability.

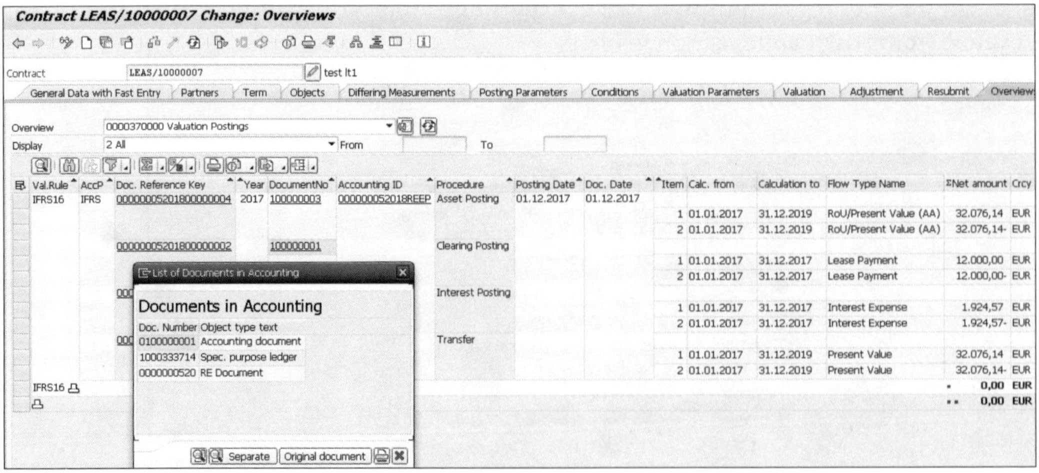


**Figure 5.40** Clearing Posting Accounting Documents

Figure 5.40 shows an example of the posting overview screen in SAP RE-FX, which shows the clearing posting entry. Clicking on the posting information pulls up the general ledger document, where we clearly can see the reduction (in Figure 5.41, 12,000 EUR) of the lease liability by crediting the clearing account and debiting the liability account.

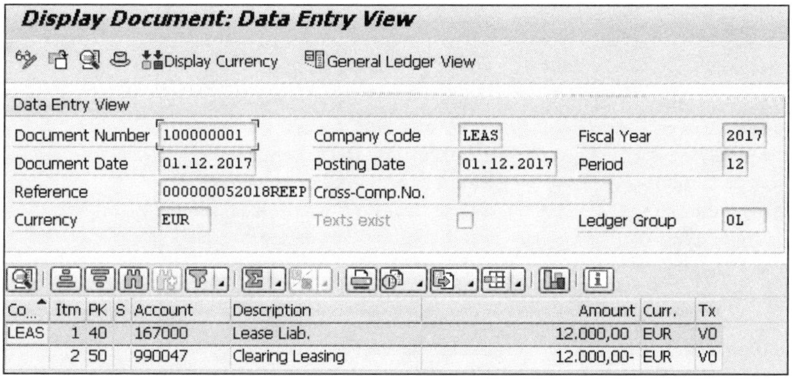


**Figure 5.41** Reduced Lease Liability

Again, the **Real Estate Document** shows the relevant flow type from the valuation rule. As shown in Figure 5.42, the effect of the valuation rule can be traced down to the general ledger document level using the flow types; in our example, the flow types are **I400**.

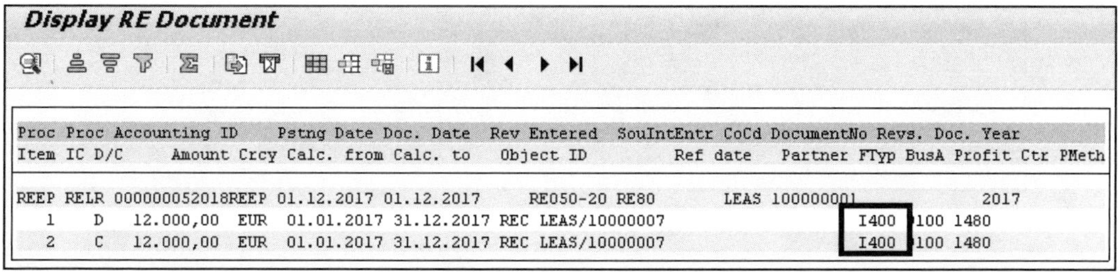


**Figure 5.42** Flow Types for Clearing Posting

These flow types have account symbols assigned to them, as shown in Figure 5.43. Recall from Section 5.3.1 that account symbols can be classified as debit or credit account symbols: You can choose from the standard predelivered symbols or create your own.

To assign account symbols to flow types, follow the IMG menu path: **Flexible Real Estate Management (RE-FX) • Accounting • Automatically Generated Accounting Documents • Account Determination • Assign Account Symbol to Flow Type**.

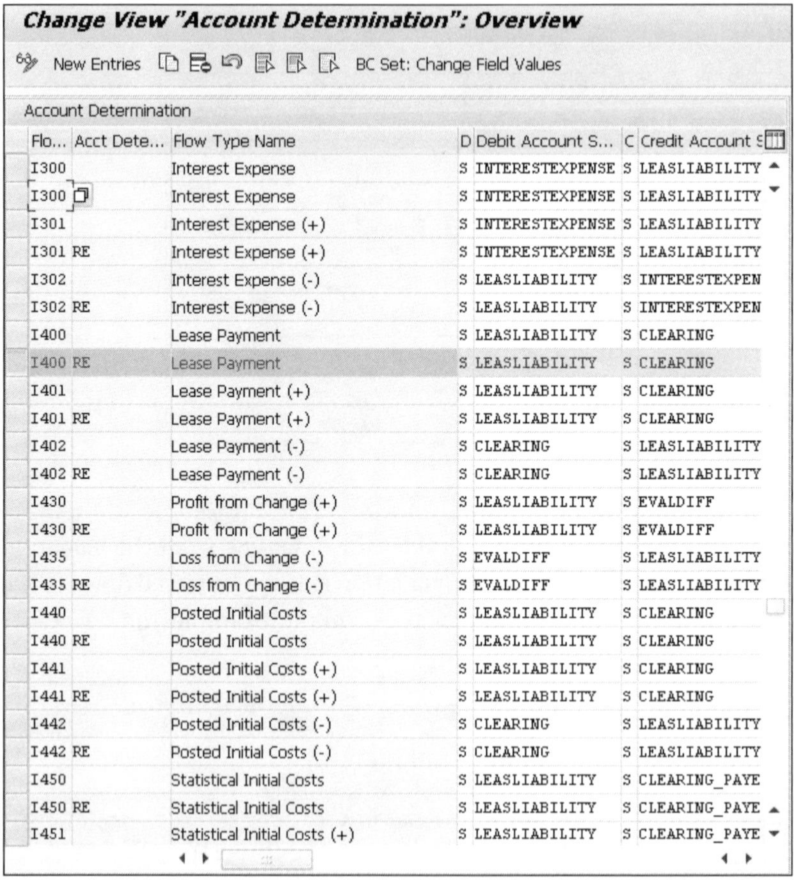


| Flo... | Acct Dete... | Flow Type Name | D | Debit Account S... | C | Credit Account S |
|---|---|---|---|---|---|---|
| I300 | | Interest Expense | S | INTERESTEXPENSE | S | LEASLIABILITY |
| I300 | | Interest Expense | S | INTERESTEXPENSE | S | LEASLIABILITY |
| I301 | | Interest Expense (+) | S | INTERESTEXPENSE | S | LEASLIABILITY |
| I301 | RE | Interest Expense (+) | S | INTERESTEXPENSE | S | LEASLIABILITY |
| I302 | | Interest Expense (-) | S | LEASLIABILITY | S | INTERESTEXPEN |
| I302 | RE | Interest Expense (-) | S | LEASLIABILITY | S | INTERESTEXPEN |
| I400 | | Lease Payment | S | LEASLIABILITY | S | CLEARING |
| I400 | RE | Lease Payment | S | LEASLIABILITY | S | CLEARING |
| I401 | | Lease Payment (+) | S | LEASLIABILITY | S | CLEARING |
| I401 | RE | Lease Payment (+) | S | LEASLIABILITY | S | CLEARING |
| I402 | | Lease Payment (-) | S | CLEARING | S | LEASLIABILITY |
| I402 | RE | Lease Payment (-) | S | CLEARING | S | LEASLIABILITY |
| I430 | | Profit from Change (+) | S | LEASLIABILITY | S | EVALDIFF |
| I430 | RE | Profit from Change (+) | S | LEASLIABILITY | S | EVALDIFF |
| I435 | | Loss from Change (-) | S | EVALDIFF | S | LEASLIABILITY |
| I435 | RE | Loss from Change (-) | S | EVALDIFF | S | LEASLIABILITY |
| I440 | | Posted Initial Costs | S | LEASLIABILITY | S | CLEARING |
| I440 | RE | Posted Initial Costs | S | LEASLIABILITY | S | CLEARING |
| I441 | | Posted Initial Costs (+) | S | LEASLIABILITY | S | CLEARING |
| I441 | RE | Posted Initial Costs (+) | S | LEASLIABILITY | S | CLEARING |
| I442 | | Posted Initial Costs (-) | S | CLEARING | S | LEASLIABILITY |
| I442 | RE | Posted Initial Costs (-) | S | CLEARING | S | LEASLIABILITY |
| I450 | | Statistical Initial Costs | S | LEASLIABILITY | S | CLEARING_PAYE |
| I450 | RE | Statistical Initial Costs | S | LEASLIABILITY | S | CLEARING_PAYE |
| I451 | | Statistical Initial Costs (+) | S | LEASLIABILITY | S | CLEARING_PAYE |

**Figure 5.43** Assigning Account Symbols

When the posting process is executed, the account symbols are replaced by real general ledger accounts. To replace the account symbols, follow the IMG menu path: **Flexible Real Estate Management (RE-FX) • Accounting • Integration FI-GL, FI-AR, FI-AP • Account Determination • Replace Account Symbols**.

In our example shown in Figure 5.44, the **Clearing** account symbol now has a general ledger account of **990047** in the **G/L Account** column.

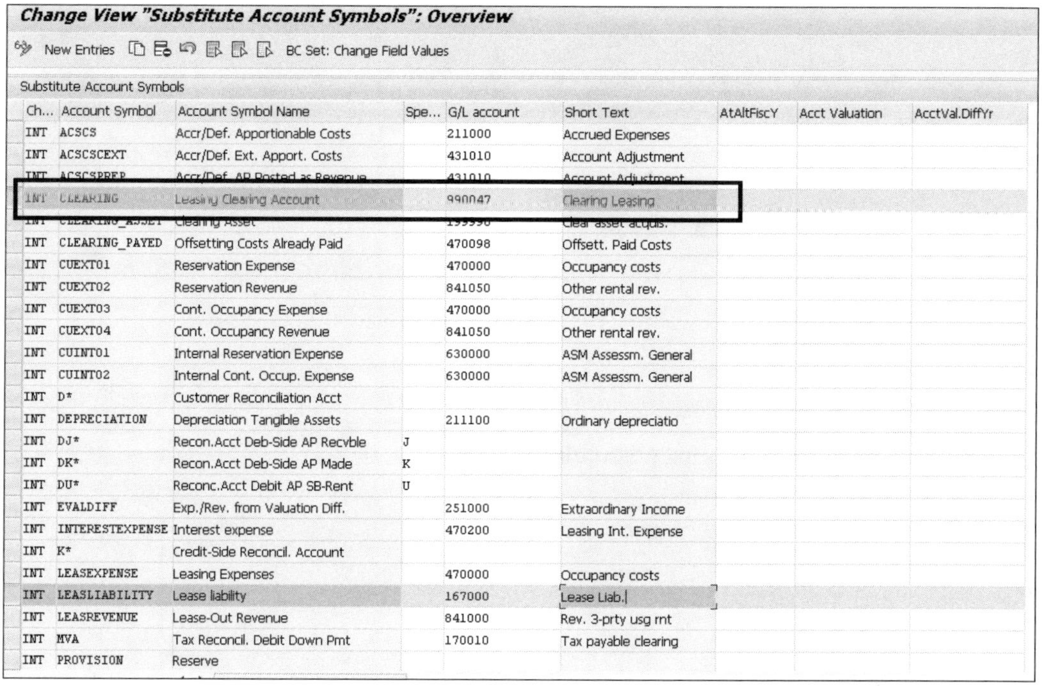

Change View "Substitute Account Symbols": Overview

New Entries BC Set: Change Field Values

Substitute Account Symbols

| Ch... | Account Symbol | Account Symbol Name | Spe... | G/L account | Short Text | AtAltFiscY | Acct Valuation | AcctVal.DiffYr |
|---|---|---|---|---|---|---|---|---|
| INT | ACSCS | Accr/Def. Apportionable Costs | | 211000 | Accrued Expenses | | | |
| INT | ACSCSCEXT | Accr/Def. Ext. Apport. Costs | | 431010 | Account Adjustment | | | |
| INT | ACSCSPREP | Accr/Def. AP Posted as Revenue | | 431010 | Account Adjustment | | | |
| INT | CLEARING | Leasing Clearing Account | | 990047 | Clearing Leasing | | | |
| INT | CLEARING_ASSET | Clearing Asset | | 199990 | Clear asset acquis. | | | |
| INT | CLEARING_PAYED | Offsetting Costs Already Paid | | 470098 | Offsett. Paid Costs | | | |
| INT | CUEXT01 | Reservation Expense | | 470000 | Occupancy costs | | | |
| INT | CUEXT02 | Reservation Revenue | | 841050 | Other rental rev. | | | |
| INT | CUEXT03 | Cont. Occupancy Expense | | 470000 | Occupancy costs | | | |
| INT | CUEXT04 | Cont. Occupancy Revenue | | 841050 | Other rental rev. | | | |
| INT | CUINT01 | Internal Reservation Expense | | 630000 | ASM Assessm. General | | | |
| INT | CUINT02 | Internal Cont. Occup. Expense | | 630000 | ASM Assessm. General | | | |
| INT | D* | Customer Reconciliation Acct | | | | | | |
| INT | DEPRECIATION | Depreciation Tangible Assets | | 211100 | Ordinary depreciatio | | | |
| INT | DJ* | Recon.Acct Deb-Side AP Recvble | J | | | | | |
| INT | DK* | Recon.Acct Deb-Side AP Made | K | | | | | |
| INT | DU* | Reconc.Acct Debit AP SB-Rent | U | | | | | |
| INT | EVALDIFF | Exp./Rev. from Valuation Diff. | | 251000 | Extraordinary Income | | | |
| INT | INTERESTEXPENSE | Interest expense | | 470200 | Leasing Int. Expense | | | |
| INT | K* | Credit-Side Reconcil. Account | | | | | | |
| INT | LEASEXPENSE | Leasing Expenses | | 470000 | Occupancy costs | | | |
| INT | LEASLIABILITY | Lease liability | | 167000 | Lease Liab. | | | |
| INT | LEASREVENUE | Lease-Out Revenue | | 841000 | Rev. 3-prty usg rnt | | | |
| INT | MVA | Tax Reconcil. Debit Down Pmt | | 170010 | Tax payable clearing | | | |
| INT | PROVISION | Reserve | | | | | | |

**Figure 5.44** Account Symbols for Clearing Posting

### 5.3.3 Interest Posting

Next, let's look at postings for the interest expense on the profit-and-loss statement, which increases the lease liability. As shown in Figure 5.45, this process generates several documents: **Accounting Document**, **Profit Center Document**, **Special Purpose Ledger**, **Controlling Document**, and (most important for our purposes) the **Real Estate Document**.

Notice that the screens shown Figure 5.46 are similar to the **Display Document** screens for the asset postings and clearing postings, but the data is different. On this screen, the leasing interest expense and the lease liability should always match; in our example, the value is the same (1,924.57 Euros).

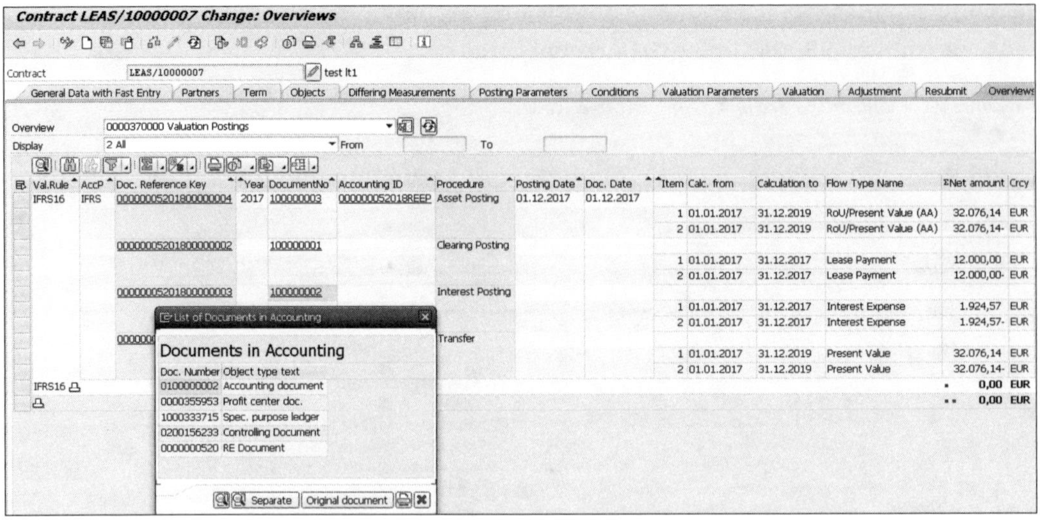


**Figure 5.45** Interest Posting Accounting Documents

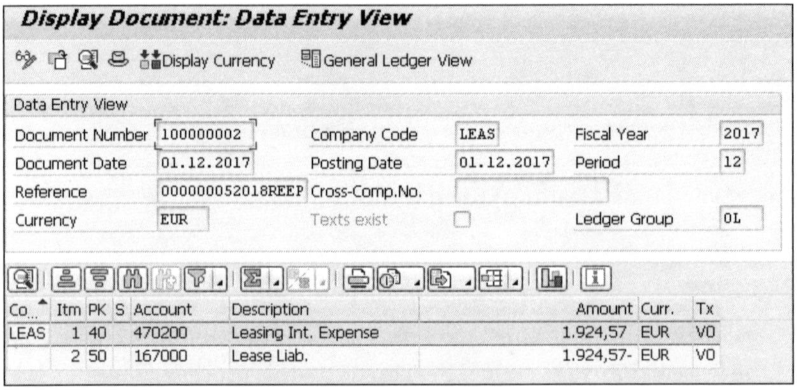


**Figure 5.46** Interest Posting

The **Real Estate Document** shows the relevant flow type from the valuation rule. In our example shown in Figure 5.47, the flow type is **I300**.

As for asset postings and clearing postings, flow types for interest postings have account symbols assigned to them, as shown in Figure 5.48. To configure these symbols, follow the IMG menu path: **Flexible Real Estate Management (RE-FX) • Accounting • Automatically Generated Accounting Documents • Account Determination • Assign Account Symbol to Flow Type**.

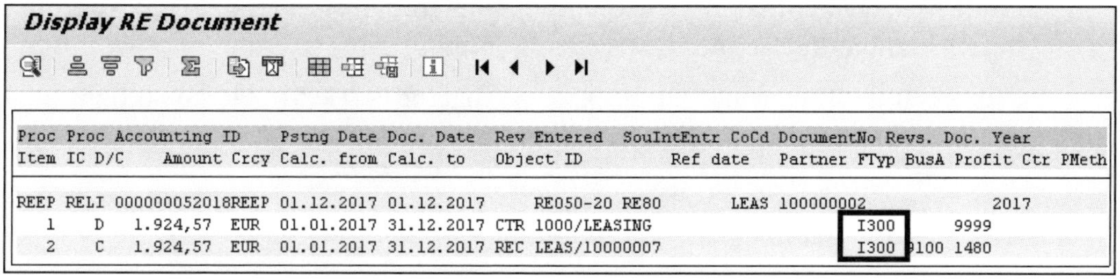

**Display RE Document**

```
Proc Proc Accounting ID      Pstng Date Doc. Date  Rev Entered  SouIntEntr CoCd DocumentNo Revs. Doc. Year
Item IC D/C    Amount Crcy Calc. from Calc. to   Object ID            Ref date    Partner FTyp BusA Profit Ctr PMeth

REEP RELI 000000052018REEP 01.12.2017 01.12.2017      RE050-20 RE80       LEAS 100000002                2017
  1     D    1.924,57  EUR  01.01.2017 31.12.2017 CTR 1000/LEASING                    I300         9999
  2     C    1.924,57  EUR  01.01.2017 31.12.2017 REC LEAS/10000007                   I300 9100 1480
```

**Figure 5.47** Real Estate Flow Type

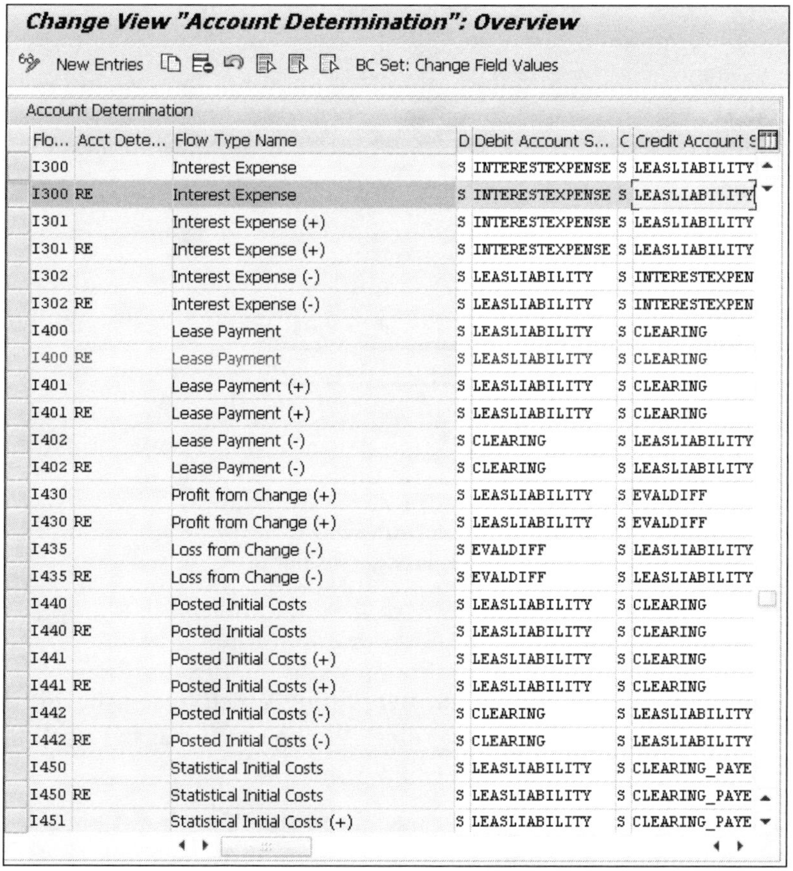

**Change View "Account Determination": Overview**



| Flo... | Acct Dete... | Flow Type Name | D | Debit Account S... | C | Credit Account S |
|---|---|---|---|---|---|---|
| I300 | | Interest Expense | S | INTERESTEXPENSE | S | LEASLIABILITY |
| I300 | RE | Interest Expense | S | INTERESTEXPENSE | S | LEASLIABILITY |
| I301 | | Interest Expense (+) | S | INTERESTEXPENSE | S | LEASLIABILITY |
| I301 | RE | Interest Expense (+) | S | INTERESTEXPENSE | S | LEASLIABILITY |
| I302 | | Interest Expense (-) | S | LEASLIABILITY | S | INTERESTEXPEN |
| I302 | RE | Interest Expense (-) | S | LEASLIABILITY | S | INTERESTEXPEN |
| I400 | | Lease Payment | S | LEASLIABILITY | S | CLEARING |
| I400 | RE | Lease Payment | S | LEASLIABILITY | S | CLEARING |
| I401 | | Lease Payment (+) | S | LEASLIABILITY | S | CLEARING |
| I401 | RE | Lease Payment (+) | S | LEASLIABILITY | S | CLEARING |
| I402 | | Lease Payment (-) | S | CLEARING | S | LEASLIABILITY |
| I402 | RE | Lease Payment (-) | S | CLEARING | S | LEASLIABILITY |
| I430 | | Profit from Change (+) | S | LEASLIABILITY | S | EVALDIFF |
| I430 | RE | Profit from Change (+) | S | LEASLIABILITY | S | EVALDIFF |
| I435 | | Loss from Change (-) | S | EVALDIFF | S | LEASLIABILITY |
| I435 | RE | Loss from Change (-) | S | EVALDIFF | S | LEASLIABILITY |
| I440 | | Posted Initial Costs | S | LEASLIABILITY | S | CLEARING |
| I440 | RE | Posted Initial Costs | S | LEASLIABILITY | S | CLEARING |
| I441 | | Posted Initial Costs (+) | S | LEASLIABILITY | S | CLEARING |
| I441 | RE | Posted Initial Costs (+) | S | LEASLIABILITY | S | CLEARING |
| I442 | | Posted Initial Costs (-) | S | CLEARING | S | LEASLIABILITY |
| I442 | RE | Posted Initial Costs (-) | S | CLEARING | S | LEASLIABILITY |
| I450 | | Statistical Initial Costs | S | LEASLIABILITY | S | CLEARING_PAYE |
| I450 | RE | Statistical Initial Costs | S | LEASLIABILITY | S | CLEARING_PAYE |
| I451 | | Statistical Initial Costs (+) | S | LEASLIABILITY | S | CLEARING_PAYE |

**Figure 5.48** Assigning an Account Symbol to a Flow Type

Account symbols are replaced by real general accounts when the posting process is executed. To configure these symbols, follow the IMG menu path: **Flexible Real**

**Estate Management (RE-FX) • Accounting • Integration FI-GL, FI-AR, FI-AP • Account Determination • Replace Account Symbols.**

In our example shown in Figure 5.49, we see that the **INTERESTEXPENSE** account symbol has been replaced by the general ledger account **470200**.

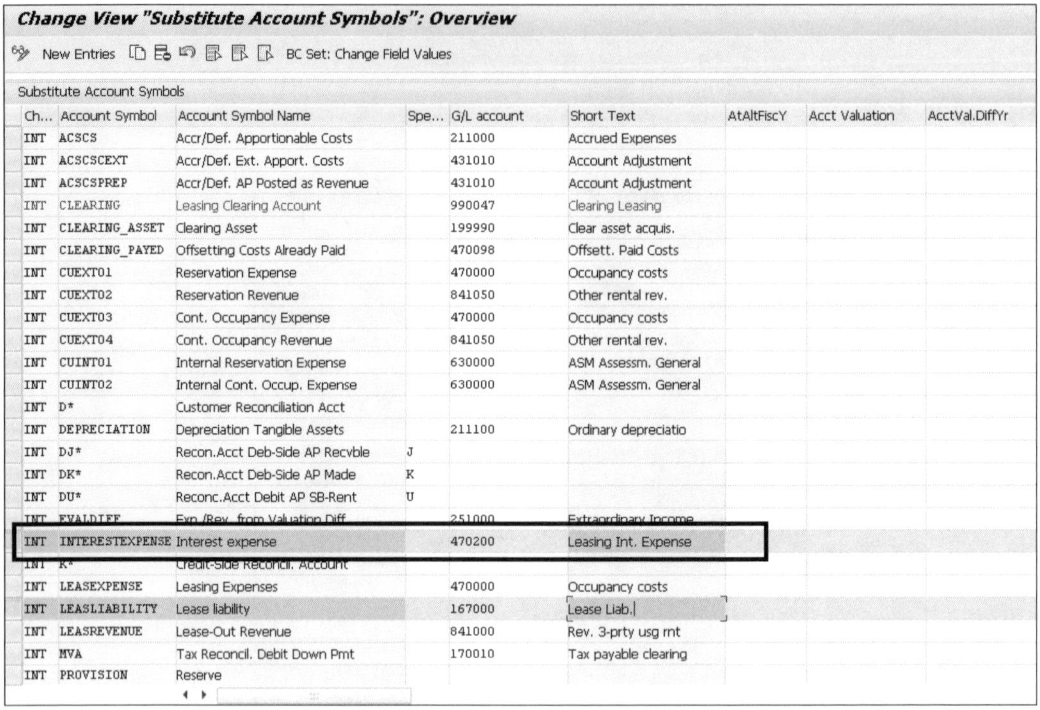

Change View "Substitute Account Symbols": Overview

New Entries BC Set: Change Field Values

Substitute Account Symbols

| Ch... | Account Symbol | Account Symbol Name | Spe... | G/L account | Short Text | AtAltFiscY | Acct Valuation | AcctVal.DiffYr |
|---|---|---|---|---|---|---|---|---|
| INT | ACSCS | Accr/Def. Apportionable Costs | | 211000 | Accrued Expenses | | | |
| INT | ACSCSCEXT | Accr/Def. Ext. Apport. Costs | | 431010 | Account Adjustment | | | |
| INT | ACSCSPREP | Accr/Def. AP Posted as Revenue | | 431010 | Account Adjustment | | | |
| INT | CLEARING | Leasing Clearing Account | | 990047 | Clearing Leasing | | | |
| INT | CLEARING_ASSET | Clearing Asset | | 199990 | Clear asset acquis. | | | |
| INT | CLEARING_PAYED | Offsetting Costs Already Paid | | 470098 | Offsett. Paid Costs | | | |
| INT | CUEXT01 | Reservation Expense | | 470000 | Occupancy costs | | | |
| INT | CUEXT02 | Reservation Revenue | | 841050 | Other rental rev. | | | |
| INT | CUEXT03 | Cont. Occupancy Expense | | 470000 | Occupancy costs | | | |
| INT | CUEXT04 | Cont. Occupancy Revenue | | 841050 | Other rental rev. | | | |
| INT | CUINT01 | Internal Reservation Expense | | 630000 | ASM Assessm. General | | | |
| INT | CUINT02 | Internal Cont. Occup. Expense | | 630000 | ASM Assessm. General | | | |
| INT | D* | Customer Reconciliation Acct | | | | | | |
| INT | DEPRECIATION | Depreciation Tangible Assets | | 211100 | Ordinary depreciatio | | | |
| INT | DJ* | Recon.Acct Deb-Side AP Recvble | J | | | | | |
| INT | DK* | Recon.Acct Deb-Side AP Made | K | | | | | |
| INT | DU* | Reconc.Acct Debit AP SB-Rent | U | | | | | |
| INT | EVALDIFF | Exp./Rev. from Valuation Diff. | | 251000 | Extraordinary Income | | | |
| INT | INTERESTEXPENSE | Interest expense | | 470200 | Leasing Int. Expense | | | |
| INT | K* | Credit-Side Reconcil. Account | | | | | | |
| INT | LEASEXPENSE | Leasing Expenses | | 470000 | Occupancy costs | | | |
| INT | LEASLIABILITY | Lease liability | | 167000 | Lease Liab. | | | |
| INT | LEASREVENUE | Lease-Out Revenue | | 841000 | Rev. 3-prty usg rnt | | | |
| INT | MVA | Tax Reconcil. Debit Down Pmt | | 170010 | Tax payable clearing | | | |
| INT | PROVISION | Reserve | | | | | | |

**Figure 5.49** Account Symbols Replaced by General Ledger Accounts

## 5.3.4 Transfer Posting

The last posting shown in Figure 5.24 is the transfer posting, which creates the initial lease liability. This value is posted against the same clearing account as the creation of the ROU asset, as shown in Figure 5.50 and Figure 5.51.

Note that the lease liability matches the clear asset acquisition, as shown in Figure 5.51; in our example shown in Figure 5.51, the values are both 32,076.14 Euros.

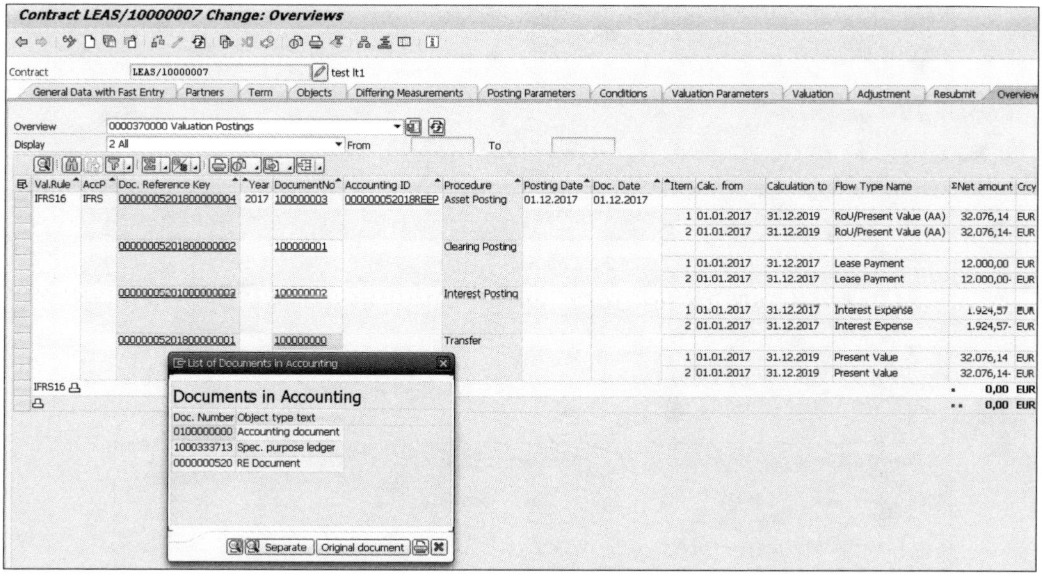


**Figure 5.50** Transfer Posting Accounting Documents

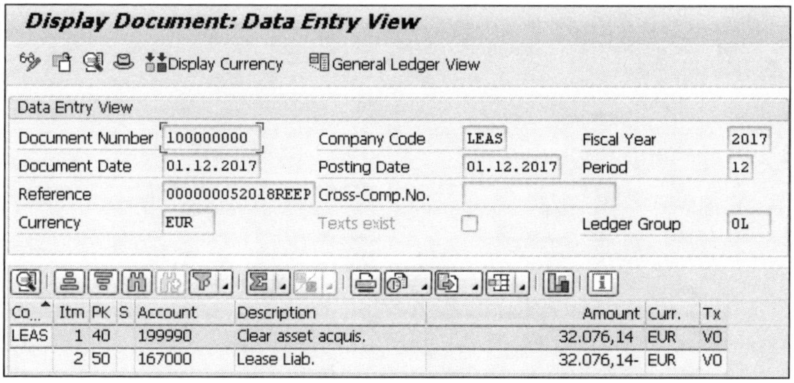


**Figure 5.51** Transfer Posting

The **Real Estate Document** shows the relevant flow type.

With certain business transactions, postings cannot be made using the flow type that was originally assigned (the flow type derived from valuation rule—in our example shown in Figure 5.52, this flow type is **I150**). Instead, *reference flow types* must be assigned to the original flow type in Customizing using a relationship key (here **CEK**, **Asset Transaction Allocation**), as shown in Figure 5.53.

Now, the reference flow type will be used to determine the correct general ledger account(s).

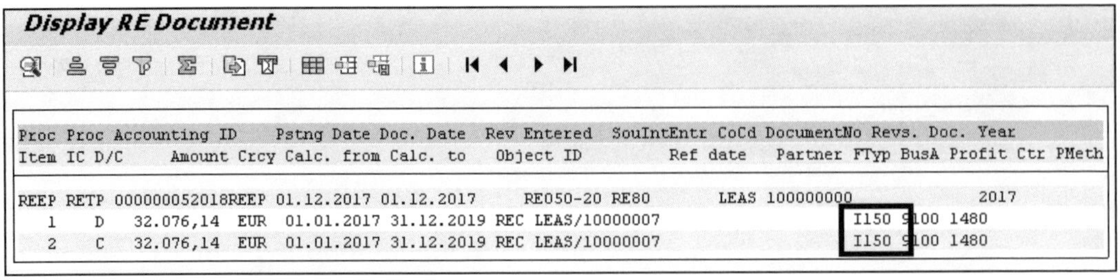


**Figure 5.52** Reference Flow Types

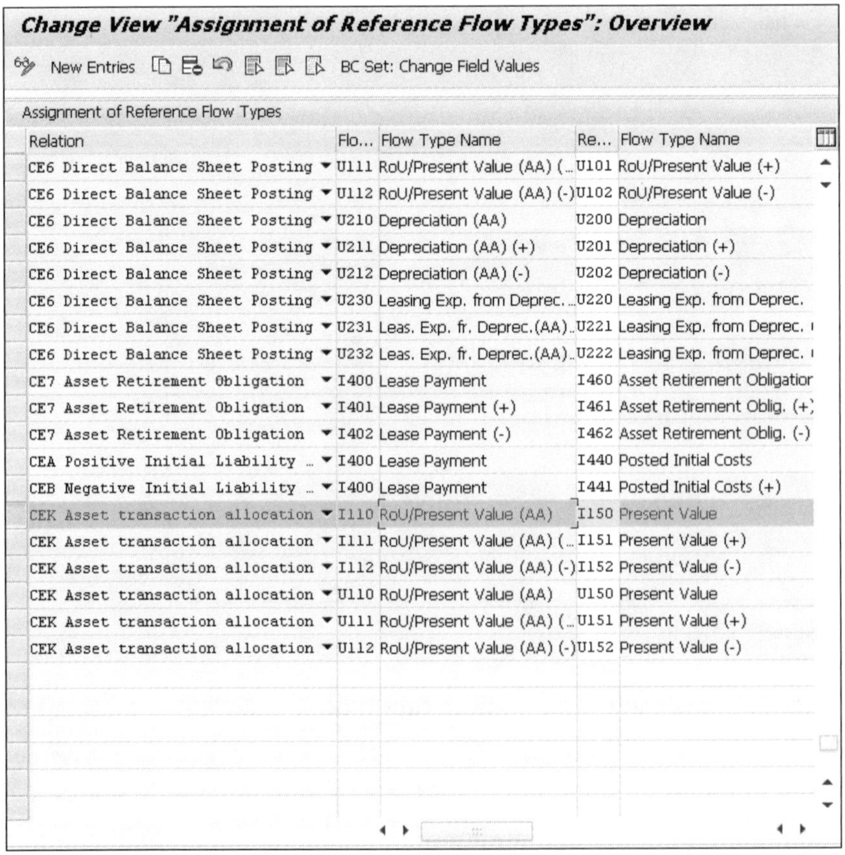


| Relation | Flo... | Flow Type Name | Re... | Flow Type Name |
|---|---|---|---|---|
| CE6 Direct Balance Sheet Posting | U111 | RoU/Present Value (AA) (... | U101 | RoU/Present Value (+) |
| CE6 Direct Balance Sheet Posting | U112 | RoU/Present Value (AA) (-) | U102 | RoU/Present Value (-) |
| CE6 Direct Balance Sheet Posting | U210 | Depreciation (AA) | U200 | Depreciation |
| CE6 Direct Balance Sheet Posting | U211 | Depreciation (AA) (+) | U201 | Depreciation (+) |
| CE6 Direct Balance Sheet Posting | U212 | Depreciation (AA) (-) | U202 | Depreciation (-) |
| CE6 Direct Balance Sheet Posting | U230 | Leasing Exp. from Deprec. ... | U220 | Leasing Exp. from Deprec. |
| CE6 Direct Balance Sheet Posting | U231 | Leas. Exp. fr. Deprec.(AA)... | U221 | Leasing Exp. from Deprec. ( |
| CE6 Direct Balance Sheet Posting | U232 | Leas. Exp. fr. Deprec.(AA)... | U222 | Leasing Exp. from Deprec. ( |
| CE7 Asset Retirement Obligation | I400 | Lease Payment | I460 | Asset Retirement Obligatior |
| CE7 Asset Retirement Obligation | I401 | Lease Payment (+) | I461 | Asset Retirement Oblig. (+) |
| CE7 Asset Retirement Obligation | I402 | Lease Payment (-) | I462 | Asset Retirement Oblig. (-) |
| CEA Positive Initial Liability ... | I400 | Lease Payment | I440 | Posted Initial Costs |
| CEB Negative Initial Liability ... | I400 | Lease Payment | I441 | Posted Initial Costs (+) |
| CEK Asset transaction allocation | I110 | RoU/Present Value (AA) | I150 | Present Value |
| CEK Asset transaction allocation | I111 | RoU/Present Value (AA) (... | I151 | Present Value (+) |
| CEK Asset transaction allocation | I112 | RoU/Present Value (AA) (-) | I152 | Present Value (-) |
| CEK Asset transaction allocation | U110 | RoU/Present Value (AA) | U150 | Present Value |
| CEK Asset transaction allocation | U111 | RoU/Present Value (AA) (... | U151 | Present Value (+) |
| CEK Asset transaction allocation | U112 | RoU/Present Value (AA) (-) | U152 | Present Value (-) |

**Figure 5.53** Assigning Reference Flow Types

Flow types have account symbols assigned to them, as shown in Figure 5.54. To configure these symbols, follow the IMG menu path: **Flexible Real Estate Management (RE-FX) • Accounting • Automatically Generated Accounting Documents • Account Determination • Assign Account Symbol to Flow Type**.

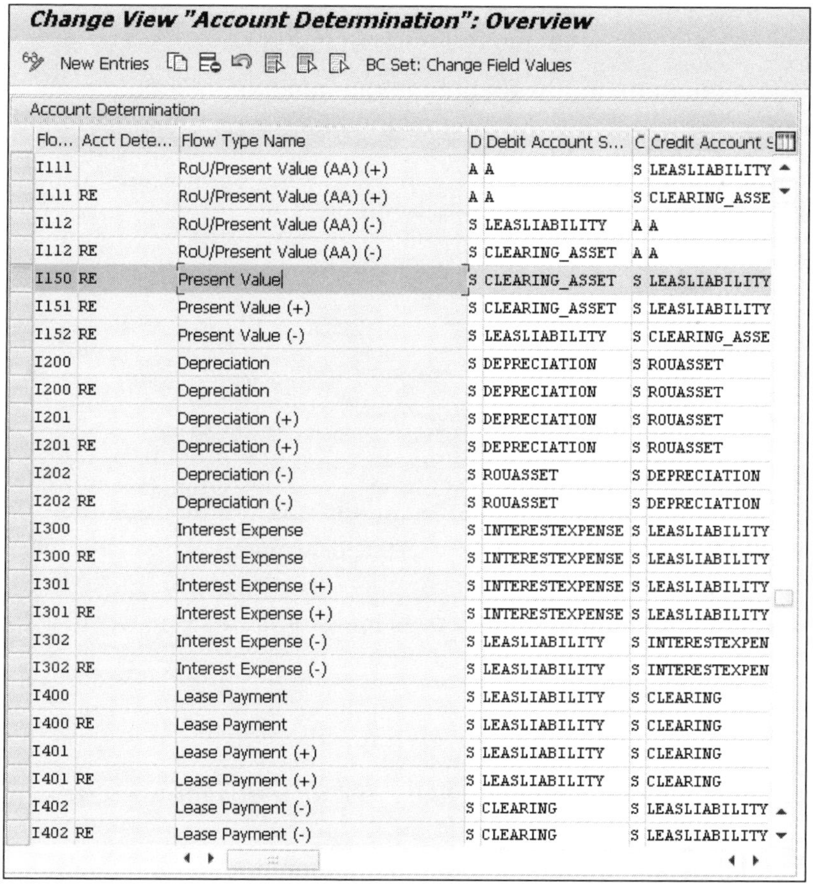

Change View "Account Determination": Overview

New Entries BC Set: Change Field Values

Account Determination

| Flo... | Acct Dete... | Flow Type Name | D | Debit Account S... | C | Credit Account S |
|---|---|---|---|---|---|---|
| I111 | | RoU/Present Value (AA) (+) | A | A | S | LEASLIABILITY |
| I111 | RE | RoU/Present Value (AA) (+) | A | A | S | CLEARING_ASSE |
| I112 | | RoU/Present Value (AA) (-) | S | LEASLIABILITY | A | A |
| I112 | RE | RoU/Present Value (AA) (-) | S | CLEARING_ASSET | A | A |
| I150 | RE | Present Value | S | CLEARING_ASSET | S | LEASLIABILITY |
| I151 | RE | Present Value (+) | S | CLEARING_ASSET | S | LEASLIABILITY |
| I152 | RE | Present Value (-) | S | LEASLIABILITY | S | CLEARING_ASSE |
| I200 | | Depreciation | S | DEPRECIATION | S | ROUASSET |
| I200 | RE | Depreciation | S | DEPRECIATION | S | ROUASSET |
| I201 | | Depreciation (+) | S | DEPRECIATION | S | ROUASSET |
| I201 | RE | Depreciation (+) | S | DEPRECIATION | S | ROUASSET |
| I202 | | Depreciation (-) | S | ROUASSET | S | DEPRECIATION |
| I202 | RE | Depreciation (-) | S | ROUASSET | S | DEPRECIATION |
| I300 | | Interest Expense | S | INTERESTEXPENSE | S | LEASLIABILITY |
| I300 | RE | Interest Expense | S | INTERESTEXPENSE | S | LEASLIABILITY |
| I301 | | Interest Expense (+) | S | INTERESTEXPENSE | S | LEASLIABILITY |
| I301 | RE | Interest Expense (+) | S | INTERESTEXPENSE | S | LEASLIABILITY |
| I302 | | Interest Expense (-) | S | LEASLIABILITY | S | INTERESTEXPEN |
| I302 | RE | Interest Expense (-) | S | LEASLIABILITY | S | INTERESTEXPEN |
| I400 | | Lease Payment | S | LEASLIABILITY | S | CLEARING |
| I400 | RE | Lease Payment | S | LEASLIABILITY | S | CLEARING |
| I401 | | Lease Payment (+) | S | LEASLIABILITY | S | CLEARING |
| I401 | RE | Lease Payment (+) | S | LEASLIABILITY | S | CLEARING |
| I402 | | Lease Payment (-) | S | CLEARING | S | LEASLIABILITY |
| I402 | RE | Lease Payment (-) | S | CLEARING | S | LEASLIABILITY |

**Figure 5.54** Assigning Account Symbols

As for the previous postings, account symbols are replaced by real general ledger accounts when the transfer posting process is executed, as shown in Figure 5.55.

To replace account symbols, follow the IMG menu path: **Flexible Real Estate Management (RE-FX) • Accounting • Integration FI-GL, FI-AR, FI-AP • Account Determination • Replace Account Symbols**.

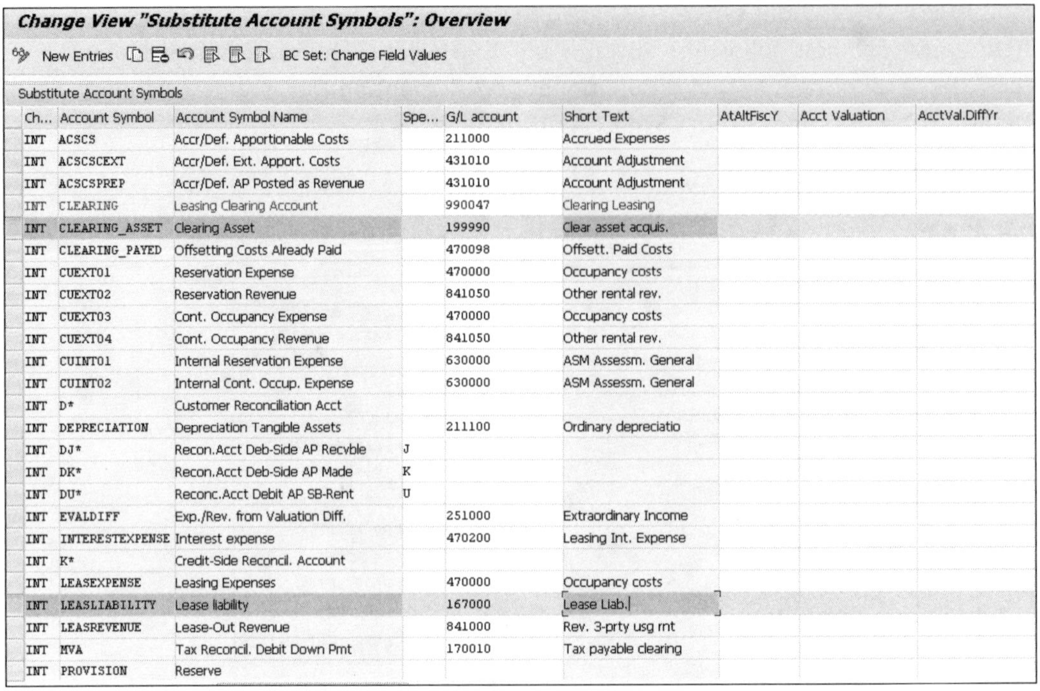
Change View "Substitute Account Symbols": Overview

New Entries BC Set: Change Field Values

Substitute Account Symbols

| Ch... | Account Symbol | Account Symbol Name | Spe... | G/L account | Short Text | AtAltFiscY | Acct Valuation | AcctVal.DiffYr |
|---|---|---|---|---|---|---|---|---|
| INT | ACSCS | Accr/Def. Apportionable Costs | | 211000 | Accrued Expenses | | | |
| INT | ACSCSCEXT | Accr/Def. Ext. Apport. Costs | | 431010 | Account Adjustment | | | |
| INT | ACSCSPREP | Accr/Def. AP Posted as Revenue | | 431010 | Account Adjustment | | | |
| INT | CLEARING | Leasing Clearing Account | | 990047 | Clearing Leasing | | | |
| INT | CLEARING_ASSET | Clearing Asset | | 199990 | Clear asset acquis. | | | |
| INT | CLEARING_PAYED | Offsetting Costs Already Paid | | 470098 | Offsett. Paid Costs | | | |
| INT | CUEXT01 | Reservation Expense | | 470000 | Occupancy costs | | | |
| INT | CUEXT02 | Reservation Revenue | | 841050 | Other rental rev. | | | |
| INT | CUEXT03 | Cont. Occupancy Expense | | 470000 | Occupancy costs | | | |
| INT | CUEXT04 | Cont. Occupancy Revenue | | 841050 | Other rental rev. | | | |
| INT | CUINT01 | Internal Reservation Expense | | 630000 | ASM Assessm. General | | | |
| INT | CUINT02 | Internal Cont. Occup. Expense | | 630000 | ASM Assessm. General | | | |
| INT | D* | Customer Reconciliation Acct | | | | | | |
| INT | DEPRECIATION | Depreciation Tangible Assets | | 211100 | Ordinary depreciatio | | | |
| INT | DJ* | Recon.Acct Deb-Side AP Recvble | J | | | | | |
| INT | DK* | Recon.Acct Deb-Side AP Made | K | | | | | |
| INT | DU* | Reconc.Acct Debit AP SB-Rent | U | | | | | |
| INT | EVALDIFF | Exp./Rev. from Valuation Diff. | | 251000 | Extraordinary Income | | | |
| INT | INTERESTEXPENSE | Interest expense | | 470200 | Leasing Int. Expense | | | |
| INT | K* | Credit-Side Reconcil. Account | | | | | | |
| INT | LEASEXPENSE | Leasing Expenses | | 470000 | Occupancy costs | | | |
| INT | LEASLIABILITY | Lease liability | | 167000 | Lease Liab. | | | |
| INT | LEASREVENUE | Lease-Out Revenue | | 841000 | Rev. 3-prty usg rnt | | | |
| INT | MVA | Tax Reconcil. Debit Down Pmt | | 170010 | Tax payable clearing | | | |
| INT | PROVISION | Reserve | | | | | | |

**Figure 5.55** Replacing Account Symbols with General Ledger Accounts

You've now completed the required configuration for lease valuation in SAP RE-FX.

## 5.4 Special Topics

Before we close this chapter on configuring SAP RE-FX for lease valuations, we want to offer some guidance on a few additional settings.

### 5.4.1 Parallel Accounting for Multiple Accounting Principles

The balance sheet valuation of real estate contracts and leases allows parallel valuations and postings for different accounting principles. While the periodic posting transaction (Transaction RERAPP) always posts to *all ledgers*, the valuation posting transaction (Transaction RECEEP) can post on an *accounting principle-specific basis*. You control which accounting principle is used at the valuation rule level.

If you are using the *ledger solution*, you'll need to make an assignment to the accounting principle in the valuation rule. If you are using the *account solution*, you'll need to control the account determination for the individual valuation rules in such a way that the posting is made to the correct accounts assigned to the respective balance sheet variant. In the valuation rule, you'll need to assign the relevant depreciation area to FI-AA on a company code-specific basis.

### 5.4.2 Changing Account Determination for Periodic Posting

In the periodic posting transaction (Transaction RERAPP), payment-relevant postings are carried out based on the partner-related cash flow. In the case of vendor contracts, the posting will equal:

*Costs of rent/leasing to vendor*

To ensure consistency when the valuation is active, posting rent/leasing rates in Transaction RERAPP must be redirected from the *costs of rent/leasing account* to the *allocation of rental payments account* as soon as the valuation is active.

To set up this redirection, you'll need to enter the *allocation of rental payments account* under **Replace Account Symbols** in the **Account Valuation** field, as shown in Figure 5.56.

**Change View "Substitute Account Symbols": Overview**

New Entries BC Set: Change Field Values

Substitute Account Symbols

| Ch... | Account Symbol | Account Symbol Name | Special G/L ind. | G/L account | Short Text | AtAltFiscY | Acct Valuation | AcctVal.DiffYr |
|---|---|---|---|---|---|---|---|---|
| INT | LEASLIABILITY | Lease liability | | 7000 | Lease Liab. | | | |
| INT | LEASREVENUE | Lease-Out Revenue | | 841000 | Rev. 3-prty usg rnt | | | |
| INT | MVA | Tax Reconcil. Debit Down Pmt | | 170010 | Tax payable clearing | | | |
| INT | PROVISION | Reserve | | | | | | |
| INT | SCSSUCST | Cost Accnt Acct.Determ.Ext ... | | 470400 | App.operating costs | | | |
| INT | SERVICEEXPEN... | Service Expense | | 415000 | External procurement | | | |
| INT | T* | | | | | | | |
| INT | TC01 | | | 470900 | Exp. non-ded.inpt tx | | | |
| INT | TC02 | | | 841910 | Rev.ded.input tax | | | |
| INT | TCST | Credit Contract Costs Transfer | | 470000 | Occupancy costs | | | |
| INT | TREV | Credit Contract Revenue Tran... | | 888900 | Rntl sales deduct. | | | |
| INT | V100 | Credit-Side Lease-In Costs | | 470000 | Occupancy costs | | 470099 | |
| INT | V110 | Credit-Side Other Costs | | 470000 | Occupancy costs | | 470099 | |
| INT | V130 | Credit-Side Service Charges | | 470400 | App.operating costs | | | |
| INT | V140 | Revenue frm Int. Rental (CCtr) | | 841099 | Clg op.cst adv.pyt | | | |
| INT | V150 | | | 470420 | RE Apport.oper.costs | | | |

**Figure 5.56** Substituting Account Symbols

### 5.4.3 Asset Accounting

Configuring FI-AA is, of course, outside the scope of this book, but we do have a few tips to offer about key asset accounting definitions.

Let's first look at asset classes: According to IFRS 16 and ASC 842, ROU assets must be managed separately from other fixed assets. Therefore, you'll need to set up the corresponding asset classes.

Valuation postings to assets are managed using FI-AA. For example, for acquisition postings, a *leasing liabilities account* is posted to as the offsetting account. In contrast, with other asset classes for which a *clearing account* is posted to as the offsetting account, you'll need to set up a separate account determination for your assets so that you can assign separate general ledger accounts.

When you're using classic FI-AA, you'll need to assign accounting-specific postings to the ROU asset to the asset depreciation areas that represent the respective accounting principle. This assignment is made using asset transaction types, which are limited to the specific depreciation areas. These asset transaction types are derived from the flow type stored in the valuation rule Assign Asset Transaction Types.

During the depreciation run, the depreciation calculated in the real estate contracts and leases is read from the contract valuations by means of a special depreciation key. You can create the *depreciation key* in several ways, as follows:

- Transaction AFAMR: Checks whether the LERE base method exists. If it exists, use it. Otherwise, create a base method with the text **Normal: Depreciation from Real Estate Leasing**. The method is for ordinary depreciation and uses the depreciation method **B - Depreciation from Real Estate Leasing**. All other indicators are set to **No**. Save and activate the method.
- Transaction AFAMS: Creates a new multilevel method (such as ZLE) **Leasing from Real Estate** with the validity **From Ordinary Depreciation Start Date**. The multilevel method has only one level with acquisition year 9999 and a validity of 999 years. The base value is **29 - External Base Value from Real Estate Leasing**. Save and activate the method.
- Transaction AFAMA: Creates the new depreciation key: **Depreciation from Real Estate Leasing** (such as ZLEA). The key has exactly one phase for ordinary depreciation with the base method and multilevel method described above. As the period control method, you can use a standard method (depending on what is required, 001, for example). For multiple shift, scrap value, and shutdown, you should set **No Effect, Cutoff Value is Ignored**, or **No**. Save and activate the key.

Assign this key to the asset classes that you want to use for the ROU assets: **Enter Default Values in Asset Classes**.

### 5.4.4 Controlling

If balance sheet valuation is not active, costs that are assigned to the contract after the partner-related cash flow has been posted are transfer-posted to the originating objects during the periodic posting (Transaction RERAPP) based on the object cash flow.

*Costs of rent/leasing (object)* to *costs of rent/leasing (contract)*

The function of this transfer posting is replaced by the valuation postings. Costs on controlling objects arise if the leading ledger (such as IFRS or US GAAP) capitalizes a right of use no longer during the periodic posting but through posting of depreciation and interest. This normally leads to a different cost distribution over the term of the contract.

### 5.4.5 New Authorization Objects for Valuation

SAP RE-FX users need specific authorizations. The following authorization objects are available in the valuation area:

- `F_RECE_TM` (valuation term): This object defines the company codes, contract types, and valuation rules for how certain activities relating to valuation rule assignment in the contract are carried out.
- `F_RECE_CD` (valuation term and conditions): This object defines the company codes, contract types, and valuation rules for how certain activities relating to condition assignment for the valuation rule in the contract are carried out.
- `F_RECE_PR` (valuation process): This object defines the company codes, contract types, and valuation rules for how certain activities relating to the actual valuation are out.
- `F_RECE_PO` (valuation postings): This object defines the company codes, contract types, and valuation rules for how certain activities for the periodic posting of valuations are carried out.

The following fields are available for the authorization check:

- **BUKRS** (company code): Possible values depend on Customizing
- **SMVART** (contract type): Possible values depend on Customizing

- **CERULE** (valuation rule): Possible values depend on Customizing
- **ACTVT** (activity): Possible activities differ per authorization object, as follows:
  - F_RECE_TM
    - 02 Change (rule assignment in contract can be changed)
    - 03 Display (rule assignment in contract can be displayed)
  - F_RECE_CD
    - 02 Change (condition assignment for rule in contract can be changed)
    - 03 Display (condition assignment for rule in contract can be displayed)
  - F_RECE_PR
    - 03 Display (process data for valuation can be displayed)
    - 06 Delete (process data for valuation can be deleted)
    - 16 Execute (the valuation can be executed and saved)
    - 48 Simulate (the valuation can be simulated)
  - F_RECE_PO
    - 10 Post (the periodic posting of the valuation can be executed and saved)
    - 48 Simulate (the periodic posting of the valuation can be simulated)
    - 85 Cancel (the periodic posting can be canceled)

## 5.5 Summary

In this chapter, we taught you how to configure SAP RE-FX for lease valuation. Though configuring integrated components like FI-AA and broader SAP RE-FX configurations are outside the scope of this chapter, the information we've presented here will help you meet the requirements set by IFRS 16 and ASC 842.

# Chapter 6
# Transition Accounting

*As the effective date for leasing regulation compliance approaches, planning the transition from your previous accounting practices is important for demonstrating your compliance with the new rules.*



The two new leasing regulations—International Financial Reporting Standards 16 and Accounting Standards Codification 842—will be applied for most entities at the beginning of the first annual reporting period, which is the date of initial application.

As shown at the top of Figure 6.1, IFRS 16 is effective for annual reporting periods beginning on or after January 1, 2019. Note that an entity may adopt the standard early, but the standard must be applied after or at the same time that IFRS 15 (Revenue from Contracts with Customers) is adopted. An entity that opts for early adoption for IFRS 16 is required to disclose that fact.

Under ASC 842, the effective date for annual reporting periods begins after December 15, 2018, for public businesses and certain other entities. For all the other entities, the effective date for annual reporting periods begins after December 15, 2019. Early adoption of the new standard is allowed.

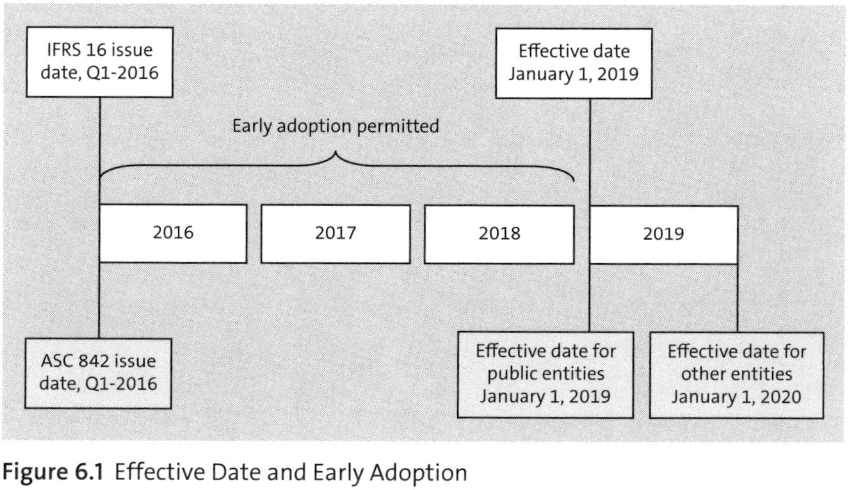


**Figure 6.1** Effective Date and Early Adoption

As we'll explain throughout this chapter, how an organization should transition depends on the standard to which they must comply.

An entity may elect one of two approaches to transition to the new IFRS 16 standard:

- A *full retrospective approach* (as if IFRS 16 had always been applied)
- A *modified retrospective approach* (with the cumulative effect of applying IFRS 16 recognized at the date of initial application)

Organizations bound by ASC 842 have fewer options because they cannot conduct a full retrospective approach. Under ASC 842, an entity, whether lessee and lessor, can only transition to the new standard with a modified retrospective approach.

## 6.1 Practical Expedients

Transitioning to the new standard may incur significant costs for an entity. As such, the standard includes several *practical expedients* that are intended to allow an entity to minimize the costs of transition without significantly compromising the quality of the financial statement.

Under IFRS 16, an entity can choose whether to apply the new standard to all their contracts, or an entity can apply a practical expedient to grandfather prior assessments of whichever existing contracts contain leases and only apply the new standard to these contracts. Table 6.1 summarizes the transition approaches and expedients for IFRS 16.

| Approach/Practical Expedient | Lessor or Lessee? | Scope |
|---|---|---|
| Early adoption | Both lessor and lessee | Accounting policy choice |
| Definition of lease: grandfather assessment | Both lessor and lessee | Accounting policy choice |
| Recognition exemption: short-term lease | Lessee only | Class of underlying asset |
| Recognition exemption: leases of low-value items | Lessee only | Lease-by-lease basis |
| Full retrospective vs. modified retrospective | Lessee only | Accounting policy choice |
| Modified retrospective: practical expedients | Lessee only | Lease-by-lease basis |

**Table 6.1** IFRS 16 Transition Approaches and Practical Expedients

Like IFRS 16, ASC 842 also provides a number of practical expedients to minimize cost and complexity of the transition. However, fewer expedients are available, and these expedients are also less flexible in their application. Table 6.2 summarizes the transition approaches and practical expedients for ASC 842.

| Approach/Practical Expedient | Lessor or Lessee? | Scope |
|---|---|---|
| Early adoption | Both lessor and lessee | Accounting policy choice |
| Definition of lease: grandfather assessment | Both lessor and lessee | Accounting policy choice |
| Recognition exemption: short-term lease | Lessee only | Class of underlying asset |
| Modified retrospective | Both lessor and lessee | Accounting policy choice |
| Practical expedient: use of hindsight | Both lessor and lessee | Accounting policy choice |

**Table 6.2** ASC 842 Transition Approaches and Practical Expedients

Let's look closer at these practical expedients.

### 6.1.1 Definition of a Lease

Let's first look at IFRS 16. The entity that chooses to take advantage of the practical expedient is permitted to apply IFRS 16 to leases previously identified in accordance with IAS 17 (Leases) and IFRIC 4 (Determining Whether an Arrangement Contains a Lease). The entity assumes that existing leases continue to be leases under IFRS 16, that existing service contracts continue to be service contracts, and that the entity is not required to apply IFRS 16 to contracts previously identified as not containing leases in accordance with IAS 17 and IFRIC 4.

If the practical expedient is chosen, an entity is required to disclose that fact. The expedient applies to all contracts of the entity entered into *before* the date of initial application or none of the contracts. All contracts entered into (or changed) *on or after* the date of initial application are required to apply IFRS 16 requirements.

If the practical expedient is not applied, an entity is required to examine all contracts in the context of IFRS 16 to determine whether the contracts contain leases.

Under ASC 842, a group of practical expedients have been provided similar to IFRS 16. To apply these practical expedients, the entity must apply them as a package and to all its leases regardless of whether the entity is the lessee or lessor. Some practical expedients include the following:

1. An entity need not reassess whether any expired or existing contracts are or contain leases.
2. An entity need not reassess the lease classification for any expired or existing leases. In other words, all existing leases that had been classified as operating leases in accordance with ASC 840 will be classified as operating leases, and all existing leases that were classified as capital leases in accordance with ASC 840 will be classified as finance leases.
3. An entity need not reassess the initial direct costs for any existing leases.

### 6.1.2 Transition for Lessors

For lessors, the accounting requirements under the new standard are identical to the existing standard in many aspects. Therefore, an entity is not generally required to make any adjustments for leases in which it is a lessor on transition.

However, one specific exception exists with respect to intermediate lessors (who issue *subleases* to a sublessee). Figure 6.2 shows the structure of a sublease.

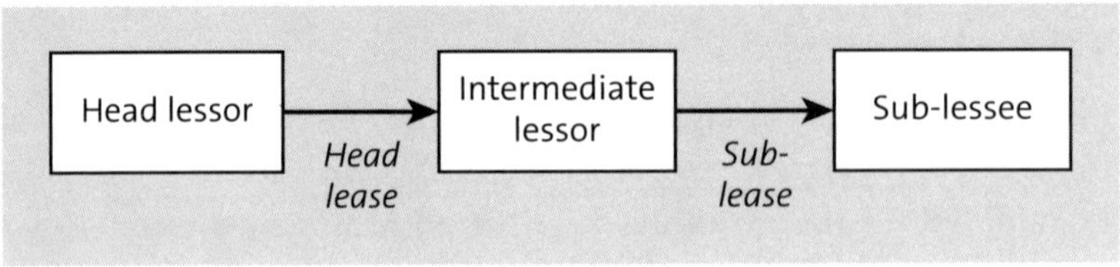


**Figure 6.2** Structure of a Sublease

As shown in Figure 6.3, at the date of initial application, an intermediate lessor is required to reassess each existing operating sublease to determine whether it should be classified as an operating lease or a finance lease under the new standard:

- For a sublease classified as an operating lease under both old and new standard, you will continue to account for the lease as an operating lease.
- For a sublease classified as finance lease under both old and new standards, you will continue to account for the lease as finance lease. Figure 6.3 shows the type of sublease and its assessment.
- For a sublease previously classified as an operating lease, but now classified as a finance lease under the new standard, the intermediate lessor accounts for

the sublease as a new finance lease entered into on the date of initial application. Any gain or loss arising on the sublease arrangement is included in the cumulative catch-up adjustment to retained earnings at the date of initial application.

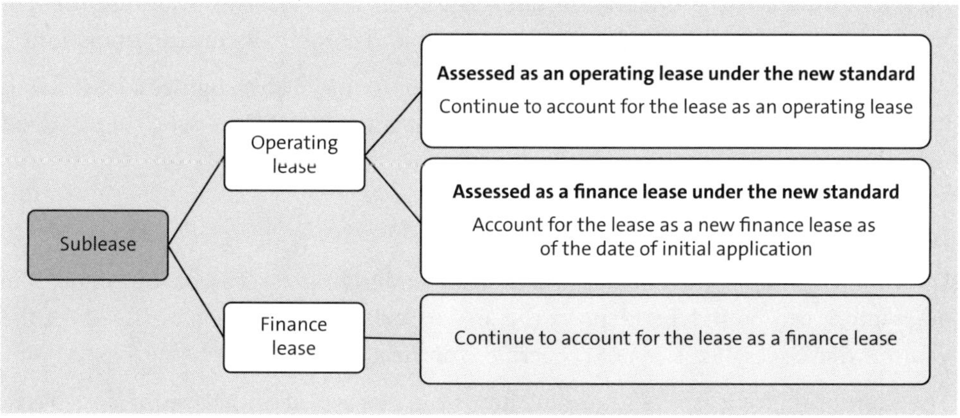


**Figure 6.3** Sublease Assessment

### 6.1.3 Transition for Lessees

Under IFRS 16, lessees are required to be recognized as an asset (ROU asset) and a liability (lease liability) on all the leases except for short-term leases and for leases of low-value assets.

Acknowledging the potentially significant impact of the new lease standard on a lessee's financial statement, IFRS 16 does not require a full retrospective approach in accordance with IAS 8 but does allow a simpler approach: a modified retrospective approach. A lessee can choose either the full retrospective approach or the modified retrospective approach but must apply their selected approach to their entire lease portfolio.

Under ASC 842, an entity can only transition to the new standard with a modified retrospective approach for both lessee and lessor. The full retrospective approach is not permitted under ASC 842.

### 6.1.4 Recognition Exemption

A lessee may elect not to apply the new standard to, or *exempt*, short-term leases and leases of low-value items. However, if one of these recognition exemptions is elected, an entity is required to make additional disclosures on its financial statements.

#### Short-Term Leases

For both IFRS 16 and ASC 841, a short-term lease is defined as a lease that, at the commencement date, has a lease term of 12 months or less and does not include an option to purchase the underlying asset. The short-term lease exemption provided by the new standard is intended to reduce costs and complexity during transition.

A lessee that elects to apply this exemption is not required to recognize a lease liability and an ROU asset. However, this exemption must be applied consistently to all underlying assets in the same class.

#### Leases of Low-Value Items

Under IFRS 16, a lessee assesses whether an underlying asset is of low-value. The assessment can be independent of the size or nature of the lease or based on the value of the asset when it is new, regardless of the age of the asset being leased.

The exemption for leases of low-value items can be applied on a lease-by-lease basis.

Under ASC 842, there is no exemption for leases of low-value assets.

### 6.1.5 Sale-and-Leaseback Transactions

If an entity (the seller-lessee) transfers an asset to another entity (the buyer-lessor) and leases that asset back from the buyer-lessor, both the seller-lessee and buyer-lessor are required, under IFRS 16, to account for the transfer contract and the lease as shown in Figure 6.4.

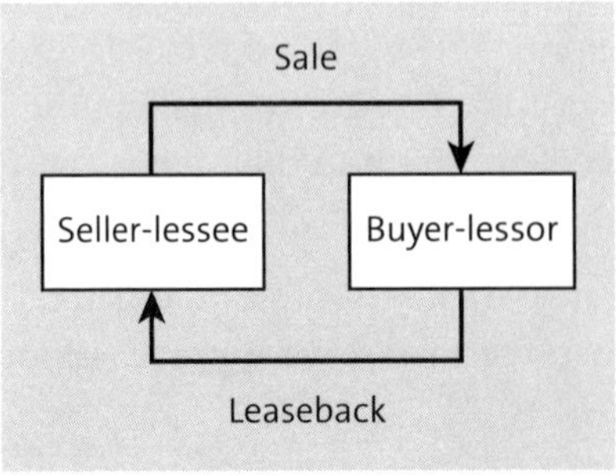


**Figure 6.4** Structure of a Sale-and-Leaseback Scenario

For sale-and-leaseback scenarios, the seller-lessee need not reassess any transactions entered into before the date of application to determine whether a sale occurred according to IFRS 15. The leaseback component of such transactions is generally accounted for just as any other lease, whether a finance or an operating lease. However, depending on the leaseback classification under IAS 17, transitional adjustments may be required, as shown in Figure 6.5.

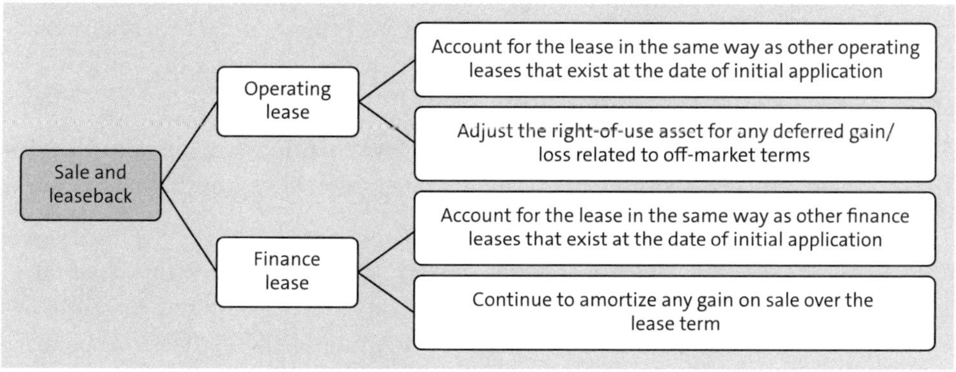


**Figure 6.5** Sale-and-Leaseback Accounting under IFRS 16

For sale-and-leaseback transactions classified as *operating leases* in accordance with IAS 17, an entity should account for lease in the same way as other operating leases that exist at the date of initial application. The ROU asset is adjusted for any deferred gain/loss related to off-market terms.

For sale-and-leaseback transactions classified as *finance leases* in accordance with IAS 17, an entity should account for lease in the same way as other finance leases that exist at the date of initial application. The gain on sales over the lease term continues to be amortized.

Under ASC 842, sale-and-leaseback transactions should *not* be reassessed to determine if these transactions would have qualified as sales according to ASC 606. The only exceptions to this rule are transactions accounted for previously as failed sales—these need to be reassessed during the transition. Lessees and lessors should account for the leaseback in accordance with the standard lessee and lessor transition requirements. Additionally, ASC 842, paragraph 10-65-1, provides guidance on the accounting for any deferred gain or loss balance after transition, which is required for sale-and-leaseback scenarios.

## 6.2 Choosing a Transition Approach

Recall that, under IFRS 16, an entity may either adopt the new standard with full retrospective approach or follow the modified retrospective approach.

If the full retrospective approach is elected, the entity is required to restate the comparative data as if IFRS 16 had always applied. On the other hand, if the modified retrospective approach is chosen, the entity is not required to restate the comparative data.

Practical expedients that are included in IFRS 16 for transitions are only available for the modified retrospective approach. The full retrospective approach does not allow you to apply any practical expedients.

Under ASC 842, an entity may only adopt the new standard with the modified retrospective approach. The modified retrospective approach is required for all leases existing at, or entered into on or after, the beginning of the earliest comparative period presented in the financial statements. Under ASC 842, practical expedients are available for transitions, which are less extensive than those under IFRS 16.

### 6.2.1 The Full Retrospective Approach

The full retrospective approach requires an entity to apply the new standard to each period presented in the financial statements, as required by IAS 8 (Accounting Policies, Changes in Accounting Estimates and Errors). In other words, the entity is required to apply the new IFRS 16 standard to all contracts in which the entity is a lessee and restate the lease's prior financial information.

The entity is also required to restate its opening balance sheet at the beginning of the earliest comparative period presented in the financial statements, as if IFRS 16 had always been applied, in accordance with IAS 1.

To present the comparative financial information, the lessee is required to report on two accounting standards simultaneously. Doing so shows the difference between IAS 17 and IFRS 16 and the effect of the new standard on the financial statements. Figure 6.6 shows an entity that has selected the full retrospective approach and presents one year of comparative financial information in two different accounting standards concurrently.

This approach provides a more detailed overview of the financial information and the effect of the new IFRS 16 standard. The approach also increases the quality of reported financial information captured for the first-year audit and provides a comparable and transparent set of data for financial users.

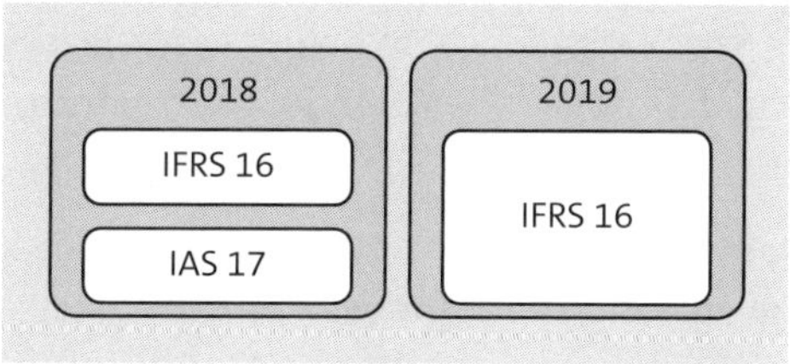


**Figure 6.6** The Full Retrospective Approach

On the other hand, this approach will also need to report comparative figures, which requires a great deal of historical information about the leases. An entity effectively needs to produce two annual reports (IAS 17 and IFRS 16). However, the full retrospective approach is likely to be more expensive, since it requires more resources and more reports and disclosures. Furthermore, this approach does not allow you to apply any practical expedients, which would be available with modified retrospective approach.

### 6.2.2 The Modified Retrospective Approach

Under IFRS 16, an entity is not required to restate comparative information when the modified retrospective approach is elected. Instead, the information in the comparative period is reported on the basis of IAS 17, but the entity recognizes the cumulative effect of initially applying IFRS 16 as an adjustment to opening equity on the date of initial application. Figure 6.7 shows an entity that has selected the modified retrospective approach; here, the entity presents its comparative financial information based on IAS 17 and reports an adjustment, in compliance with the new standard, in its financial statements on the date of initial application.

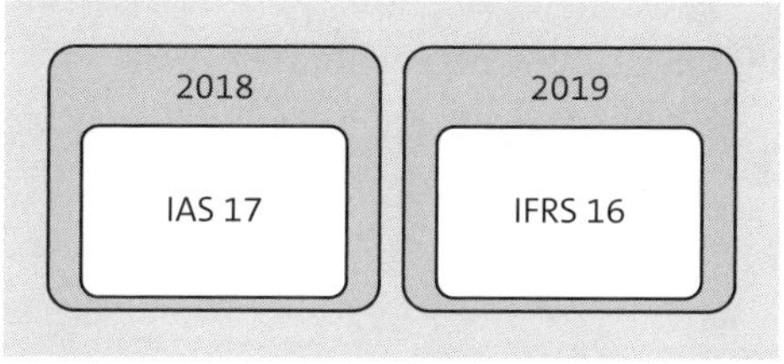


**Figure 6.7** The Modified Retrospective Approach

This approach helps reduce the scope of reports, significantly lowering the cost of transitioning by requiring fewer resources. With this approach, you won't need parallel accounting reports nor will you need to restate comparative financial information. You'll also have the option of applying specific practical expedients for leases previously identified as operational leases, which is not available under the full retrospective approach.

However, this approach may potentially generate less relevant financial reports because the financial information within the current and prior year financial statements may not be comparable. (In this approach, prior period financial information is not restated.) If this approach is selected, an entity is required to make additional disclosures on its financial statements.

Under ASC 842, an entity is required to restate comparative information when the modified retrospective approach is selected.

## 6.3 Adopting the Modified Retrospective Approach

If a lessee elects to apply IFRS 16 using the modified retrospective approach, the lessee will no longer distinguish between operating leases and finance leases but instead recognize lease liabilities and an ROU asset for each lease.

A lease liability represents the lessee's contractual obligation to make lease payments over the term of the lease. An ROU asset represents the lessee's right to use the leased asset over the term of the lease. The modified retrospective approach accounts for these concepts, depending on the kind of lease, as shown in Table 6.3.

| | |
|---|---|
| **Operating lease** | **Lease liability**: Measured at the present value of the remaining lease payments |
| | **Right-of-use asset**: Measured at the amount of lease liability of carrying amount as if IFRS 16 had been applied since the beginning |
| **Finance lease** | **Lease liability**: Measured at the same amount as under IAS 17 |
| | **Right-of-use asset**: Measured at the same amount as under IAS 17 |

**Table 6.3** The Modified Retrospective Approach under IFRS 16

Under ASC 842, the lessee is still required to classify leases as operating or finance lease. Transition for each classification differs only slightly, as we'll now explain.

### 6.3.1 Lease Liability for Operating Leases

Under IFRS 16, for leases that were previously classified as operating leases and that will *continue* to be classified as operating leases under the new standard, the lease liability is initially measured at the present value of the remaining lease payments using the incremental borrowing rate at the date of initial application.

For the same leases under ASC 842, the lease liability should be similarly calculated as the present value of the sum of the remaining minimum rental payments and any amounts that the lessee likely owes as guaranteed residual value. The discount rate used to calculate the present value should be determined at the later of the earliest period presented or the lease commencement date. This requirement is different and more complicated than the IFRS 16 requirement of using the rate at the date of initial application.



### 6.3.2 Right-of-Use Asset for Operating Leases

Under IFRS 16, for leases previously classified as operating lease, the ROU asset is initially measured with one of two provided options on a lease-by-lease basis:

1. Option 1 measures the ROU asset retrospectively as if IFRS 16 had always been applied since the beginning (but using the incremental borrowing rate at the date of initial application of IFRS 16).
2. Option 2 measures the ROU asset at an amount equal to the lease liability minus any prepaid or accrued lease payments.

Under ASC 842, lessees don't have the option of using a retrospective calculation for the right-of-use-asset. Instead, lessees must use a method similar to option 2 above, where the ROU asset is measured equally to the lease liability, but with the following adjustments:

- Prepaid or accrued rent (like IFRS 16)
- Remaining balance of any lease incentives
- Unamortized initial direct costs that would have qualified for capitalization under ASC 842
- Impairments
- Carrying amount of any liability related to the lease recognized in accordance with ASC 420 (Exit or Disposal Cost Obligations)

If unamortized initial direct costs would not have qualified for capitalization under ASC 842, the cost should be written off with an offsetting entry to equity. If an entity elects to apply the practical expedients package according to ASC 842, paragraph 10-65-1(f), the accounting for unamortized initial direct costs may be different.

Recall from Section 6.1 that a lessee can choose to apply a recognition exemption for short-term leases (generally less than a 12-month term). In that case, the organization doesn't need to recognize ROU assets and lease liabilities but instead continues to recognize lease payments on a straight-line basis and recognizes variable payments in the period in which the obligation for such payments is incurred.

### 6.3.3 Lease Liability and Right-of-Use Asset for Finance Leases

The accounting requirements for managing finance leases in IFRS 16 are similar to the accounting requirements in IAS 17. The leases that were previously classified as finance leases are unlikely to encounter substantial matters during transition to the new IFRS 16 standard.

Consequently, the lease liability and ROU asset are measured at the same amount of the lease liability and finance lease asset under IAS 17. The carrying forward balances from IAS 17 are applied in IFRS 16 aligned with the new requirements from the date of initial application.

Similar to IFRS 16, ASC 842 doesn't expect a lot of changes for finance leases. In general, the existing finance lease asset should be reclassified as the ROU asset and existing lease obligations shall become lease liabilities for each period the lease was outstanding beginning with the earliest period presented.

Any unamortized initial direct costs that meet this definition under the new standard should be included in the ROU asset. Costs that do not qualify for capitalization should be written off with an offsetting entry to equity. Keep in mind the practical expedient regarding initial direct costs, which can result in different accounting treatments.

### 6.3.4 Practical Expedients

When applying a modified retrospective approach to transition a lease previously classified as operating lease, a lessee may use one or more of the following practical expedients on a lease-by-lease basis. Let's discuss the five available practical expedients:

- Discount rate
- Impairment and onerous leases
- Use of hindsight
- Leases with a short remaining term
- Initial direct costs

Note that, under ASC 842, the only allowed practical expedient is the use of hindsight and, to some extent, the practical expedient for initial direct costs, although this expedient cannot be applied separately. Both expedients cannot be applied on a lease-by-lease basis like IFRS 16; instead, they must be applied to the whole lease portfolio.



#### Discount Rate

Under the modified retrospective transition approach, the discount rate plays a significant role in the initial measurement of the lease liability.

An entity may apply a single discount rate to a portfolio of leases with reasonably similar characteristics (such as leases with a similar remaining lease term for a similar class of underlying asset in a similar economic environment), as defined by IFRS 16. Otherwise, the incremental borrowing rate is to be applied at the date of transition for each lease separately.

#### Impairment and Onerous Leases

As defined by IFRS 16, an entity may rely on a previous assessment of whether leases are onerous in accordance with IAS 37 (Provision, Contingent Liabilities and Contingent Assets) immediately before the date of initial application as an alternative to performing an impairment review. If a lessee chooses this practical expedient, the lessee shall adjust the ROU asset at the date of initial application by the amount of any provision for onerous leases recognized in the statement of financial position immediately before the date of initial application.

The practical expedient only applies to measurement during the transition. Subsequently, the company accounts for the ROU asset in accordance with IFRS 16.

#### Leases with Short Remaining Terms

As defined by IFRS 16, an entity may not recognize leases with terms ending within 12 months of the date of initial application. In this case, a lessee shall:

1. Account for those leases in the same way as short-term leases
2. Include the cost associated with those leases within the disclosure of short-term lease expense in the annual reporting period that includes the date of initial application

If an entity decides to apply this practical expedient, it can choose not to restate these leases. For example, the entity can continue to treat them in the same way as operating leases under IAS 17.

This practical expedient does not relate to the recognition exemption for short-term leases, which is a choice of the accounting policy made for an underlying class of asset. On the contrary, this expedient can be applied on a lease-by-lease basis even if the recognition exemption for short-term leases is not used.

#### Initial Direct Costs

An entity may exclude initial direct costs from the measurement of the ROU asset at the date of initial application, as defined by IFRS 16.

If selected, this practical expedient will help reduce the cost of the transition for the company, as you won't have to identify the initial direct costs of leases that were classified as operating leases under IAS 17.

Under ASC 842, an entity need not reassess initial direct costs for any leases, but this practical expedient can only be applied as a package as described in ASC 842, paragraph 10-65-1(f) and, unlike IFRS 16, must be applied to all leases or not at all.

#### Use of Hindsight

An entity may use hindsight, for example, to determine the lease term if the contract contains options to extend or terminate the lease, as defined by IFRS 16.

Hindsight is the only practical expedient that can be applied without regard for other expedients under ASC 842.

## 6.4 Summary

This chapter explained how to transition from pre-IFRS 16 and pre-ASC 842 accounting practices to the new standards using the modified and full retrospective approaches.

Chapter 7

# Managing Leases with SAP Lease Administration by Nakisa

*Now that your SAP Lease Administration by Nakisa system is live, you'll be able to process leases in compliance with the new regulations.*

7

The purpose of this chapter is to walk through the lease lifecycle in SAP Lease Administration by Nakisa (hereafter, SAP Lease Administration) using step-by-step instructions and system screenshots. We'll cover all the steps you'll need to take, from creating a lease to generating the corresponding financial schedules and journal entries to managing the lease events.

As shown in Figure 7.1, the lease lifecycle in SAP Lease Administration is composed of different objects or data elements, as we'll see in each section of this chapter.

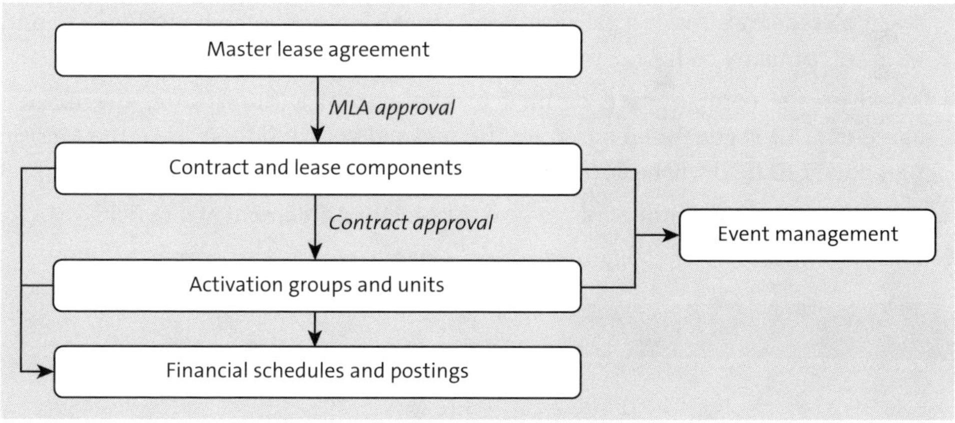


**Figure 7.1** SAP Lease Administration Leasing Data Structure

The first object required to set up a lease is the master lease agreement (MLA), which we'll define in Section 7.1. A single MLA could have one more multiple contracts with their leases components, which are defined in Section 7.2. Once the contract and lease component are approved, the system will generate an activation group, where the units and accounting details such as financial schedules and period postings are maintained; we'll define these in Section 7.3. Once the lease is active, SAP Lease Administration can handle certain events such as lease modifications; we'll manage those in Section 7.4.

## 7.1 Master Lease Agreement

The *master lease agreement* (MLA) is an umbrella agreement for multiple lease contracts and is also where the lease hierarchy is defined. You can enter an MLA manually in the system or, alternatively, mass upload MLAs via an Excel file.

In this section of the chapter, we'll walk through how to manually set up an MLA within SAP Lease Administration.

### 7.1.1 Creating a New MLA

To create a new MLA, follow these steps:

1. Click **Main Menu • Create Master Agreement**.
2. Select the master agreement year from the **Master Agreement Year** dropdown menu.
3. Select the lease area from the **Lease Area** dropdown menu. The lease area represents a regional area or legal entity. Note that a lease area can be assigned to one or more company codes.
4. Based on the configuration defined by the system administrator, the master agreement ID is generated based on the selected year and lease area; the **Master Agreement ID** field will be autopopulated.
5. Enter the master agreement name into the **Master Agreement Name** field.
6. Click **Submit**, as shown in Figure 7.2.

**Figure 7.2** Creating a New Master Lease Agreement

Once the master agreement has been created, three new pages will appear on the left-hand side of the screen:

1. **Definitions** page: On this page, the MLA definitions (such as hierarchy, legal information, and additional reporting details) are defined.
2. **Partners** page: On this page, the MLA lenders and suppliers may be added for informational purposes. You can also set up user notifications, such as the approval requested, at this level for MLA events.
3. **Contract List** pages: This page will provide a view of all the contracts that belong to the MLA.



We'll examine each of these pages in this section, beginning with the **Definitions** page and its three sections: **General Information**, **Hierarchy**, and **Signature**. Note that, when defining a new MLA or any new object in SAP Lease Administration, certain fields are mandatory; these fields are identified with a red asterisk.

In the **General Information** section, shown in Figure 7.3, the MLA identification fields are specified. The following information is available in the **General Information** section:

- The **Master Agreement ID** field shows the generated ID.
- The **Created By** field indicates the user who created the MLA.
- The **Master Agreement Name** may be modified if needed.
- A **Description** of the MLA may be entered.
- The **Valid From** and **Valid To** fields are automatically populated based on the earliest start date and latest end date of all of the contracts under the MLA.
- A **Target Value** may be entered for the MLA. The target value can be used to indicate the line of credit value, or the budget value for the contracts.
- The **Agreement Group** may be selected based on the preconfigured values in the AdminConsole.
- The **Language** of the MLA and all of the attached contracts may be selected.
- The **Currency** for the MLA may be selected. Note that, if a currency is selected, all contracts under the MLA will use the specified currency. If this field is left empty, each contract can use a different currency.
- The **MLA Category** may be selected based on values preconfigured in the AdminConsole.

- The **Legal Jurisdiction** may be entered to indicate the area where the leases are subject to their own distinct tax regulations, such as city or country.
- The **Principal Position** for the attached contracts is automatically set to the value "Lessee."

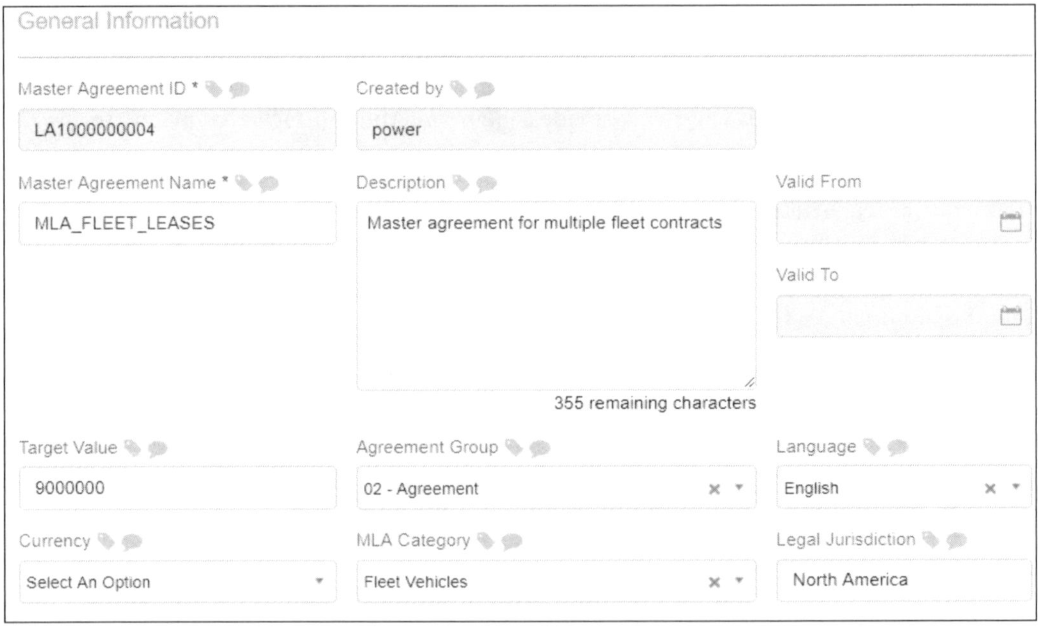


**Figure 7.3** General Information Section of the MLA Definitions Page

In the **Hierarchy** section shown in Figure 7.4, the MLA hierarchy is identified. All of the fields set in this section will be copied down to contracts of the MLA and cannot be overridden. If optional fields are left blank, different values can be set for each contract:

- The **Lease Area** represents a regional area or legal entity.
- The **Lease Business Unit** represents a line of business belonging to the lease area; this information must be set at this level.
- The **Company** represents the legal entity used for accounting purposes; this information may be set at this level. The available list of companies is based on the selected lease area and lease business unit.
- The **Lease Department**, which can represent a corporate department, may be set at this level. The lease department is assigned to a company code.

- The **Lease Group**, which can represent an asset type, may be set at this level. The lease group is assigned to a lease department.
- The **Trading Partner**, which represents a legally independent company, may be set at this level.

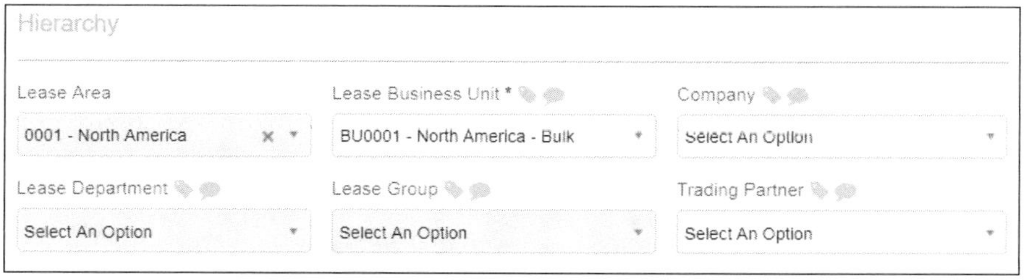


**Figure 7.4** Hierarchy Section of the MLA Definitions Page

The final section of the **Definitions** page is the **Signature** section, which is where you'll enter the legal signing information of the MLA. The following three optional fields are available:

- **Signing Person**: The name of the person signing the lease agreement
- **Place of Signature**: The location where the lease agreement was signed
- **Date of Signature**: The date when the lease agreement was signed

**Uploading and Tagging PDFs**

All pages within SAP Lease Administration allow users to upload PDF documents and to apply data tagging to any fields by selecting locations on the PDF document.

You can add one or more PDF files to any page of SAP Lease Administration. The document viewer is available by clicking the left-facing two-arrow icon. To upload a document, click on the icon in the middle of the panel and upload the relevant file. Once you've uploaded a file, you'll have the following options:

- Use the page navigation buttons to navigate through the file.
- Use the **Document** dropdown list to select the file to be viewed.
- Adjust the zoom level of the document.
- Click the **Cancel** icon (an X) to delete the document.
- Click the **Upload** icon (up arrow) to upload additional files.
- Click the **Download** icon (down arrow) to download the file being viewed.

SAP Lease Administration's data tagging functionality allows you to highlight areas of attached PDFs. Along with data tagging, users can also enter a comment for each field.

To add a data tag, follow these steps:

1. Click on the **Add Tag** icon to open the document panel.
2. Locate the information on the PDF document that needs to be tagged.
3. Create a box around the relevant information. As a result, an icon appears next to the associated field for each created tag as shown in Figure 7.5.

To add a comment, follow these steps:

1. Click on the **Comment** icon to open a dialog box where you may enter a comment related to that field. For example, you might add a note about the page where information may be found (e.g., "Information found on page 2/12") or the internal user this field was reviewed by (e.g., "reviewed by VP leasing").
2. Click on **Submit** to save the comment along with the associated user name, date, and time stamp for internal audit purposes.

Figure 7.5 Data Tagging

The next page of the MLA creation workflow is the **Partners** page, shown in Figure 7.6. On this page, a user with the right security role (such as a lease administrator, for example) may add applicable lenders and suppliers to the master lease agreement. Lenders and suppliers are added for informational purposes only at this level. The lists of lenders and suppliers are based on the vendors configured in the ERP system for the company codes in the selected lease area. Lessors are added at the contract level.

Lease administrators may also add users that should be notified at each MLA event (such as a request for approval) in the **User Notifications** section, as shown in Figure 7.6. Note that any user with the appropriate role and access to the MLA or contract can perform the MLA or contract action; this section only determines who will *receive* the notification.

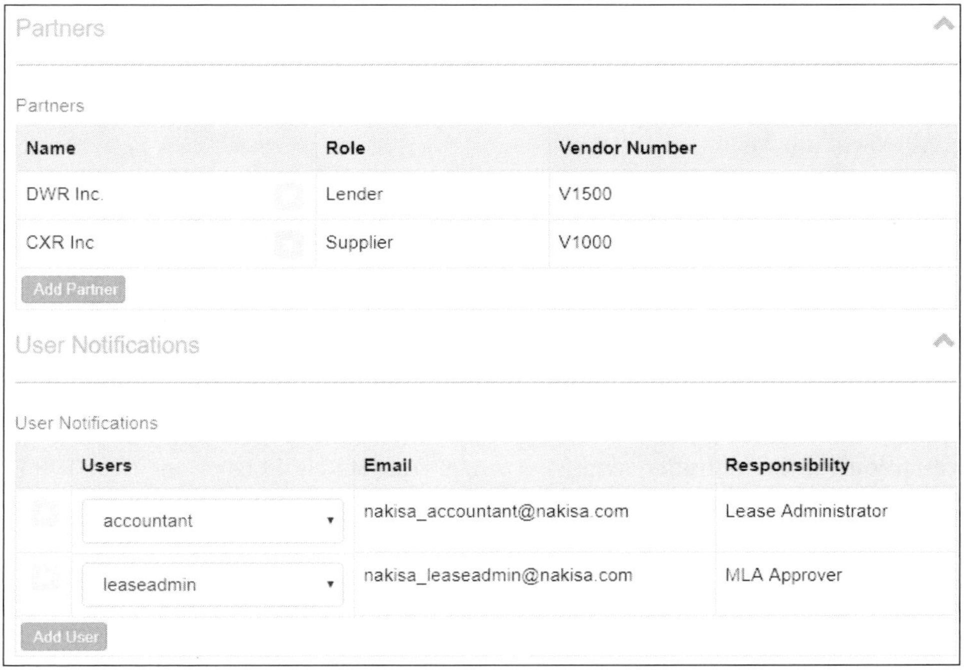


**Figure 7.6** Partners Page of the MLA

### 7.1.2 Approving an MLA

When the MLA has been completed with all of the required information, the user with the right security role (e.g., the lease administrator) must request approval for the MLA by clicking on **Send to Approval** button found at the top of all pages within the MLA.

Once sent for approval, the *master agreement status* will change from "Define" to "Waiting for Approval." The user with the approval security role (e.g., the VP of leasing), who has been added to the **User Notification** section of the MLA in the **Partners** tab, will automatically receive an alert in the notification center as well as an email notification.

Once ready for approval, the approver has the following options:

- Approve the MLA
- Discard the MLA
- Send the MLA back to be reworked
- Call back the approval if no contract has been added (available for approved MLAs only)

Once the MLA has been approved, the master agreement status will change from "Waiting for Approval" to "Active," and new contracts may now be added under the umbrella of this MLA.

## 7.2 Contracts and Lease Components

Once an MLA has been approved, users such as lease administrators can create contracts; the list of contracts belonging to an MLA will appear in the **Contract List** page of the MLA.

Contracts make up all the financial information of a lease and include the terms and conditions of the identified asset(s). A single contract could have one or multiple lease components; the contract identifies the general information of a lease.

The asset is defined as a collection of *lease components* in SAP Lease Administration. Lease components identify the specific terms and conditions for the lease asset(s). For example, if a lease contract exists for trucks and trailers from the same lessor, and both have unique terms and conditions, then in SAP Lease Administration, one contract may be set up with two different lease components (one for trucks and the other for the trailers), and each of their terms and conditions can be set up individually.

Note that you can enter contracts and lease components manually in SAP Lease Administration, or alternatively mass upload the contracts and lease components via an Excel file.

In this section, we'll walk through manually creating contracts and lease components in SAP Lease Administration.

### 7.2.1 Creating a New Contract

Once you've created an MLA, follow these steps to create a new contract:

1. From the MLA level, click the **Context Menu** button (three vertical dots) and then click **Create Contract**.

2. Select the year that the contract starts from the **Year** dropdown list, as shown in Figure 7.7.
3. The data in the **Lease Area** and **Lease Business Unit** fields are inherited from the MLA.
4. If the company code was not set in the MLA, then specify it in the **Company** field.
5. Based on the configuration defined by the system administrator, the data in the **Contract ID** field is generated based on the selected year and company code.
6. Enter a name for the contract in the **Contract Name** field.
7. Click **Submit**.



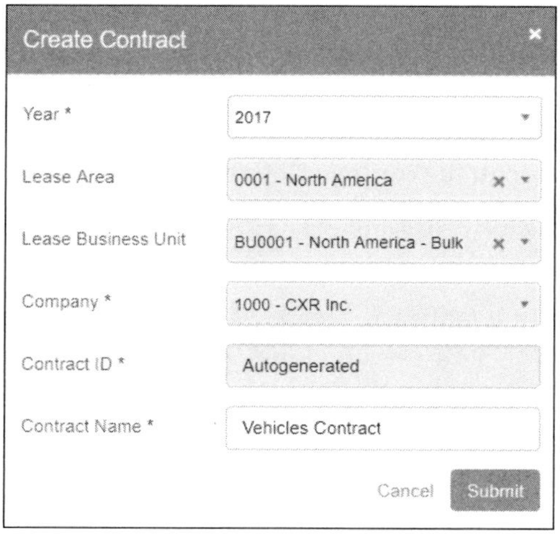


**Figure 7.7** Creating a New Contract

Once the contract has been created, five new pages will appear on the left-hand side of the screen:

1. **Lease Determination**: Identify the lease type.
2. **Definition**: Specify contract definitions such as hierarchy (if not defined at the MLA), legal information, and additional reporting details.
3. **Partners**: Define the lessor, supplier, and user notifications.
4. **Accounting**: Define the entry of financing terms of the lease along with cost objects.
5. **Lease Component List**: View all the lease components that belong to the contract.

Let's walk through the actions you'll take in each of these pages.

#### Lease Determination

Once a contract has been created, the user with the right security role (such as lease administrators or accountants) must complete the lease determination questionnaire to determine the lease type.

The list of questions available out of the box have been gathered from the Financial Accounting Standards Board (FASB) and the International Accounting Standards Board (IASB) to allow the end users to determine whether the contract being entered is a lease or not; as shown in Figure 7.8, these questions can also help identify whether the lease contains an identified asset, whether it is a service contract, whether the customer has the right to obtain substantially all of the economic benefits from the use of the asset, and so on. Based on the answers provided, SAP Lease Administration displays a suggested lease type on the **Lease Determination** page in the **Lease Type** field. If the lease determination is performed outside of SAP Lease Administration, then this step may be skipped, and the lease type may be selected in the contract **Definition** page.

The five lease types available in SAP Lease Administration are as follows:

- **Lease contract (fix)**
  This lease type identifies that the contract qualifies as a lease. SAP Lease Administration will generate a right-of-use asset (ROU asset) and long-term lease liability once the lease is activated.
- **Lease short-term**
  This lease type identifies that the contract qualifies as a short-term lease. SAP Lease Administration will generate an expense entry once the lease is activated. SAP Lease Administration will *not* generate an ROU asset or lease liability; instead, this lease will be treated as on an accrue-and-pay basis (in other words, the system will generate an accrual entry and make a payment when due). Per International Financial Reporting Standards 16 and Accounting Standards Codification 842 standards, a short-term lease contract has a lease term of 12 months or less. For ASC 842, if no extension or purchase options exist that the lessee is reasonably certain to exercise at lease start, the lease would still be considered a short-term lease.
- **Lease low value**
  This lease type identifies that the asset being leased qualifies as a low-value asset. SAP Lease Administration will generate an expense entry once the lease is activated. SAP Lease Administration will *not* generate an ROU asset or lease liability; this lease will be treated as on an accrue-and-pay basis. Per IFRS 16, a low-value asset has a fair market value of $5,000 or less when new. Per ASC 842, the fair market value of a low-value asset may differ for each company; the threshold is usually defined with an advisory firm.

- **Non-lease service contract**
  This lease type identifies that the contract does not qualify as a lease; however, the contract may be tracked. SAP Lease Administration will generate an expense entry once the lease is activated. SAP Lease Administration will *not* generate an ROU asset or lease liability; instead, this lease will be treated as on an accrue-and-pay basis.
- **Non-lease**
  This lease type identifies that the contract does not qualify as a lease; however, the contract may be tracked. SAP Lease Administration allows users to set up a contract with lease components, but no activation groups or units will be created. This lease type is maintained in the system only for reference purposes.

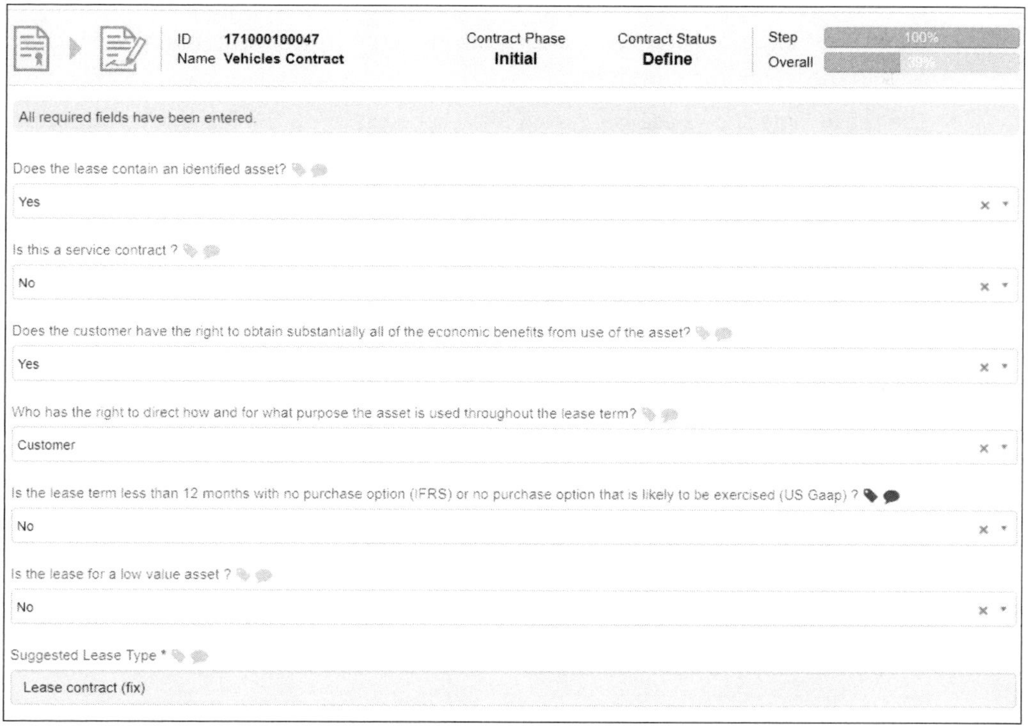


**Figure 7.8** Lease Determination Questionnaire for a Lease Contract (Fix)

### Contract Definitions

Once the lease determination information has been entered, lease administrators or accountants can enter information on the contract's **Definition** page, which is divided into four sections: **General Information**, **Hierarchy**, **Groups**, and **Signature**. Let's look at each section in detail.

The contract identification fields are specified along with the contract currency. The following information is available in the **General Information** section, shown in Figure 7.9:

- The **Contract ID** field shows the generated ID.
- The **Contract Name** may be modified if needed.
- The **Created By** field indicates the user who created the contract.
- The **External Contract Reference** of the contract may be entered; for example, you might populate this field with a purchase order number.
- The **Description** of the contract may be entered.
- The **Validity Period From** and **To** fields are generated by the application based on the earliest expected start date and latest end date from the standard term category in the terms and conditions.
- The **Lease Type** shows the suggested lease type based on the lease determination questionnaire. If lease determination is performed outside of SAP Lease Administration, then users can select the lease type here.
- The **Contract Category** may be selected based on the preconfigured values in the AdminConsole.

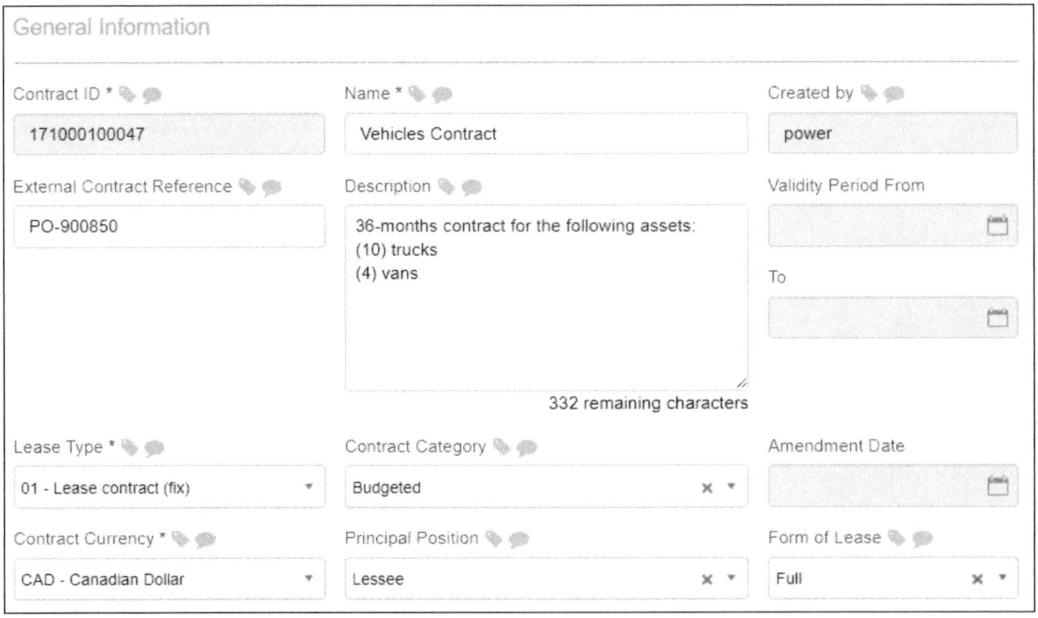


**Figure 7.9** General Information Section in the Contract Definition Page

- The **Amendment Date** is used to indicate whether a lease modification or reassessment was undertaken; this field will display the last date of modification.
- The **Contract Currency** must be defined (if not defined at MLA).
- The **Principal Position** is automatically set to "Lessee."
- The **Form of Lease** may be selected based on the preconfigured values in the AdminConsole.

The **Hierarchy** page shown in Figure 7.10 is where the contract hierarchy is identified, if not already set at the MLA level. If the hierarchy *has* been defined at the MLA, then the contract inherits these details, which cannot be overridden. You can set different values for each contract in any optional fields not previously set in the MLA.



If the optional **Lease Department** and **Lease Group** fields are not set, this information can be set at the contract level. If the **Trading Partner** is specified, this data will be available in all general ledger postings for the contract.

**Figure 7.10** Hierarchy Section in the Contract Definition Page

On the **Groups** page, users can specify additional details that can be used for reporting purposes, internal coding, and/or lease identification. System administrators can modify the captions and list of values in the dropdown menus in the AdminConsole.

As shown in Figure 7.11, two dropdown fields (**Group 1** and **Group 2**) and two free text fields (**Group 3** and **Group 4**) are immediately available out of the box.

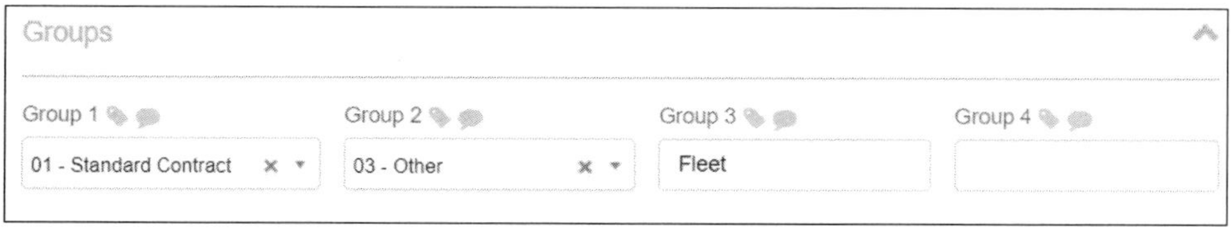


**Figure 7.11** Groups Section in the Contract Definition Page

The final section of the contract **Definitions** page is the **Signature** section, where users may add signing information regarding the contract. The following fields are available:

- **Signing Person**: The name of the person signing the lease agreement
- **Place of Signature**: The location where the lease agreement was signed
- **Date of Signature**: The date when the lease agreement was signed

#### Contract Partners

After the contract **Definition** page comes the contract **Partners** page.

On the **Partners** page, the lease administrator can add applicable lessors and suppliers to the contract. Adding a lessor to the contract is mandatory since this information will be used during posting to identify the vendor, but you can only add one lessor per lease contract. Adding a supplier is optional, since this information will be used for informational purposes only. The dropdown list of lessors and suppliers on this page is loaded from the master data, which is synchronized with the SAP vendor master for the selected company code.

To add lessors and suppliers to the contract, follow these steps:

1. Open the contract and click **Partners** in the left-panel.
2. In the **Partners** section, click **Add Partner**.
3. Search for the required partner and set their role to either "Lessor" or "Supplier."
4. Click **Submit**.

To edit, hover over the row for the partner that was just added and click on the row. The edit form will appear below the table. To add additional contact information, click on **Add Contact**. Enter the valid contact information and click **Submit**. The partner information will be saved, as shown in Figure 7.12.

Lease administrators may also add the users to be notified at each contract event (such as a request for approval). Note that any user with the appropriate role and access to the contract may perform the contract action. This section only determines who will receive the notification.

To add user notifications to the contract, follow these steps:

1. In the **Users** column, select the user that will receive the notification. The **Responsibility** is listed by default in the right column, as shown in Figure 7.13.
2. If required, click **Add User** to add additional users and responsibilities.

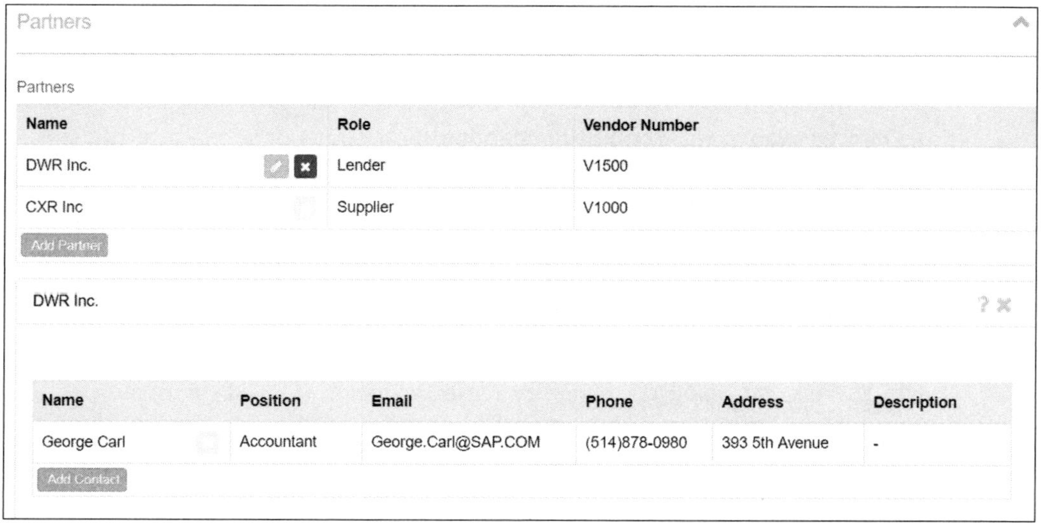


**Figure 7.12** Contacts in the Contract Partners Page

**Figure 7.13** User Notifications in the Contract Partners Page

### Contract Accounting Information

The fourth page you'll see when creating a new contract is the **Contract Accounting Information** page. On this page, users with the right security roles (such as lease administrators or accountants) can enter accounting information for the contract to identify the interest calculation methods and the cost object.

The accounting page is divided into four different sections: **Financing Terms**, **Default Cost Object**, **Payable**, and **Accounting Standards**.

***Financing Terms***

In this section, you'll identify the interest calculation drivers of the contract. Let's walk through the fields available in this section, which are shown in Figure 7.14:

- The **Contract Rate (%)** may be entered if known. In this field, the contract implicit rate, which is provided by the lessor, can be entered. This rate will be used to calculate the *present value of minimum lease payments* (PVMLP) and the periodic accrued interest values. If the rate is not provided by the lessor, this field may be left blank, and the *incremental borrowing rate* (IBR), which is maintained in the AdminConsole, will be used for calculations instead. The IBR will be populated once the lease is assessed based on the company code, validity period, and contract length. Chapter 4, Section 4.3.2, includes additional details on setting up the IBR.

  Note that the **Contract Rate (%)** field is only enabled when the lease type is **Lease contract (fix)**; the field is disabled for short-term leases, low-value leases, non-lease service contracts, and other non-lease contracts.
- Setting the *consumer price index* (CPI) in the **CPI/Indexation** field, which determines the type of indexation, is optional. The values are defined in the AdminConsole.
- Selecting the **Embedded Derivative** checkbox is optional. This field is used for informational purposes only.
- The **Compounding Frequency** identifies the number of times that interest is calculated. Six compounding frequencies are available out of the box: **Daily**, **Monthly**, **Bi-Monthly**, **Quarterly**, **Semi-Annually**, and **Annually**.
- Selecting the **360 Convention** checkbox is optional. This convention assumes a year contains 30 days in a month and 360 days a year. If this checkbox is not selected, the calculation will be based on the actual number of days for each month.
- Select the **Payments in Arrears** checkbox if the terms and conditions in the contract are in arrears (on the last day of the month).

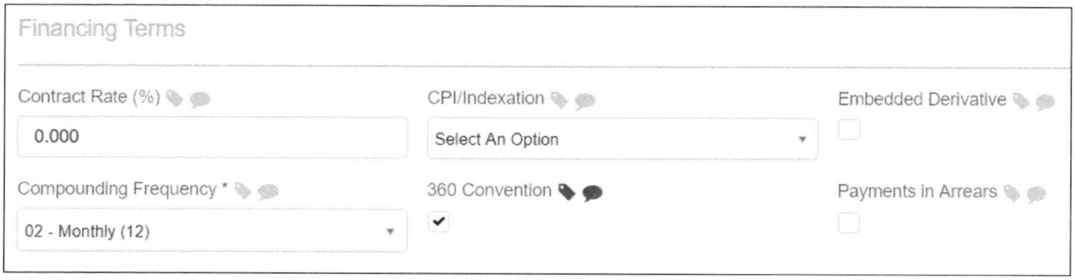


**Figure 7.14** Financing Terms Section of the Contract Accounting Page



### *Default Cost Object*

In this section, you'll set default values for the cost objects related to the posting of the lease. At the activation group level, certain cost objects may be overridden. The following fields are available in this section and shown in Figure 7.15:

- The data in the **Company Code** field is set at either the MLA or contract level. This field cannot be modified and is available for information purposes.
- The default **Cost Center** must be selected. The cost center is an organizational unit within a controlling area that represents a defined location where costs are incurred.

However, some fields in the **Default Cost Object** section are optional, such as:

- The **WBS** (work breakdown structure) field represents a model of the project that organizes project tasks into a hierarchy. The WBS can also be a cost collector for the corporation.
- The **Functional Area** field is used to analyze cost-of-sales accounting. This field allows users to analyze the organization's expenses by functional area (such as finance, marketing, production, and human resources).
- The **Business Area** field is used to differentiate transactions that come from different lines of business in a company.
- To use internal orders in SAP, select the **Track Costs** checkbox and select the **Internal Order Type.** To generate internal orders in SAP, leave the **Internal Order** field empty; SAP Lease Administration will display the internal order value once the order has been created in SAP. To use an existing internal order from SAP, select the required one from the **Internal Order** dropdown menu.

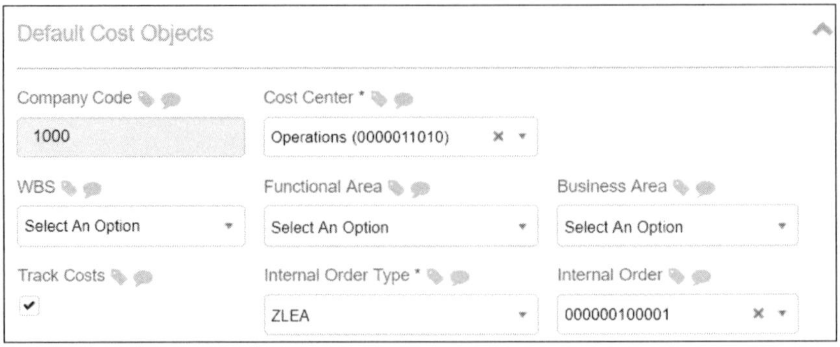


**Figure 7.15** Default Cost Objects Section of the Contract Accounting Page

***Payable***

In the **Payable** section shown in Figure 7.16, you'll be able to choose whether the contract will generate an accounts payable entry directly in the Accounts Payable (AP) module or to the SAP General Ledger (GL) module of SAP ERP.

The following fields are available in this section:

- The **Vendor** field displays the lessor selected on the **Partner** page.
- The **Contract Currency** field displays the currency selected on the **Definition** page.
- The **Generate Vendor Invoices** checkbox determines how payable entries will be posted in SAP. If this checkbox is selected, SAP Lease Administration will generate an entry directly in the AP module, where the vendor accounts payable will be credited with the total payment value of the invoice. If this checkbox is not selected, SAP Lease Administration will make a general ledger posting only, where the credit line item of the journal entry will be offset by a clearing or reconciliation account. If the AP process in place prior to implementing SAP Lease Administration is satisfactory and does not need to change, you should deselect the **Generate Vendor Invoices** checkbox if it had been selected.

In addition, you can set the following fields only if the **Generate Vendor Invoices** checkbox is selected:

- The **Payment Terms** field allows users to select the term for determining when the invoice is due for payment (e.g., pay 30 days after receiving the invoice). This field may be different from the default payment terms of the lessor (vendor).
- The **Tax Code** field specifies the SAP tax code that is assigned to the posting transaction. This information represents the rate of the city/region/province where the goods are used.

- The **Tax Jurisdiction** field specifies the SAP tax jurisdiction that is assigned to the posting transaction. This information represents a geographical area in countries where taxes are levied at more than one level.

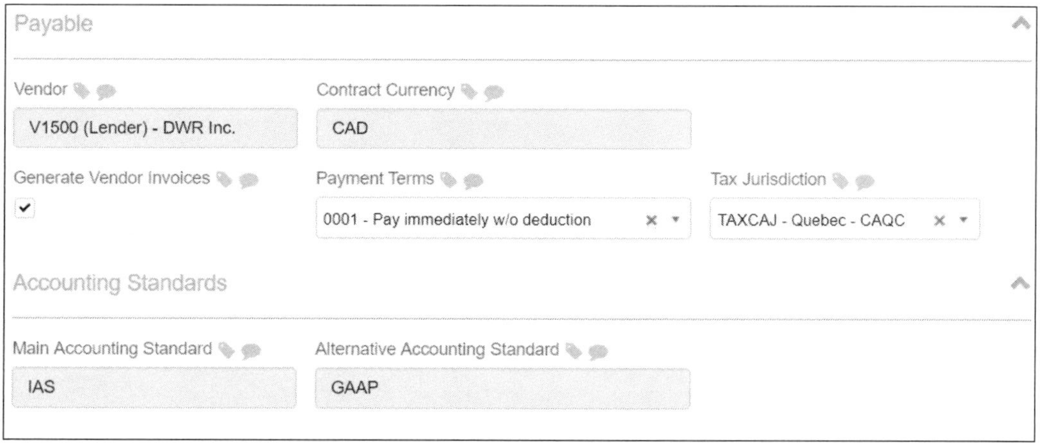


**Figure 7.16** Payable and Accounting Standards Sections of the Contract Accounting Page

***Accounting Standards***

The last section of the contract **Accounting** page is the **Accounting Standards** section, which displays the main and alternate accounting standards for the selected company code, as shown in Figure 7.16. The accounting standards for each company code are configured in the AdminConsole. One company code could be associated with multiple accounting standards depending on the SAP system configuration. SAP Lease Administration supports current and future accounting standards from the IASB (i.e., IAS 17 and IFRS 16) and following United States Generally Accepted Accounting Principles (i.e., ASC 840 and ASC 842).

### 7.2.2 Creating a New Lease Component

Once you've set up the mandatory fields for the contract, you can set up a lease component by following these steps:

1. From the contract level, click the **Context Menu** icon (three vertical dots) and then click **Create Lease Component**.
2. Based on the configuration defined by the system administrator, the data in the **Lease Component ID** field is generated based on the year and company code.
3. Enter a name for the lease component in the **Name** field shown in Figure 7.17.

4. Click **Submit**.

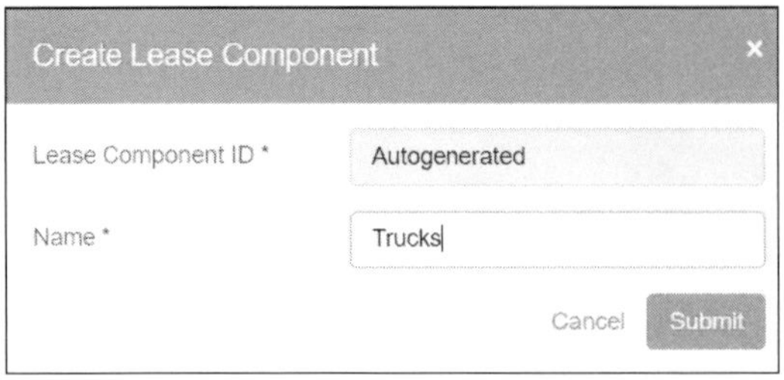


**Figure 7.17** Creating a New Lease Component

Once the lease component has been created, three new pages will appear on the left-hand side of the screen:

- **Definition**: Set the lease component definitions, such as asset class, fair market value, and number of assets.
- **Terms & Conditions**: Define the minimum lease payments and other financial terms and conditions.
- **Activation Group List**: View all the activation groups that belong to the contract and lease component.

Let's walk through the actions you'll take on each of these pages.

### Lease Component Definitions

On the lease **Definition** page, you must identify the type of asset(s) being leased and any carry-over values. The **Definition** page is divided into two different sections: **Definition** and **Carry-Over Balance per Unit**.

In the **Definition** section shown in Figure 7.18, you'll identify the asset(s) being leased and may include additional asset parameters.

The following fields are available in this section:

- The **Lease Component ID** is automatically generated, based on the year and company code.
- Modify the **Name** field if needed.
- The **Quantity** field indicates the number of assets being leased that share the same terms and conditions. The maximum allowed quantity per lease component is 100 units, unless the lease component is managed as a bulk asset (explained later in this section).

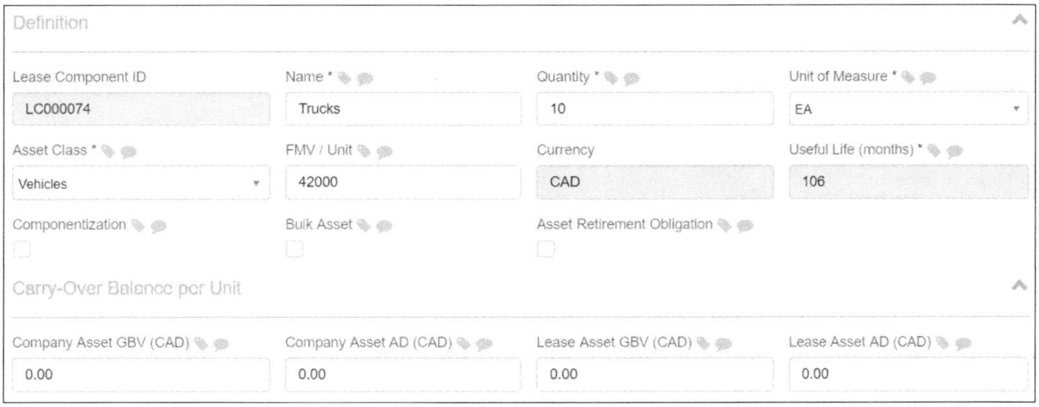


**Figure 7.18** Definition Section of the Lease Component Page

- Select the **Unit of Measure** for the quantity field. This field is configured in the AdminConsole by the user administrator.
- Select the **Asset Class**. This field is configured in the AdminConsole by the user administrator, when SAP Lease Administration asset classes are mapped to SAP asset classes.

  Note that the **Asset Class** field is only available if the lease type is **Lease contract (fix)**; this field is disabled for other types of contracts.
- The **FMV/Unit** is the *fair market value* (FMV) per unit and represents the value of the asset as though the asset were being sold on the market. This field is optional and is used to determine the accounting classification for the asset.

  Note that the **FMV/Unit** field is only available if the lease type is **Lease contract (fix)**; this field is disabled for other types of contracts.
- The **Currency** field displays the currency defined at the MLA or contract level.
- The **Useful Life (Months)** is automatically populated based on the configured values per asset class, where each asset class has a specific useful life associated with it. The useful life represents the timeline used for depreciating an asset.

  Note that the **Useful Life (Months)** field is only available if the lease type is **Lease contract (fix)**; this field is disabled for other types of contracts.
- Select the **Componentization** checkbox to break down the leased asset into subassets. This functionality can be used if a leased asset has multiple subassets with different FMVs and depreciate using different useful lives.

  A good example of componentization is a lease contract for an airplane, where multiple subassets exist such as the engine, seats, and the body. Each of these subassets depreciate using different useful lives and FMV. The componentization functionality generates separate asset numbers for each subasset (in SAP Lease Administration and SAP ERP's fixed asset module, Asset Accounting [FI-AA]) to better track the depreciation. This functionality is only available for finance lease compliance under IFRS 16 and ASC 842, as required by IASB and FASB. With regard to lease liability and the payment schedules, only one entry and one payment schedule will be generated.

If the **Componentization** checkbox is selected, you must set the **Quantity** field to "1" and click on **Add New Sub-Component**, where the following fields must be completed:

- The **Sub-component ID** is automatically generated.
- A **Description** for the subcomponent can be entered.
- The **Quantity** field is automatically set to "1."
- The **PVMLP (%)** must be entered. The PVMLP represents the percent value of the subasset in comparison to the total asset value.
- The **Asset Class** must be selected.
- The **GRV% Split** must be entered. This value represents the percent value of the subasset's *guaranteed residual value* (GRV) in comparison to the total GRV of the asset. If there is no GRV, this field may be set to "0."
- The **Useful Life (Months)** is automatically populated based on the configured values for the asset class.

Click **Submit** and repeat the same steps for all subassets.

- Select the **Bulk Asset** checkbox to indicate that the assets should be managed as a group rather than individual units. If this field is selected, only one asset will be generated when the lease is activated (in SAP Lease Administration and FI-AA). For lease liability and payment schedules, only one entry and one payment schedule will be generated.

  Note that the **Bulk Asset** option is only available if the lease type is **Lease contract (fix)**; this checkbox is disabled for other types of contracts.

- The **Asset Retirement Obligation** checkbox may be selected if the payment amount associated with the retirement of the leased asset at lease end is known.

  Note that the **Asset Retirement Obligation** field is currently available for informational purposes and is only available if the lease type is **Lease contract (fix)**; this checkbox is disabled for other types of contracts.

The second section of the **Definition** page is the **Carry-Over Balance per Unit** section, shown in Figure 7.18.

When bringing in contracts that have already started and were not entered in SAP Lease Administration at inception, the carry-over balance information may be defined in the lease component.

The following fields are available in this section:

- The **Company Asset GBV** field is where the asset's *gross book value* (GBV) on the contract date may be entered into SAP Lease Administration in the company code currency.
- The **Company Asset AD** field is where the *accumulated depreciation* (AD) on the contract date may be entered into SAP Lease Administration in the company code currency.
- The **Lease Asset GBV** field is where the asset's GBV on the contract date may be entered into SAP Lease Administration in the contract currency.
- The **Lease Asset AD** field is where the AD on the contract date may be entered into SAP Lease Administration in the contract currency.

Since both the GBV and AD values are entered, SAP Lease Administration will calculate the *net book value* (NBV), which is the difference between GBV and AD. The NBV will override the asset opening value on the lease activation date.



#### Lease Component Terms and Conditions

Users such as lease administrators and accountants must enter terms and conditions in the lease components. The terms and conditions represent payments that are agreed upon with the lessor in the contract agreement. This information will be pushed down to the activation groups, where users will be able to specify which terms will likely be exercised at lease inception.

Six term types are available in SAP Lease Administration to identify the lease payments:

- **Standard**
  Minimum lease payments. The payments can be fixed (i.e., the same payment amounts throughout the lease term) or variable (i.e., different payment amounts, such as escalating or sawtooth payments, throughout the lease term—variable payments may be imported through the Excel template). This term is mandatory and is the first term that must be set up; once entered, other payment terms are enabled and then defined.

Additional standard terms are available:

- Extension payments: Lease renewal period to prolong the base rent
- Supplemental payments: Additional lease payment amounts, to be added to the base rent
- Reduction: Deduction in lease payment amounts, to be reduced from the base rent

- **Prepaid**
  Prepayment prior to lease commencement.
- **Index**
  The incremental payment due to changes in index/rate can be entered.
- **Incentive**
  In-cash or in-kind incentives, such as free rent period(s).
- **Initial direct costs**
  Initial direct costs (IDC) encountered at lease commencement.
- **Lease end**
  Termination prior to contract end date with a payment amount. Purchase option of the leased asset.

Note that a single lease component can have multiple terms and conditions set up, as shown in Figure 7.19.

| Name | Category | Lease Amount / Unit | Non Lease Amount / Unit | Total Amount / Unit | Contract Currency | Amount Frequency | Payment Frequency | First Payment Date | Last Payment Date | GRV / Unit |
|---|---|---|---|---|---|---|---|---|---|---|
| Base Rent | Standard Term | 500.00 | 50.00 | 550.00 | CAD | OneTime | Monthly | Jan 1, 2017 | Dec 31, 2019 | 0.00 |
| Extension 1 | Standard Term | 475.00 | 50.00 | 525.00 | CAD | OneTime | Monthly | Jan 1, 2020 | Dec 31, 2020 | 0.00 |
| Extension 2 | Standard Term | 475.00 | 50.00 | 525.00 | CAD | OneTime | Monthly | Jan 1, 2021 | Dec 31, 2021 | 0.00 |
| Initial Direct cost (IDC) | Initial Direct Cost | 0.00 | 100.00 | 100.00 | CAD | OneTime | OneTime | Jan 1, 2017 | Jan 1, 2017 | 0.00 |
| Termination Option | Lease End | 800.00 | 0.00 | 800.00 | CAD | OneTime | OneTime | Jul 1, 2018 | Jul 1, 2018 | 0.00 |

**Figure 7.19** Lease Component with Multiple Term Types

Let's set up new standard terms for base rent as an example. Note that, if you set up term types other than standard terms, the page will look identical; however, certain fields will be disabled based on the accounting impact that the term has. For example, if an **IDC** term is selected, the contract has a one-time payment payable at lease commencement. SAP Lease Administration will set the **Amount Frequency** and **Payment Frequency** fields to **One Time** by default, and users will not be allowed to edit these values.

To add a base rent term, follow these steps while referring to Figure 7.20:

1. From the lease component's **Terms & Conditions** page, click on **Add New Term • Standard Term**.
2. In the **Term Type** field, select **Base Rent**.
3. The **Name** field defaults to the **Term Type** ID, but can be modified.
4. Enter the lease payment amount in the **Lease Amount/Unit** field. This value will be used to calculate the present value of the minimum lease payment.

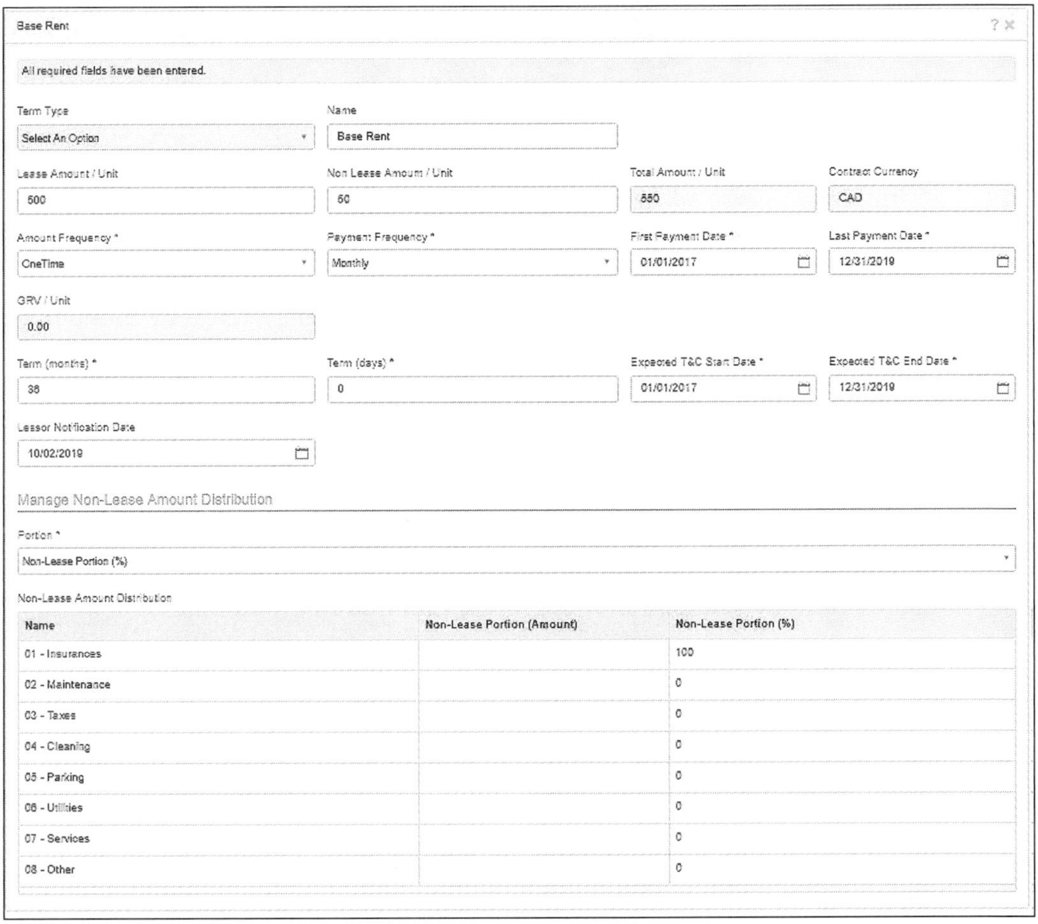


**Figure 7.20** Standard Term with a Non-Lease Amount in the Lease Component Terms & Conditions Page

5. Enter the payment amount related to an expense tied to the lease in the **Non-Lease Amount/Unit** field. This amount will not impact the calculation of the *present value of minimum lease payments* (PVMLP). For example, these amounts may represent payments for services, maintenance, or any other kind of accommodation fee. The non-lease amount must be allocated to expense categories that are defined in the AdminConsole, where each expense category is mapped to a GL account. The amount can be split between different categories through amount or percent.
6. The **Total Amount** field displays the sum of the lease and non-lease amounts entered.
7. The **Contract Currency** field displays the currency selected at the MLA or contract.
8. The **Amount Frequency** field indicated the rate at which the total amount is applied. The list of values available for amount frequency include: **OneTime**, **Day**, **Month**, and **Year**. For example, when an asset with a daily rate is leased, such a drill rig, SAP Lease Administration will calculate the payment amount at the end of the payment period using the daily rate specified.
9. The **Payment Frequency** field indicates how frequently payments will be made. The following values are available for payment frequency: **OneTime**, **Bi-Monthly**, **Monthly**, **Quarterly**, **Semi-Annually**, and **Yearly**.
10. Specify the date of the first payment in the **First Payment Date** field.
11. By default, the system will use the most recent payment in the **Last Payment Date** field.
12. The **GRV/Unit** may be entered if a maximum GRV exists.
13. Enter the lease term in the **Term (months)** and **Term (days)** fields.
14. Enter the expected lease start date in the **Expected T&C Start Date** field.
15. By default, the system will populate the data in the **Expected T&C End Date** field.
16. The **Lessor Notification Date** field may be configured in the AdminConsole to generate notifications to internal users or external contacts to alert them that this lease is nearing its end.

### 7.2.3 Approving Contracts and Lease Components

Once you've entered the lease contract details and completed all the lease components, your contract is ready for approval.

The approval must occur at the contract level and not the lease component level because one contract can have one or more lease components that should be approved only once. Think back to the example of the trucks and trailers leased out where two different lease components belong to the same contract. Once details about the trucks' and trailers' terms and conditions are entered, you must go back to the contract level to approve both the lease components at once.

Thus, to start the approval process, the user with the right security role (such as a lease administrator, for example) must request approval for the contract by clicking on the **Send to Approval** button found at the top of all pages on the contract level. Once sent to approval, the contract's status will change from "Define" to "Waiting for Approval." Another user with the approval security role (e.g., the VP of leasing) who has been added to the **User Notification** section of the contract in the **Partners** tab will automatically receive an alert in the notification center as well as receive an email notification.

Once ready for approval, the approver has the following options, as shown in Figure 7.21, which are available on at the top of all SAP Lease Administration pages by clicking the information icon (the blue "i"):

- Approve the contract
- Discard the contract approval
- Send back the contract to be reworked
- Call back the approval if the activation group has not yet been activated (applies for approved contracts only)

Once the contract has been approved, the contract's status will change from "Waiting for Approval" to "Active." The only remaining step is to close the contract.

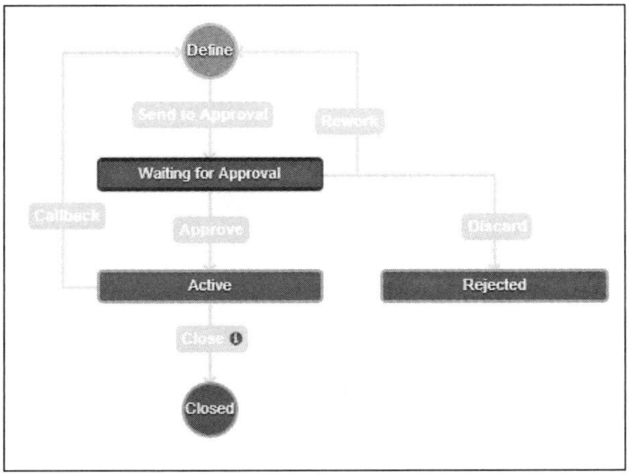


**Figure 7.21** Contract Approval Workflow

## 7.3 Activation Groups and Units

Once a contract has been approved, SAP Lease Administration will automatically generate an activation group, which groups together all the assets or units that share the same terms and conditions.

*Activation groups* are mini-leases within a contract and serve different purposes. For example, referring back to our trucks and trailers example, let's say the total number of trucks was 10, which were received in two batches of five trucks each on different dates from the lessor. In this case, each group of trucks will have a different right-of-use start date (also referred to as the *activation date*) and, hence, different terms and conditions. In SAP Lease Administration, this difference is handled by splitting the activation group in two to reflect the correct activation date for each group of assets. At the activation group level, the financial schedules are accessible for the first time. When a lease is activated in SAP Lease Administration, FI-AA will generate asset ID numbers.

In this section, we'll cover activation group pages and describe the workflow required to activate a lease. Figure 7.22 shows a detailed version of the data hierarchy and the lease lifecycle objects, where a many-to-one relationship exists. An MLA could have multiple contracts: Each contract could have multiple lease components, and each lease component could have multiple activation groups with many units in each group.

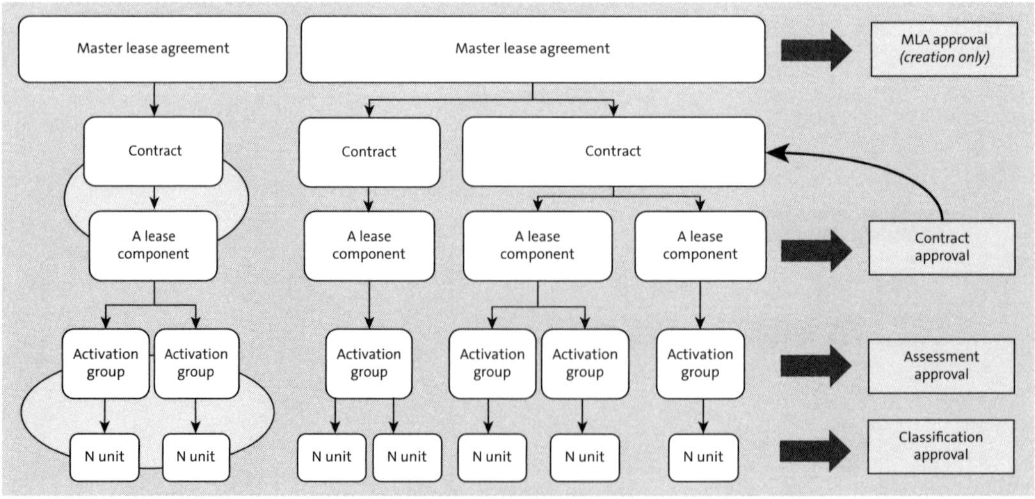


**Figure 7.22** SAP Lease Administration Data Hierarchy

### 7.3.1 Managing an Activation Group

Once an activation group is generated, six new pages appear on the left-hand side of the screen:

1. **Definition**: View the activation group description and the expected activation date.
2. **Accounting**: View all the accounting information entered at the contract for information purposes and edit some fields.
3. **Terms & Conditions**: View all the terms and conditions entered at the lease component. Users can select which ones they are likely to exercise.
4. **Classification**: Review and confirm the system-recommended classification, along with the contract summary.
5. **Unit List**: Maintain the individual asset details.
6. **Charge List**: Enter any additional expense charges.



#### Activation Group Definitions

On the activation group's **Definition** page, shown in Figure 7.23, the following fields are available and are mainly used for reference purposes only:

- The **Name** field defaults to the lease component name we specified when we created the lease component (in Section 7.2.2) but can be modified if needed.
- The **Description** field defaults to the contract description provided but can be modified if needed.
- The **Activation Date** field represents the expected activation date of the lease; the default is the earliest expected terms and conditions start date specified in the lease component terms and conditions. This field is not editable; once the lease is activated, the actual activation date will be determined.
- The **End Date** field represents the expected end date of the lease; the default is the latest expected terms and conditions end date generated in the lease component terms and conditions. This field is not editable; once the lease is terminated, the actual end date will be determined.
- The **Reassessment Effective Date** field is populated if a lease event takes place that requires reassessment. This field is not editable; if a reassessment takes place, the effective date will be determined.

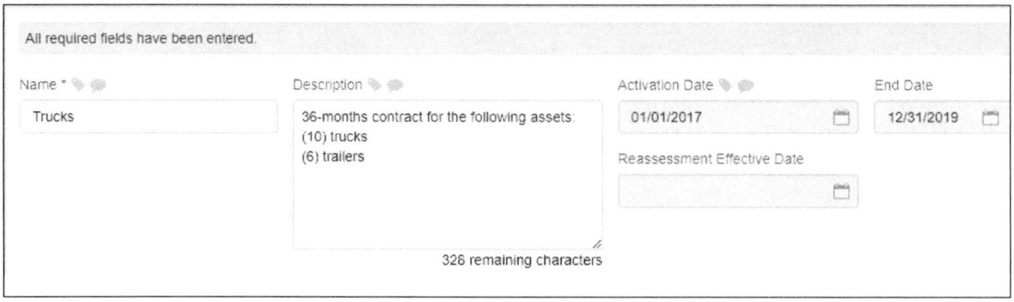


**Figure 7.23** Definition Section of the Activation Group Page

## Activation Group Accounting

On the **Accounting** page, the information from the contract-level **Accounting** tab cascades down to the activation group, where some fields are available for modification.

Note that the same four sections from the **Accounting** page on the contract level (Section 7.2.1) are available. For the **Accounting** page on the activation group level, each section, with its fields, is listed below and shown in Figure 7.24.

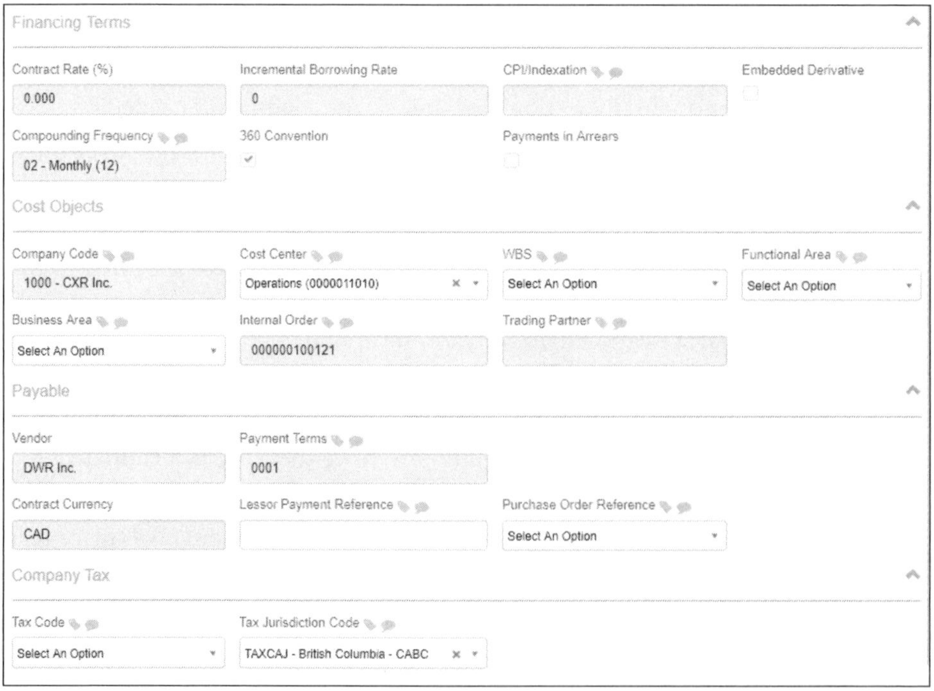


**Figure 7.24** Accounting Page of the Activation Group

#### *Financing Terms*

The following fields cascade down from the contract level and are not editable: **Contract Rate (%)**, **CPI/Indexation**, **Embedded Derivative**, **Compounding Frequency**, **360 Convention**, and **Payments in Arrears**.

Another non-editable field should be mentioned. The **Incremental Borrowing Rate** field is only populated once the activation group has been sent for assessment (Section 7.2.1). Activation group assessment is covered in detail in Section 7.3.2.

#### *Cost Objects*

The following fields cascade down from the contract level and are not editable: **Company Code**, **Internal Order**, and **Trading Partner**.

The following fields cascade down from the contract level and may be edited if needed: **Cost Center**, **WBS**, **Functional Area**, and **Business Area**.

#### *Payable*

The following fields cascade down from the contract level and are not editable: **Vendor**, **Payment Terms**, and **Contract Currency.**

Two editable fields are newly introduced:

- The **Lessor Payment Reference** is a free text field that may be added to include a reference for the payment.
- The **Purchase Order Reference** is a dropdown list of the existing purchase orders belonging to the vendor. If a purchase order related to the lease exists, you may select the purchase order for this field for reference purposes.

#### *Company Tax*

The tax code and tax jurisdiction may be assigned. If assigned in this section, the calculation of the sales tax will be generated after lease activation.

### Activation Group Terms and Conditions

The **Terms & Conditions** page of the activation group lists all the terms and conditions that were entered at the lease component level. You can see the details of each term by clicking on the term; details will appear at the bottom of the page, as shown in Figure 7.25.

You can select the terms and conditions that are likely to be exercised. Based on what you select, SAP Lease Administration will generate the calculation of the present value of minimum lease payments and the financial schedules once you click the

**Send to Assessment** button. Terms and conditions that are *not* likely to be exercised are kept for reference purposes but can also be used later for reassessment if terms are later exercised at any point in the lease lifecycle. Instructions for assessing an activation group are described in Section 7.3.2.

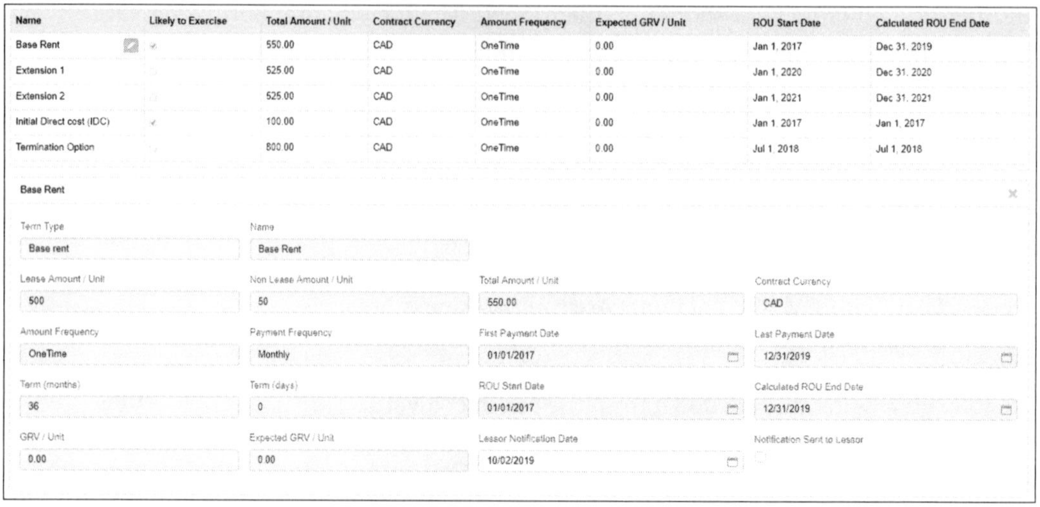


**Figure 7.25** Terms & Conditions Page of the Activation Group (Base Rent Term Type)

### Activation Group Classification

The **Classification** page of the activation group includes the accounting classification generated SAP Lease Administration; you must confirm this classification, which we'll cover in Section 7.3.2. As shown in Figure 7.26, this page is divided into three different sections: **Classification**, **Carry-Over Balance per Unit**, and **Contract Classification Summary**.

In the **Classification** section, the company code accounting standards are displayed with an automatically populated "system classification." The fields and their definitions are as follows:

- The **Main Accounting Standard** field displays the accounting standards assigned to the particular company code in the AdminConsole.
- The **System Classification** field represents the system-recommended classification of the lease. The classification will default to the actual lease type for the following three lease types: short-term leases (**Lease Short-Term**), low-value leases (**Lease Low Value**), and non-lease service contracts (**Non-Lease Service Contract**). For **Lease Contract (Fix)**, SAP Lease Administration will default the lease classification to

**Finance** for IFRS 16. The bright line test will be applied to all other standards to identify the classification (either "operating" or "finance" lease for ASC 842 and either "operating" or "capital" lease for IAS 17 and ASC 842). The bright line test threshold is configured in the AdminConsole.

- The **Confirm Classification** field allows you to confirm the classification of the lease. SAP Lease Administration does not force you to select the same classification as the **System Classification** field. For example, if the system classification is "operating" for an ASC 842 lease, and you select "finance" as a classification, the system will not block you; however, this information will be stored in the audit log and it must be directed through the right approval workflow.
- The **Last Classification Date** field is a system-generated date that tracks the last day that the lease was classified.

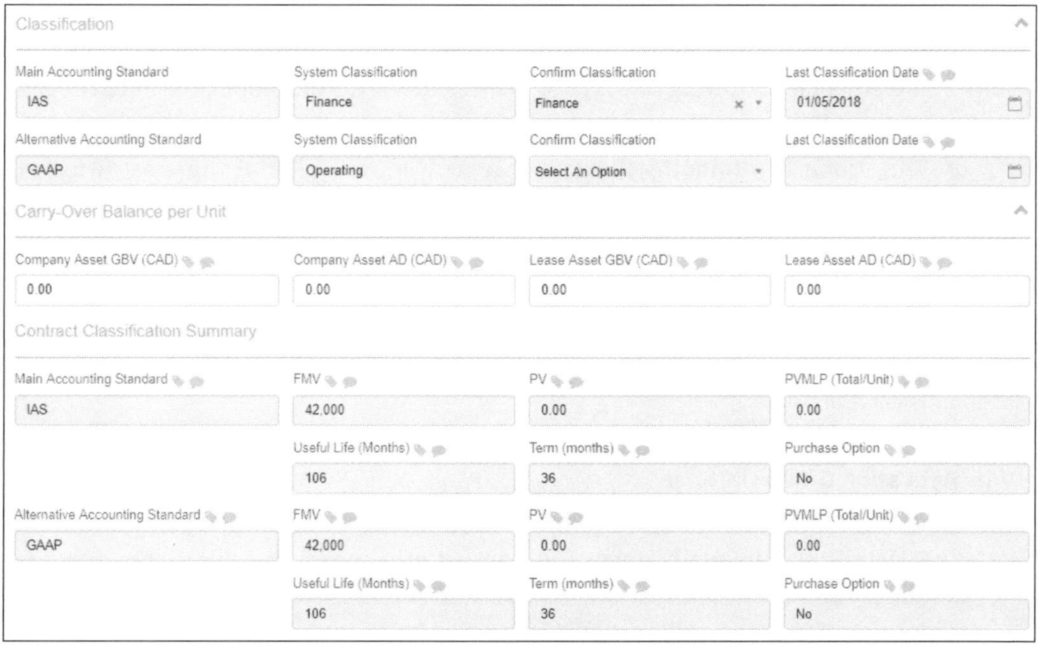


**Figure 7.26** Classification Page of an Activation Group

In the **Carry-Over Balance per Unit** section, carry-over balance information that that has been added in the lease component definition page is displayed and can be modified if needed. Refer to our earlier discussion about carry-over information in Section 7.2.2.

In the **Contract Classification Summary** section, SAP Lease Administration summarizes the information you have provided. The following fields are available but not editable:

- The **Main Accounting Standard** field displays the accounting standard configured for the company code.
- The **FMV** field represents the FMV/unit entered on the lease component definition page (Section 7.2.2).
- The **PV** field represents the *present value* (PV) calculated based on the terms and conditions that are likely to be exercised, expected GRV, and the contract rate (if not entered, the incremental borrowing rate is used). This field will only be populated once the activation group has been sent for assessment.
- The **PVMLP (Total/Unit)** field represents the *present value of minimum lease payment* (PVMLP) per unit, calculated based on the terms and conditions that are likely to be exercised, the maximum GRV, and the contract rate (if not entered, the incremental borrowing rate is used). This field will only be populated once the activation group has been sent for assessment.
- The **Useful Life (Months)** field represents the useful life of the asset, which is assigned to the asset class.
- The **Term (months)** field represents the total number of months that make up the lease term. This field combines the total length of the terms and conditions that are likely to be exercised.
- The **Purchase Option** field indicates whether a purchase option is associated with the lease.

### Activation Group Unit List

On this page, all the assets belonging to the activation group are listed, and individual unit details may be maintained. The unit list grid shown in Figure 7.27 provides a summary of the unit information. Users can click on the edit icon (pencil) to view the unit information in detail, as shown in Figure 7.28. The following fields are available:

- The data in the **Unit ID** field is automatically generated by SAP Lease Administration.
- The **Name** field is defaulted to the lease component name, but you can modify it as necessary.
- The **Reference ID** is a free text field which may be entered.
- The **GBV** field is read from FI-AA. This field is non-editable and is populated once the lease has been activated.

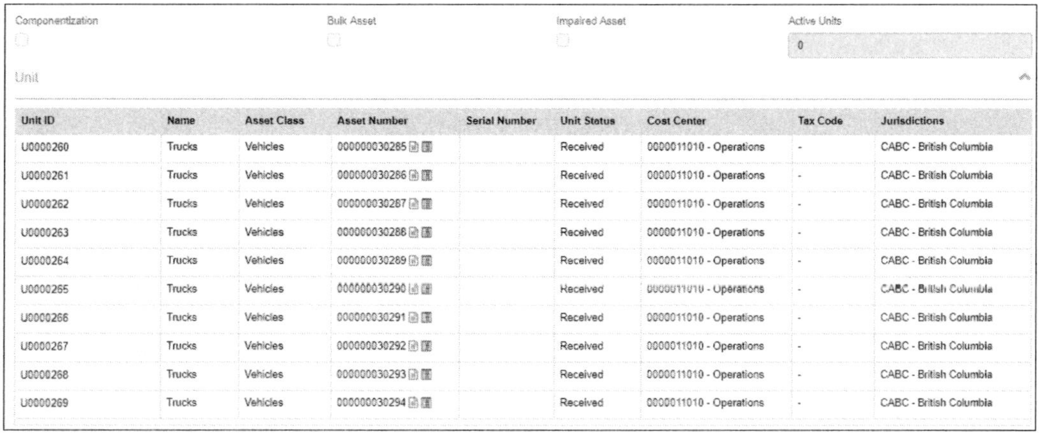


| Unit ID | Name | Asset Class | Asset Number | Serial Number | Unit Status | Cost Center | Tax Code | Jurisdictions |
|---|---|---|---|---|---|---|---|---|
| U0000260 | Trucks | Vehicles | 000000030285 | | Received | 0000011010 - Operations | - | CABC - British Columbia |
| U0000261 | Trucks | Vehicles | 000000030286 | | Received | 0000011010 - Operations | - | CABC - British Columbia |
| U0000262 | Trucks | Vehicles | 000000030287 | | Received | 0000011010 - Operations | - | CABC - British Columbia |
| U0000263 | Trucks | Vehicles | 000000030288 | | Received | 0000011010 - Operations | - | CABC - British Columbia |
| U0000264 | Trucks | Vehicles | 000000030289 | | Received | 0000011010 - Operations | - | CABC - British Columbia |
| U0000265 | Trucks | Vehicles | 000000030290 | | Received | 0000011010 - Operations | - | CABC - British Columbia |
| U0000266 | Trucks | Vehicles | 000000030291 | | Received | 0000011010 - Operations | - | CABC - British Columbia |
| U0000267 | Trucks | Vehicles | 000000030292 | | Received | 0000011010 - Operations | - | CABC - British Columbia |
| U0000268 | Trucks | Vehicles | 000000030293 | | Received | 0000011010 - Operations | - | CABC - British Columbia |
| U0000269 | Trucks | Vehicles | 000000030294 | | Received | 0000011010 - Operations | - | CABC - British Columbia |

**Figure 7.27** Unit List Grid of the Activation Group

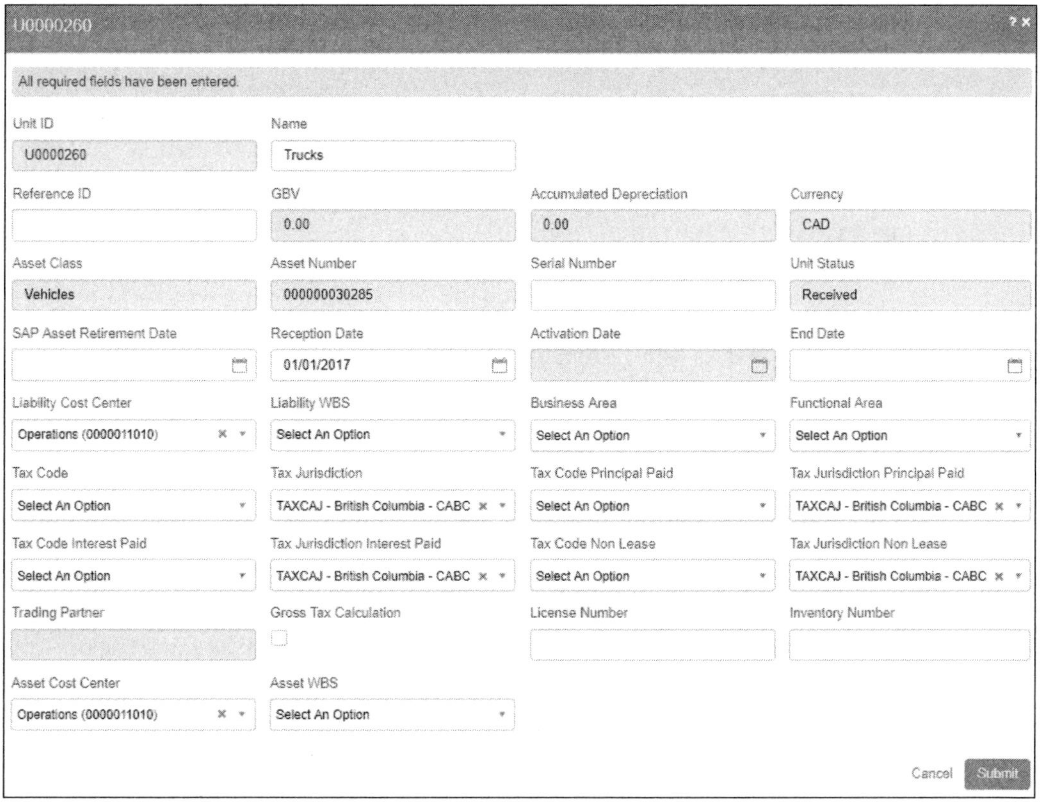


**Figure 7.28** Details Maintained at the Unit Level

- The **Accumulated Depreciation** field is read from FI-AA. This field is non-editable and is populated once the lease has been activated and the asset depreciation postings are produced.
- The **Currency** field displays the currency defined in the MLA or contract.
- The **Asset Class** field displays the asset class defined in the lease component **Definition** page.
- The **Asset Number** field is read from FI-AA. This field is non-editable and is populated once the lease has been activated.
- The **Serial Number** is a free text field that may be edited.
- The **Unit Status** field is set by SAP Lease Administration. The following statuses are available:
  - **Received**: Once the reception date is entered.
  - **Activated**: Once the activation group is activated.
  - **Casualty**: Once a casualty event has been entered.
  - **Purchased**: When a purchase option term is applied.
  - **Returned**: Once the returned date is entered.
  - **Replaced**: Once a unit replacement event has been entered for a selected unit.
  - **Cancelled**: If all of the units in the activation group were never received, and the user cancels the activation group.
- The **SAP Asset Retirement Date** is automatically set when an asset is returned or purchased.
- The **Reception Date** is the date that goods are received or are ready to be used.
- The **Activation Date** is the date selected to activate the activation group.
- The **End Date** represents the termination date of a leased asset.
- The **Cost Center** is set by default to the value defined in the activation group but may be modified if needed. The same concept applies for **WBS**, **Business Area**, and **Functional Area** fields.
- The **Tax Code** field specifies the SAP tax code assigned to the posting transaction.
- The **Tax Jurisdiction** field specifies the SAP tax jurisdiction assigned to the posting transaction. If this field is set and the **Generate Vendor Invoices** checkbox (see Section 7.2.1) was enabled for the contract, the tax jurisdiction will be generated in the payment posting.

- If the following fields are set, SAP Lease Administration will calculate the tax amount for the principal paid and generate the posting for it (this applies if the **Generate Vendor Invoices** checkbox is selected):
  - **Tax Code Principal Paid**
  - **Tax Jurisdiction Principal Paid**
- If the following fields are set, SAP Lease Administration will calculate the tax amount for interest and generate the posting for it (this applies if the **Generate Vendor Invoices** checkbox is selected):
  - **Tax Code Interest Paid**
  - **Tax Jurisdiction Interest Paid**
- If the following fields are set, SAP Lease Administration will calculate the tax amount for the non-lease payments and generate the posting for it (this applies if the **Generate Vendor Invoices** checkbox is selected):
  - **Tax Code Non Lease**
  - **Tax Jurisdiction Non Lease**
- The **Gross Tax Calculation** checkbox will allow SAP Lease Administration to calculate the tax amount for the principal, interest, and non-lease amount if selected.
- The **Trading Partner** field displays partner selected in the MLA or contract.
- The **License Number** is a free text field that may be edited and is passed to SAP ERP.
- The **Inventory Number** is a free text field that may be edited and is passed to SAP ERP.

#### Activation Group Charge List

This page is used to enter one-time charges, as needed, once a lease has been activated.

*One-time charges* are expenses that are encountered throughout the lease lifecycle that had not been accounted for during lease creation. Those charges do not impact the value of the lease liability and the ROU asset; they simply are extra expense charges tied to the lease. For example, going back to our trucks and trailers example, an additional maintenance charge may be levied as one-time charge if, for example, a truck has a flat tire.

To enter a one-time charge, follow these steps while referring to Figure 7.29:

1. Click on **Add Charge**; a new popup window will appear.
2. Enter the name of the charge in the **Name** field.

3. In the **Charge Type** field, identify to which general ledger expense category this one-time charge would be applied. This list is the same as the one used in the lease component terms and conditions (see Section 7.2.2).
4. Input the expected payment date in the **Due Date** field.
5. Input the payment value in the **Amount** field.
6. In the **Unit** field, select the asset that is related to this one-time charge. You'll be able to track the additional charges per unit.
7. You can add additional details in the **Description** field, as necessary.
8. Click on **Submit**.

Once submitted, a user with the right security role may post or delete this one-time charge. If posted, the journal entry will be available in SAP.

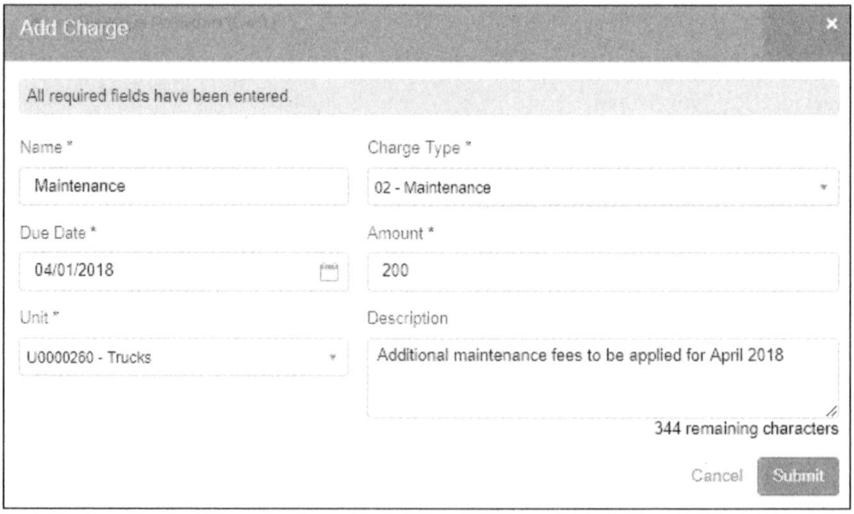


**Figure 7.29** Adding a One-Time Charge

### 7.3.2 Activating a Lease

Before a lease becomes active, the activation group must go through multiple approval steps, as shown in Figure 7.30. Let's walk through the different steps required to activate an activation group.

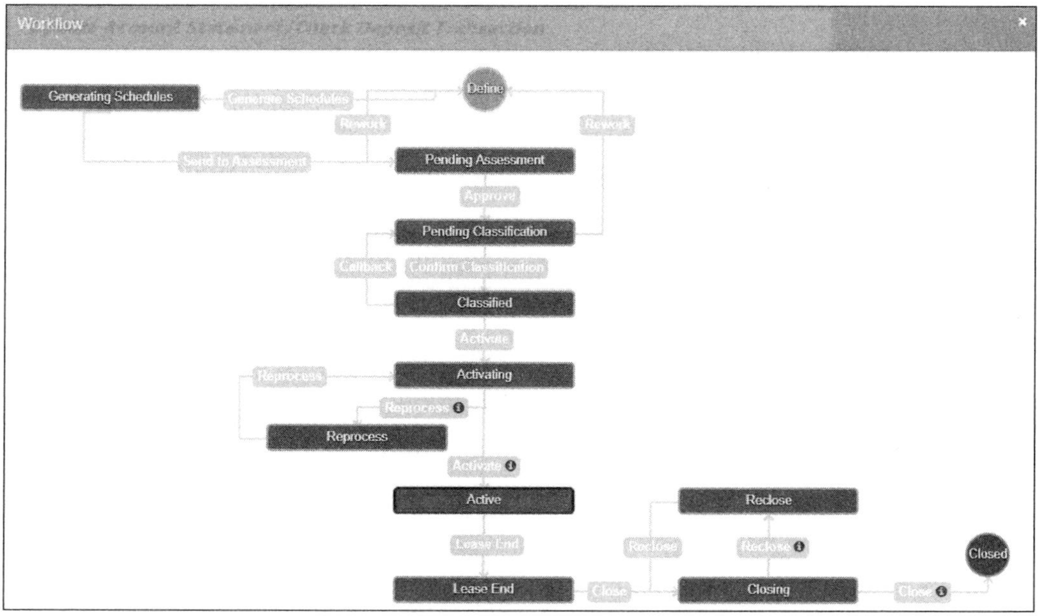


**Figure 7.30** Activation Group Approval Workflow

## Assessing and Approving Activation Groups

Once you select the terms and conditions likely to be exercised at the activation group level, you can generate financial schedules by clicking on the **Send to Assessment** button, which is available on the top of all pages for the activation group.

Clicking on this button will also send email notifications to the users that are responsible for assessment approvals (if configured and if users have been added on the **Partners** page). Once sent for assessment, the activation group status will change from "Define" to "Pending Classification"; at that time, you may access financial schedules by clicking on the context menu (three vertical dots) and choosing **View Schedules**. The **Financial Schedules** tab will open, as shown in Figure 7.31.

On the left, the **Level** dropdown menu allows you to select on which level to view the schedules. The lowest level available is the individual asset level; the schedules are also available at the activation group, lease component, and contract level.

The **Standard** dropdown menu allows you to select the accounting standard. The standards available are the ones set up for the particular company code; for example, if the company code is set up for both IFRS 16 and ASC 842, then the schedules for both standards will be available.

Level: Trucks - U0000260 ▾ | Standard: IFRS Finance ▾ | View: Total Payments - Accounting ▾ | Year: All Years ▾ | Refresh | Export to Excel

| | | | | | Total Payments Month-end Closing | | |
|---|---|---|---|---|---|---|---|
| Period Count | Period Month Start Date | Period Payment Date | Standard Term Total Payment (CAD) | Standard Term 2 Total Payment (CAD) | Prepaid Total Payment (CAD) | Index Total Payment (CAD) | Incentive Total Payment (CAD) |
| 1 | 01/01/2017 | 01/01/2017 | 550.00 | 0.00 | 0.00 | 0.00 | 0.00 |
| 2 | 02/01/2017 | 02/01/2017 | 550.00 | 0.00 | 0.00 | 0.00 | 0.00 |
| 3 | 03/01/2017 | 03/01/2017 | 550.00 | 0.00 | 0.00 | 0.00 | 0.00 |
| 4 | 04/01/2017 | 04/01/2017 | 550.00 | 0.00 | 0.00 | 0.00 | 0.00 |
| 5 | 05/01/2017 | 05/01/2017 | 550.00 | 0.00 | 0.00 | 0.00 | 0.00 |
| 6 | 06/01/2017 | 06/01/2017 | 550.00 | 0.00 | 0.00 | 0.00 | 0.00 |
| 7 | 07/01/2017 | 07/01/2017 | 550.00 | 0.00 | 0.00 | 0.00 | 0.00 |
| 8 | 08/01/2017 | 08/01/2017 | 550.00 | 0.00 | 0.00 | 0.00 | 0.00 |
| 9 | 09/01/2017 | 09/01/2017 | 550.00 | 0.00 | 0.00 | 0.00 | 0.00 |
| 10 | 10/01/2017 | 10/01/2017 | 550.00 | 0.00 | 0.00 | 0.00 | 0.00 |
| 11 | 11/01/2017 | 11/01/2017 | 550.00 | 0.00 | 0.00 | 0.00 | 0.00 |

**Figure 7.31** Financial Schedules Tab

The **Year** dropdown menu allows you to view the schedules for one year only or for all years of the lease term.

The **View** dropdown menu allows you to view different financial schedules in either **Accounting** or **Treasury** view. The **Accounting** view generates schedules based on calendar month-end closings. The **Treasury** view generates schedules based on lease accrual periods. The following schedules are available for all views:

- **Total Payment**: This schedule displays the expected payment amounts throughout the lease lifecycle. The schedule separates the payments based on the different terms defined.
- **Liability**: This schedule provides a breakdown of the lease liability on periodic basis by showing the principal liability opening balance, month-end principal paid, month-end accrued interest, and principal liability closing balance.
- **Non-Lease**: This schedule displays the expected non-lease payment amounts throughout the lease lifecycle. The schedule separates the payments based on the different terms defined.
- **Posting**: This schedule provides a view of the posted and open periods for the particular lease contract. This schedule only becomes enabled once the lease is activated.

- **Asset Transition:** This schedule provides a breakdown of the asset depreciation schedule on a periodic basis at the unit level in company code currency. This schedule includes the closing gross book value (GBV), opening accumulated depreciation (AD), depreciation, closing accumulated depreciation (AD), and net book value (NBV).

  For ASC 842 operating leases, the guidance from FASB mandates that the ROU asset amortization should be the difference between the straight-line lease expense and interest accretion. For IFRS 16 finance and ASC 842 finance leases, SAP Lease Administration will generate the schedules based on straight-line depreciation method where all periods will have the same depreciation value.
- **All Columns**: This schedule provides a view of all the schedules listed above combined together in one view.



Once a user with the right role has reviewed the schedules and concluded that the right numbers are generated based on the terms and conditions, then the activation group may be approved by clicking on **Approve** on top of any page of the activation group. Once approved, the activation group status will change from "Pending Assessment" to "Pending Classification." If a mistake had occurred and the user forgot to include a term and condition, then the **Rework** button may be used to return the activation group to the "Define" status.

#### Classifying an Activation Group

Once a lease has been assessed and SAP Lease Administration has generated the system classification, you must confirm the classification of the activation group by following these steps:

1. From the **Classification** page, select a value from the **Confirm Classification** dropdown menu if it is not defaulted by the system.
2. Click on **Confirm Classification** on top of the page.

Once confirmed, the activation group's status will change from "Pending Classification" to "Classified."

#### Activating an Activation Group

Once the lease has been assessed and classified, a user must enter the date the assets are received. This step is required for tangible assets to indicate the date at which the lessor has delivered the leased items.

The reception date of an asset can be set in one of two ways:

- You can manually enter the reception date for each unit by going through the unit details (Section 7.3.1).
- You can mass-update reception dates for all units in an activation group by clicking on the context menu (three vertical dots) and selecting **Set Reception Date**. Select and submit the relevant date.

After all the activation groups belonging to a contract have been classified and the reception date has been entered, then the activation group may be activated by clicking on the **Activate** button on the top of the page.

A new popup window will appear with the following dates:

- **Activation Date**: This date defaults to the expected start date of the lease based on the terms and conditions but may be modified if needed. This date represents the date on which the asset will be created and capitalized in FI-AA.
- **Posting Date**: This date defaults to the system date but may be modified if needed. This date represents the date on which the journal entry is posted to the general ledger.
- **Document Date**: This date defaults to the expected start date of the lease based on the terms and conditions but may be modified if needed. This date represents the date on which the journal entry is issued.

Once the dates are submitted, SAP Lease Administration will activate the lease; the activation group status will change from "Classified" to "Active," and the following postings will be generated:

- Initial recognition entry of the ROU asset and lease liability: To access the initial recognition entry, click on the document icon next to the generated asset number on the unit list page of the activation group, as shown in Figure 7.32, which also allows you to drill down to SAP (see Figure 7.33). The journal entry of the asset recognition will generate the following line items:
  - Dr. ROU Asset (B/S)
  - Cr. Asset Clearing (B/S)
- The journal entry of the lease liability will generate the following line items:
  - Dr. Asset Clearing (B/S)
  - Cr. ROU LT Liability (B/S)

- Asset capitalization in SAP, where an asset number is generated in SAP and visible in SAP Lease Administration: A user may drill down to FI-AA by clicking on the document icon next to the asset number, as shown in Figure 7.34.

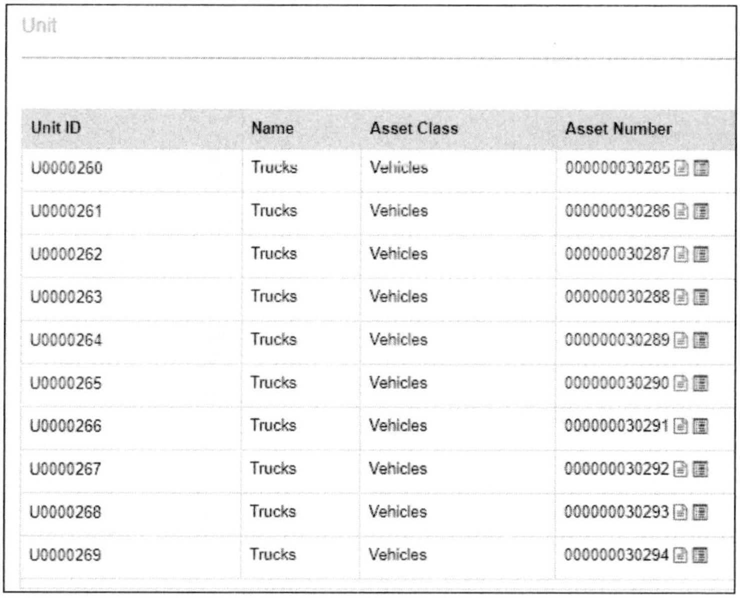

Unit

| Unit ID | Name | Asset Class | Asset Number |
| --- | --- | --- | --- |
| U0000260 | Trucks | Vehicles | 000000030285 |
| U0000261 | Trucks | Vehicles | 000000030286 |
| U0000262 | Trucks | Vehicles | 000000030287 |
| U0000263 | Trucks | Vehicles | 000000030288 |
| U0000264 | Trucks | Vehicles | 000000030289 |
| U0000265 | Trucks | Vehicles | 000000030290 |
| U0000266 | Trucks | Vehicles | 000000030291 |
| U0000267 | Trucks | Vehicles | 000000030292 |
| U0000268 | Trucks | Vehicles | 000000030293 |
| U0000269 | Trucks | Vehicles | 000000030294 |

**Figure 7.32** List of Units with Drilldown to SAP ERP

Document(s)

Document: Liability - 010000402110002017

| | | | |
| --- | --- | --- | --- |
| Document Number | 0100004021 | Status | Posted |
| Fiscal Year | 2017 | Company Code | 1000 |
| Document Date | 01/01/2017 | Posting Date | 12/01/2017 |
| Period Count | 0 | Reference | 171000100055 |
| Currency | CAD | Ledger Group | IAS |

| Item | Payment | Account | Description | Amount | Currency |
| --- | --- | --- | --- | --- | --- |
| 1 | Debit | 0000159999 | AA-Asset Clearing | 17,676.05 | CAD |
| 2 | Credit | 0000250000 | ROU LT Liability | 17,676.05 | CAD |

**Figure 7.33** Lease Liability Recognition Entry

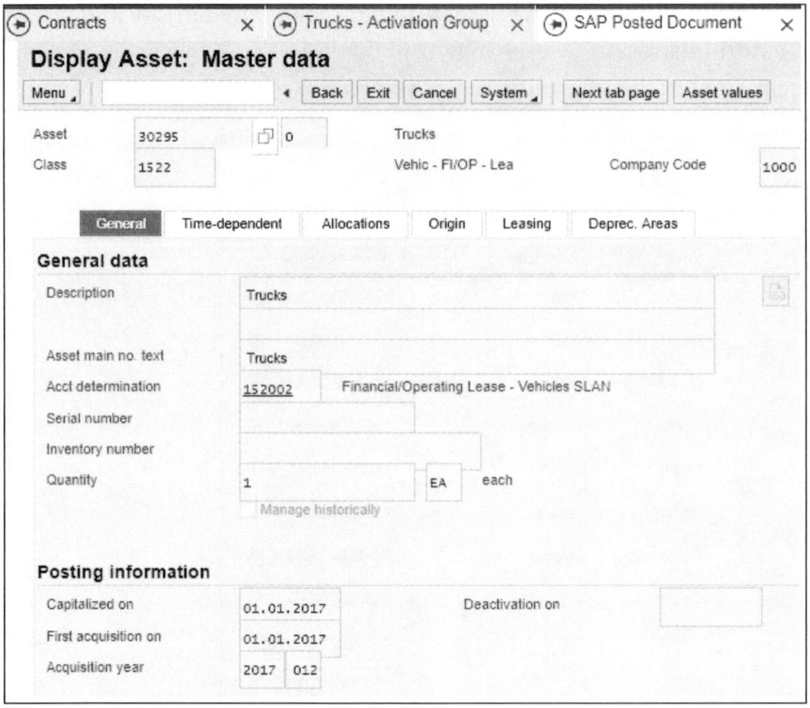


**Figure 7.34** Drilldown to SAP ERP FI-AA

## Posting Journal Entries for an Activation Group

Once the activation group has been activated, future periodic postings are enabled. To access the postings, click on the context menu and select **View Postings**. A new tab will appear with the available postings for the activation group. Postings are scheduled through the job scheduler available in the AdminConsole, but you can also run the postings manually. Postings may be set to appear as either "parked" or "posted" in SAP.

The following postings are generated for all leases:

- Payment posting: Recognizes the payments being generated for the lease. If connected to the AP module, an AP posting will be generated. If not connected to the AP module, a GL posting will be generated.
- Accrual posting: Recognizes the interest charge for the period. This entry will post the reclassification of the lease liability from long term to short on a periodic basis.

The following posting is generated for ASC 842 operating leases only:

- Asset depreciation: Recognizes the period depreciation values based on the accounting standards. For all other types of fix lease contracts, FI-AA will generate the asset depreciation entry.

## 7.4 Lease Event Management



Once a lease is active and is producing journal entries, any changes required by modifications in the lease terms and conditions may be handled in SAP Lease Administration to account for the following events:

- Activation group reassessment
- Activation group casualty
- Unit replacement
- Lease contract modification
- Lease contract change

In this section, we'll walk through the different lease events and demonstrate how they are handled in SAP Lease Administration.

### 7.4.1 Reassessing Activation Groups

During the operating phase of a lease, an activation group may go through reassessment for various reasons. Reassessment allows the ROU asset and lease liability to be revaluated by exercising new terms and conditions to the lease. For example, during the inception phase of the lease, a base rent and an extension option may have been identified, but only the base rent was reasonably likely to be exercised. If some time after the lease started, the parties to the lease decided that the extension option *was* to be applied, then this modification would be handled through reassessment.

During a reassessment, SAP Lease Administration will create a draft copy of the activation group. While the draft is open, the master version remains active, thus still allowing periodic postings to occur.

To reassess an activation group, follow these steps:

1. Open the activation group and click on the **Context Menu • Reassessment**.

2. From the **Reason Code** dropdown list, select the reason code for reassessment (reason codes are defined in the AdminConsole). Out of the box reason codes include the following:
   - **Early Buyout**: A purchase option will be applied.
   - **Early Termination**: A termination option will be applied.
   - **Impairment**: The ROU asset value has been marked down to a value less than what the contract states. Impairment will be reflected in FI-AA.
   - **Reassessment**: Other terms and conditions will be applied such as an extension, a supplement, or a reduction.
3. Enter the contract rate into the **Contract Rate** field if known. This rate will be used for liability calculations. If this field is not set, then the incremental borrowing rate (IBR) will be used.
4. Enter a description for the reassessment in the **Description** field displayed in Figure 7.35.

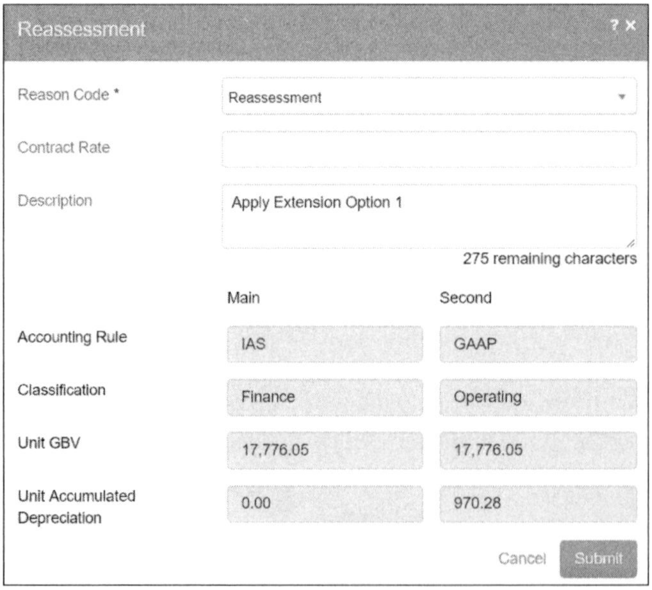


**Figure 7.35** Reassessment Page of the Activation Group

5. Several fields are available for view only:
   - **Accounting Rule**: Displays the accounting standard(s).
   - **Classification**: Displays the accounting classification selected for the standard(s).

- **Unit GBV**: Displays the unit gross book value.
- **Unit Accumulated Depreciation**: Displays the accumulated depreciation value.

6. Click on **Submit.** Some fields will now be editable, and the activation group's status will change from "Active" to "Define." To go back to the master version, click on the **Context Menu • Show Master**. To return to the draft version, click on the **Open Draft** button.
7. Go to the **Terms & Conditions** page of the activation group. Select the term types that will be used for the reassessment.
8. Click on **Send to Assessment**.
9. Select the effective date, which is the date on which the remeasurement of the ROU asset and liability will take effect. This date must be a payment date.
10. Click **Submit** to generate the revised financial schedules, which are accessed by clicking on the **Context Menu • View Schedules**.
11. Click on **Approve**.
12. Click on **Confirm Classification**.
13. Click on the **Context Menu • Complete Remeasurement**.
14. A popup with the following message will appear: "All of the changes made in the draft will be merged to the master version. Do you want to continue?" Click **Confirm.**



### 7.4.2 Applying a Casualty Activation Groups

During the operating phase of a lease contract, sometimes one or several units may be destroyed or damaged to the point where they are no longer useful. This loss is handled through a *casualty event* for the activation group, which will retire all related units. (Note that, if an activation group has multiple units, and you only need to apply the casualty event to one unit, you must split the activation group in order to apply the event to the group that contains the damaged unit, while the first group remains active.)

Follow these steps to apply a casualty event to an activation group:

1. Open the activation group and click on the **Context Menu • Casualty**. If a unit needs to be spilt from the activation group, click on **Context Menu • Split Activation Group** and select the unit that needs to be split off from the group.
2. The **Reason Code** field will be default to **Casualty**.

3. Enter the payment date in the **Payment Date** field. The payment date is the date on which the casualty (lease-end) amount will be posted.
4. Enter the contract rate into the **Contract Rate** field if known. This rate will be used for liability calculations. If this field is not set, then the IBR will be used.
5. Enter the casualty amount (the payment that will be paid to the lessor) in the **Casualty Amount** field, if any.
6. Enter a description for the casualty.
7. Click **Submit** and confirm that all of the units in the activation group will be retired.
8. Click **Terms & Conditions** in the left panel. Note that a casualty term has been automatically added.
9. Click **Send to Assessment.**
10. Select the effective date, which reflects the date on which the remeasurement of the ROU asset and liability will take effect. This date must be a payment date.
11. Click **Submit** to generate the revised financial schedules, which are accessed by clicking on the **Context Menu • View Schedules**.
12. Click on **Approve.**
13. Click on **Confirm Classification**.
14. Click on the **Context Menu • Complete Remeasurement**.
15. A popup with the following message will appear: "All of the changes made in the draft will be merged to the master version. Do you want to continue?" Click **Confirm**.

### 7.4.3 Replacing a Unit in the Activation Groups

During the operating phase of a lease contract, one or several units may be replaced by the lessor at no additional cost to the lessee. This event is handled in SAP Lease Administration through a *unit replacement*. For example, going back to our trucks and trailers example, if the model of trucks being leased is recalled by the manufacturer due to a defect, then a unit replacement will be made.

Note that the unit replacement functionality is only available for leases that are in active status; unit replacements cannot be performed on draft leases.

To replace a unit, follow these steps:

1. Load the activation group and click **Context Menu • Replace Unit**.
2. Select the required unit in the **Unit To Be Replaced**.

3. Enter the **New Unit Name**.
4. Enter the **Replacement Date** of the unit.
5. Click **Submit**. A new unit is created in the unit list page.
6. Click on the replaced unit to view all of the unit information:
   - The **Unit Status** shows the unit is now "Replaced."
   - The **End Date** field shows the **Reception Date** that was entered for the new unit.
7. Click on the new unit to view all of the unit's information:
   - The **Unit Status** shows that the unit is "Activated."
   - The **Reception Date** field shows the reception date that was entered for the new unit.
   - The **Asset ID** field shows the same ID as that of the replaced unit.



### 7.4.4 Modifying a Lease Contract

During the operating phase of a lease contract, new lease terms might be offered by the lessor that will have a financial impact on future postings. This scenario may be handled through a *lease modification*. For example, going back to our trucks and trailers example, let's say, a year later, the lessor wanted provide the option of adding additional trucks to the contract and reducing the lease payments on the existing trucks; this new option would be handled in SAP Lease Administration through a lease modification.

During a lease modification, a full draft copy of the contract, its lease components, and its activation groups is created, and all of these objects may be modified. While the draft is open, the master version of the contract is still active, and postings and unit replacements can still be performed.

Follow these steps to apply a lease modification:

1. Open the contract and click **Context Menu • Lease Modification**.
2. Select the **Amendment Date.** This date represents the date on which the contract change was recognized.
3. Select the reason code from the **Reason Code** field to specify why the contract needs to be modified. Out of the box, the following reason codes are available:
   - **Add New Lease Component**: A new lease component needs to be created.
   - **Addendum to Contract – New Contract Rate**: The contract rate needs to be modified.

- **Addendum to Contract – New Terms**: Additional terms need to be added.
- **Addendum to Contract – Payment Adjustment**: A payment modification needs to be made.
- **Decrease Lease Terms**: Lease term needs to be reduced.
- **Decrease Lease Values**: A payment reduction needs to be applied.

4. Enter the current contract rate in the **Contract Rate** field if required. If this field is not set, then the IBR will be used instead.
5. Enter a description for the lease modification in the **Description** field.
6. Click **Submit**. A draft of the contract is created and loaded automatically.
7. Make the changes required in the draft version. For example, if you need to make a payment adjustment, go to the lease component's **Terms & Conditions** page and make the needed adjustments, such as adding a supplemental payment or reduction. To go back to the master version, click on the **Context Menu • Show Master**. To return to the draft version, click the **Open Draft** button.
8. Go through the contract approval flow. Click on **Send to Approval** and then **Approve**.
9. Go to the activation groups and select the terms and conditions likely to be exercised that were added in the lease modification.
10. Click on **Send to Assessment**.
11. Select the effective date in the **Effective Date** field, which reflects the date on which the remeasurement of the ROU asset and liability will take effect. This date must be a payment date. This step will generate the revised financial schedules.
12. Click on **Approve** and then **Confirm Classification**.
13. Go back to the contract level and click on **Context Menu • Complete Assessment**.
14. A popup with the following message will appear: "All of the changes made in the draft will be merged to the master version. Do you want to continue?" Click **Confirm**.

### 7.4.5 Applying a Contract Change

During the operating phase of a lease contract, certain changes may arise that need to be made to a contract that do not have any financial impact on the future accounting postings; in SAP Lease Administration, you would handle this development through a contract change. For example, if the lessor is acquired by another company, this change needs to be reflected in the contract by modifying the lessor (vendor).

Follow these steps to apply a lease modification:

1. Open the contract and click **Context Menu • Change Contract**.
2. Select the reason code to explain why the contract needs to be changed. Out of the box reason codes include the following:
   - **Change Lessor**: The lessor in the **Partners** page needs to be modified.
   - **Change Notification**: Users in the **User Notification** section of the **Partners** page needs to be modified.
   - **Other Changes**: Other changes need to be made, such as an update of the **Description** field.
3. Add a description and then click **Submit**. The draft of the contract is created and loaded automatically.
4. Make the changes required. To go back to the master version, click on the **Context Menu • Show Master**. To return to the draft version, click the button **Open Draft**.
5. Go through the contract approval flow. Click on **Send to Approval** and then click on **Approve**.
6. A popup with the following message will appear: "All of the changes made in the draft will be merged to the master version. Do you want to continue?" Click **Confirm**.

## 7.5 Summary

In this chapter, we discussed how you can use SAP Lease Administration by Nakisa for lease accounting. In the next chapter, we'll provide the equivalent instructions for using SAP RE-FX.

# Chapter 8
# Managing Leases with SAP Flexible Real Estate Management

*Once SAP Flexible Real Estate Management has been properly configured for your organization, you'll be ready to use its powerful functionalities to accurately abstract, calculate, and post lease valuations. Let's learn how.*



SAP Flexible Real Estate Management (SAP RE-FX) is a robust solution that supports residential, commercial, and corporate real estate processes and is fully integrated with SAP ERP. SAP RE-FX has been available within SAP ERP since version 4.7. SAP developers saw that thousands of customers required data to accurately calculate and post lease valuations, as required by the new lease accounting standards, and that the necessary data was already available within their SAP ERP systems. Therefore, SAP extended the contract management functionality already found within SAP RE-FX to simplify the transition to the new lease accounting standards for current SAP RE-FX customers.

Though SAP RE-FX covers the entire real estate lifecycle, you don't have to implement the entire solution when undertaking a leasing project. Portions of the solution, such as portfolio management, contract management, maintenance and repair, or investment and construction, may be implemented independently to meet your most critical and pressing real estate requirements but are probably outside the scope of your International Financial Reporting Standards 16 or Accounting Standards Codification 842 compliance project.

The objective of this chapter is to teach you how to manage your leases using the available functionality found within SAP RE-FX in compliance with the new lease accounting standards. Note that, in this chapter, we'll only cover the data entry points and functionality available to help comply with these new leasing standards. This chapter will not provide a full description of all functionalities and features found within the real estate contract.

**Note**

SAP Note 2255555 (Valuation of Leasing Contracts) describes the minimum system release and support package requirements to utilize the new lease accounting functionality found in SAP's real estate solutions. Additionally, this SAP Note provides a list of support notes containing newly released functionality and system documentation.

The real estate contract is a key component of the contract management and lease administration real estate process and is the basis for all leasing activities within the solution. An accurately abstracted lease provides the solution all the information required to support both IFRS 16 and ASC 842 as well as local GAAP lease accounting standards.

Before we dive into step-by-step instructions, let's review the lease management process in SAP RE-FX. A lease has its own lifecycle, and each step within this lifecycle may have a significant impact on lease valuation. SAP RE-FX breaks this lifecycle into three major phases, as shown in Figure 8.1:

- Contract and lease management: Abstracting the contours of the lease
- Valuation and classification: Assigning valuation and classification rules
- Multi-GAAP posting: Enabling postings that comply with GAAP regulations in multiple countries

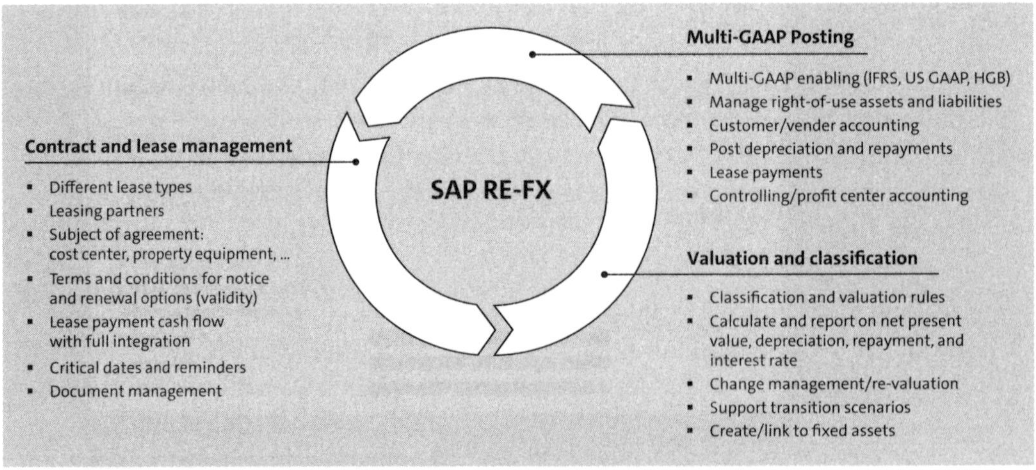


**Figure 8.1** Lease Valuations Integrated into the Contract Lifecycle

The first step of the lease valuation process is to abstract the lease agreement. The abstraction of the lease serves as the basis of accurate lease valuations, so any errors or inconsistencies within the lease abstraction process may have significant impacts on the valuation amounts recorded within the general ledger.

A properly abstracted lease includes the following critical information:

- The type of lease, like an office, warehouse, or store
- The landlord or other payees related to the contract
- The subject of the lease and the identification of the asset behind the lease agreement
- The terms and conditions of the agreement, such as contract start dates and renewal or termination options
- Lease payment amounts (e.g., for rent, services charges, payment penalties, etc.) identified on the agreement
- Critical dates and reminders around important leasing tasks



SAP RE-FX not only supports the manual abstraction of lease data but also provides mass uploading tools and integration into advanced deep learning applications to systematically interpret and abstract the lease agreement.

Once a lease has been properly abstracted, your next step is to assign valuation rules to the contract. Each assigned valuation rule supports a lease accounting standard such as IFRS 16, ASC 842 (either an operating lease or a finance lease), or local GAAP. A single contract can contain one or more valuation rules, and each valuation rule operates independently by calculating and posting its own financial entries.

Once you've created valuation rules and assigned the critical terms and conditions, the SAP RE-FX system will calculate the valuation amounts. You can review and analyze these valuation cash flow entries through standard SAP reports. You can also extract them into business intelligence or disclosure management applications using standard business intelligence extraction tools.

Each valuation rule supports a lease accounting standard with financial postings generated for each rule using the lease valuation posting transaction. International-, US-, or local GAAP-compliant postings can be made to individual ledgers or general ledger accounts based on your organizational requirements and system settings.

Historically, lease administrators had full control of the lease administration process. They are experts at abstracting leases, monitoring critical dates, and maintaining relationships with landlords and service providers. However, with the adoption of the new lease accounting standards, tight coordination is required between the lease administrator and the lease accountant.

This coordination between the lease administrator and accountant is shown in Figure 8.2. The lease administrator continues to abstract the lease, manage the terms of the lease agreement, and generate payments. These users will continue to use Transaction RECN or RE80 to manage lease agreements. The lease accountant must review the lease; classify the lease as low value, short term, or for US GAAP; and determine whether the lease is an operating or finance lease. Lease accountants also generate the lease valuation postings and provide key metrics to support disclosure reporting.

For organizations to maintain proper financial and systematic controls over leasing information, SAP has provided specific authorization objects for lease valuations and has created a new transaction (Transaction RECECN, Edit Contract Valuation) specifically for accountants. This transaction is specifically designed to reduce the number of fields available for display and maintenance on the contract and ensures only information related to the lease valuation process may be modified by a user with the authorization to change this transaction.

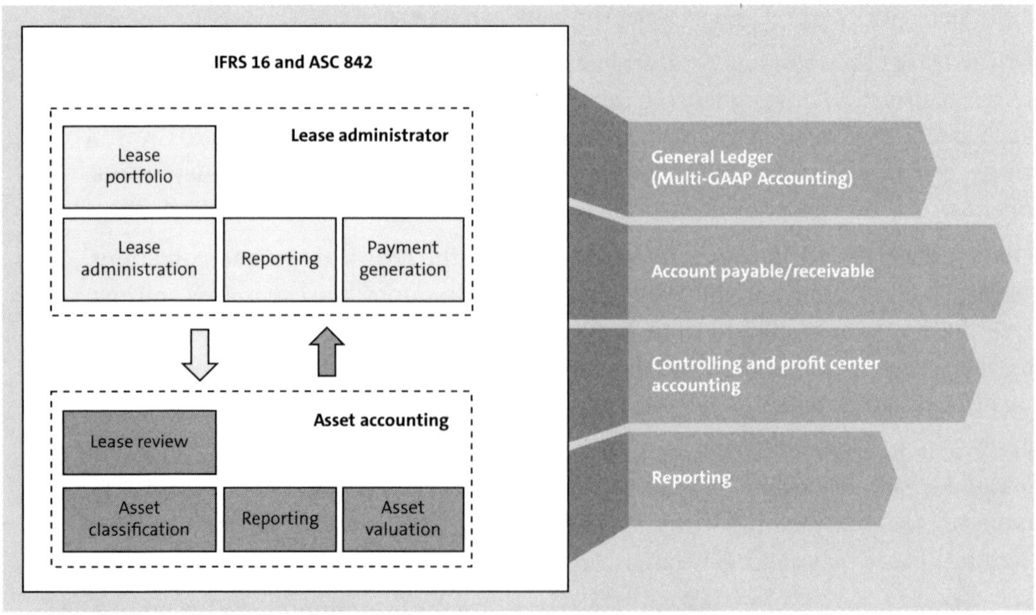


**Figure 8.2** Separate Responsibilities but Shared Leasing Information

Now that we've surveyed the lease management process in SAP RE-FX from 10,000 feet, let's walk through the process step by step.

## 8.1 Lease Valuation Data

Let's begin with how to properly abstract leasing data, which is critical to the accurate valuation of leases.

Note that this section will only focus on the data attributes required to calculate lease valuations and won't take into consideration ancillary leasing processes like service charge settlements, sales based/income rents, consumer price index (CPI) rent adjustments, or common area maintenance reconciliation. Support around these topics is available at *http://help.sap.com*. Depending on how you configure your screens within SAP RE-FX, your input screens may be different, but the data elements will remain the same.



The following screens contain the data elements required for lease valuation:

- **General Data**: Basic information around the contract
- **Partners**: Vendors and key contacts for the lease
- **Term**: Lease terms and renewal/termination options
- **Objects**: Assets related to the lease
- **Conditions**: Payment amounts or other financial considerations related to the lease

Let's walk through each screen in detail.

### 8.1.1 General Data

The first step in the lease abstraction and classification process takes place in the **General Data** tab shown in Figure 8.3. The following fields influence the lease valuation:

- **Contract Type**: This field contains a dropdown list of available contract types in the system such as commercial, residential, office, warehouse, service, or equipment. It's imperative that you correctly assign this field because the contract type determines the screen layouts, available payment types, and valuation procedures.
- **Company Code**: This field contains the list of companies that have been defined within the SAP ERP Financials system. The company code is one of the central

posting blocks for all financial entries, as the assignment influences all financial postings from the real estate contract.

- **Contract**: The contract number may be either internally or manually assigned and is the tracking number for the lease agreement.
- **Contract Currency**: This field is for the currency on which the *lease agreement* is based. This currency may be different from the company code or condition currencies.
- **Valuation Relevance**: This dropdown menu identifies whether the lease should be valuated or classified as a short-term and low-value lease.

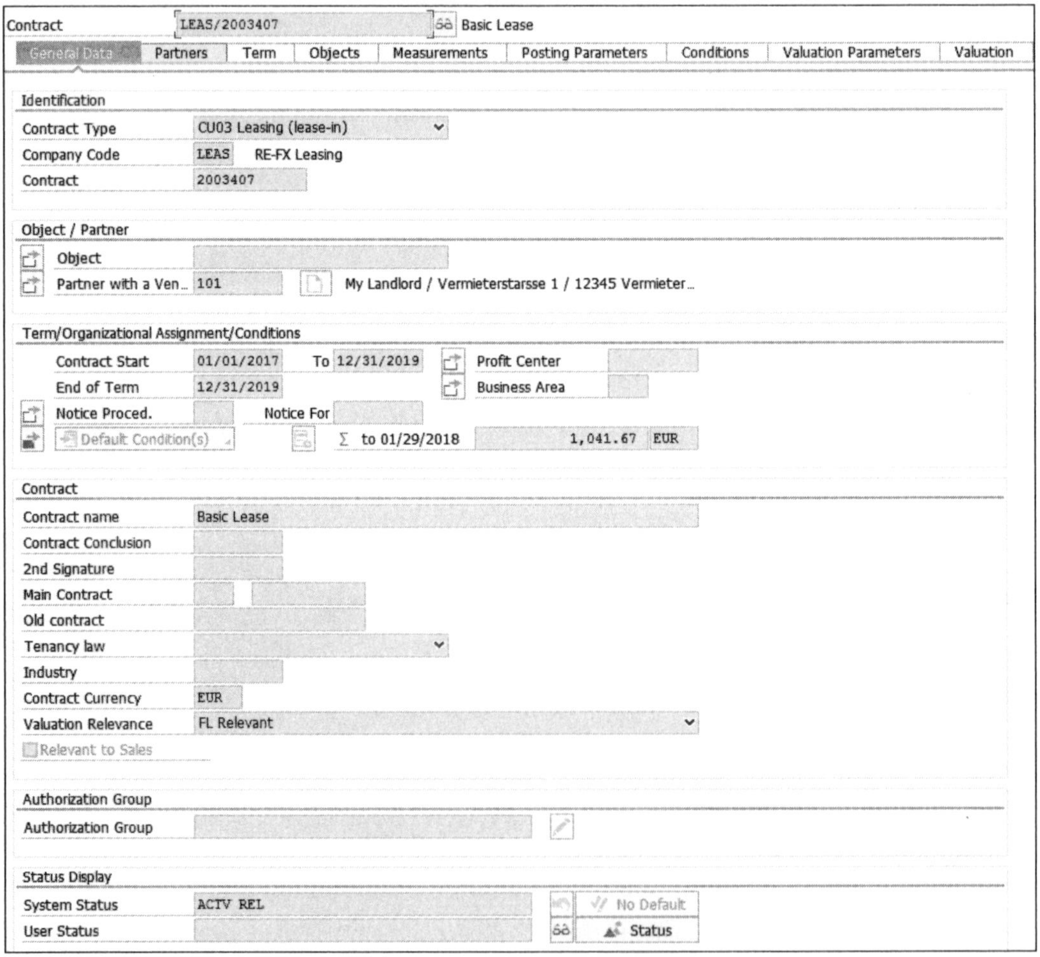


**Figure 8.3** General Data Tab

> **Foreign Currency Valuations**
>
> A contract in SAP RE-FX can utilize three different currencies: company code, contract, and condition.
>
> All three currencies may be different based on the terms of the lease agreement. For example, an organization headquartered in Germany but with operations in Mexico may have lease agreements utilizing the following currencies: company code (EUR), contract (MXN), and a payment condition (USD).
>
> Refer to SAP Note 2474141 (RE-FX Leasing: Foreign Currencies) for a detailed explanation on how foreign currencies can impact lease valuations.



### 8.1.2 Partners

The **Partners** tab is used to document both financial and non-financial business partners. A business partner with a financial role (e.g., landlords or vendors) is linked to a vendor or customer account. Business partners with non-financial roles (lease administrators, assigned accountants, or the primary contact with the vendor) only contain contact information. The number of financial or non-financial business partners that can be assigned to the contract is unlimited.

As shown in Figure 8.4, enter the key information for a business partner as follows:

- **BP Role**: The field marks the type of business partner being assigned.
- **Business Partner**: This internally assigned number represents the business partner. A single business partner may have multiple business partner roles.
- **Start Relationship**: This field contains the date on which the relationship with a partner starts.
- **End of Relat.**: This field contains the date on which the relationship with a partner ends.
- **Vendor**: This field is for the alphanumeric key that uniquely identifies the vendor in the SAP system.

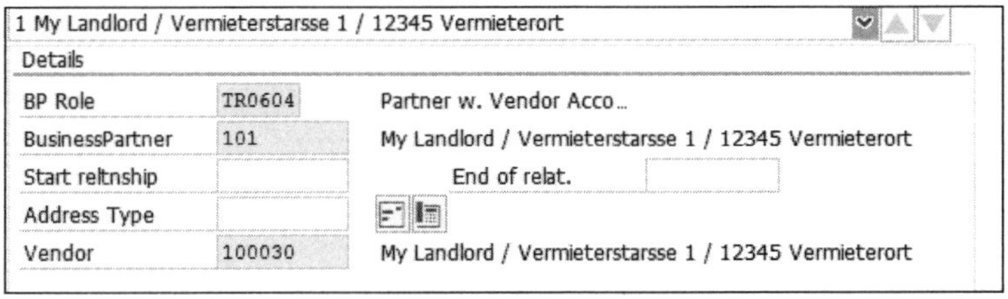


**Figure 8.4** Key Business Partner Information

### 8.1.3 Terms

The **Term** tab documents the most important dates related to the contract. All payments, renewals, and termination options are driven from the dates entered in this tab. With real estate, you can take possession of a property prior to the official start date of the lease agreement or continue occupying the property after a contract has expired; for these scenarios, you'll need to maintain dates in the **Possession From** and **Possession To** fields.

The following data elements are available on the **Term** tab, as shown in Figure 8.5:

- **Contract Start Date**: This field marks the start date of the lease agreement. All date calculations and validations are driven from this date.
- **1st Contract End**: This field marks the end date of the initial lease term. You can enter this date directly, or alternatively, you can enter the length of the contract in the **Term in Months** field, and system will calculate the **1st Contract End** date automatically.
- **First Posting From**: This date is relevant for legacy data transfers. The date of first posting (which should be greater than or equal to the date in the **Cash Flow From** field) specifies the date on which the system should begin *posting* financial transactions.
- **Possession Date From**: This field shows the date the tenant received access to the property.
- **Possession Date To**: This field shows the date when the tenant vacates the property.

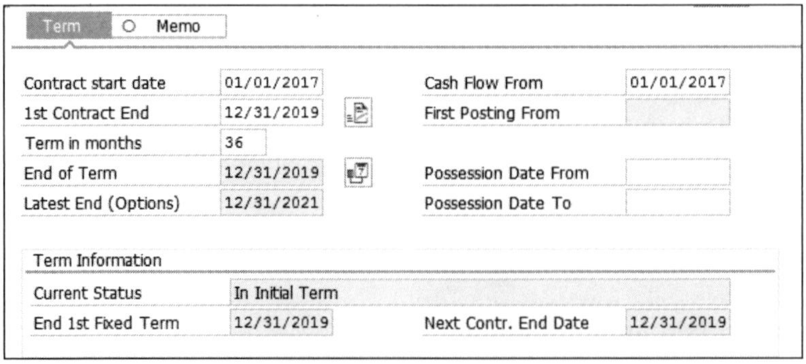


**Figure 8.5** Term Tab Information

### 8.1.4 Objects

With the introduction of the new lease accounting functionality found within SAP RE-FX, a new object was introduced: the contract object. A contract object is a placeholder that lets you assign an asset related to the contract without having to create all the dependent master data within the ERP. For example, previously, if you wanted to assign a building to a contract, the lease administrator would create a building within portfolio management. She would then assign this newly created building to the contract as a building object. With a contract object, the maintenance of master data is significantly reduced for certain types of organizations.



The **Objects** tab identifies what assets are controlled or impacted by a lease agreement. The valuation of the contract is carried out based on the contract objects assigned to the contract. As a result, a separate right-of-use asset (ROU asset) can be entered and posted for each object assigned to the contract. The following are examples of objects that may be assigned to the contract:

- Assets
- Buildings
- Land
- Contract objects
- Cost centers
- Equipment
- Projects

Customers can configure and define this list based on their business requirements.

Figure 8.6 shows an example of a contract object, which has the following fields:

- **Contract Object**: This field is for the name of the object. Choose an easy-to-identify name so that your colleagues can quickly understand the underlying asset of the lease. For our example, we'll enter "Potsdam Building #2."
- **Relnship Valid From**: This field is for the start date of the object assignment. If left blank, then the contract start date from the **Term** tab is utilized.
- **Relnship Valid To**: This field is for the end date of the object assignment. If left blank, the contract end date from the **Term** tab is utilized. The end of term date considers all active renewal and termination options.
- **Possession Date From**: This field shows the date the tenant received access to the property.

- **Possession Date To**: This field shows the date when the tenant vacated the property.
- **Account Assignment**: This field is for the SAP cost object intended to receive the expense postings from the contract. All valid SAP cost objects are available for assignment to the **Account Assignment** field.

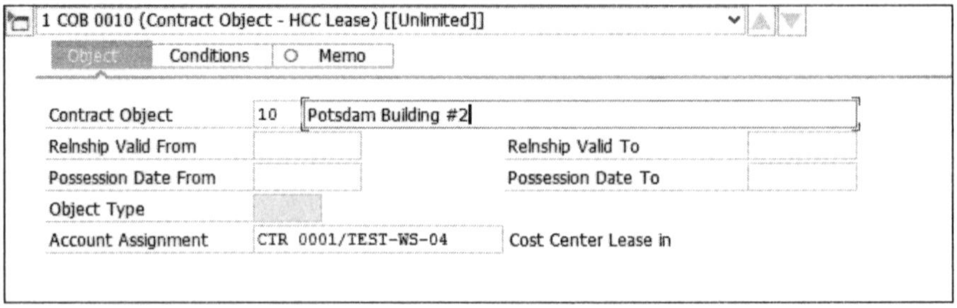


**Figure 8.6** Contract Object

### 8.1.5 Conditions

Conditions are the amounts to be paid or considered by the contract. Sometimes referred to as *payment types* or *rent categories*, conditions are entered on the **Conditions** tab.

Each payment amount listed on the lease agreement should be entered as a condition on the contract. A condition may be used to generate payments to the landlord as well as serve as a basis to calculate the present value of the lease agreement. Customers can configure the list of available conditions based on their implementation needs through Customizing.

A condition type identifies the purpose of the payment. Figure 8.7 shows some examples of condition types.

You can add multiple conditions to the contract as required or specified by the agreement. Note that the same condition may be repeated within a contract but cannot exist for the same time frame. An example of repeating a condition but utilizing different time periods is known as *step rent*. Figure 8.8 shows an example of setting up multiple conditions to represent steps in rent payments: one from January 1, 2017, to December 31, 2017; the next from January 1, 2018, to December 31, 2018; and the final one from January 1, 2019, onward.

| CTyp | Condition Type Name |
|---|---|
| V100 | Credit side basic rent |
| V101 | Credit Side Service |
| VNVV | Credit side basic rent |
| V900 | Cr. Side Reduction |
| V400 | Credit Leasing Rate |
| V110 | Credit side energy supply |
| V127 | Credit Side Service |
| V126 | Credit Side Service |
| V125 | Credit side basic rent |
| V112 | Credit-Side Initial Costs |
| V120 | Credit side security deposit |
| V210 | Minimum Rent - Credit Side |
| V250 | Sales-Based Ad.Fees- Credit |
| V108 | IFRS Incentive |
| V103 | Credit Side Residual Value |
| V102 | Credit-Side Initial Costs |
| V902 | Cred. Incentive prior 1.comm |
| V911 | Credit-Side Initial Costs |
| V104 | Credit-Side Surrender Value |
| V105 | Credit-Side Penalty Payment |
| V107 | Asset Default Value |
| I104 | Extraordinary Depreciation |
| I105 | Extraordinary Write-up |
| V109 | NPV Default Value |
| V106 | Asset Retirement Obligation |
| V811 | Asset retirement |
| V810 | Asset acquisition |

**Figure 8.7** Sample List of Condition Types

Notice in Figure 8.8 that the condition types are the same (credit basic rent), but the dates in the **Valid From** and **Valid To** fields define the specific time interval of each step rent increase.

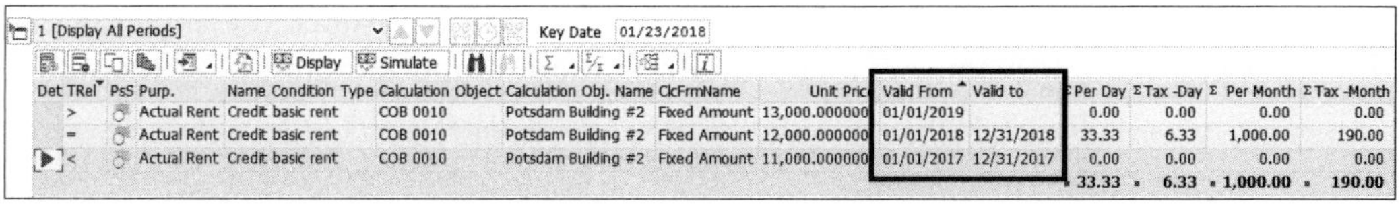


| Det | TRel | PsS | Purp. | Name Condition Type | Calculation Object | Calculation Obj. Name | ClcFrmName | Unit Price | Valid From | Valid to | Per Day | Tax -Day | Per Month | Tax -Month |
|---|---|---|---|---|---|---|---|---|---|---|---|---|---|---|
| | > | | Actual Rent | Credit basic rent | COB 0010 | Potsdam Building #2 | Fixed Amount | 13,000.000000 | 01/01/2019 | | 0.00 | 0.00 | 0.00 | 0.00 |
| | = | | Actual Rent | Credit basic rent | COB 0010 | Potsdam Building #2 | Fixed Amount | 12,000.000000 | 01/01/2018 | 12/31/2018 | 33.33 | 6.33 | 1,000.00 | 190.00 |
| | < | | Actual Rent | Credit basic rent | COB 0010 | Potsdam Building #2 | Fixed Amount | 11,000.000000 | 01/01/2017 | 12/31/2017 | 0.00 | 0.00 | 0.00 | 0.00 |
| | | | | | | | | | | | 33.33 | 6.33 | 1,000.00 | 190.00 |

**Figure 8.8** Multiple Conditions Assigned as Step Rent on a Contract

Once the condition type has been selected and assigned to the contract, the following data may be assigned per condition, as shown in Figure 8.9:

- **Calculation Object**: Input the calculation object or object group that the condition applies to.
- **Condition Purpose**: This field is for the condition purpose (e.g., actual rent, market rent, cost rent, and so on).

- **Valid From**: This field is for the starting date of the condition (expense type)
- **Valid To**: This field is for the date when the condition ends.
- **Unit Price**: This field is for the unit to be paid—either a price per unit or a fixed amount.
- **Formula**: The condition formula will automatically calculate the condition amount based on numerous factors. The calculation formula may be based on the measurement of the building in a price-per situation (e.g., square meters or square feet) or even based on a percentage of another condition. See the **Calculations** subtab for more information.
- **Currency**: This field is for the currency of the condition.

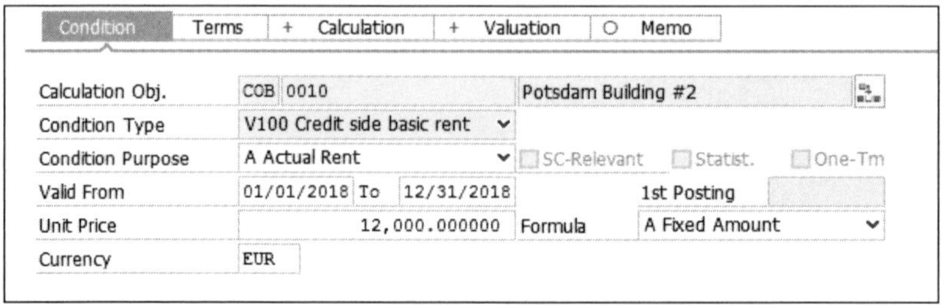


**Figure 8.9** Key Input Parameters for a Payment Condition

The condition purpose defines whether the contract generates a payment for that condition on a recurring basis, whether the condition is a one-time entry, or whether the condition is listed on the contract only for informational purposes. An informational condition is called a *statistical condition*, and while a statistical condition will not generate any payments in the system, you can use them to influence the valuation of the contract. Statistical conditions are often used in the following situations:

- Asset acquisition amounts
- Incentives received
- Surrender amounts
- Initial costs
- Asset retirement obligations

In these cases, the valuation of the ROU asset is impacted but a payment is not necessarily sent to the landlord.

The **Conditions** tab breaks into several smaller subtabs: **Terms**, **Calculation**, and **Valuations**.

In the **Terms** tab, condition terms are assigned to each condition. As a result, each condition can have its own posting rule, frequency, organizational assignment, or CPI adjustment rule.

Data concerning the frequency of posting and organizational assignments are defined on the **Posting Parameters** tab. With SAP RE-FX, the system automatically assigns the condition to the standard terms (**Postings**, **Frequency**, and **Organizational Assignment**). If you want to assign a condition to a different (non-standard) term, you may assign it manually on the condition **Terms** subtab, as shown in Figure 8.10.

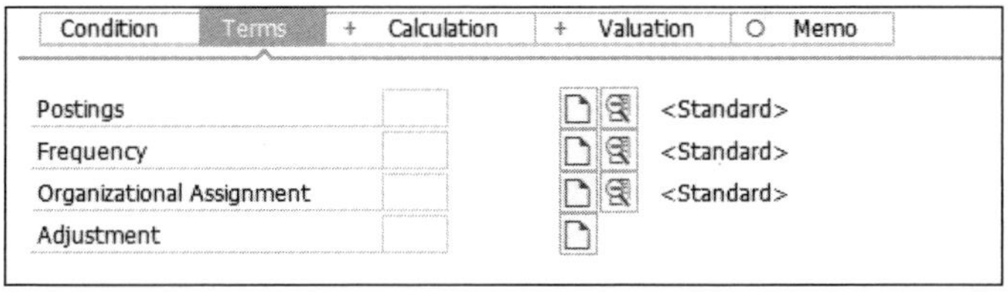


**Figure 8.10** Conditions Terms Subtab

In the **Calculation** subtab shown in Figure 8.11, you can assign a calculation formula to each condition. For example, the condition amount can be calculated by multiplying the unit price by the size of the assigned object (e.g., price per square meter or amount per parking space).

When configuring the system, calculation formulas can be predefined (defaulted) or maintained directly within the contract. If a calculation formula is based on a measurement, then the system will require that you indicate the measurement type and measurement unit.

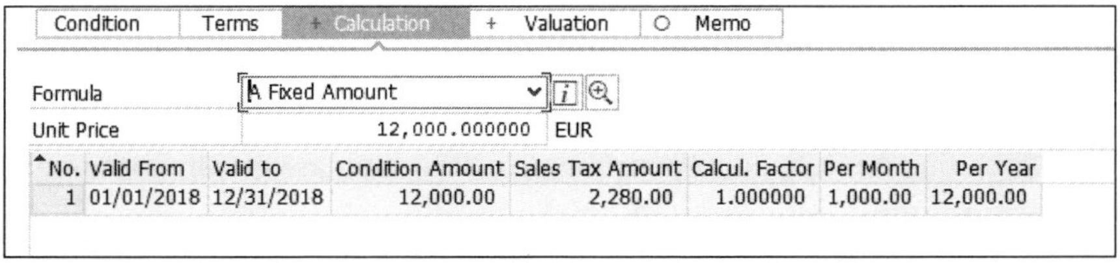


**Figure 8.11** Condition Calculation Subtab

Condition valuations will be covered in the next section.

## 8.2 Valuation Rules and Calculations

To support the new lease accounting standards, SAP developers have extended the contract management functionality long found within SAP RE-FX by adding two new tabs to the real estate contract:

- The **Valuation Parameter** tab is used to specify the settings used to calculate lease valuations.
- The **Valuation** tab is where lease valuations are processed and displayed according to US GAAP.

### 8.2.1 Assigning Valuation Parameters

The **Valuation Parameters** tab on the contract is the central element for lease valuation. At the highest level, a *valuation rule* (defined through configuration) is assigned to the contract and typically represents an accounting principle—in this case, IFRS 16, ASC 842, or a local GAAP.

On this tab, you can assign valuation rules to the contract and maintain contract-specific values for each rule. You can also maintain the rule assignments for each relevant condition.

Within each valuation rule, specific fields are used as parameters to control how the lease is valuated. Each valuation rule operates independently, meaning an IFRS valuation rule may be set up, reviewed, approved, and valuated prior to creating a US GAAP valuation rule on the same contract.

The following quick info options are available from the icon bar on the **Valuation Parameter** tab:

- **Create Term**: This is where the required valuation rules are assigned. The SAP RE-FX system automatically assigns numbers to these rules.
- **Delete Selected**: Clicking this icon removes a valuation rule from the **Valuation Parameters** tab.
- **Fast Entry**: Clicking this icon opens a single screen to assign all parameters within a valuation rule.
- **Cut Time Slice**: Clicking this icon controls **Valid From** and **Valid To** dates for each valuation rule. This functionality will be discussed in greater detail in Section 8.4.

- **Rule Complete**: This icon marks a rule complete, signifying the approval step for a rule. When a valuation rule is marked as complete, a fixed asset number is automatically assigned, creating the link between the valuation rule and the ROU asset in Asset Accounting (FI-AA).
- **Invalidate Rule**: This icon marks a rule as incomplete and prevents valuations from being calculated until the rule is reviewed and marked as complete.
- **Display Tree**: Clicking this icon displays all valuation rules assigned to the contract.



Figure 8.12 provides an example where multiple valuation rules have been assigned to the same contract. Notice in this example that the **INT** valuation rule has a rule status of complete, but the **US-GAAP OL** valuation rule is incomplete. Because no valuation is required for the local GAAP (the valuation rule **HGB**), the rule status and the valuation status are marked complete.

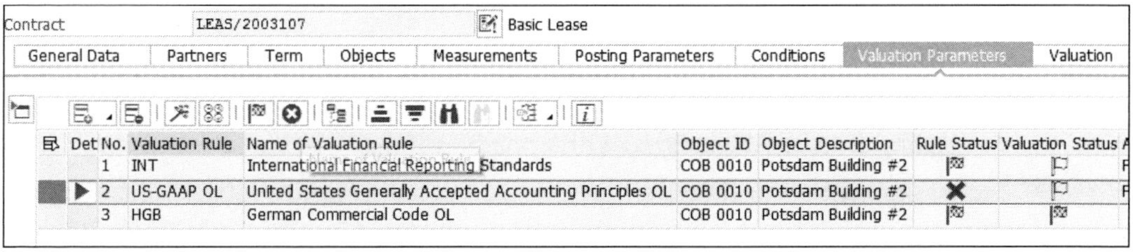


**Figure 8.12** Example of Valuation Rules with Quick Info Icons

For each valuation rule, three subtabs are available: **Valuation**, **Conditions**, and **Memo**. The **Valuation** subtab, shown in Figure 8.13, is used to enter the detailed parameters for each valuation rule and has the following fields:

- **Start of Consideration**: This field is for the valuation start date. The present value is calculated beginning on this date for the calculation of the ROU asset and offsetting liability.
- **1st Pstg**: This field defines the start date for the valuation *postings*. This date can be after the date in the **Start of Consideration** field.
- **Asset** (only for FI-AA integration): This field contains the fixed asset number of the ROU asset. When FI-AA integration is utilized, this value may be automatically assigned or manually entered depending on your organization's defined business process.

- **End of Usage ROU**: Enter data in this field when the useful life of the asset is *different* from the lease term. If you specify a date, the depreciation amount is linearized, so the ROU asset is fully depreciated by this date.
- **Probable End**: This field is for the expected end date of the contract, including all renewal and termination options that are expected to be exercised. By selecting the **Simulate Renewal** icon, all renewal options are displayed, and the user can select the radio button of the desired renewal option. The probable end date will then be populated with this system date. If the **Probable End** field is left blank, the default values based on the legal contract terms will be utilized.
- **Interest Rate**: This field contains the interest rate that will be used to calculate the present value of the balance sheet calculations. The interest rate may be defaulted into the **Valuation Parameters** tab through configuration, manually entered by the user, or calculated by the system as an implicit interest rate.
- **Frequency Term**: This field controls the frequency of the valuation calculations and postings.
- **Val. Behavior**: This dropdown menu controls the valuation of the balance sheet capitalization. Depending on the value selected, a new ROU asset will be created or an existing asset will be utilized with updated values.
- **Acct Assignment**: This field is where the expenses or revenue entries will be posted from the valuation. This value is typically populated by the account assignment entered on the object.
- **Memo**: In this field, you can document decisions around the input valuation parameters.

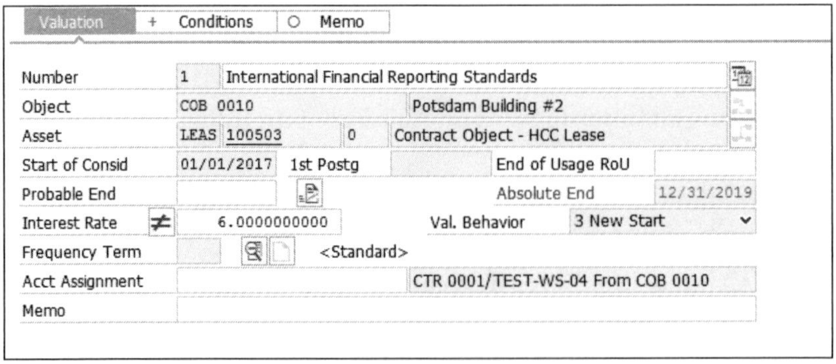


**Figure 8.13** Fields Available on the Valuations Subtab

You can create time slices within the valuation parameters to enter valuation changes (condition increases, term changes, interest changes, scope changes, and so on). To add a time slice, select the **Add Validity Period** icon New and enter the corresponding dates for the desired valuation rule in the **Valid From** and **Valid To** fields (see Figure 8.14). The input the appropriate information in the **Interest Rate** and **Consideration Start** field (and add a note, as necessary). All valuations based on these changes will be based on this time forward.

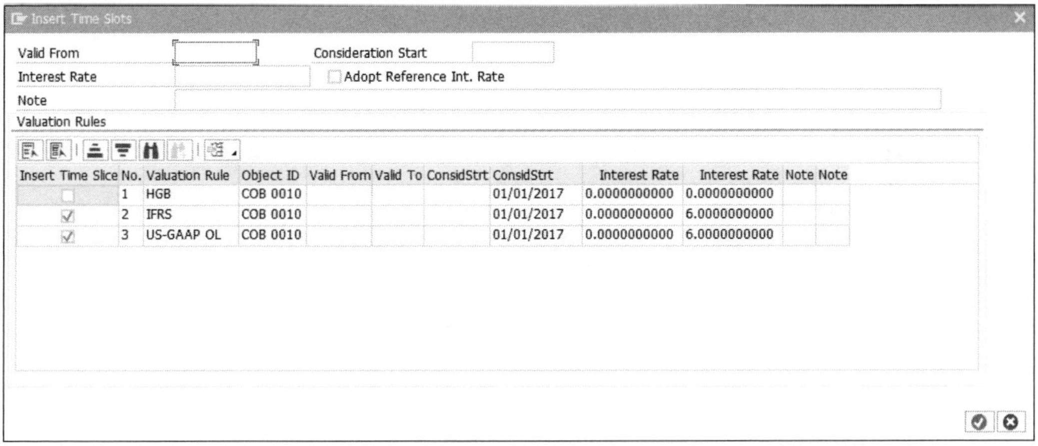


**Figure 8.14** Valuation Parameter Time Slice

### SAP RE-FX Integration with Asset Accounting

SAP RE-FX contains provides extensive integration with FI-AA. SAP Note 2568784 (Evaluation of Leasing Contracts and Integration with Asset Accounting) describes the available integration options between these two solutions.

During Customizing, you'll define which condition types impact the lease valuation. How a condition is considered during the valuation process is defined on the **Conditions** subtab. Every condition that influences the lease valuation for the selected valuation rule is automatically listed in this subtab. Figure 8.15 shows an example of conditions assigned to the **Conditions** subtab and the selection options for each item.

Notice the **Consider** column, which flags the condition to be considered in the valuation calculation. The condition consideration controls how the valuation is performed, taking into account whether the full condition amount is to be included, excluded, or partially considered.

The following options are available in the dropdown menu for the **Condition Consideration** field:

- **Full Consideration**: The full condition amount is valuated.
- **Do Not Consider**: The condition amount is excluded from valuation.
- **Linearization**: The condition amount is excluded from valuation but included in local GAAP postings.
- **As Specified**: A percentage or absolute amount can be defined for valuation.

Use the **Percentage Consideration** field to valuate just a percentage of the condition amount. This option is convenient for triple net lease payments. For example, if "80%" is entered in the **Percentage Consideration** field, then 20% of the payment amount is excluded in the valuation as service costs are not valuated. The remaining 80% of the condition amount is included in the valuation.

Finally, use the **Absolute Share** field to valuate a fixed amount regardless of condition amount.

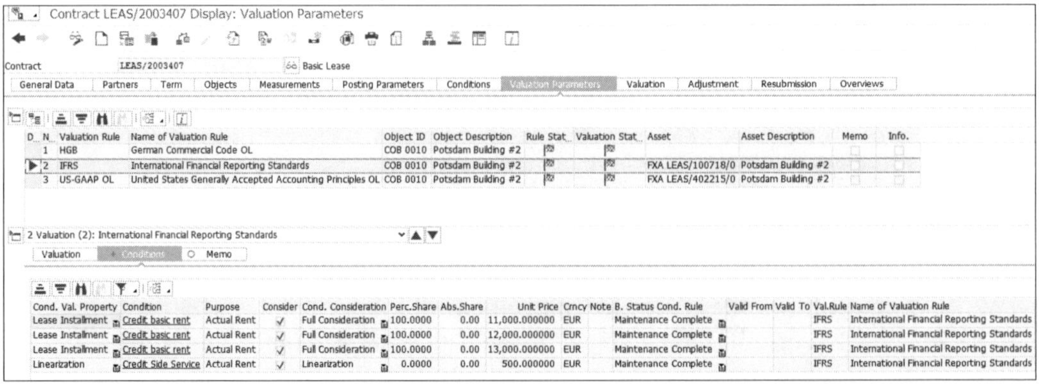


**Figure 8.15** Condition Subtab for IFRS Valuation Rule

Notice each condition contains its own consideration parameters. Both real and statistical conditions are available for assignment on the **Conditions** subtab.

Statistical conditions do not create payments to landlords or vendors but can influence lease valuations. Therefore, a statistical condition lets you specify a *condition valuation property* that will impact the lease valuation. Assigning a valuation property can be made for each condition on the conditions subtab. The following available valuation properties can be defined within the system:

- Lease installment payments
- Initial costs
- Incentives
- Present value specification
- Net worth value specification
- Unscheduled depreciation
- Redemption value
- Residual value guarantees
- Obligations to return property in original condition
- Penalty payments
- Transfer postings/linearization
- Subleases



**CPI Adjustments for US GAAP**

Under ASC 842, leases are not adjusted based on changes to the consumer price index. Valuations based on the original condition amount, and all future CPI rent increases are excluded.

To simply comply with the standard, enter the following parameters for the condition on the **Valuation Parameter** tab:

- Select the **US GAAP** valuation rule.
- Go to the **Conditions** subtab and select the impacted rent condition.
- Assign **As Specified** in the **Condition Consideration** field.
- Enter the original condition amount in the **Absolute Share** field.

Finally, the **Memo** subtab is available to document decisions made when defining the valuation parameters. This is a true SAP memo field, so there are no technical limitations on the amount of information you can store on this tab.

When a valuation rule is fully defined, select the rule and click on the **Rule Complete** icon. Save the contract to complete the definition of the valuation parameters.

### 8.2.2 Performing and Viewing Valuations

The **Valuation** tab shown in Figure 8.16 displays the valuation calculations and a record of each valuation. Each time the valuation is calculated for the contract, an additional log is stored in the system, thus providing a clear audit trail and record of the contract valuation changes and updates.

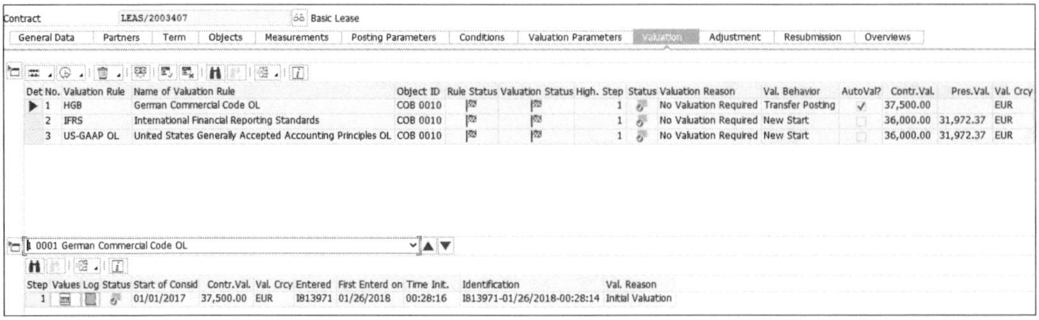


**Figure 8.16** Valuation Processing

Valuation for a contract can be executed directly from the contract screen or using the mass run transaction, Transaction RECEPR (Perform Contract Valuations). When executing the valuation, all valuation *cash flows* are generated. These valuation cash flows provide the basis on which the valuation postings are later created.

The SAP RE-FX system generates a "cash flow set" for each valuation parameter (combination of valuation rule and valuation object). Depending on the valuation type, this cash flow set consists of the following:

- Changes to assets (e.g., asset acquisition/retirement or leasing receivable)
- Depreciation (made available to FI-AA)
- Clearing (of payments)
- Interest
- Transfer postings/linearization
- Special flows (e.g., extraordinary loss from change, initial costs, retroactive changes, and so on)

The ROU asset amount, depreciation, interest, and repayment are calculated using the simulated payment cash flows based on the valuation rules. When executing these calculations, the system uses the simulated due dates.

The following quick links are available on the menu bar:

- **Simulate Valuation** : Clicking this icon simulates the valuation cash flows for single or multiple valuation rules. A simulated valuation does not allow the saving of cash flow results after execution.

- **Perform Valuation**: Clicking this icon calculates the valuation cash flows for a single or for multiple valuation rules. At the end of the valuation, you'll be given the option to save the valuation results. The cash flow amounts are recorded in posting log.
- **Delete Last Valuation Step**: Clicking this icon deletes the last valuation cash flow. This process may be executed for a single or multiple valuation rules.
- **Cash Flow**: Clicking this icon simulates the condition cash flow. This payment cash flow is not related to valuation postings.
- **Post Valuation**: Clicking this icon enables the posting of valuation entries into the general ledger. When using the quick link icon, only one valuation rule may be posted at a time.
- **Reverse Valuation**: Clicking this icon executes the reversal of a valuation posting. When using the quick link icon, only one valuation rule may be reversed at a time.

To perform a valuation, select the desired valuation rule and the **Perform Valuation** quick link icon. The option is given to execute the valuation for a single valuation rule or multiple valuation rules. You can then review the valuation calculations prior to saving the valuation cash flow results.

The **Assets** tab, shown in Figure 8.17, displays the calculated ROU asset values based on the contract values. The fixed asset number, posting flow type, and status are displayed for each. The **Acct. Assignment** column contains links to quickly access the relevant asset master in FI-AA.

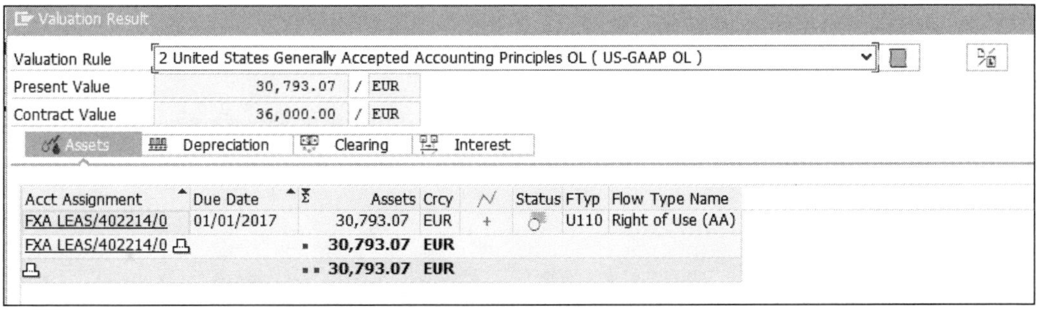


**Figure 8.17** Asset Results for ASC 842 Operating Lease Valuation

The **Depreciation** tab, shown in Figure 8.18, displays the planned depreciation entries for the ROU asset. Recall that SAP RE-FX will calculate the depreciation values. The depreciation run in FI-AA will utilize these amounts to depreciate the ROU asset.

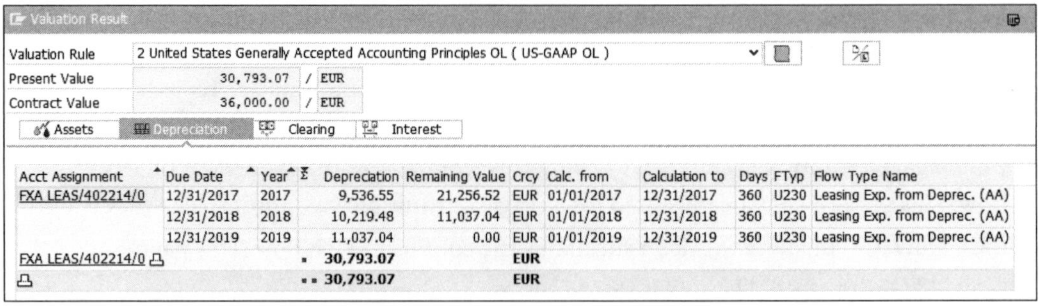


**Figure 8.18** Depreciation Results for ASC 842 Operation Lease Valuations

The **Clearing** tab, shown in Figure 8.19, displays the reduction of the liability based on payments to the landlord.

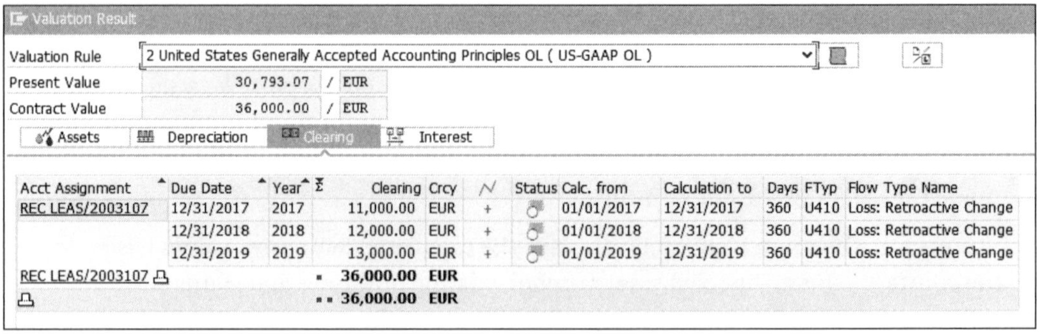


**Figure 8.19** Clearing Results for ASC 842 Operating Lease Valuations

The **Interest** tab, shown in Figure 8.20, displays the calculated interest, by period, based on the balance of the liability.

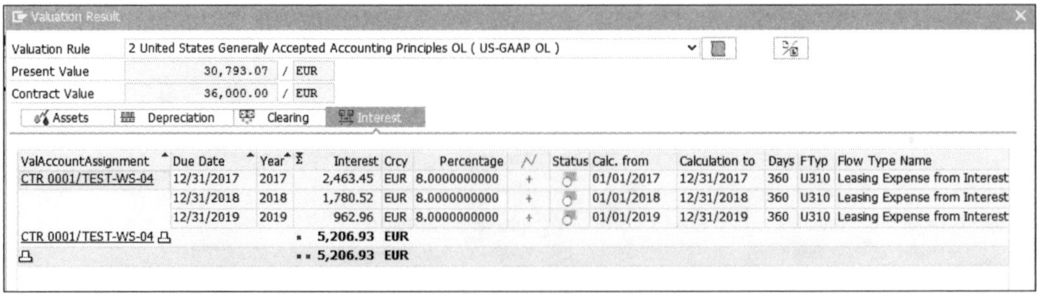


**Figure 8.20** Interest Results for ASC 842 Operating Lease Valuations

The **Linearization** tab, shown in Figure 8.21, displays the condition amounts included on the contract but not included in the lease valuation. These amounts simply post to the expense account during the valuation process.

| ValAccountAssignment | Due Date | Year | Linearization | Crcy | | Status | Calc. from | Calculation to | Days | FTyp | Flow Type Name |
|---|---|---|---|---|---|---|---|---|---|---|---|
| CTR 0001/TEST-WS-04 | 12/31/2017 | 2017 | 500.00 | EUR | + | | 01/01/2017 | 12/31/2017 | 360 | I600 | Cred. Linearization |
| | 12/31/2018 | 2018 | 500.00 | EUR | + | | 01/01/2018 | 12/31/2018 | 360 | I600 | Cred. Linearization |
| | 12/31/2019 | 2019 | 500.00 | EUR | + | | 01/01/2019 | 12/31/2019 | 360 | I600 | Cred. Linearization |
| CTR 0001/TEST-WS-04 | | | ▪ 1,500.00 | EUR | | | | | | | |
| | | | ▪▪ 1,500.00 | EUR | | | | | | | |

**Figure 8.21** Linearization Results for US GAAP Operating Lease

### Explanation of Calculations

SAP Note 2555105 (Explanation of Calculations IFRS 16/US GAAP ASC 842) describes how the present value and interest amounts are calculated by the system. This SAP Note also provides options on how different interest rates may be defaulted to the contract and lists the available interest calculation methods available within SAP.

After the lease valuations have been calculated and saved, the valuation cash flow results are stored within the system, and the valuation status is marked as complete (shows a checkered flag icon in the **Valuation Status** field).

The SAP RE-FX system generates a log that records who performed the valuation, the time created, an internal identification code, and the valuation reason. In our example shown in Figure 8.22, the log notes that the start of consolidation was on January 1, 2017; that the contracted value was for $36,000; that the present value is 30,793.07 Euros; and so on.

You can view the results of the valuation run by selecting the **Values** icon. The same results listed in the previous section will be displayed.

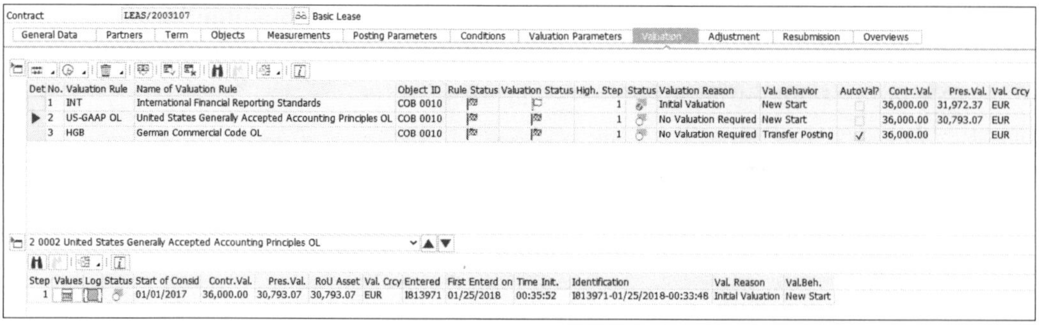


**Figure 8.22** Example of Valuation Posting Log

### 8.2.3 Running Valuation Reports

The contract **Overviews** tab is frequently overlooked by users, but this tab can be a rather helpful tool by providing a list of reports that can be executed for the contract. Instead of having to execute a specific report using the SAP menu or transaction code, you can select just the desired report from the **Overviews** tab. This functionality is especially helpful for lease valuations because two very helpful reports are located on this tab: the Valuation Process report and the Valuation Cash Flow report.

The Valuation Process report quickly displays each valuation rule, status, value, and valuation reason. The format of this report is similar what is shown on the **Valuation** tab but summarized more succinctly. In our example in Figure 8.23, we see the most important information around each valuation rule. If multiple valuation runs have been generated for a single rule, you'll see from this screen the cash flow amounts generated for each valuation run as well as why a new valuation was performed.

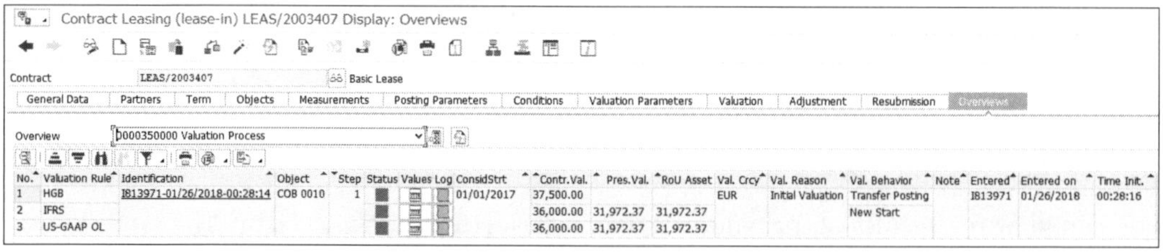


**Figure 8.23** Valuation Process Report

The Valuation Cash Flow report shown in Figure 8.24 provides a single report to view all valuation-related cash flow entries by valuation rule (in this case, GAAP). This report is usually executed by the lease accountant to ensure all valuation cash flow entries are being calculated as expected prior to generating valuation postings. This report displays the contract value, present value, a list of linearization postings, the amortization schedule for the ROU asset, and the corresponding liability.

Note that, for quick reference, all asset information is displayed in orange, and all liability information is highlighted in green. The repayment and lease expense/revenue amounts are also listed by period on this report.

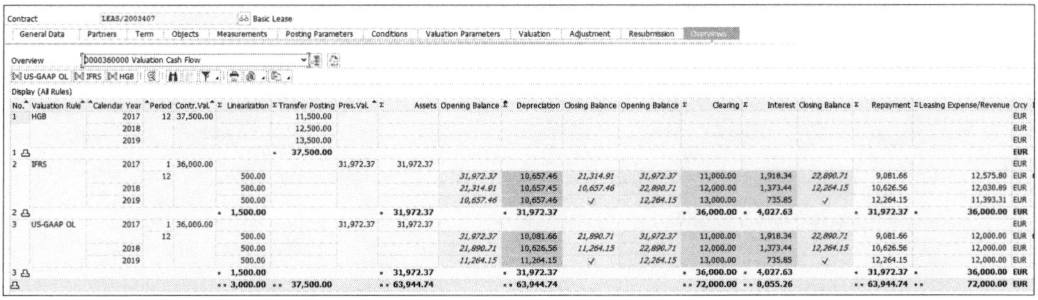
Contract LEAS/2003407 Basic Lease

General Data | Partners | Term | Objects | Measurements | Posting Parameters | Conditions | Valuation Parameters | Valuation | Adjustment | Resubmission

Overview 0000360000 Valuation Cash Flow

US-GAAP OL | IFRS | HGB

Display (All Rules)

| No. | Valuation Rule | Calendar Year | Period | Contr.Val. | Linearization | Transfer Posting | Pres.Val. | Assets | Opening Balance | Depreciation | Closing Balance | Opening Balance | Clearing | Interest | Closing Balance | Repayment | Leasing Expense/Revenue | Crcy |
|---|---|---|---|---|---|---|---|---|---|---|---|---|---|---|---|---|---|---|
| 1 | HGB | 2017 | 12 | 37,500.00 | | 11,500.00 | | | | | | | | | | | | EUR |
| | | 2018 | | | | 12,500.00 | | | | | | | | | | | | EUR |
| | | 2019 | | | | 13,500.00 | | | | | | | | | | | | EUR |
| 1 | | | | | | • 37,500.00 | | | | | | | | | | | | EUR |
| 2 | IFRS | 2017 | 1 | 36,000.00 | | | 31,972.37 | 31,972.37 | | | | | | | | | | EUR |
| | | | 12 | | 500.00 | | | | 31,972.37 | 10,657.46 | 21,314.91 | 31,972.37 | 11,000.00 | 1,918.34 | 22,890.71 | 9,081.66 | 12,575.80 | EUR |
| | | 2018 | | | 500.00 | | | | 21,314.91 | 10,657.45 | 10,657.46 | 22,890.71 | 12,000.00 | 1,373.44 | 12,264.15 | 10,626.56 | 12,030.89 | EUR |
| | | 2019 | | | 500.00 | | | | 10,657.46 | 10,657.46 | ✓ | 12,264.15 | 13,000.00 | 735.85 | ✓ | 12,264.15 | 11,393.31 | EUR |
| 2 | | | | | • 1,500.00 | | | • 31,972.37 | | • 31,972.37 | | | • 36,000.00 | • 4,027.63 | | • 31,972.37 | • 36,000.00 | EUR |
| 3 | US-GAAP OL | 2017 | 1 | 36,000.00 | | | 31,972.37 | 31,972.37 | | | | | | | | | | EUR |
| | | | 12 | | 500.00 | | | | 31,972.37 | 10,081.66 | 21,890.71 | 31,972.37 | 11,000.00 | 1,918.34 | 22,890.71 | 9,081.66 | 12,000.00 | EUR |
| | | 2018 | | | 500.00 | | | | 21,890.71 | 10,626.56 | 11,264.15 | 22,890.71 | 12,000.00 | 1,373.44 | 12,264.15 | 10,626.56 | 12,000.00 | EUR |
| | | 2019 | | | 500.00 | | | | 11,264.15 | 11,264.15 | ✓ | 12,264.15 | 13,000.00 | 735.85 | ✓ | 12,264.15 | 12,000.00 | EUR |
| 3 | | | | | • 1,500.00 | | | • 31,972.37 | | • 31,972.37 | | | • 36,000.00 | • 4,027.63 | | • 31,972.37 | • 36,000.00 | EUR |
| | | | | | •• 3,000.00 | •• 37,500.00 | | •• 63,944.74 | | •• 63,944.74 | | | •• 72,000.00 | •• 8,055.26 | | •• 63,944.74 | •• 72,000.00 | EUR |

**Figure 8.24** Valuation Cash Flow Report

## 8.3 Valuation Postings

Once you've calculated and saved the valuation cash flows, SAP RE-FX is ready to post the planned cash flow entries into the general and fixed asset ledgers. The posting valuation transaction (Transaction RECEEP) generates the following types of transactions:

- Asset acquisition or retirement
- Leasing liability
- Interest
- Clearing (part of the repayment)
- Linearized service costs
- Transfer postings (e.g., according to HGB)
- Retroactive changes
- Repayment from initial costs or incentive
- Owner financing differences
- Asset retirement obligations

Before we walk through the valuation posting program, let's look at how the system will record the financial transactions by using a leased building as an example. As shown in Figure 8.25, the lease payments for this building are paid annually (for simplicity) over three years. During each year of the agreement, the rent increases by 1,000 EUR. The discount rate for this lease is 6%.

| | | |
|---|---|---|
| **Liability** | 31.972,37 € | |
| Present value lease payments | 31.972,37 € | Interest rate 6% |
| **Sum = Asset value** | **31.972,37 €** | |

| Periods | | 1 | 2 | 3 | Sum |
|---|---|---|---|---|---|
| Lease payments | | 11.000 € | 12.000 € | 13.000 € | **36.000 €** |
| Total payments | | 11.000 € | 12.000 € | 13.000 € | **36.000 €** |
| **Right-of-use asset** | | | | | |
| Depreciation | | 10.657 € | 10.657 € | 10.657 € | **31.972 €** |
| Residual value of RoU asset | 31.972 € | 21.315 € | 10.657 € | 0 € | |
| **Liability** | | | | | |
| Interest | | 1.918 € | 1.373 € | 736 € | **4.028 €** |
| Repayment | | 9.082 € | 10.627 € | 12.264 € | **31.972 €** |
| Residual value at end of period | 31.972 € | 22.891 € | 12.264 € | 0 € | |

**Figure 8.25** Lease Example

Within our example, we will support IFRS, US GAAP, and HGB (a local German GAAP). For simplicity, each of these GAAP versions is posted to a parallel ledger, as shown in Figure 8.26.

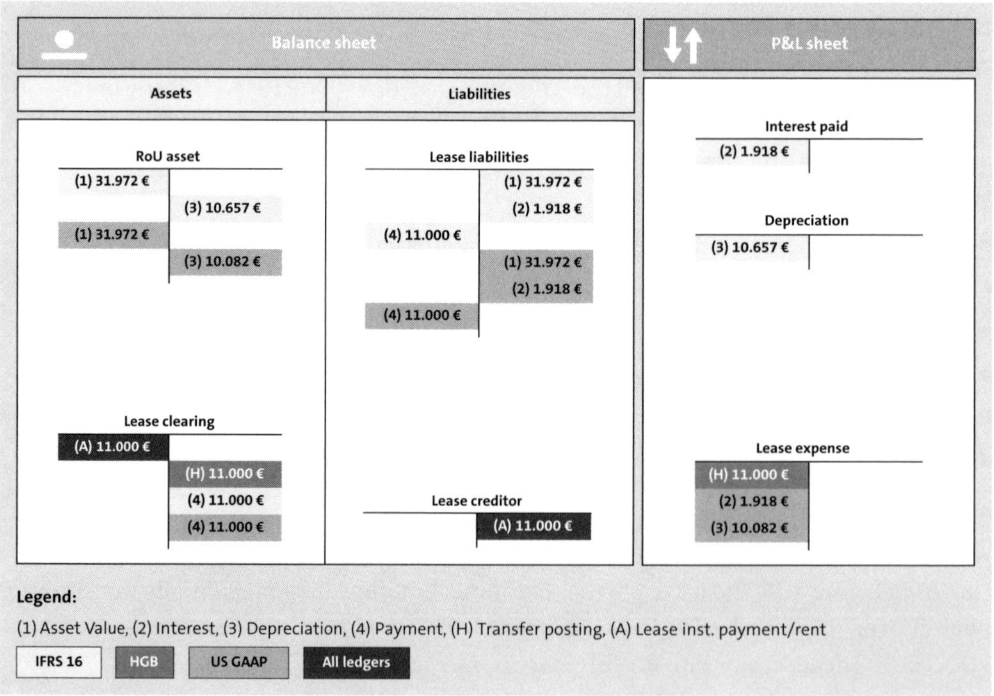


**Figure 8.26** Sample Postings

**IFRS 16**

Period 0

(1) ROU asset/liability acquisition – 31,972€

Period 1

(2) Interest paid/liability – 1,918€

(3) Depreciation expense/depreciate ROU asset – 10,657€

(4) Reduction of liability/lease clearing account – 11,000€

(A) Lease clearing account/payment to creditor – 11,000€

**US GAAP for Operating Leases**

Period 0

(1) ROU asset/liability acquisition – 31,972€

Period 1

(2) Lease expense/liability – 1,918€

(3) Lease expense/depreciate ROU asset – 10,082€

(4) Reduction of liability/lease clearing account – 11,000€

(A) Lease clearing account/payment to creditor – 11,000€

**HGB (Local German GAAP)**

Period 1

(1) Lease expense/lease clearing account – 11,000€

(A) Lease clearing account/payment to creditor – 11,000€

In all cases, the clearing account is used to offset the valuation postings with lease payments. As all condition amounts are either valuated and offset through the reduction of the liability or linearized and posted directly to the appropriate expense account, then the clearing account is periodically fully cleared by lease.

### 8.3.1 Posting Contract Valuations

SAP RE-FX uses a new posting transaction to post valuation cash flows: Transaction RECEEP (Post Contract Valuation). This transaction enables the posting of the pending cash flows for each individual accounting principle, all accounting principles assigned to a contract or for a group of contracts.

The **Post Valuation for Contracts** screen, shown in Figure 8.27, is broken down into several subsections. The key fields in the **Contract Selection** section are as follows:

- **Company Code**: Input the individual company code or a range or list of company codes to perform the lease valuation.
- **Contract**: Input the individual contract number or a range or list of contracts to perform the lease valuation.
- **Contract Type**: Input the contract type or a range or list of contracts to perform the lease valuation.

The key fields in the **Filter** section are as follows:

- **Person Responsible**: This field represents the person responsible for the contract. The default for the contract is the person who created the contract. You can change the **Person Responsible** field en masse using Transaction RECNRP (Change Person Responsible: Contracts).
- **Group Responsible**: This group is made up of one or more responsible users. When selecting by group responsible, all objects or reminder dates that are assigned to one of the members of the group are displayed.

The key fields in the **Period** section are as follows:

- **Month for Posting Run**: Input the calendar month for the valuation posting run.
- **Year for Posting Run**: Input the calendar year for the valuation posting run.
- **Due Date**: Input the due date for the lease valuations. The valuation program will pick up all unposted valuation cash flow entries that are less than or equal to this date.

The key fields in the **Further Selection Criteria** section are as follows:

- **Accounting Principle**: These options include IFRS, HGB, US GAAP, etc. A valuation rule is assigned when the accounting principle is configured.
- **Valuation Rule**: Input the valuation rule or a range or list of valuation rules to perform the lease valuation.

The key fields in the **Posting** section are as follows:

- **Document Header Text**: Input the text to be posted to the accounting document header.

- **Posting Date**: Input the posting date to be recorded in the financial accounting document.
- **Document Date**: Input the document date to be recorded in the financial accounting document.
- **Posting Period**: Input the fiscal period for the posting.
- **Posting Run Mode**: This dropdown menu offers two options: The **Simulation** option will only display planned valuation postings. The **Update Run** option will post planned valuation entries into the financial ledgers.



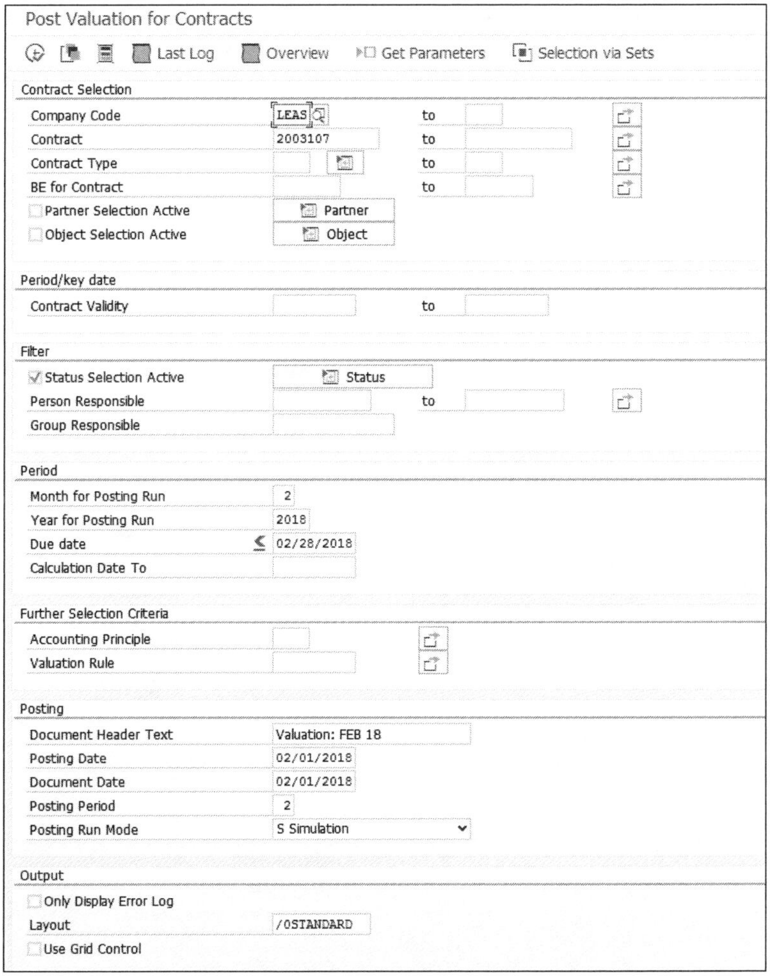


**Figure 8.27** Post Valuation Entry Screen

After you run Transaction RECEEP (Post Contract Valuation), SAP RE-FX will display the results, as shown in Figure 8.28.

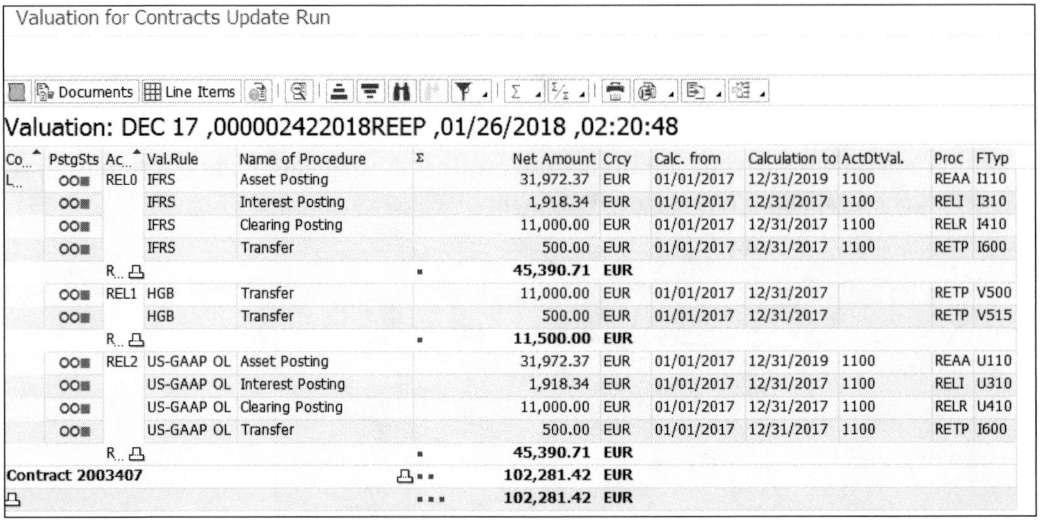


Valuation: DEC 17 ,000002422018REEP ,01/26/2018 ,02:20:48

| Co... | PstgSts | Ac... | Val.Rule | Name of Procedure | Σ | Net Amount | Crcy | Calc. from | Calculation to | ActDtVal. | Proc | FTyp |
|---|---|---|---|---|---|---|---|---|---|---|---|---|
| L... | OO■ | REL0 | IFRS | Asset Posting | | 31,972.37 | EUR | 01/01/2017 | 12/31/2019 | 1100 | REAA | I110 |
| | OO■ | | IFRS | Interest Posting | | 1,918.34 | EUR | 01/01/2017 | 12/31/2017 | 1100 | RELI | I310 |
| | OO■ | | IFRS | Clearing Posting | | 11,000.00 | EUR | 01/01/2017 | 12/31/2017 | 1100 | RELR | I410 |
| | OO■ | | IFRS | Transfer | | 500.00 | EUR | 01/01/2017 | 12/31/2017 | 1100 | RETP | I600 |
| | | R... | | | ■ | **45,390.71** | **EUR** | | | | | |
| | OO■ | REL1 | HGB | Transfer | | 11,000.00 | EUR | 01/01/2017 | 12/31/2017 | | RETP | V500 |
| | OO■ | | HGB | Transfer | | 500.00 | EUR | 01/01/2017 | 12/31/2017 | | RETP | V515 |
| | | R... | | | ■ | **11,500.00** | **EUR** | | | | | |
| | OO■ | REL2 | US-GAAP OL | Asset Posting | | 31,972.37 | EUR | 01/01/2017 | 12/31/2019 | 1100 | REAA | U110 |
| | OO■ | | US-GAAP OL | Interest Posting | | 1,918.34 | EUR | 01/01/2017 | 12/31/2017 | 1100 | RELI | U310 |
| | OO■ | | US-GAAP OL | Clearing Posting | | 11,000.00 | EUR | 01/01/2017 | 12/31/2017 | 1100 | RELR | U410 |
| | OO■ | | US-GAAP OL | Transfer | | 500.00 | EUR | 01/01/2017 | 12/31/2017 | 1100 | RETP | I600 |
| | | R... | | | ■ | **45,390.71** | **EUR** | | | | | |
| **Contract 2003407** | | | | | ■■ | **102,281.42** | **EUR** | | | | | |
| | | | | | ■■■ | **102,281.42** | **EUR** | | | | | |

**Figure 8.28** Valuation Results

Select the **Documents** button to display the posting documents, as shown in Figure 8.29.

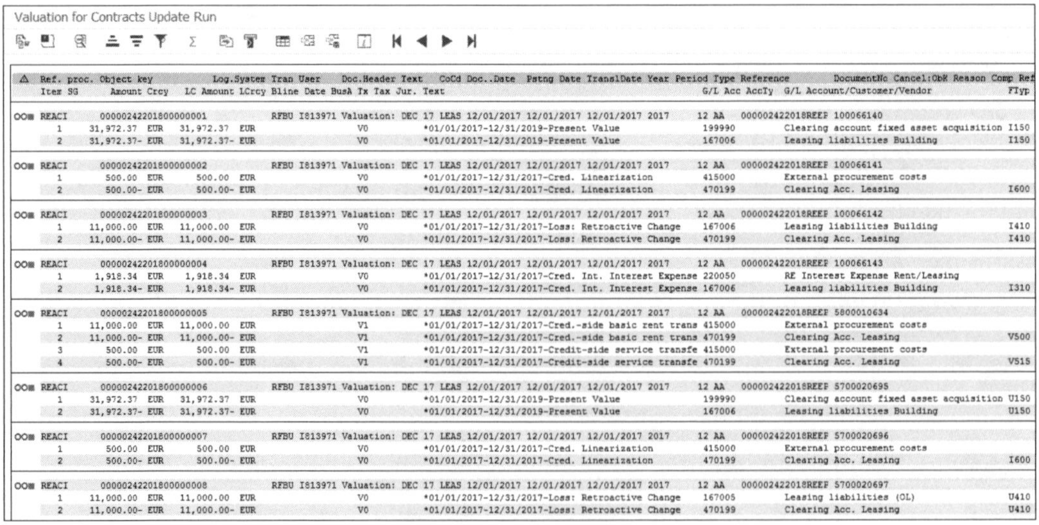


| △ | Ref. proc. | Object key | Log.System | Tran | User | Doc.Header Text | CoCd | Doc..Date | Pstng Date | TranslDate | Year | Period | Type | Reference | DocumentNo | Cancel:ObK | Reason | Comp | Ref |
|---|---|---|---|---|---|---|---|---|---|---|---|---|---|---|---|---|---|---|---|
| | Item SG | Amount | Crcy | LC Amount | LCrcy | Bline Date | BusA | Tx | Tax Jur. | Text | G/L Acc | AccTy | G/L Account/Customer/Vendor | FTyp | | | | | |
| OO■ | REACI | 000002422018000000001 | | RFBU | I813971 | Valuation: DEC 17 | LEAS | 12/01/2017 | 12/01/2017 | 12/01/2017 | 2017 | 12 | AA | 000002422018REEP | 100066140 | | | | |
| | 1 | 31,972.37 | EUR | 31,972.37 | EUR | | | V0 | | *01/01/2017-12/31/2019-Present Value | 199990 | | Clearing account fixed asset acquisition | I150 | | | | | |
| | 2 | 31,972.37- | EUR | 31,972.37- | EUR | | | V0 | | *01/01/2017-12/31/2019-Present Value | 167006 | | Leasing liabilities Building | I150 | | | | | |
| OO■ | REACI | 000002422018000000002 | | RFBU | I813971 | Valuation: DEC 17 | LEAS | 12/01/2017 | 12/01/2017 | 12/01/2017 | 2017 | 12 | AA | 000002422018REEP | 100066141 | | | | |
| | 1 | 500.00 | EUR | 500.00 | EUR | | | V0 | | *01/01/2017-12/31/2017-Cred. Linearization | 415000 | | External procurement costs | | | | | | |
| | 2 | 500.00- | EUR | 500.00- | EUR | | | V0 | | *01/01/2017-12/31/2017-Cred. Linearization | 470199 | | Clearing Acc. Leasing | I600 | | | | | |
| OO■ | REACI | 000002422018000000003 | | RFBU | I813971 | Valuation: DEC 17 | LEAS | 12/01/2017 | 12/01/2017 | 12/01/2017 | 2017 | 12 | AA | 000002422018REEP | 100066142 | | | | |
| | 1 | 11,000.00 | EUR | 11,000.00 | EUR | | | V0 | | *01/01/2017-12/31/2017-Loss: Retroactive Change | 167006 | | Leasing liabilities Building | I410 | | | | | |
| | 2 | 11,000.00- | EUR | 11,000.00- | EUR | | | V0 | | *01/01/2017-12/31/2017-Loss: Retroactive Change | 470199 | | Clearing Acc. Leasing | I410 | | | | | |
| OO■ | REACI | 000002422018000000004 | | RFBU | I813971 | Valuation: DEC 17 | LEAS | 12/01/2017 | 12/01/2017 | 12/01/2017 | 2017 | 12 | AA | 000002422018REEP | 100066143 | | | | |
| | 1 | 1,918.34 | EUR | 1,918.34 | EUR | | | V0 | | *01/01/2017-12/31/2017-Cred. Int. Interest Expense | 220050 | | RE Interest Expense Rent/Leasing | | | | | | |
| | 2 | 1,918.34- | EUR | 1,918.34- | EUR | | | V0 | | *01/01/2017-12/31/2017-Cred. Int. Interest Expense | 167006 | | Leasing liabilities Building | I310 | | | | | |
| OO■ | REACI | 000002422018000000005 | | RFBU | I813971 | Valuation: DEC 17 | LEAS | 12/01/2017 | 12/01/2017 | 12/01/2017 | 2017 | 12 | AA | 000002422018REEP | 5800010634 | | | | |
| | 1 | 11,000.00 | EUR | 11,000.00 | EUR | | | V1 | | *01/01/2017-12/31/2017-Cred.-side basic rent trans | 415000 | | External procurement costs | | | | | | |
| | 2 | 11,000.00- | EUR | 11,000.00- | EUR | | | V1 | | *01/01/2017-12/31/2017-Cred.-side basic rent trans | 470199 | | Clearing Acc. Leasing | V500 | | | | | |
| | 3 | 500.00 | EUR | 500.00 | EUR | | | V1 | | *01/01/2017-12/31/2017-Credit-side service transfe | 415000 | | External procurement costs | | | | | | |
| | 4 | 500.00- | EUR | 500.00- | EUR | | | V1 | | *01/01/2017-12/31/2017-Credit-side service transfe | 470199 | | Clearing Acc. Leasing | V515 | | | | | |
| OO■ | REACI | 000002422018000000006 | | RFBU | I813971 | Valuation: DEC 17 | LEAS | 12/01/2017 | 12/01/2017 | 12/01/2017 | 2017 | 12 | AA | 000002422018REEP | 5700020695 | | | | |
| | 1 | 31,972.37 | EUR | 31,972.37 | EUR | | | V0 | | *01/01/2017-12/31/2019-Present Value | 199990 | | Clearing account fixed asset acquisition | U150 | | | | | |
| | 2 | 31,972.37- | EUR | 31,972.37- | EUR | | | V0 | | *01/01/2017-12/31/2019-Present Value | 167006 | | Leasing liabilities Building | U150 | | | | | |
| OO■ | REACI | 000002422018000000007 | | RFBU | I813971 | Valuation: DEC 17 | LEAS | 12/01/2017 | 12/01/2017 | 12/01/2017 | 2017 | 12 | AA | 000002422018REEP | 5700020696 | | | | |
| | 1 | 500.00 | EUR | 500.00 | EUR | | | V0 | | *01/01/2017-12/31/2017-Cred. Linearization | 415000 | | External procurement costs | | | | | | |
| | 2 | 500.00- | EUR | 500.00- | EUR | | | V0 | | *01/01/2017-12/31/2017-Cred. Linearization | 470199 | | Clearing Acc. Leasing | I600 | | | | | |
| OO■ | REACI | 000002422018000000008 | | RFBU | I813971 | Valuation: DEC 17 | LEAS | 12/01/2017 | 12/01/2017 | 12/01/2017 | 2017 | 12 | AA | 000002422018REEP | 5700020697 | | | | |
| | 1 | 11,000.00 | EUR | 11,000.00 | EUR | | | V0 | | *01/01/2017-12/31/2017-Loss: Retroactive Change | 167005 | | Leasing liabilities (OL) | U410 | | | | | |
| | 2 | 11,000.00- | EUR | 11,000.00- | EUR | | | V0 | | *01/01/2017-12/31/2017-Loss: Retroactive Change | 470199 | | Clearing Acc. Leasing | U410 | | | | | |

**Figure 8.29** Valuation Posting Documents

Thanks to the integration of SAP RE-FX with SAP ERP Financials, all these entries are recorded to the general and fixed asset ledgers in real time with no need to maintain cumbersome interfaces.

### 8.3.2 Reversing Contract Valuations

To reverse posted cash flow valuations, you can use another new posting transaction: Transaction RECEEPRV (Reverse Contract Valuation). Valuation posting runs may be reversed either by contract number or by process ID. If by *contract number*, only the valuation entries for that individual contract will be reversed. A *process ID* is automatically assigned to each posting run, so when reversing a valuation by process ID, all posted documents under that ID will be reversed.



### 8.3.3 Depreciating Right-of-Use Assets

You can depreciate ROU assets using the standard FI-AA depreciation program.

To process depreciation, run Transaction AFAB (Depreciation Run: Execute). The depreciation amounts are calculated by SAP RE-FX and stored as valuation cash flow entries. Due to the special depreciation key provided by SAP, the stored cash flow entries for depreciation are utilized by asset accounting.

### 8.3.4 Deactivating Leased Assets

As leases reach the end of their term or are terminated through early termination options, leases will be fully depreciated (a process controlled by the lease valuation process). However, a right-of-use fixed asset will still be active even though the acquisition and production cost (APC) is zero. For deactivating ROU assets, SAP has developed two new transactions:

- Transaction RECEASSETDEACT (Deactivate Lease Assets)
- Transaction RECEASSETDEACTRV (Deactivate Lease Assets: Reversal)

The Deactivate Lease Assets report will deactivate ROU assets en masse. In addition to the usual contract report selection criteria, two sets of fields are available, as shown in Figure 8.30.

The key fields in the **Selection** section are as follows:

- **Valuation Rule**: With these two fields, you can filter the deactivation of ROU assets by a specific valuation rule.

- **Asset Class**: With these two fields, you can only deactivate specific asset classes.
- **Assets for Contracts**: Select this checkbox to deactivate the assets for the contract identified on the selection screen.
- **Assets for Object Groups**: Select this checkbox to deactivate all assets for the items listed in the object group.
- **Only Assets That Can Be Deact.**: Select this checkbox to select only assets that have a zero balance and can be deactivated.

The key fields in the **Posting** section are as follows:

- **Month for Posting Run**: Input the calendar month of the deactivation run.
- **Year for Posting Run**: Input the calendar year of the deactivation run.
- **Document Header Text**: Add short text to be included on the fixed asset posting document.
- **Deactivation Date**: Input the date the deactivation is effective.
- **Posting Date**: Input the posting date on the fixed asset document.
- **Document Date**: Input the document date on the fixed asset posting document.
- **Posting Period**: Input the fiscal period for the deactivation posting.
- **Execution Mode**: Choose the execution mode from the dropdown menu—either **Simulation** (to display deactivation results without posting) or **Update Run** (to post deactivation results).

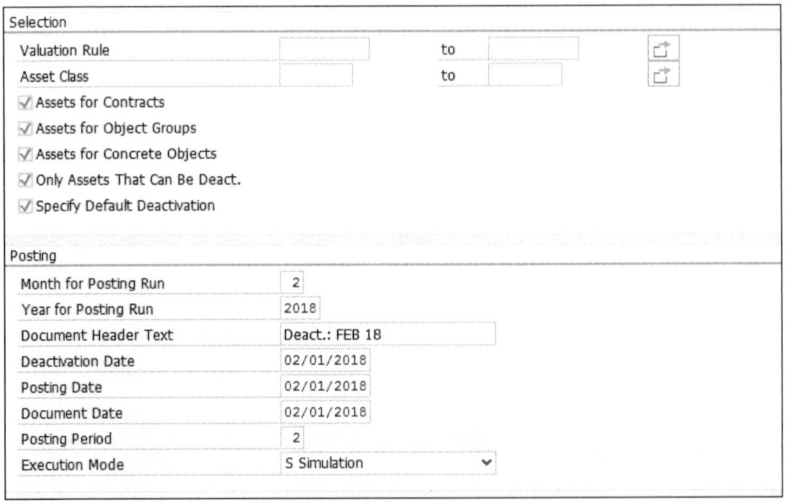


**Figure 8.30** Deactivate Lease Assets Selection Screen

Once you execute the report, the SAP RE-FX system displays the results as shown in Figure 8.31.

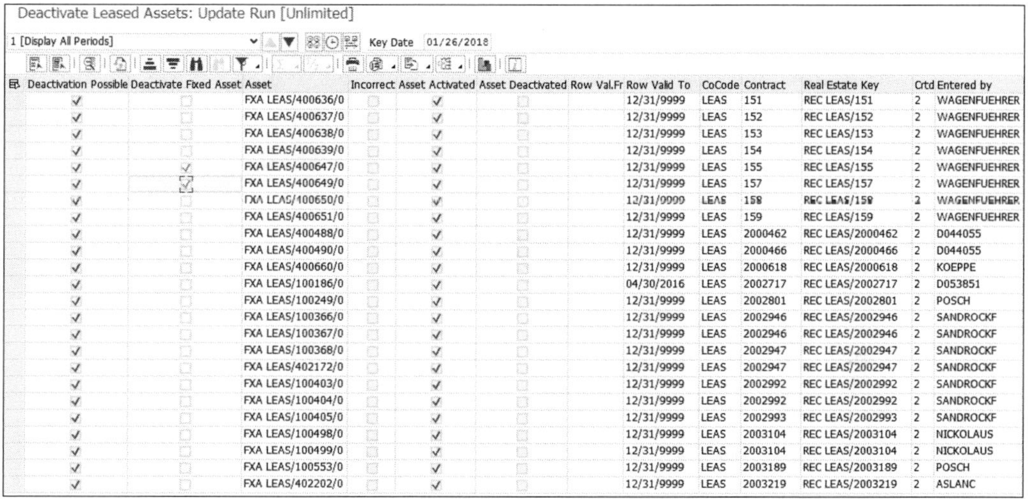
Deactivate Leased Assets: Update Run [Unlimited]

1 [Display All Periods] Key Date 01/26/2018

| Deactivation Possible | Deactivate Fixed Asset | Asset | Incorrect | Asset Activated | Asset Deactivated | Row Val.Fr | Row Valid To | CoCode | Contract | Real Estate Key | Crtd | Entered by |
|---|---|---|---|---|---|---|---|---|---|---|---|---|
| ✓ | | FXA LEAS/400636/0 | | ✓ | | | 12/31/9999 | LEAS | 151 | REC LEAS/151 | 2 | WAGENFUEHRER |
| ✓ | | FXA LEAS/400637/0 | | ✓ | | | 12/31/9999 | LEAS | 152 | REC LEAS/152 | 2 | WAGENFUEHRER |
| ✓ | | FXA LEAS/400638/0 | | ✓ | | | 12/31/9999 | LEAS | 153 | REC LEAS/153 | 2 | WAGENFUEHRER |
| ✓ | | FXA LEAS/400639/0 | | ✓ | | | 12/31/9999 | LEAS | 154 | REC LEAS/154 | 2 | WAGENFUEHRER |
| ✓ | ✓ | FXA LEAS/400647/0 | | ✓ | | | 12/31/9999 | LEAS | 155 | REC LEAS/155 | 2 | WAGENFUEHRER |
| ✓ | ✓ | FXA LEAS/400649/0 | | ✓ | | | 12/31/9999 | LEAS | 157 | REC LEAS/157 | 2 | WAGENFUEHRER |
| ✓ | | FXA LEAS/400650/0 | | ✓ | | | 12/31/9999 | LEAS | 158 | REC LEAS/158 | 2 | WAGENFUEHRER |
| ✓ | | FXA LEAS/400651/0 | | ✓ | | | 12/31/9999 | LEAS | 159 | REC LEAS/159 | 2 | WAGENFUEHRER |
| ✓ | | FXA LEAS/400488/0 | | ✓ | | | 12/31/9999 | LEAS | 2000462 | REC LEAS/2000462 | 2 | D044055 |
| ✓ | | FXA LEAS/400490/0 | | ✓ | | | 12/31/9999 | LEAS | 2000466 | REC LEAS/2000466 | 2 | D044055 |
| ✓ | | FXA LEAS/400660/0 | | ✓ | | | 12/31/9999 | LEAS | 2000618 | REC LEAS/2000618 | 2 | KOEPPE |
| ✓ | | FXA LEAS/100186/0 | | ✓ | | | 04/30/2016 | LEAS | 2002717 | REC LEAS/2002717 | 2 | D053851 |
| ✓ | | FXA LEAS/100249/0 | | ✓ | | | 12/31/9999 | LEAS | 2002801 | REC LEAS/2002801 | 2 | POSCH |
| ✓ | | FXA LEAS/100366/0 | | ✓ | | | 12/31/9999 | LEAS | 2002946 | REC LEAS/2002946 | 2 | SANDROCKF |
| ✓ | | FXA LEAS/100367/0 | | ✓ | | | 12/31/9999 | LEAS | 2002946 | REC LEAS/2002946 | 2 | SANDROCKF |
| ✓ | | FXA LEAS/100368/0 | | ✓ | | | 12/31/9999 | LEAS | 2002947 | REC LEAS/2002947 | 2 | SANDROCKF |
| ✓ | | FXA LEAS/402172/0 | | ✓ | | | 12/31/9999 | LEAS | 2002947 | REC LEAS/2002947 | 2 | SANDROCKF |
| ✓ | | FXA LEAS/100403/0 | | ✓ | | | 12/31/9999 | LEAS | 2002992 | REC LEAS/2002992 | 2 | SANDROCKF |
| ✓ | | FXA LEAS/100404/0 | | ✓ | | | 12/31/9999 | LEAS | 2002992 | REC LEAS/2002992 | 2 | SANDROCKF |
| ✓ | | FXA LEAS/100405/0 | | ✓ | | | 12/31/9999 | LEAS | 2002993 | REC LEAS/2002993 | 2 | SANDROCKF |
| ✓ | | FXA LEAS/100498/0 | | ✓ | | | 12/31/9999 | LEAS | 2003104 | REC LEAS/2003104 | 2 | NICKOLAUS |
| ✓ | | FXA LEAS/100499/0 | | ✓ | | | 12/31/9999 | LEAS | 2003104 | REC LEAS/2003104 | 2 | NICKOLAUS |
| ✓ | | FXA LEAS/100553/0 | | ✓ | | | 12/31/9999 | LEAS | 2003189 | REC LEAS/2003189 | 2 | POSCH |
| ✓ | | FXA LEAS/402202/0 | | ✓ | | | 12/31/9999 | LEAS | 2003219 | REC LEAS/2003219 | 2 | ASLANC |

**Figure 8.31** Deactivate Lease Asset Results

During the update run, you'll have the option to deactivate specific fixed assets using the checkbox. When you've selected the desired assets, save the report, and the fixed ROU assets will be deactivated. A fixed asset document will be generated, as shown in Figure 8.32.

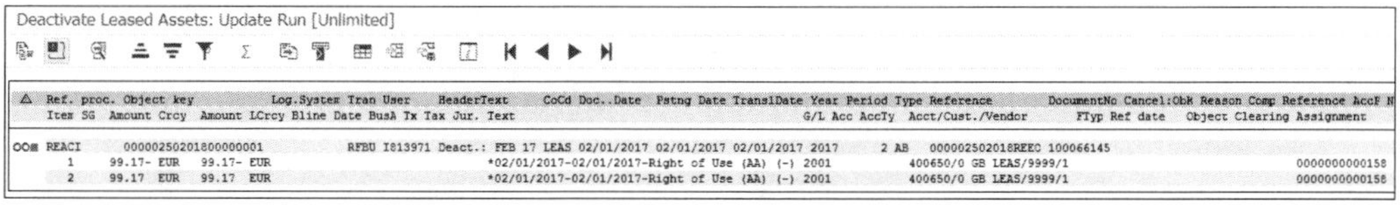


**Figure 8.32** Deactivate Lease Accounting Document

## 8.4 Lease Modifications and Updates

Over the life of a real estate contract, the terms and conditions of a lease agreement may change. A central requirement of the new leasing standards is for detailed processing of changes, which must be transparent and visible.

For example, perhaps you perform an analysis of a property and determine that you expect to occupy that property longer than originally intended and that you will exercise all renewal options instead of the first available option only. In this case, the probable end date is updated to a new contract end date, and the lease must be revaluated.

Within the valuation rule, you can enter, calculate, and post (per accounting principle) the following modifications in SAP RE-FX with full visibility into the valuation adjustment amounts and a posting log of who made the changes:

- Condition changes (e.g., increase, reduction, scale, and so on)
- Index adjustments
- Term changes (shortened, extended)
- Notices and terminations
- Scope changes (scope reduction or widened scope)
- Changes to basic principles (e.g., interest)
- New elements
- Switch between operate and finance lease
- Extraordinary depreciations
- Change of options to buy, residual value guarantees, or asset retirement obligations
- Retroactive condition changes in already closed periods (as profit and loss posting)
- Changes to the account assignment elements
- Profit center or trading partner changes

With each valuation-relevant contract change, a user can create a new time slot in the valuation parameters. Based on this change, SAP RE-FX will create a new version of the "cash flow set" that contains all cash flow records of the old time slices that have already been posted and the changed cash flow records for the new time slice. The old cash flow set is retained and can be viewed for analysis.

## 8.5 Reporting and Disclosure Statements

The last step in the lease management lifecycle in SAP RE-FX is to follow reporting and disclosure requirements.

### 8.5.1 Displaying and Maintaining Valuation Rules

The developers at SAP understand that lease administrators and lease accountants need to manage and maintain many contracts all at once. During a contract's lifecycle, multiple updates to the lease classification or discount rates can occur, or terms and conditions can be modified.

Thus, to accelerate the handling of contract changes, SAP introduced Transaction RECEISRULECN (Display and Maintain Valuation Rules). This transaction serves as both a report to view the valuation rules assigned to a contract and as a mass change/maintenance tool.

Besides the usual selection criteria available on most real estate contract reports, this report also has an **Activity** section, shown at the bottom of Figure 8.33, in which two kinds of parameters may be assigned.



First, the **Activity** dropdown menu gives you two options: Select **Display** for a static report. If you select **Change**, then data elements related to valuation rules may be maintained through the report. Changes made through the report update each contract and will be reflected in the valuation process log.

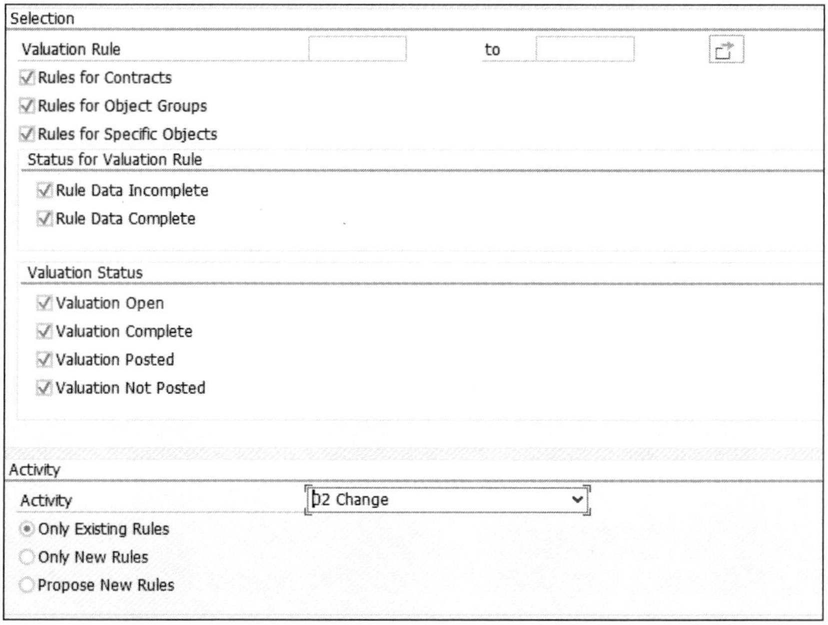


**Figure 8.33** Display/Maintain Valuation Rule Entry Screen

Second, choose one from among three radio buttons:

- **Only Existing Rules**: This radio button allows users to only display or change existing valuation rules.

- **Only New Rules**: This radio button only allows users to maintain new valuation rules.
- **Propose New Rules**: The SAP RE-FX system will propose valuation rules for each contract where a valuation rule has not been assigned.

Within the report shown in Figure 8.34, the following quick link icons are available:

- **Rule Data Complete**: This icon is for marking a valuation rule as complete if the report is executed in change mode.
- **Rule Data Incomplete**: This icon is for marking a valuation rule as incomplete. You might use this icon if a lease modification occurred and the valuation rule requires additional analysis.
- **Mass Change**: This icon enables change to a value in multiple contracts or valuation rules simultaneously. You should first select the valuation rules to be maintained and then select this icon to display the screen shown in Figure 8.35. You can now populate the values to be maintained and select the **Continue** icon.
- **Add Time Slots**: This icon provides the ability to specify additional time slots, as we described earlier in Section 8.4.

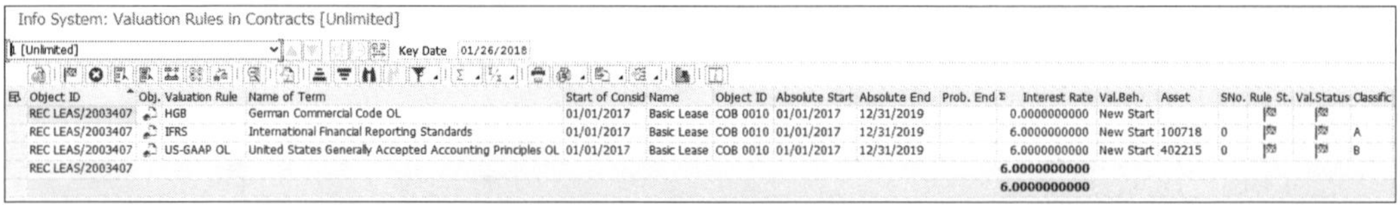


**Figure 8.34** Maintain Valuation Rule Report

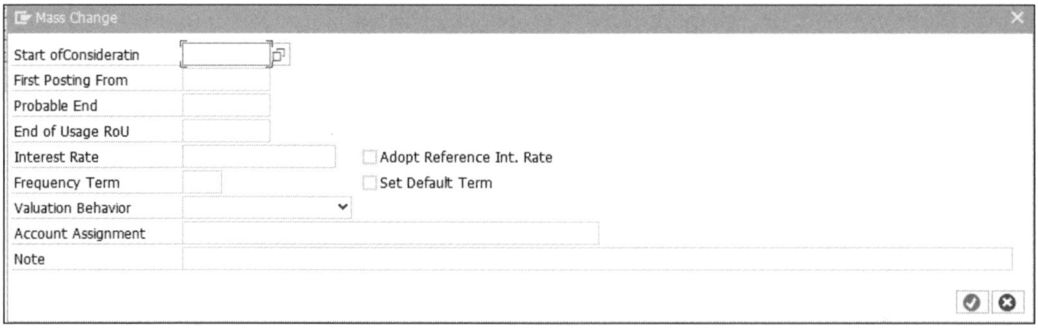


**Figure 8.35** Mass Change Valuation Rules

If you make any changes in this report, be sure to save them by clicking the save icon.

## 8.5.2 Viewing Leased Assets for Contracts

A fixed asset is generally assigned to each valuation rule; thus, a leasing analyst needs to understand what assets are assigned to each contract.

Transaction RECEISASSETCN (Lease Assets for Contracts) provides this listing. Besides providing the standard real estate contract selection fields, the system also lets you filter by valuation rule, asset class, valuation rule status (top of Figure 8.36), and by valuation status (bottom of Figure 8.36).

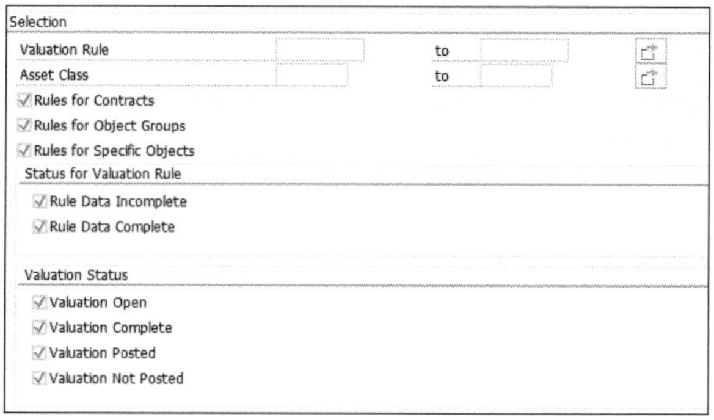


**Figure 8.36** Lease Assets Report Selection Screen

The results of the Leased Assets for Contracts report displays a listing of contracts and their assigned fixed asset numbers. You can also quickly check the posting status and the valuation status of each lease by consulting the **Posting Status** and **Valuation Status** columns on the right side of the report, as shown in Figure 8.37.

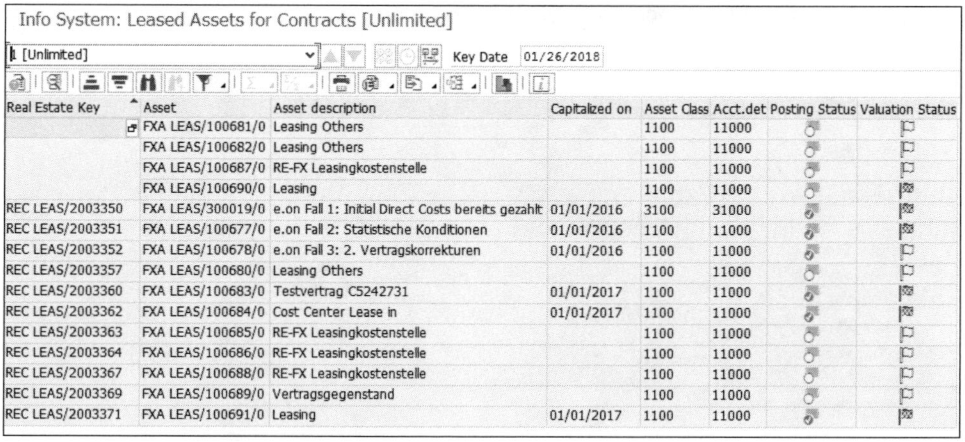
Info System: Leased Assets for Contracts [Unlimited]

[Unlimited] Key Date 01/26/2018

| Real Estate Key | Asset | Asset description | Capitalized on | Asset Class | Acct.det | Posting Status | Valuation Status |
|---|---|---|---|---|---|---|---|
| | FXA LEAS/100681/0 | Leasing Others | | 1100 | 11000 | | |
| | FXA LEAS/100682/0 | Leasing Others | | 1100 | 11000 | | |
| | FXA LEAS/100687/0 | RE-FX Leasingkostenstelle | | 1100 | 11000 | | |
| | FXA LEAS/100690/0 | Leasing | | 1100 | 11000 | | |
| REC LEAS/2003350 | FXA LEAS/300019/0 | e.on Fall 1: Initial Direct Costs bereits gezahlt | 01/01/2016 | 3100 | 31000 | | |
| REC LEAS/2003351 | FXA LEAS/100677/0 | e.on Fall 2: Statistische Konditionen | 01/01/2016 | 1100 | 11000 | | |
| REC LEAS/2003352 | FXA LEAS/100678/0 | e.on Fall 3: 2. Vertragskorrekturen | 01/01/2016 | 1100 | 11000 | | |
| REC LEAS/2003357 | FXA LEAS/100680/0 | Leasing Others | | 1100 | 11000 | | |
| REC LEAS/2003360 | FXA LEAS/100683/0 | Testvertrag C5242731 | 01/01/2017 | 1100 | 11000 | | |
| REC LEAS/2003362 | FXA LEAS/100684/0 | Cost Center Lease in | 01/01/2017 | 1100 | 11000 | | |
| REC LEAS/2003363 | FXA LEAS/100685/0 | RE-FX Leasingkostenstelle | | 1100 | 11000 | | |
| REC LEAS/2003364 | FXA LEAS/100686/0 | RE-FX Leasingkostenstelle | | 1100 | 11000 | | |
| REC LEAS/2003367 | FXA LEAS/100688/0 | RE-FX Leasingkostenstelle | | 1100 | 11000 | | |
| REC LEAS/2003369 | FXA LEAS/100689/0 | Vertragsgegenstand | | 1100 | 11000 | | |
| REC LEAS/2003371 | FXA LEAS/100691/0 | Leasing | 01/01/2017 | 1100 | 11000 | | |

**Figure 8.37** Leased Assets Report Results

### 8.5.3 Displaying Contract Valuations

The Display Contract Valuations report is similar to the Valuation Cash Flow report provided on the **Overviews** tab of the contract.

Transaction RECESH (Display Contract Valuations) provides a single report to view all valuation-related cash flow entries by valuation rule (in our example, US GAAP). Accountants execute this report to ensure all valuation cash flow entries are being calculated as expected prior to generating valuation postings. Unlike the Valuation Cash Flow report, the Display Contract Valuation report displays the valuations for multiple contracts, supporting aggregate reporting for disclosures.

In addition to the standard selection criteria available on a real estate contract, several selection options are available for Display Contract Valuation report.

The key fields in the **Output Options** section of Figure 8.38 are as follows:

- **View**: Your options in this dropdown menu are **Process** or **Cash Flow**.
  - The **Process** output will display each valuation rule, status, values, and valuation reason. The format is similar to what's found on the **Valuation** tab of the contract but displayed in a clear and concise format.
  - The **Cash Flow** output provides a single report to view all valuation related cash flow entries by valuation rule (GAAP). This simple report is executed by accountants to ensure all valuation cash flow entries are being calculated as expected prior to generating valuation postings.
- **Use Fiscal Year**: This checkbox is applicable for organizations that do not operate on a calendar year basis. Instead of displaying all valuation amounts by calendar year, values will be allocated to the appropriate fiscal year to support disclosure reporting.

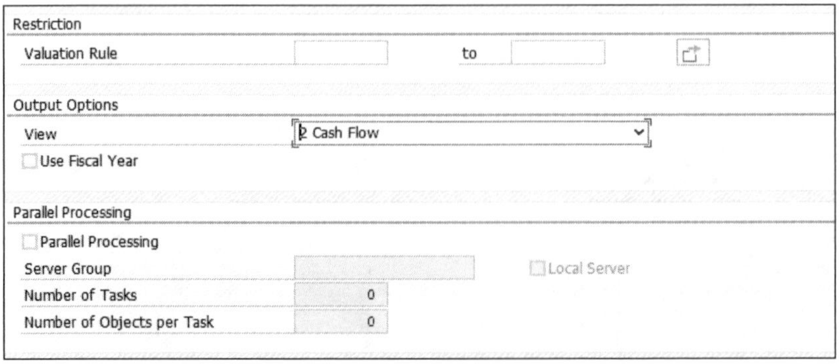


**Figure 8.38** Display Contract Valuations Selection Screen

As shown in Figure 8.39 and Figure 8.40, the Display Contract Valuation report provides the contract value, the present value, and a list of linearization postings as well as the amortization schedule for ROU assets as well as their corresponding liability. Note that, for quick reference, all asset information is displayed in orange, and all liability information is highlighted in green. The repayment and lease expense/revenue amounts are also listed by period on this report.

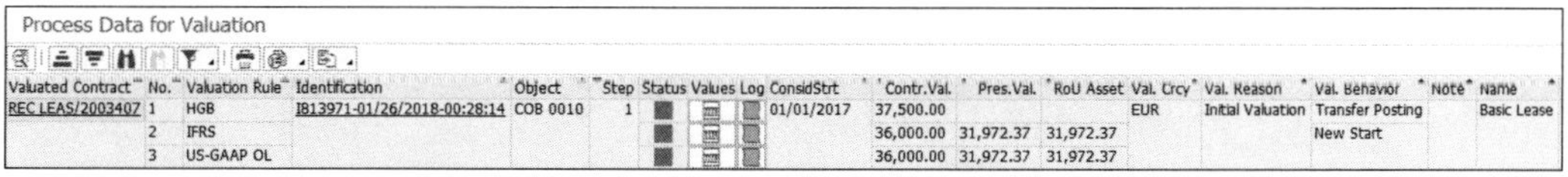

Process Data for Valuation

| Valuated Contract | No. | Valuation Rule | Identification | Object | Step | Status | Values | Log | ConsidStrt | Contr.Val. | Pres.Val. | RoU Asset | Val. Crcy | Val. Reason | Val. Behavior | Note | Name |
|---|---|---|---|---|---|---|---|---|---|---|---|---|---|---|---|---|---|
| REC LEAS/2003407 | 1 | HGB | IB13971-01/26/2018-00:28:14 | COB 0010 | 1 | | | | 01/01/2017 | 37,500.00 | | | EUR | Initial Valuation | Transfer Posting | | Basic Lease |
| | 2 | IFRS | | | | | | | | 36,000.00 | 31,972.37 | 31,972.37 | | | New Start | | |
| | 3 | US-GAAP OL | | | | | | | | 36,000.00 | 31,972.37 | 31,972.37 | | | | | |

Figure 8.39 Display Contract Valuation Process Report

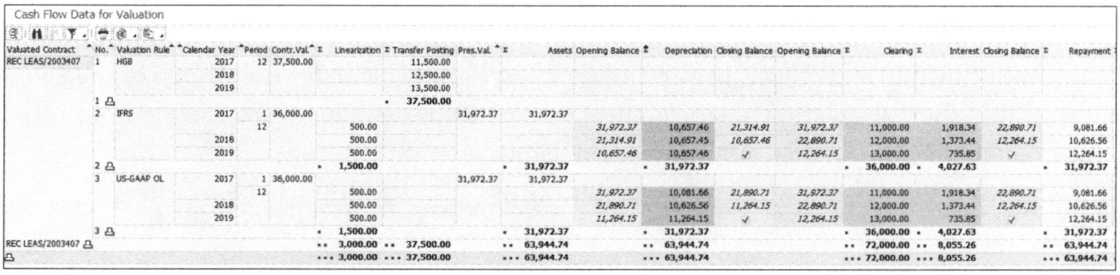

Cash Flow Data for Valuation

| Valuated Contract | No. | Valuation Rule | Calendar Year | Period | Contr.Val. | Linearization | Transfer Posting | Pres.Val. | Assets | Opening Balance | Depreciation | Closing Balance | Opening Balance | Clearing | Interest | Closing Balance | Repayment |
|---|---|---|---|---|---|---|---|---|---|---|---|---|---|---|---|---|---|
| REC LEAS/2003407 | 1 | HGB | 2017 | 12 | 37,500.00 | | 11,500.00 | | | | | | | | | | |
| | | | 2018 | | | | 12,500.00 | | | | | | | | | | |
| | | | 2019 | | | | 13,500.00 | | | | | | | | | | |
| | 1 | | | | | | • 37,500.00 | | | | | | | | | | |
| | 2 | IFRS | 2017 | 1 | 36,000.00 | | | 31,972.37 | 31,972.37 | | | | | | | | |
| | | | | 12 | | 500.00 | | | | 31,972.37 | 10,657.46 | 21,314.91 | 31,972.37 | 11,000.00 | 1,918.34 | 22,890.71 | 9,081.66 |
| | | | 2018 | | | 500.00 | | | | 21,314.91 | 10,657.45 | 10,657.46 | 22,890.71 | 12,000.00 | 1,373.44 | 12,264.15 | 10,626.56 |
| | | | 2019 | | | 500.00 | | | | 10,657.46 | 10,657.46 | ✓ | 12,264.15 | 13,000.00 | 735.85 | ✓ | 12,264.15 |
| | 2 | | | | | • 1,500.00 | | | • 31,972.37 | | • 31,972.37 | | | • 36,000.00 | • 4,027.63 | | • 31,972.37 |
| | 3 | US-GAAP OL | 2017 | 1 | 36,000.00 | | | 31,972.37 | 31,972.37 | | | | | | | | |
| | | | | 12 | | 500.00 | | | | 31,972.37 | 10,081.66 | 21,890.71 | 31,972.37 | 11,000.00 | 1,918.34 | 22,890.71 | 9,081.66 |
| | | | 2018 | | | 500.00 | | | | 21,890.71 | 10,626.56 | 11,264.15 | 22,890.71 | 12,000.00 | 1,373.44 | 12,264.15 | 10,626.56 |
| | | | 2019 | | | 500.00 | | | | 11,264.15 | 11,264.15 | ✓ | 12,264.15 | 13,000.00 | 735.85 | ✓ | 12,264.15 |
| | 3 | | | | | • 1,500.00 | | | • 31,972.37 | | • 31,972.37 | | | • 36,000.00 | • 4,027.63 | | • 31,972.37 |
| REC LEAS/2003407 | | | | | | •• 3,000.00 | •• 37,500.00 | | •• 63,944.74 | | •• 63,944.74 | | | •• 72,000.00 | •• 8,055.26 | | •• 63,944.74 |
| | | | | | | ••• 3,000.00 | ••• 37,500.00 | | ••• 63,944.74 | | ••• 63,944.74 | | | ••• 72,000.00 | ••• 8,055.26 | | ••• 63,944.74 |

Figure 8.40 Display Contract Valuation Report Results

### 8.5.4 Reclassifying Liabilities

To make accurate disclosures, you'll need to separate lease liabilities into short-term (less than one year) and long-term (greater than one year) categories. SAP RE-FX automatically posts the lease liability when the ROU asset is created, so SAP created Transaction RECEISRECLASSIFY (Reclassification) to properly recognize the lease liabilities in short-term and long-term components.

In addition to providing the standard real estate contract selection fields, this report also provides the ability to filter by valuation rule, sort method, and key date (see Figure 8.41). Valuation cash flows must be posted to the liability account to be considered for reclassification. With this report, you can also drill down to the original contract master record if needed.

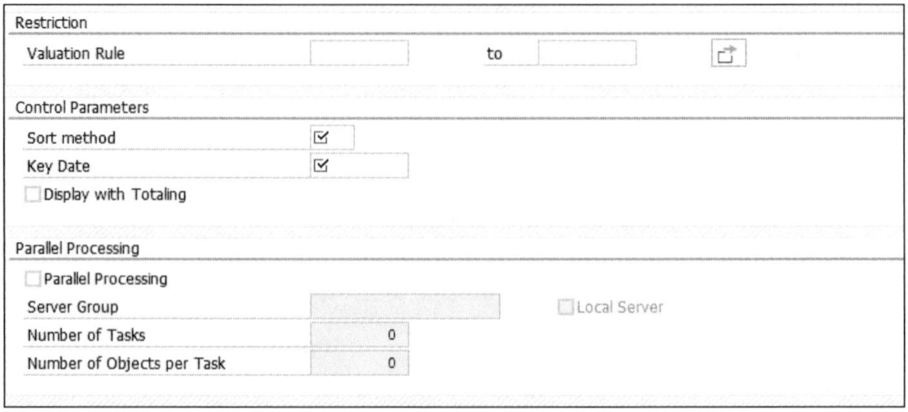


**Figure 8.41** Reclassification Report Selection Screen

As shown in Figure 8.42, the Reclassification report calculates how much of the liability is short term and recognized in the **Start Absolute** field, which is the amount that should be reclassified as a short-term liability.

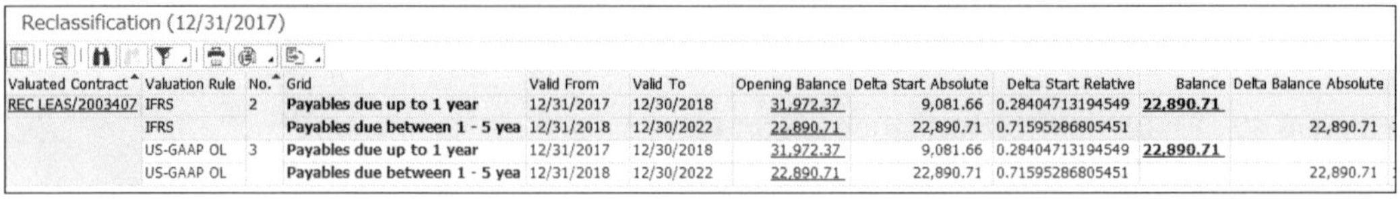

Reclassification (12/31/2017)

| Valuated Contract | Valuation Rule | No. | Grid | Valid From | Valid To | Opening Balance | Delta Start Absolute | Delta Start Relative | Balance | Delta Balance Absolute |
|---|---|---|---|---|---|---|---|---|---|---|
| REC LEAS/2003407 | IFRS | 2 | **Payables due up to 1 year** | 12/31/2017 | 12/30/2018 | 31,972.37 | 9,081.66 | 0.28404713194549 | **22,890.71** | |
| | IFRS | | **Payables due between 1 - 5 yea** | 12/31/2018 | 12/30/2022 | 22,890.71 | 22,890.71 | 0.71595286805451 | | 22,890.71 |
| | US-GAAP OL | 3 | **Payables due up to 1 year** | 12/31/2017 | 12/30/2018 | 31,972.37 | 9,081.66 | 0.28404713194549 | **22,890.71** | |
| | US-GAAP OL | | **Payables due between 1 - 5 yea** | 12/31/2018 | 12/30/2022 | 22,890.71 | 22,890.71 | 0.71595286805451 | | 22,890.71 |

**Figure 8.42** Reclassification Report Results

## 8.6 Summary

As shown in this chapter, SAP's comprehensive real estate solution supports many different leasing scenarios. Due to its tight integration with SAP ERP Financials, SAP RE-FX can properly calculate and record valuation entries for multiple accounting standards simultaneously. The solution also supports lease modifications and tracks all changes made to leases over their lifecycles. With powerful reporting features, lease accounting disclosure requirements are greatly simplified.

# Chapter 9
# Disclosures, Reporting, and Analytics

*Beyond complying with the corresponding legal standards for financial disclosures, every company can use out-of-the-box functionality to fulfill internal reporting and analysis requirements.*



This chapter introduces the disclosure requirements introduced with the new regulations according International Financial Reporting Standards 16 and Accounting Standards Codification 842. We'll describe the differences in regards to lease costs and the new requirements for right-of-use assets (ROU assets) and lease liabilities in Section 9.1. In Section 9.2 and Section 9.3, we'll focus on SAP Flexible Real Estate Management (SAP RE-FX) and SAP Lease Administration by Nakisa, focusing on the reporting functionalities provided by both applications out of the box, along with examples.

## 9.1 Standard Required Disclosures

According the International Accounting Standards Board (IASB), the objective of IFRS 16 is to report information that faithfully represents lease transactions and provides a basis for users of financial statements to assess the amount, timing, and uncertainty of cash flows arising from leases. To meet that objective, a lessee should recognize assets and liabilities arising from a lease.

IFRS 16 introduces a single lessee accounting model and requires a lessee to recognize assets and liabilities for all leases with a term of more than 12 months, unless the underlying asset is of low value. A lessee is required to recognize an ROU asset, representing its right to use the underlying leased asset, and a lease liability, representing its obligation to make lease payments.

### 9.1.1 Lease Cost

With accounting regulations before IFRS 16, a separation existed between an operating lease and a finance lease (IAS 17). With this separation, for operating leases, no values represented either assets or liabilities. Only leasing rates were shown, and those amounts were accounted for directly as costs. Such operating lease contracts were not represented in the balance sheet of the lessee (off-balance), whereas finance lease contracts were shown in the balance sheet (on-balance).

With the new valuation according to IFRS 16, you will no longer distinguish between operating leases and finance leases contracts. For all contracts that are or contain leases, all acquired rights of use must be shown within assets as ROU assets and as lease liabilities.

### 9.1.2 Right-of-Use Assets and Lease Liabilities

A lessee measures ROU assets similarly to other non-financial assets (such as property, plant, and equipment) and lease liabilities similarly to other financial liabilities. Consequently, a lessee recognizes the depreciation of the ROU asset, usually on a straight-line basis, and recognizes interest on the lease liability. In the statement of cash flows, a lessee separates the total amount of cash paid into the principal (presented within financing activities) and the interest (presented within either operating or financing activities) in accordance with IAS 7.

Assets and liabilities arising from a lease are initially measured on a present value basis. The measurement includes non-cancellable lease payments (including inflation-linked payments) and also includes payments to be made in optional periods if the lessee is reasonably certain to exercise an option to extend the lease, or not to exercise an option to terminate the lease. The initial lease asset equals the lease liability in most cases.

The lease asset is the right to use the underlying asset and is presented in the statement of financial position either as part of property, plant, and equipment or as its own line item.

#### Right-of-Use Assets

The ROU asset is measured with the value of the lease liabilities, corrected by the following (per IFRS 16, paragraph 23ff.):

- Lease rates at or before contract start date
- Received subventions or incentives

- Initial direct costs
- Estimated costs for fulfilling an obligation for removing or reconstructing the underlying asset (if applicable)

According IFRS 16, a revaluation of the ROU asset is carried out with amortized costs. In other words, the value of the asset is reduced by the planned accumulated depreciation and possibly other decreases in value (IFRS 16, paragraph 32).

For the depreciation period, according to IFRS 16 (and similar to IAS 17), the shorter of the asset's useful life or the duration of the lease contract must be chosen. If the leased object is transferred to the lessee at the end of the asset's useful life, or if a purchase option exists, then only the asset's useful life is relevant.



If the lessee is using the "Fair Value Model" according to IAS 40, this approach is also obligatory for corresponding lease circumstances.

According IFRS 16, ROU assets have to be shown either in the balance sheet or attached to the balance sheet. If there is no separate balance sheet position, the ROU assets have to be assigned to the balance sheet position, they would belong to, if they were own property. (This assignment must be explained according to IFRS 16, paragraph 47.) If the asset constitutes real estate for financial investment, the asset must be accounted for as investment property.

### Lease Liability

According IFRS 16, lease liabilities must be disclosed separately from other liabilities or explained as an attachment to the balance sheet. If not disclosed separately, lease liabilities must be commented on in the attachment, describing to what extent lease liabilities are included within other liabilities.

Lease liabilities are measured based on the present value of future lease payments (IFRS 16, paragraph 26ff.), taking the following items into consideration:

- Fixed future payments for lease agreements including de facto fixed leasing payments
- Variable leasing payments, which depend on a rate or index
- Price of the purchase option, if the purchase option is likely to be executed
- Expected payments for guaranteed residual value

Unaccrued interest must be added to lease liabilities over contract's lifetime. Lease payments have to be captured as repayments at once. In case of contract modifications, a re-evaluation must be made, so that the book value of the liability will correspond to the changed circumstances (IFRS 16, paragraph 36).

IFRS 16 substantially carries forward the lessor accounting requirements in IAS 17. Accordingly, a lessor continues to classify its leases as operating leases or finance leases and continues to account for those two types of leases differently.

### 9.1.3 Differences between ASC 842 and IFRS 16

Let's examine the differences between the disclosure requirements under ASC 842 and IFRS 16 and see which reports are needed for which regulations.

The quantitative disclosure requirements under IFRS 16 are similar, but not identical to, ASC 842. ASC 842 guidance provides an explicit list of quantitative disclosures. In contrast, IFRS 16 does *not* include a list of prescriptive disclosures, instead setting out objectives and requiring companies to determine the information that would satisfy those objectives on their own. In addition, for leases that contain complex features (e.g., variable lease payments, extension options, and guaranteed residual value), IFRS 16 requires a company to disclose material, company-specific information that is not covered elsewhere in the financial statements.

Table 9.1 and Table 9.2 show the required lease cost disclosures and the required quantitative disclosures according IFRS 16 and ASC 842.

| Disclosure | | IFRS 16 | ASC 842 |
|---|---|---|---|
| Finance lease cost | | | |
| | Amortization of ROU assets | X | X |
| | Interest on lease liabilities | X | X |
| Operating lease cost | | | X |
| Short-term lease cost | | X | X |
| Low-value asset lease cost | | X | |
| Variable lease cost | | X | X |

**Table 9.1** Lease Cost Disclosures

| Disclosure | | IFRS 16 | ASC 842 |
|---|---|---|---|
| Cash paid for amounts included in the measurement of lease liabilties | | X | X |
| | Operating cash flows from finance leases | X | X |
| | Operating cash flows from operating leases | | X |
| | Financing cash flows from finance leases | X | X |
| Additions of all ROU assets during the period (prepaid leases) | | X | |
| ROU assets obtained in exchange for new finance lease liabilities | | | X |
| ROU assets obtained in exchange for new operating lease liabilities | | | X |
| Carrying amount of ROU assets disclosed by underlying asset classes | | X | |
| Weighted-average remaining lease term (finance and operating leases) | | | X |
| Weighted-average discount rate (finance and operating leases) | | | X |
| Maturity analysis of finance and operating lease liabilities | | X | X |

**Table 9.2** Quantitative Disclosures for IFRS 16 and ASC 842

Let's turn our attention to the reporting functionalities available in SAP's two solutions for lease accounting, starting with SAP RE-FX.

## 9.2 Reporting and Analytics with SAP RE-FX

SAP RE-FX provides different categories of information systems such as contracts, conditions, cash flows, periodic postings, and balance sheet valuation of contracts out of the box. Let's look at each.

### 9.2.1 Contracts

Contract data can be analyzed via the contract reporting tool, which can be found in the information system for contracts. SAP RE-FX provides the following twelve reports for contract data, shown in Figure 9.1 and accessed by following the menu path **Flexible Real Estate Management • Contract • Information System**:

- Transaction REISCN (Overview)
- Transaction REISCNPE (Term)
- Transaction REISCNNT (Notice)
- Transaction REISCNNTRULE (Notice Rules)
- Transaction REISCNRN (Renewal)
- Transaction REISCNRNRULE (Renewal Rules)
- Transaction REISCNDP (Security Deposit Agreements)
- Transaction RECARSCN (Reminder Dates)
- Transaction REISCNBP (Business Partner for Contracts)
- Transaction REISCNMS (Contract Measurements)
- Transaction REISCNOA (Objects for Contracts)
- Transaction REISCHGDOCCN (Change Documents)

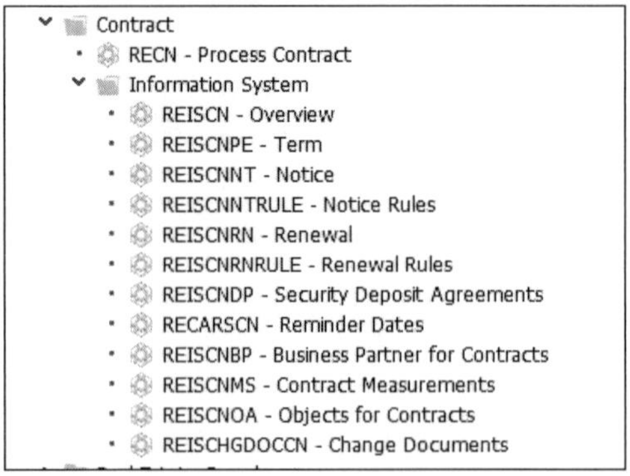


**Figure 9.1** Contract Information System

Let's look at an example: Transaction REISCN (Info System Contracts). In the selection screen shown in Figure 9.2, you'll input contract data, period and key date data, filter data, and output options.

For specific information on an individual contract, the reporting functionality is provided directly in the contract dialog, which can be found under the **Overview** tab, as shown in Figure 9.3.

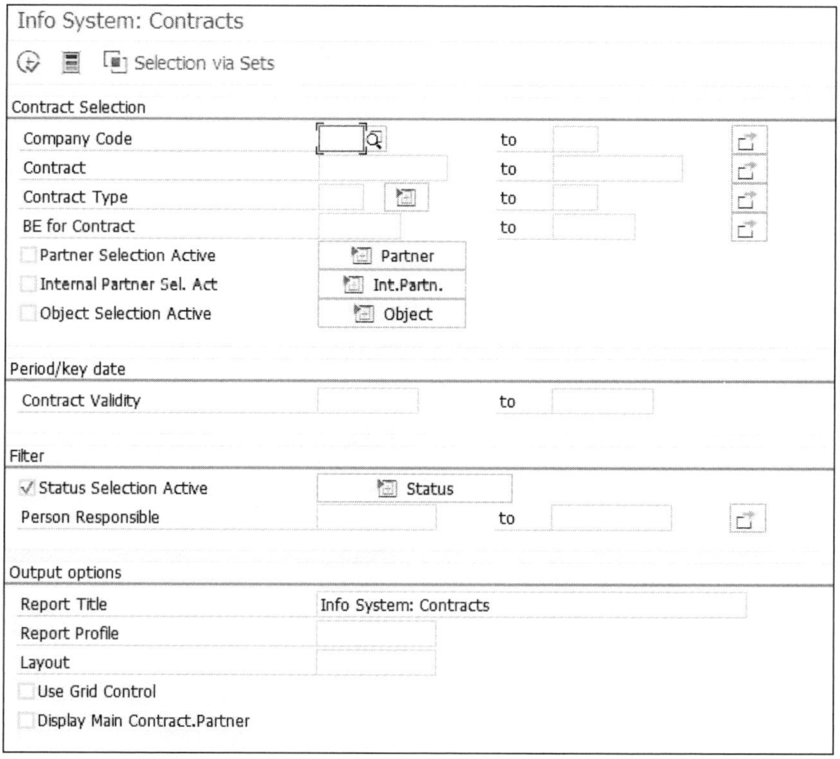


**Figure 9.2** Transaction REISCN (Info System Contracts)

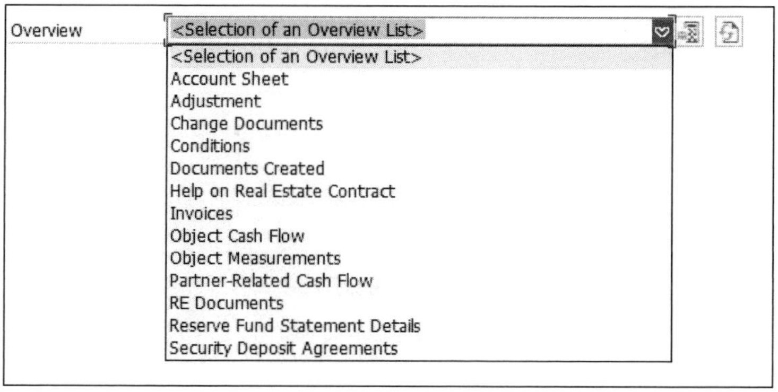


**Figure 9.3** Report List in the Overview Tab

### 9.2.2 Conditions

You can use Transaction REISCN (Overview) for conditions reporting as well. Therefore, you'll have to use the **Report Profile** field and assign condition groups relevant for leasing contracts.

You can also find additional reports for conditions in the generic information system of SAP RE-FX:

- Transaction REISCDCN (Conditions for Contracts)
- Transaction REISCDCNAJ (Conditions and Adjustment Rule for Contract)

### 9.2.3 Cash Flows

You can find reporting for an individual contract's cash flows either directly in the contract under the **Conditions** tab, as shown in Figure 9.4, where you can display the cash flow, or under the **Overview** tab, where you can select the requested report.

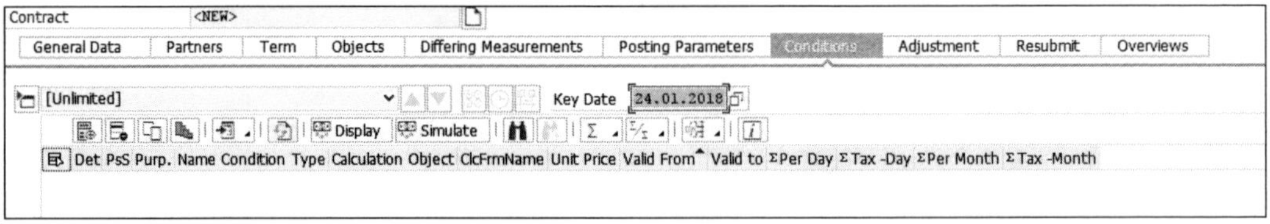


**Figure 9.4** Conditions Tab with Cash Flow Display and Simulation

If you want to analyze cash flows of more than one contract, two transactions are provided within the reporting in the accounting area:

- Transaction REISCDCF (Cash Flow)
- Transaction REISCDCFOBJ (Object Cash Flow)

### 9.2.4 Periodic Postings

You can get information of results of periodic postings via various transactions:

- Transaction RERAPL (Posting Log)
- Transaction REISREDOCCN (RE Documents for Contract)
- Transaction FBL5N (Customer Line Items)

- Transaction REISALIT (Accruals/Deferrals)
- Transaction REISRADOCITEM (Item Overview)

You can access the documents, which are posted via contract management, via the posting log (Transaction RERAPL). As shown in Figure 9.5, you can select documents via process ID or by using other attributes of the real estate document.

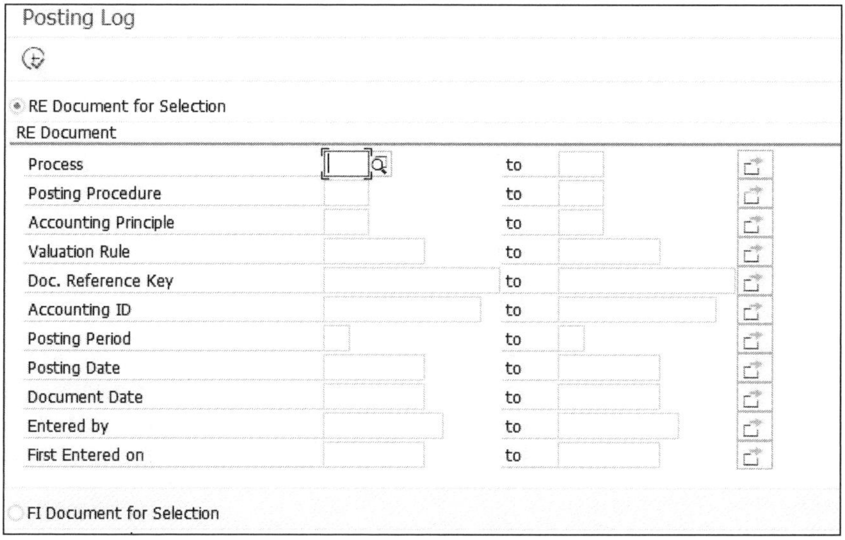


**Figure 9.5** Transaction RERAPL (Posting Log)

### 9.2.5 Balance Sheet Valuation of Contracts

To analyze the balance sheet valuation of contracts, SAP RE-FX provides several standard reports via the information system, as shown in Figure 9.6:

- Transaction RECEISRULCN (Display and Maintain Valuation Rules)
- Transition RECEISCONDRULECN (Display/Maintain Condition-Specific Valuation Rules)
- Transaction RECEISASSETCN (Leased Assets for Contracts)
- Transaction RECESH (Display Contract Valuations)
- Transaction RECEISRECLASSIFY (Reclassification)
- Transaction RECEISLIABGRAD (Liabilities Grading)

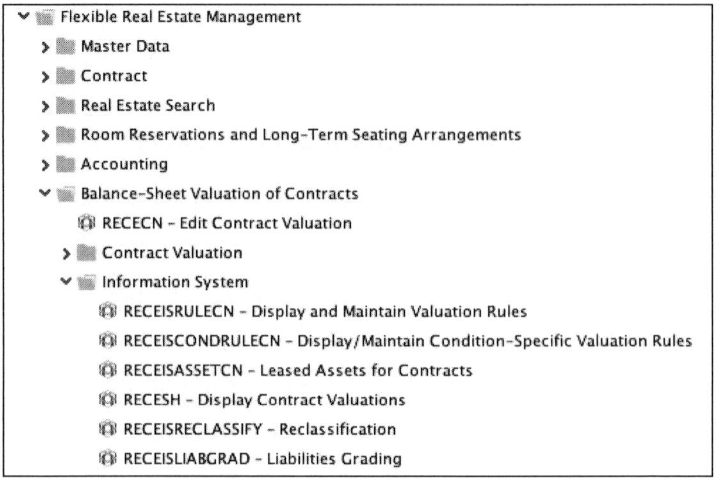


**Figure 9.6** Information System for the Balance Sheet Valuation

For specific information on an individual contract, you can access additional reporting functionality directly in the contract dialog. Under the **Valuation** tab, you'll see the calculated values or the valuation log; within the **Conditions** tab, the cash flow can be displayed or simulated. Within the **Partner** area, you can display the vendor line item list (Transaction FBL1N).

### 9.2.6 Right-of-Use-Assets

With Transaction RECEISASSETCN, you can display ROU assets assigned to the valuation parameters of the contracts. With this report, you can display the individual valuation steps for the selected contract. The report is time-based, so you can select between different time slices or enter the due date for the report.

In the selection screen for Transaction RECEISASSETCN, shown in Figure 9.7, you'll input contract selection data, period/key date data, filter data, output options, and selection data and make selections for valuation rule status and valuation status.

**Figure 9.7** Transaction RECEISASSETCN (Leased Assets for Contracts)

## 9.2.7 Lease Liabilities

To follow the disclosure requirements, lease liabilities must be clustered according the residual term of the contracts. With Transaction RECEISRECLASSIFY, you can group the lease liabilities.

**Example**

A common lease liability grouping is as follows:

- Lease liabilities shorter than one year
- Lease liabilities with residual terms between one and five years
- Lease liabilities with residual terms greater than five years

To display the liability grid, use Transaction RECEISLIABGRAD. In this transaction, you'll also be able to use the defined clustering or select periods directly via the selection screen shown in Figure 9.8.

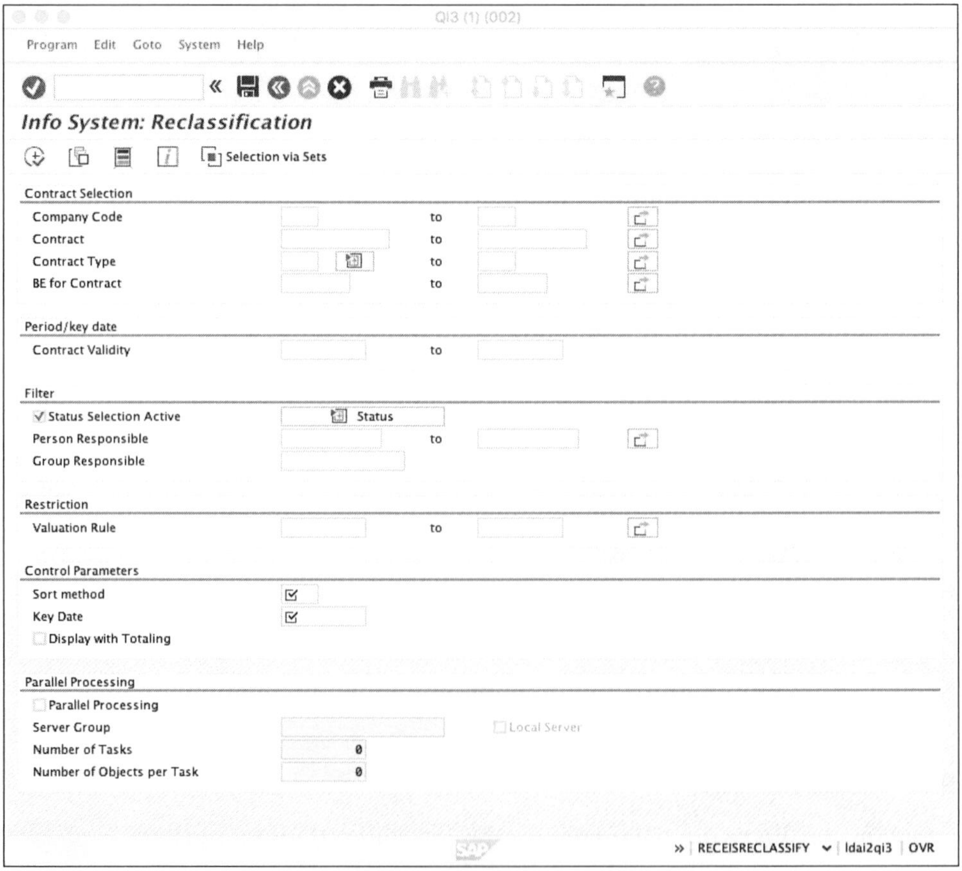


**Figure 9.8** Transaction RECEISRECLASSIFY (Reclassification)

## 9.3 Reporting and Analytics with SAP Lease Administration by Nakisa

SAP Lease Administration provides three different types of standard reports: disclosure reports, management reports, and transaction reports. You can also use SAP Lease Administration to extract data from reports embedded in external sources. And finally, if necessary, you can also extract customized reports from SAP Lease Administration in either Excel format or from other business intelligence reports.

### 9.3.1 Disclosure Reports

Disclosure reports fulfill the quantitative requirements described in the new lease accounting standards. In partnership with the Big Four accounting firms, these reports have been designed to both comply with the list of disclosures under ASC 842 *and* meet the objectives set out under IFRS 16.

#### Liability Balances

Both ASC 842 and IFRS 16 require disclosures of liability balances, whereby the lessee presents lease liabilities as a separate line item, or together with other similar liabilities, in a manner relevant to understanding the lessee's financial position. A lessee will also split lease liabilities into current and non-current portions, based on the timing of payments. Figure 9.9 shows an example of the Liability Balances report in SAP Lease Administration. This report presents a yearly summary of the current and non-current liability balances for the remaining lease term.

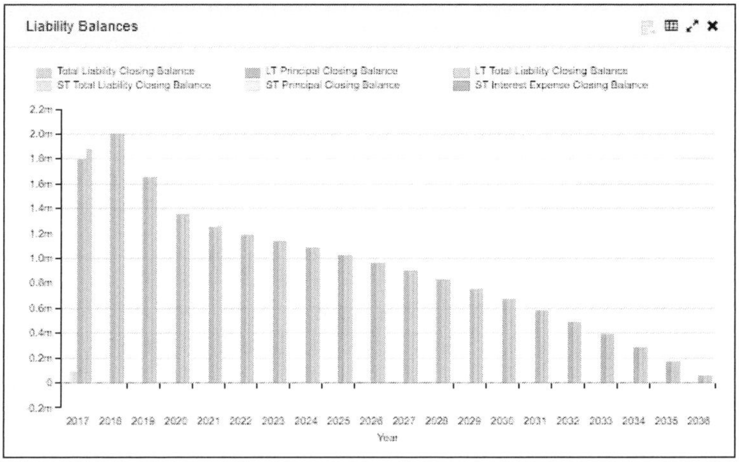


**Figure 9.9** Liability Balances Report

### ROU Asset Roll Forward

The ROU Asset Roll Forward report, shown in Figure 9.10, presents a yearly summary of the ROU asset for the remaining lease term.

This report meets the IFRS 16 requirement to present information about underlying assets in several ways:

- The opening and ending carrying balances of the ROU asset of a given reporting period
- The additions to the ROU asset (incentives, modifications/reassessment, and initial direct costs)
- The depreciation charge of the ROU asset

Although not required under ASC 842, your organization can use this information to further analyze your lease properties.

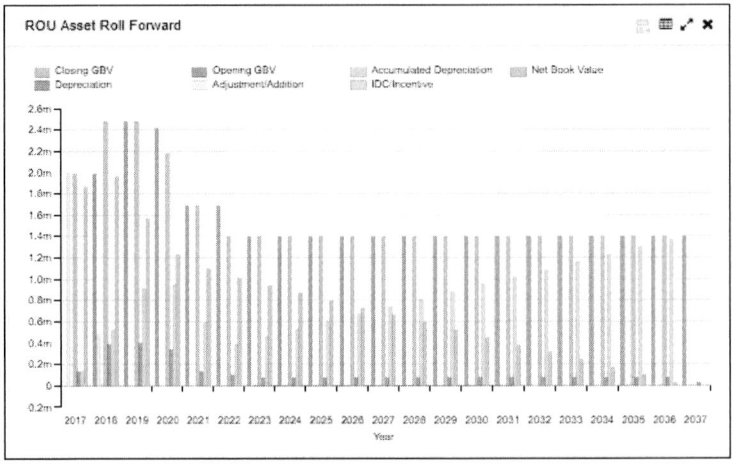


**Figure 9.10** ROU Asset Roll Forward Report

### Lease Cost

The lease cost disclosure is a requirement under both new lease accounting standards. In applying the new model, the income statement will disaggregate the presentation of lease expenses for former off-balance sheet leases—as in operating leases—splitting the expense into two components for all leases under IFRS 16 and for capital leases under ASC 842. The report shown in Figure 9.11 presents a yearly summary of the current and non-current liability balances for the remaining lease term in a manner relevant to understanding the lessees' financial position.

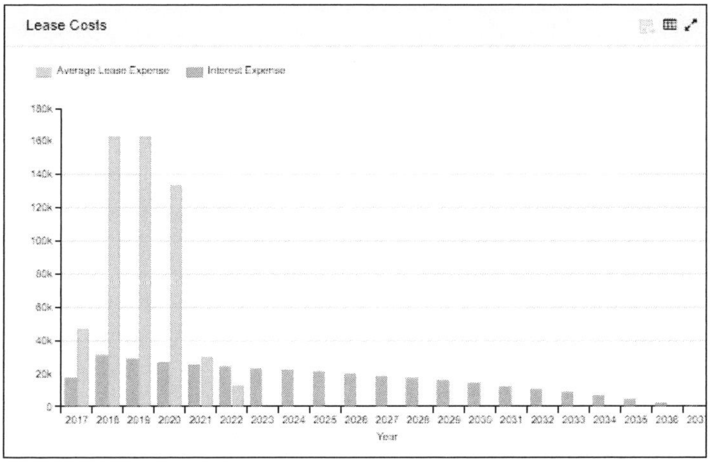


Figure 9.11 Lease Cost Report



### Cash Flow

For cash flow disclosures, you'll need to describe the cash paid for amounts included in the measurement of lease liabilities separately for ASC 842 finance and operating leases. The Cash Flow report also includes supplemental non-cash information on lease liabilities arising from obtaining ROU assets, such as maintenance costs, that are part of the rental payments. This report, a requirement under both new leasing regulations, presents a yearly summary of the impact to the cash flow statement from operating and financing activities for the remaining lease term.

Figure 9.12 shows an example of a Cash Flow report in SAP Lease Administration.

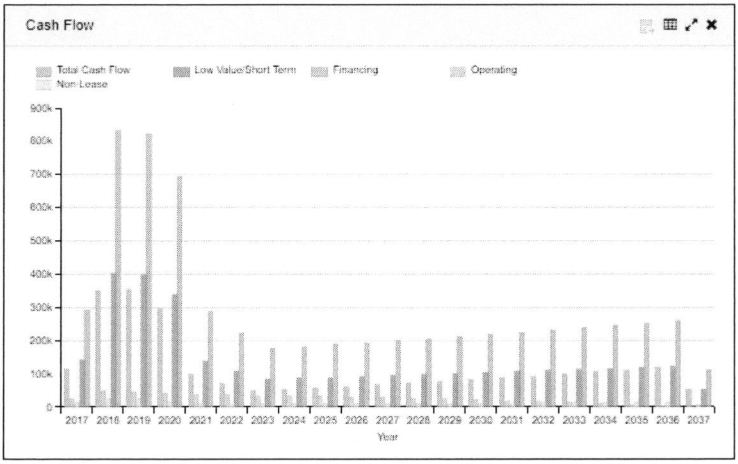


Figure 9.12 Cash Flow Report

### Weighted Average Discount Rate

This disclosure report presents the *weighted average discount rate* for each lease based on the discount rate used to calculate the lease liability balance at the reporting date and on the remaining lease payments. This information can be presented in two ways:

- Under ASC 842, entities are required to disclose the weighted average discount rate on all open leases, with finance and operating leases separated.
- Under IFRS 16, entities are required to disclose the weighted average discount rate on all open leases, calculated using the weighted average discount rate for all finance leases recorded in accordance with IFRS 16.

Figure 9.13 shows an example Weighted Average Discount Rate report.

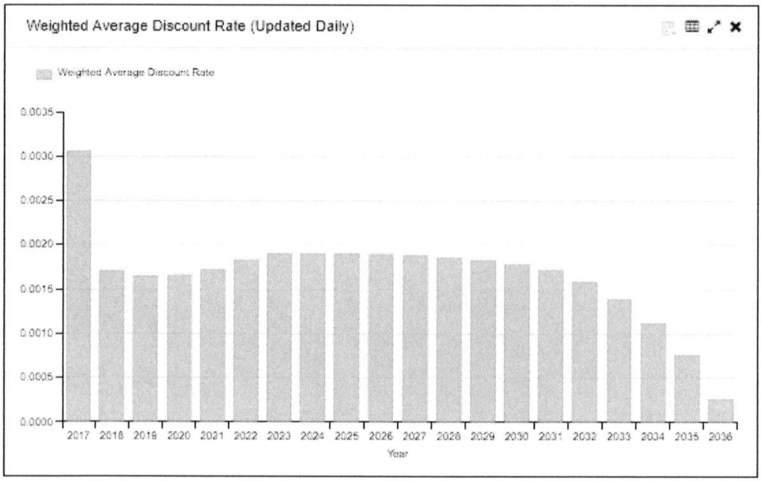


**Figure 9.13** Weighted Average Discount Rate Report

### Weighted Average Lease Term

Similar to the Weighted Average Discount Rate report, this disclosure report presents the *weighted average lease term* for each lease based on the remaining lease term and the liability balance at the reporting date. This information is to be presented in two ways:

- Under ASC 842, entities are required to disclose the weighted average remaining lease term on all open leases, with finance and operating leases separated.

- Under IFRS 16, entities are required to disclose the weighted average remaining lease term on all open leases, calculated using the weighted average remaining lease term for all finance leases recorded in accordance with IFRS 16.

As shown in Figure 9.14, the weighted average life of a lease diminishes over time.

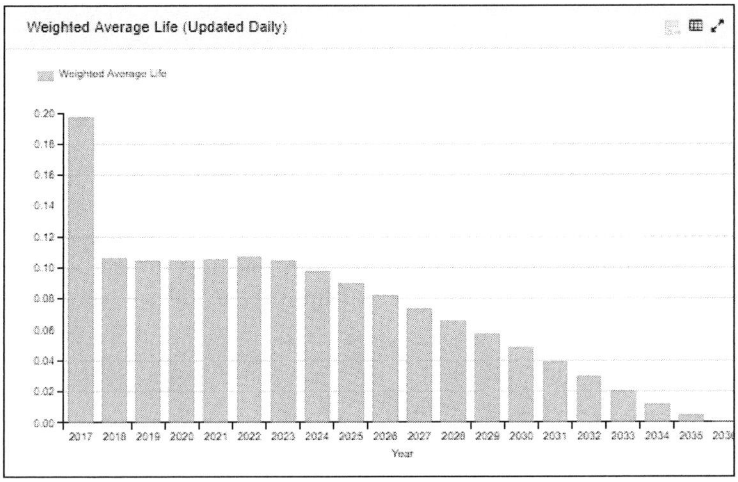


**Figure 9.14** Weighted Average Lease Term Report

### 9.3.2 Management Reports

Unlike disclosure reports, management reports are discretionary. In other words, these reports can be internally used by your organization's management to make decisions. For example, these reports can provide a complete overview of the lease contracts and are shown in separate dashboards representing the various levels of a lease contract (e.g., master agreement, contract, lease component, activation group, and unit).

**Example**

Commonly, management reports are used across departments. For example, a procurement department may like to assess the number of contracts within the company in two ways:

- By phase (open and operating or closed)
- By region

Each dashboard generates a distinct set of reports that provide financial information used for internal decision making and strategic analysis. The reports breakdown leases based on the status, lease type, lease area, business unit, company code, cost center, and other cost objects. You can use the filters on the left-hand side of the screen to drilldown to a specific view. For example, you want to view the leases that belong to a specific asset class (e.g., vehicles), then select the vehicles asset class on the left-hand side of the filters.

Management reports are interactive and are accessible in graph or table view. For example, you can select a specific area of a report (e.g., the "Active" contract status), and the remaining reports belonging to the dashboard will be updated to show the details of the "Active" contracts.

To access SAP Lease Administration's management reports, follow these steps:

1. Click on the hamburger menu (three horizontal lines).
2. Select **Dashboards**.
3. A list of available dashboards will appear as shown in Figure 9.15. Select one from the following list:
   - **Master Agreement**
   - **Contract**
   - **Lease Component**
   - **Activation Group** (shown in Figure 9.16)
   - **Unit**

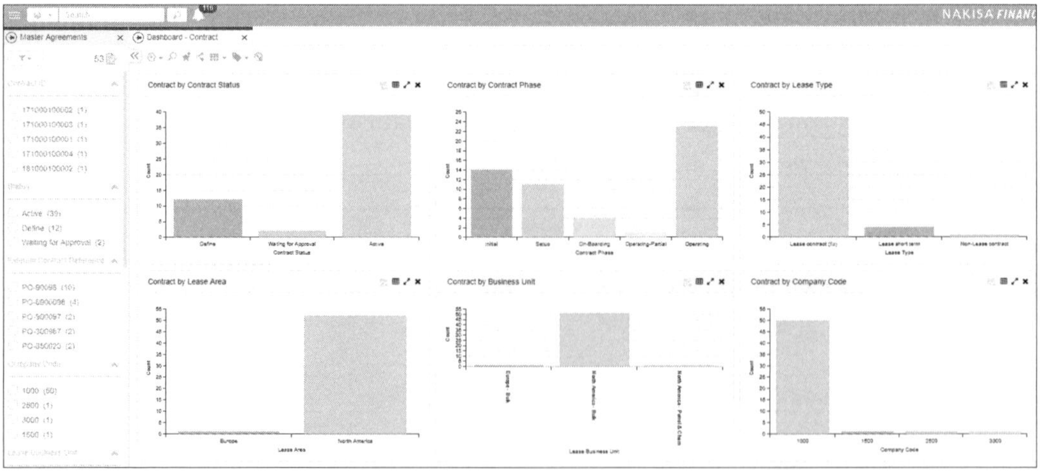


**Figure 9.15** Contract Management Dashboard in SAP Lease Administration

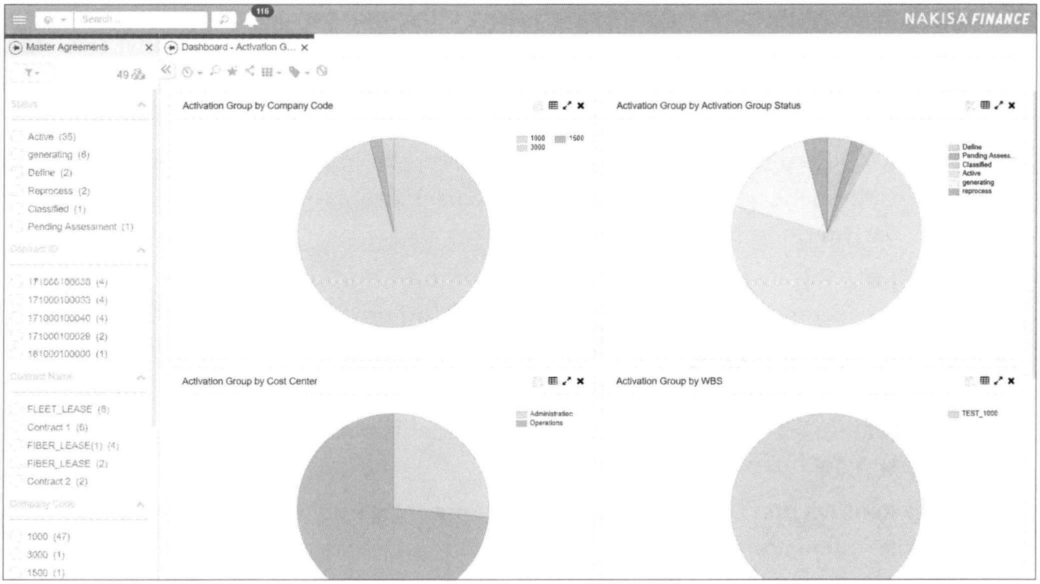


**Figure 9.16** Activation Group Management Dashboard in SAP Lease Administration



### 9.3.3 Transaction Reports

Transaction reports (or reconciliation reports) provide a detailed list of all transactions that have been posted in the ERP system from SAP Lease Administration. These reports are useful for reconciliation purposes and to create audit trails.

A different report is available for each posting type generated. Users can access the transactional line item detail of every posting based on the report type selected and can use the filters on the left-hand side of the screen to generate the details needed. For example, if you only want to view the transactions for a particular lease contract, then select the lease contract from the filters. The transactional reports are available in table view and may be exported to Excel.

To access the transaction reports, follow these steps:

1. Click on the hamburger menu (three horizontal lines).
2. Select **Transactional Reports**.
3. From the list of the following available dashboards that appears (see Figure 9.17), select the one that fits your needs:
   – Asset Capitalization Documents: As shown in Figure 9.18, this report provides information related to the asset capitalization at the inception of the lease.

- Asset Depreciation Documents: This report provides information related to asset depreciation posted from SAP Lease Administration. Note that this only applies for ASC 842 operating leases. For all other lease contracts (fix), the depreciation amount is calculated and posted in the SAP fixed asset module (FI-AA).
- Asset Retirement Documents: This report provides information related to asset retirement, which is triggered when a user creates events such as a casualty or early termination of the lease.
- Ledger Transfer Documents: This report provides information related to transfer documents generated by SAP Lease Administration. This is application when SAP Lease Administration is configured to generate invoices in AP module.
- Interest Accrual Documents: As shown in Figure 9.19, this report provides information related to interest accrual documents posted from SAP Lease Administration.
- Rent Accrual Documents: This report provides information related to rent and payment accrual documents posted from SAP Lease Administration.
- Liability Adjustment Documents: This report provides information related to liability adjustments postings when there is an event such as a casualty, lease reassessment, or lease modification.
- Liability Obligation Documents: This report provides information related to the liability obligation documents posted at the inception of the lease.
- Charge Report Documents: This report provides a summary of one-time (charge) documents posted by SAP Lease Administration throughout the lease lifecycle.

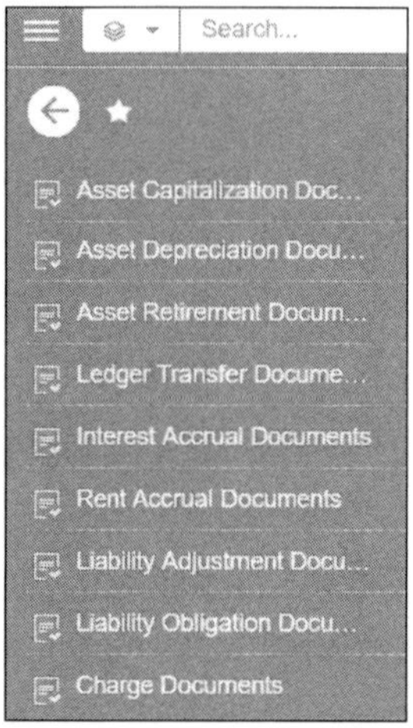


**Figure 9.17** List of Transactional Reports Available in SAP Lease Administration

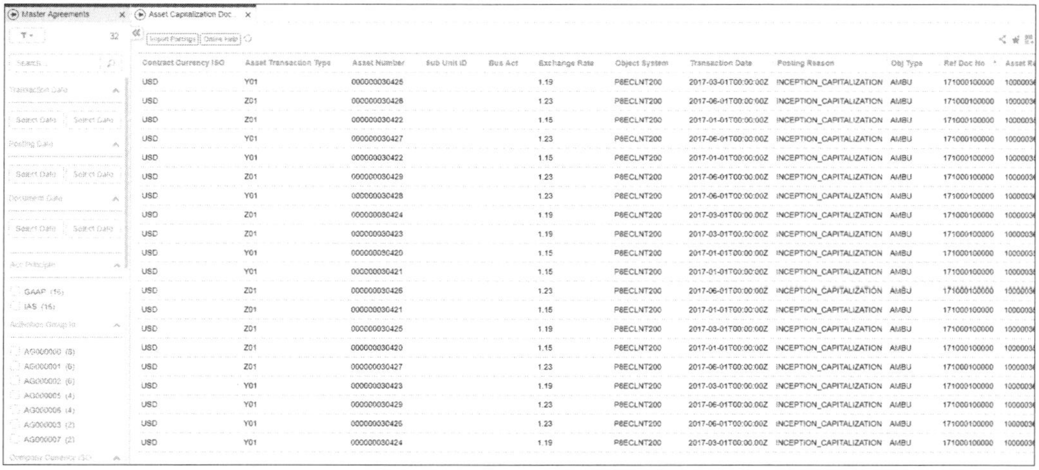

**Figure 9.18** Asset Capitalization Documents Transaction Report

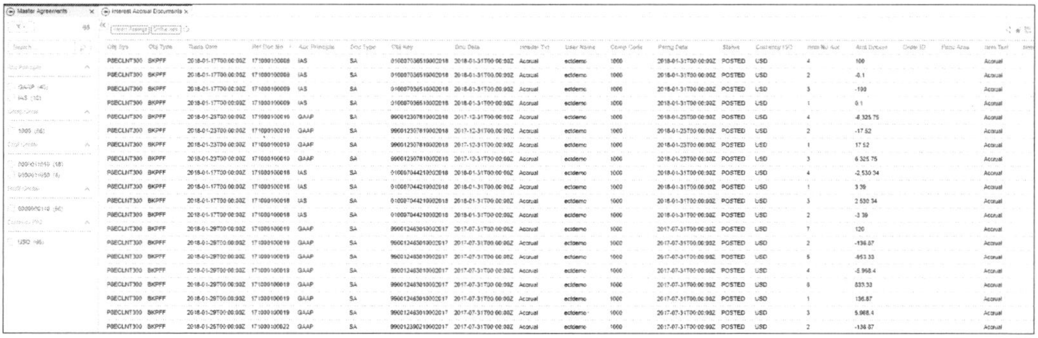

**Figure 9.19** Interest Accrual Documents Transaction Report

## 9.4 Summary

The objective of this chapter has been to explain the standard disclosures required by IFRS 16 and ASC 842 and outline out-of-the-box reporting features from both SAP RE-FX and SAP Lease Administration.

# Chapter 10
# Key Industry Considerations

*Leasing is widely used in almost every major industry. Before we close the book, let's consider businesses cases in three different industries to better understand lease accounting.*



Leasing is widely used by companies around the world to access properties, plants, and equipment without incurring large cash outflows. This flexible financing mechanism also allows companies across industries to lease assets without having to undertake residual value risks or the risk of obsolescence.

However, the volume, type, and nature of the assets routinely leased differ from one industry to the next. For example, an energy company might lease power lines, while a retailer would lease retail and storage spaces, and a professional services firm might lease computer equipment and offices. In these cases, lease structures and terms are likely to vary greatly, depending on the nature of an organization's business model and myriad other factors, such as industry regulations, pricing patterns, and existing risks unique to the line of business. Thus, when adopting International Financial Reporting Standards 16 or Accounting Standards Codification 842, firms should be mindful that accounting implications and impacts will arise differently in different industries.

This chapter will explore unique the challenges and requirements experienced by companies in the healthcare, high-tech, and air and defense (A&D) industries when implementing a leasing project and discuss how the new lease standards are likely to impact performance measures and financial ratios.

## 10.1 Healthcare

Regardless of industry, a company's individual circumstances will govern the degree of these changes. In recent years, healthcare and medical firms have seen the following strategic trends over the past decade:

- **The expansion of medical, surgical, and service centers to suburban areas**
  Real estate operators have had additional incentives to engage in new projects to construct facilities and to convert existing real estate holdings into medical centers. Several medium-term operating leases (approximately 5 to 10 years) have been undertaken by companies in the healthcare industry, allowing these lessees to avoid large influxes of recognized lease liabilities on their balance sheets and avoid large cash outflows for fixed asset investments.
- **Advancements in technology that give rise to sophisticated medical equipment**
  Operating leases have allowed firms to acquire expensive and advanced medical equipment with minimal cash outlay. This financing solution also enables firms to avoid residual value risks, as well as the risk of obsolescence because the leased equipment will be returned to the lessor after the lease term.

Organizations in the pharmaceutical industry in particular should consider new lease terms and conditions thoroughly given the following scenarios:

- Bespoke equipment such as custom pill machines/mixers is often made for customers.
- Equipment payment schedules may vary based on the quantity of consumables used with the equipment.
- Legally enforceable minimum consumable orders are common.
- Consumables such as medical pumps or thermometers are substitutable for other pharmaceutical companies' products.

Standard leases and current lease agreements in the healthcare industry are likely to meet the new definition of a lease under IFRS 16 and ASC 842, with exemptions for low-value assets and short-term leases applicable as well.

While the new lease standards' net effect on statements of financial position will see significant increase in liabilities recorded, additional changes may be required to the calculation of lease liabilities. Be sure to consider components such as contingent rent, purchase options, and other services under agreement like maintenance and installation as well as minimum consumable order levels.

Healthcare organizations should also expect key accounting metrics to be affected, with an adverse impact on debt-to-equity ratios (resulting in an increase in net debt due to lease liability spikes), and expect an increased in metrics such as the earnings before interest, taxes, depreciation, and amortization (EBITDA) due to the new recognition of interest, depreciation, and amortization on the income statement. Net assets, on the other hand, will decrease as the right-of-use asset (ROU asset) will be amortized on a straight-line basis.

In financial assessments, the new metrics often rely heavily on assessments of an entity's balance sheet. Similarly, for bond agreements and financial covenants, an increase in liabilities in your financial position will pose new challenges as lenders may hesitate to continue existing financing agreements with your business.

Renegotiation will also be required when evaluating performance metrics in share-based payments, as well as dividend policies given the change in cash flow patterns. (IFRS 16 and ASC 842 will see an increase in front-loaded lease expenses.)

Firms in the healthcare industry must therefore carefully consider the benefits of purchasing assets versus leasing assets when evaluating current leasing strategies. In the current time horizon, leases are likely to still be preferred over purchasing for three reasons:

- Leases allow organizations with low cash flow to minimize upfront cash outlays.
- Real estate leases give healthcare firms the flexibility to move to locations that prove more advantageous for their business (particularly when considering their clientele).
- Medical equipment is expensive to purchase and often entails a huge initial cash outlay followed by a financing agreement. Often, the buyer of the equipment is also left shouldering the risk of obsolescence.



Moving forward, healthcare firms may need to consider several complex scenarios under the current IAS 17 or ASC 840 and completely understand the terms encapsulated within current leases. Because existing leases at the time of adoption will not be grandfathered, healthcare companies must clearly and understandably document key provisions of these lease terms for proper review. Furthermore, IT solutions must be selected carefully to ensure that the lease information can be stored and handled in a manner that is easily accessible and understandable for stakeholders.

These entities should also assess lease versus buy options as well as lease terms, weighing the pros and cons more carefully than before. For example, firms must decide if operational goals can be achieved with longer lease terms, or if larger liability balances would be more detrimental to existing debt covenants.

**Example**

A pharmaceutical and medical device company (the lessor) enters into an arrangement with a hospital (the lessee) to provide dialysis equipment and medical blood pump consumables for six years. The lessor installs the dialysis machine at the hospital's premises, and the dialysis machine requires the use of consumables also sold by the lessor. The dialysis machine is provided to the lessee free of charge, but the hospital is legally required to purchase a minimum quantity of consumables.

Let's say the dialysis machine is then configured to run on the hospital's patented software. While the lessor owns the legal title of the dialysis machine and is permitted to substitute the machine at its discretion, the substitution of the equipment would significantly disrupt the hospital's activities and potentially trigger the lease's penalty clauses in the event of equipment downtime. The lessor only expects to substitute equipment in the event of a malfunction and will provide maintenance services for the dialysis machine.

This arrangement contains a lease, as the equipment is on the lessee's premises and is customized specifically for their use. The asset (equipment) is implicit to the lease. Furthermore, while the lessor has the right to substitute the equipment, this right is not substantive due to the disruption of substitution and downtime penalty. The hospital has the right to control the use of the asset throughout the period of use as it has the right to obtain substantially all the economic benefits of the identified asset and can direct how and when the equipment shall be used.

**Example**

The same medical device company (the lessee) leases a lab facility. This agreement includes the land on which the facility sits as well as laboratory equipment. The lessee, in this instance, can purchase equipment from a different supplier and use the laboratory equipment in other facilities. The monthly lease payments made to the lessor include a fixed amount for the lab facility, land, and equipment; a fixed amount for maintenance of the lab equipment; and a fixed maintenance fee for building upkeep. This example assumes that the right to use the land as a separate lease component is immaterial.

In this example, the lease components identified are the building (and land) and the lab equipment. The non-lease components, on the other hand, would be the maintenance services provided for the lab equipment and the building.

The right to use the laboratory equipment is determined as a separate lease component as this right is dependent neither on the building nor the facility. Maintenance services are non-lease components as they are deemed to be separate services provided to the lessee. Furthermore, as the accounting effect of the right to use the land is minimal and does not impact the classification of the lab facility even if the right to use the land is separated from the right to use of the facility, the land shall not be treated as a separate lease component.

## 10.2 High-Tech

Similar to the healthcare industry, companies in the high-tech sector should consider the substantial impact that IFRS 16 and ASC 842 will have on their financial statements, especially how the new definition of a lease will affect the number of contracts that will now be considered in scope.

For the high-tech industry, the key change to the expansion of the lease identification provision is the removal of the distinction between operating and finance leases. Remember that an ROU asset and a corresponding lease liability should now be recognized on the balance sheet, increasing reported overall assets and liabilities. Moving forward, contracts will be considered to contain a lease if the contract enables the lessee to control the use of an identified asset, through directing the use and obtaining substantially all the economic benefit for the period of use. While an asset may seemingly be available to a lessee, establishing whether the supplier is able to substitute an alternative asset during the period of the contract is essential: If the supplier can practically substitute another asset, and there is economic benefit for the supplier to do so, then the contract is said to not contain a lease.



The delivery of certain services within the technology industry include the installation of IT equipment or satellite TV dishes. These assets may require installation at a customer's office or home, and such a service must be specified. As these assets might be substitutable with others during the delivery of the service, determining whether the supplier would derive economic benefit from the substitution is important.

For example, a distinct portion of an asset (e.g., such as dark fibers in a fiber optic cable) are identifiable as an asset. However, an abstract portion of an asset (e.g., "20% of the capacity" of a fiber optic cable) is not identifiable because the lessee is not afforded the right to substantially all of this asset. Note that capacity arrangements entered into by several entities in the technology industry (e.g., network tower space arrangements) must now also be evaluated under IFRS 16. Remember that exceptions for leases with a duration of 12 months or less and for leases with low-value assets exist, where the lessee may choose to continue adopting operating lease accounting methods. IFRS 16 also excludes intangible assets, such as licensing agreements, which are within the scope of IAS 38. For licensing agreements, firms may apply the lease standards to the right to use other intangible assets.

Apart from real estate and equipment leases, technology companies can also enter into a variety of arrangements, such as outsourcing and supply agreements, covering areas such as employment, information management, intellectual property, and data center agreements. In evaluating these agreements, these entities must take care to establish processes to identify leases embedded in contracts and their respective lease and non-lease components. Observable information must also be used as much as possible in allocating consideration to each of these components. Entities should return to the lease accounting basics of the new standards, determining whether an arrangement contains an explicit or implicit asset and whether, as a lessor, they control the use of the asset in question.

In key performance metrics, high-tech companies should also anticipate changes to their operating expense patterns, as leases will become front-loaded as opposed to being accounted for with even, straight-line expense recognition. EBITDA margins will increase, which is critical because high-tech firms often use cash flows as a basis for business valuation. These organizations will now need to redefine capital expenditure (e.g., either by investing cash flows in property, plants, and equipment or as an addition to their carried lease liability).

With large increases to lease liabilities on financial positions, high-tech firms will increasingly face decisions to build their own technical infrastructure and networks as opposed to leasing them. As with other industries, individual circumstances and business models will greatly influence these operational goals, and thus the change in lease liabilities can vary widely across companies.

The new on-balance sheet accounting for leases will entail greater demands in how lease data is captured, and high-tech entities will be required to adopt sophisticated systems able to capture and track lease data in a systematic and transparent manner.

**Example**

A software company (supplier-lessor) provides cloud computing services to its customer. Its customer, Entity A (customer-lessee) enters into a contract with the supplier for a specified amount of server capacity in the supplier's data center for a duration of four years. The equipment and servers at the data center are owned and operated by the supplier. The supplier can allow other customers to use the same server simultaneously and is able to move its customers from one server to another. The supplier may also choose to upgrade or change their equipment at their sole discretion during the lease term to maximize the use of their servers and accommodate as many customers as possible in their data center.

This agreement is said to not contain a lease as the supplier has a substantive right to substitute the asset. The supplier can also change server equipment without significant cost and even benefit from increasing the number of customers the data center accommodates. While a specified amount of server capacity is spelled out in the arrangement, the supplier can direct how the equipment and servers are used to provide that service to the customer.

**Example**

Let's look at the components that can exist within a contract. From the previous example, the supplier will be in charge of maintaining the data center, while the customer has exclusive rights to a portion of the data center in that the customer's own personnel and resources operate the resource for the duration of the lease term. The yearly payments the customer makes to the supplier include a fixed rent amount, insurance premiums for the data center, and property tax for the data center's premises. The insurance premiums and property taxes are paid directly to the relevant authorities by the customer.

The lease component in the contract is the data center, and a non-lease component in the contract is the maintenance service. The maintenance service is a separate service provided to the customer, and the insurance premiums and property taxes are not components but rather reimbursements of the costs incurred by the supplier regardless of whether the data center was leased or not.



## 10.3 Air and Defense

The impact of IFRS 16 and ASC 842 will extend across air and defense (A&D) business operations, with significant effects on IT systems and key performance metrics used for both internal management and external reporting. As for other industries, the provisions of the new lease standards will increase lease-related assets and liabilities on statements of financial position, affecting the timing and classification of income and expenses derived from leases.

A long frequent practice for A&D companies has been to finance aircraft through off-balance sheet leases, with firms renting essential facilities (such as airports, airbases, and jetways) and property for corporate spaces. Because IFRS 16 no longer distinguishes between operating and finance leases, A&D lessees will expect to see all lease contracts brought on-balance sheet, recognizing ROU assets and corresponding lease liabilities. Similarly, A&D companies operating in the US will be governed by ASC 842, where operating leases will also be brought onto the balance sheet.

Lease liabilities will also need to include areas such as contingent rent, renewal and purchase options, and other services encompassed within an agreement. Forecast data has estimated that the new leasing regulations will induce additional lease obligations amounting to trillions of dollars across the industry.

For organizations in the A&D industry, the impact of the new standards on income statements will be no less significant, with the lessee's interest and depreciation expenses being expected to contribute to a front-loaded lease pattern. Lease expenses will be initially higher than the current IAS 17-based straight-line method for operating lease payments, becoming a lower cost in later stages of the lease period.

That said, this lease expense pattern may be nullified since periodic leases, such as month-to-month agreements, are common in the A&D industry. If several periodic batch leases are entered into in different periods, then the entity's income statement and other financial ratios will likely experience high volatility across these time horizons. Furthermore, the capitalization of leases will raise EBITDA and EBIT metrics for entities that heavily employ the use of operating leases outside of the US.

A&D entities will need to evaluate whether their lease arrangements have any underlying assets; wherever the supplier has a substantive right to substitute the asset in question, no identified asset exists. For example, if a supplier owns several aircraft and is contractually allowed to exchange the aircraft leased to the customer at their discretion without the permission of the customer, then there is no underlying asset. The supplier can benefit from using the aircraft when the customer is not using it, and the customer does not have the right to obtain substantively all the economic benefits from the use of the aircraft.

Other accounting implications that A&D entities should be mindful of include determining the profit and loss for sale-and-leaseback transactions in accordance to provisions of IFRS 16, paragraph 98-103, as well as agreements that include repurchase agreements.

Aircraft sold and rented back by A&D entities will be brought on-balance sheet under IFRS 16. The impact on the demand for sale-and-leaseback transactions is likely to be significant, as the strong incentive for keeping assets off-balance sheet no longer exists. Thus, lessors may move to more flexible lease arrangements and models, offering to base payments on asset utilization, as opposed to a fixed rate, to continue to keep assets off-balance sheet.

Moving forward, lease arrangements across the industry may see some restructuring to accommodate shorter lease terms with renewal positions. These arrangements will reduce overall debt as well as leverage ratios for lessees. In addition, foreign entities that lease aircraft in US dollars will also need to be mindful of currency translation when reporting liabilities on their balance sheets, thus exposing a company's financial position to currency risk; management will need to consider this risk when adopting the new lease standards.

While technical provisions under IFRS 16 can prove to be challenging to achieve, A&D companies should also be aware of the broader implications presented to their business process and operations. These challenges include the following:

- **Debt covenants, share-based payments, and dividend payments**
  Substantial increases in lease liabilities may waiver debt agreements. The ability of A&D companies to adhere to leverage-based covenants may be jeopardized. Performance metrics used in share-based payments may need to be revised, and dividend policies reassessed, because of the drastic change in lease expense patterns.
- **Lease negotiations and customer contracts**
  Commercial negotiations may change, with lessees preferring shorter lease terms and smaller lease liabilities on their balance sheets. For A&D firms with government contracts, portions of permitted cost reimbursements being allocated to interest expenses is now a point of contention during contract negotiations, because interest is not reimbursable under current government cost accounting standards.
- **Stakeholder education**
  Key performance indicators will change drastically, and A&D companies ought to consider educating investors, providing additional disclosures explaining these changes, and comparing their metrics to industry standards.
- **Data collection**
  Changes to disclosures and reporting will require substantial volumes of data of individual leases. This data will need to be transformed into digestible portions for stakeholders, as well as analyzed and validated thoroughly. Singling out and focusing on contracts that contain leases will be challenging and time consuming.
- **Technology**
  Entities will need to consider whether their existing systems are sufficient for storing key data and whether they are able to perform the necessary accounting calculations and entries moving forward. Automating IFRS 16 processes can be crucial to churning out accurate and efficient reporting for internal management and external stakeholders.

- **Taxation**
  Tax departments of A&D firms should perform overall tax accounting analysis, and must account for changes in taxes to be paid and in deferred tax positions arising from applying the new standards to their leases.

A&D entities, in identifying these potential obstacles early and engaging in thorough preparation can be better prepared to undertake a resource-intensive and elaborate IFRS 16 or ASC 842 implementation project. The demands required of adopting the new lease regulations, coupled with their broader business impact, need to be evaluated carefully so that firms can ensure compliance by the appropriate effective date.

**Example**

An A&D company enters into a three-year contract with an aircraft supplier. The A&D company will use the aircraft in the lease for commercial use every Saturday and Sunday from 9am to 5pm each day. The supplier owns more than one of the same type of aircraft and can substitute the aircraft at any time during the contract duration. The supplier is also obligated to substitute the aircraft if malfunctions occur or the aircraft is not in proper operational condition.

This contract does not contain a lease, as no asset can be identified. The supplier can benefit from the asset on the weekends even though the aircraft is specified in the contract and can substitute the aircraft at its sole discretion. The A&D company does not have the right to obtain substantively all the economic benefits from the use of the aircraft and cannot direct the use of the asset.

To determine if maintenance services should be separated as non-lease components, consider that, for airlines that incur maintenance expenses prior to returning an aircraft to the lessor because of contractually binding return conditions, IFRS 16 requires that those costs be included in the measurement of the ROU asset. A provision for maintenance costs should also be accounted for in accordance with IAS 37 guidance.

## 10.4 Summary

In this short chapter, we'll give you a look at a few industry-specific requirements and common leasing needs.

In the next and last chapter of this book, we'll share our final thoughts about using SAP software to undertake a compliance project to adopt IFRS 16 and ASC 842 requirements.

# Conclusion

*Having spent hundreds of pages guiding you through your leasing project, we'll now offer our closing thoughts.*

In this book, we covered much of what you'll need to know about the regulatory changes under Accounting Standards Codification 842 (United States) and International Financial Reporting Standards 16 (International), the impact on your business and system processes, the recommended SAP leasing software solutions with its configuration steps, the implementation timelines and budgets, and key industry-specific requirements and business cases. Let's close the book by summarizing some key takeaways and tips for implementing SAP Flexible Real Estate Management (SAP RE-FX) and SAP Lease Administration by Nakisa, and offer some tricks for supporting the solution after implementation.

## Chapter 1

Chapter 1 focused on lease accounting basics: the fundamental elements and different procedures that the lessee and lessor must take into account for their leases.

With the introduction of IFRS 16, we'll need to assess whether the lease contract contains an *identified asset* and the right of use of that asset. You must differentiate between a service contract and a lease contract. In a lease contract, the lessee has permission to benefit from the full *economic benefits* of using the identified asset during contractual period as well as the asset use (with restrictions) and holds the *right* to direct the use of the identified asset. *Protective rights* are the terms and conditions included in the leasing contract that protect the lessor's interest in the identified asset.

Under the new IFRS 16 standard, the lessee is not required to differentiate between finance leases (shown on the balance sheet) and operating leases (kept off the balance sheet). However, the lessee must identify the right-of-use asset (ROU asset) and the corresponding lease liability for nearly all lease contracts. The lessee will recognize the ROU asset and the lease liability, which is recorded as the purchase of an asset on a financed basis. The lessee will also recognize the interest on the lease liability and the depreciation on the ROU asset in the profit and loss statement. In other words, the lessee accounting model under IFRS 16 is a single lease accounting model.

The lessor accounting model under the new standard of IFRS 16 is a dual lessor accounting model. The lessor still must classify leases as either finance or operating leases, depending on whether all the risk and rewards incidental owning the underlying asset are substantially transferred. Similar to the lessor accounting model, the lease classification test for the lessor fundamentally remains the same as under IAS 17.

## Chapter 2

In Chapter 2, we discussed how the biggest impact of ASC 842 and IFRS 16 will be for the lessee in both non-movable and movable leases. Lessees who have movable leases will encounter the most implementation challenges because these arrangements can involve a varied range of lease contract scenarios. Table 1 shows the recommended leasing solutions for these particular scenarios.

| Entity | Non-Moveable Lease | Moveable Lease |
|---|---|---|
| Lessor | SAP Flexible Real Estate Management (SAP RE-FX) | SAP Lease Accounting (FI-LA) Contract Management (FI-CA)<br>SAP Lease Administration by Nakisa |
| Lessee | SAP Flexible Real Estate Management (SAP RE-FX) | SAP Lease Administration by Nakisa |

**Table 1** Recommended Leasing Solutions from SAP

After discussing the recommended leasing solution, we then proceeded to determine what master data we needed to gather, analyze, translate, and transform to fit into the new system. For this phase, we needed to identify the subject matter experts (SMEs) from the various departments in your company, such as accounting and finance, real estate and property, operations, procurement, IT, and business analysis.

The integration of both these leasing solutions can be easily implemented since SAP RE-FX is a subcomponent of SAP ERP Financials and since SAP Lease Administration is natively integrated with various SAP ERP Financials modules such as Asset Accounting (FI-AA), General Ledger (FI-GL), and Accounts Payable (FI-AP), and with

Plant Maintenance (PM) and Procure to Pay. If you are presently using an SAP ERP system, then you can use SAP's integration technologies such as remote function calls (RFCs) or intermediate documents (IDocs) to facilitate the data transfer. For non-SAP ERP systems, integration will depend on the communication interfaces that your current system supports. However, you can use web services, electronic data interchange (EDI) standards, or OData/Excel/.csv files, or other commonly used standards.

## Chapter 3

After we assessed the impact of the regulatory change on your company's master data, business processes, and IT system, we proceeded with our SAP Lease Administration and SAP RE-FX implementation project by planning project timelines, discussing methodologies, and determining our budget.

In assessing the project's timeline, for accuracy, you need to have a good project management officer (PMO), one with a good understanding of customer requirements and knowledge of the SAP software ecosystem. Key factors to consider while creating an estimate of the project timeline include the project scope (what must be done), the budget (how much is the cost), and the schedule (how long you will need). Apart from these, the PMO should be able to identify and manage risks in all phases of the project. Risks directly affecting critical path activities of the project should be mitigated with appropriate contingency plans to avoid project delays.

The duration of a project implementation is influenced by a myriad of factors. Navigating timelines with complex landscapes, cost constraints, and logistical constraints of large teams involved can be a challenge. Project duration overruns are common pitfalls in failed implementations and are often due to shortfalls in change management and a lack of cross-cultural integration. As a result, timelines, budgets, and logistic plans suffer.

The establishment of project timelines and deliverables can be undertaken using SAP's standard Accelerated SAP (ASAP) implementation methodology (ASAP 8), the latest methodology that provides prescriptive, step-by-step frameworks and structures to enable organizations to efficiently and rapidly implement SAP solutions. Some differences between ASAP and ASAP 8 make the latter the recommended implementation methodology for SAP RE-FX and SAP Lease Administration projects. ASAP 8 incorporates Agile and Scrum industry standards, using iterative development, thus allowing for greater flexibility when managing frequently changing requirements. Your company can also leverage SAP's accelerators, which provide structured, prescriptive, and scalable methods or powerful workarounds to implementing SAP software.

## Chapter 4 and Chapter 5

Chapter 4 and Chapter 5 showed you how to implement the IFRS 16 and ASC 842 requirements using SAP Lease Administration and SAP RE-FX, respectively. We described the customizing steps necessary to meet the business requirements established in the previous chapters. How the two solutions are customized and implemented also shows the different approaches SAP and Nakisa have taken towards lease accounting. SAP Lease Administration is an IFRS 16 solution focusing basically on the moveable assets, while SAP RE-FX is coming from an established customer base that focuses on non-moveable assets like real estate for all kind of business processes (including financing). For this reason, we limited our discussion from configuring FI-AA or real estate processes outside the scope of IFRS 16.

## Chapter 6

Chapter 6 discussed on the transitional approaches necessary when an entity decides to adopt a full retrospective or a modified retrospective approach, to comply with IFRS 16 for the annual reporting period beginning on or after January 1, 2019. Under ASC 842, the effective date for annual reporting periods begins December 15, 2018, for public businesses and certain other entities. For all the other entities, the effective date for annual reporting periods begins December 15, 2019. Early adoption is allowed.

Each organization will choose its own transition accounting approach. The *full retrospective approach* requires an entity to apply the new IFRS 16 standard to all lease contracts and each period presented in financial statements, as required by IAS 8 (Accounting Policies, Changes in Accounting Estimates and Errors). Under IFRS 16, an entity is not required to restate comparative information when the *modified retrospective approach* is undertaken. As a result, the information in the comparative period is reported on an IAS 17 basis.

Under ASC 842, an entity may only adopt the new standard with a modified retrospective approach. The modified retrospective approach is required for all leases existing at or entered into on or after the start of the earliest comparative period presented in the financial statements.

## Chapter 7

Once it is implemented in your company, you can then use SAP Lease Administration to manage your leases. As we now know, SAP Lease Administration is a certified solution extension developed by an SAP partner that provides enterprise lease management and accounting functionality to accelerate your compliance with leasing standards under ASC 842 and IFRS 16. SAP Lease Administration provides a unified leasing contract data repository for all your leasing contracts. The advantage this repository provides is access to lease accounting capabilities such as classification, accruals, contract status, payment obligations, and automatic generation of disclosure reports that comply with ASC 842 and IFRS 16 and that help you visualize their impact on your financial statements over time. SAP Lease Administration's end-to-end lease management process improves the efficiency and accuracy of your business processes, lays the foundation for auditability and compliance, and most importantly provides big picture clarity through comprehensive analytics and reporting mechanisms.

## Chapter 8

Similarly, once it is implemented in your company, you can then use SAP RE-FX to manage your leases.

The lease management process in SAP RE-FX has its own lifecycle, and each step within this lifecycle may have a significant impact on a lease's valuation. SAP RE-FX breaks this lifecycle into three major phases. Recall that the first step of the lease valuation process is to abstract the lease agreement. Any errors or inconsistencies within the lease abstraction process may have significant impact on the valuation amounts recorded in the general ledger.

Once the lease has been properly abstracted, the next step is to assign valuation rules to the contract. Each assigned valuation rule supports a lease accounting standard, such as IFRS 16, ASC 842 (for both operating and finance leases), or local GAAP. A single contract can contain one or more valuation rules, and each valuation rule operates independently by calculating and posting its own financial entries. Once you've created valuation rules and assigned the critical terms and conditions, SAP RE-FX will calculate the valuation amounts.

Each valuation rule supports a lease accounting standard with financial postings being generated for each rule using the lease valuation posting transaction. International,

US GAAP, or local GAAP can be posted to individual ledgers or general ledger accounts based on your organizational requirements and system settings.

Once you've calculated and saved the valuation cash flows, SAP RE-FX is ready to post planned cash flow entries into the general ledger and fixed asset ledger.

## Chapter 9

In Chapter 9, we discussed disclosure requirements under the new IFRS 16 and ASC 842 regulations, in terms of reporting and analytics. We also highlighted the differences for lease costs, ROU assets, and lease liabilities as well as introduced the various reports available in SAP RE-FX and SAP Lease Administration.

According the International Accounting Standards Board (IASB), the objective of IFRS 16 is to report information that faithfully represents lease transactions and that provides a basis for users of financial statements to assess the amount, timing, and uncertainty of cash flows arising from leases. To meet these objectives, a lessee must recognize assets and liabilities arising from a lease.

Recall that the reporting mechanisms for IFRS 16 and ASC 842 aren't identical, however. For lease cost disclosures, both standards have the same requirement, although lease costs for an operating lease are not required under IFRS 16. For qualitative disclosures, under IFRS 16, cash paid (lease liability measurements) will exclude operating cash flows, additions of all ROU assets during period, carrying amounts of ROU assets disclosed by underlying asset classes, maturity analysis of finance and operating lease liabilities. For qualitative disclosures, ASC 842 covers most scenarios, except for additions of ROU assets during the lease term and carrying amounts of ROU assets disclosed by underlying asset classes.

SAP RE-FX provides different categories of information systems (such as contracts, conditions, cash flows, periodic postings) and balance sheet valuation of contracts, ROU assets, and lease liabilities.

Meanwhile, SAP Lease Administration provides three different types of standard reports: disclosure reports, management reports, and transaction reports. You can also use SAP Lease Administration to extract data from reports embedded in external sources. In other scenarios, you can extract customized reports from SAP Lease Administration in either Excel format or from other business intelligence reports.

## Chapter 10

Chapter 10 considered how different industries implement IFRS 16 requirements, looking at special requirements in how assets are used for their respective business operations. Healthcare companies rely heavily on sales financing and must manage the impact of IFRS 15 and IFRS 16 impacts on their books. For the high-tech industry, the most impact will be from the expansion of the lease identification provision, the removal of the distinction between operating and finance leases. Finally, for air and defense (A&D) companies, the previous practice of financing aircraft through off-balance sheet leases, with firms renting essential facilities (such as airports, airbases, and jet ways) and property for corporate spaces, will be impacted. Because IFRS 16 no longer distinguishes between operating and finance leases, A&D lessees will expect to see all lease contracts brought onto the balance sheet, recognizing ROU assets and corresponding lease liabilities.

## Additional Resources

In writing this book, we have consulted the official documentation of IFRS 16 and ASC 842 and have analyzed on our own experiences implementing these requirements in order to distill the most important concepts into an actionable SAP leasing guide.

However, we know that we can't cover everything, so we recommend that you consult the following resources to supplement this book:

- The IFRS 16 standard listed at *http://www.ifrs.org/*
- The ASC 842 standard listed at *https://asc.fasb.org/*
- SAP Lease Administration by SAP (*http://www.nakisa.com/lease-accounting-software*)
  - Administration Guide
  - Deployment Guide
  - User Guide
- SAP Flexible Real Estate Management (*https://help.sap.com/*)

We wish you the best of luck with your IFRS 16 and ASC 842 leasing projects!

# Appendix A
# IFRS 16 and ASC 842 FAQs

This appendix will answer common questions arising from the release of the new leasing standards: Accounting Standards Codification 842 and International Financial Reporting Standards 16.

### What is a lease?

A lease is defined as a binding legal contract between a lessor and a lessee that outlines the terms and conditions of an agreement to use a specific asset for a period of time for a defined amount of regular payments. Both IFRS 16 and ASC 842 regulate all leases and subleases except for intangible assets, biological assets, exploration (or use of non-regenerative resources such as oil and gas), inventory, and assets under construction.

### What is a sale-and-leaseback transaction?

A sale-and-leaseback transaction is where an entity transfers an asset to another (known as the *buyer-lessor*) and leases the asset back from the buyer-lessor. Under ASC 842, the majority of leases will be brought on-balance sheet, which eliminates entities' ability to use sale-and-leaseback transactions as sources of off-balance sheet financing.

If the transfer of an underlying asset involves passing its control to the buyer-lessor, then the transfer will be deemed both a sale and a lease by both the seller and the buyer. The seller-lessee should then do four things:

1. Recognize the transaction price for the sale at the point in time the buyer-lessor obtains control of the asset.
2. Adjust the transaction price for any off-market terms and recognize the entire gain/loss on the sale of the asset.
3. De-recognize the carrying amount of the underlying asset.
4. Account for the lease in accordance with ASC 842.

The buyer-lessor recognizes the asset purchase in accordance with other ASC guidelines and accounts for the lease per ASC 842.

### How do I determine if a lease contract contains a lease?

The lease contract identification process looks for two lease components: the identified asset and the right of use of that asset.

The identified asset of a contract can either be explicitly defined in the contract, or it can be implicitly defined when the asset is made accessible to the lessee. The asset must be physically distinct, and the lessee should have the right to substantially all of the asset's economic benefits. The lessor will not have any substantive rights to substitute the asset during its period of use.

If a contract contains an identified asset, we'll then proceed to consider whether the contract includes the *right of use* for that asset. Evaluate whether the lessee has permission to do two things: first, to achieve the full economic benefits of using the identified asset throughout its contractually agreed-upon period (including economic benefits from commercial transactions with a third party, like subleasing the asset) and, second, to direct the use of the identified asset.

If the contract meets both requirements, then it is a lease.

### Do substitution rights mean the agreement does not contain a lease?

A contract or agreement is deemed to contain a lease if it conveys the right to control the use of an identified asset for a period of time in exchange for consideration. However, if the supplier has a substantive right to substitute an asset, then no specific asset can be identified.

IFRS 16, paragraph B13-14, states that substantive substitution rights exist where the supplier has the practical ability to substitute alternative assets throughout the period of use and where the supplier would economically benefit from substitution.

This distinction is a fine line, but the supplier's substitution right is not considered substantive if that right can only be exercised on or after a specified date or the occurrence of a specified event. Substitution rights alone are not sufficient to exempt a contract from being deemed a lease. The substitution right must be substantive and enforceable throughout the asset's period of use.

For example, a customer enters into a contract with a supplier for the right the control the use of an asset for three years. The supplier, although the legal owner of the asset who holds the right to substitute the asset, is subject to downtime penalty clauses if the asset is unavailable for customer use for a specified period of time. Furthermore, the supplier is only likely to substitute the asset in the event of malfunction. Thus, even though substitution rights exist, the contract contains a lease.

### Under the new lease standards, will the lessee's identified right-of-use asset (ROU asset) be regarded as tangible or intangible for regulatory capital purposes?

If the underlying asset in the lease is a tangible asset, the ROU asset shall not be deducted from regulatory capital. Additionally, the ROU asset shall be included in risk-based capital and leverage ratio denominators.

### How should I handle recurring costs?

When determining the ROU asset value, include only payments for the ROU asset, and continue to treat recurring costs on the asset, such as maintenance, rent, or license fees, as operating expenses.

However, if rental payments include fixed and variable portions, then make estimates to exclude those portions. Alternatively, you may include these rental payments in capitalized lease rentals, although doing so will increase the recognized ROU asset value and lease liability on the balance sheet. Expenses on the income statement will also be presented quite differently than if these recurring costs were accounted for separately.

### Do I need to evaluate whether service arrangements involving the use of property, plant, and equipment (PP&E) contain a lease?

Under ASC 842, paragraph 10-15-2, at contract inception, entities are required to evaluate whether a contract contains a lease—as a result, service arrangements must also be evaluated.

Certain leases may themselves be embedded in other arrangements. For example, supply agreements or oil drilling contracts may contain leases pertaining to laboratory facilities or oil rigs. If PP&E is part of an arrangement (either implicit or explicit), then both the customer and the supplier should determine who controls and directs the use of the PP&E throughout the period of its use.

If a contract that is a service arrangement does *not* contain an embedded lease, then the customer does not need to bring the contract onto the balance sheet. Entities should take care to identify leases in service arrangements, which, if missed, may lead to leases being misstated on the balance sheet.

### What happens when a lease is modified?

A lease modification is defined as a change in the terms and conditions of a contract that has implication to the scope of a lease or to the financial consideration for a lease. For example, perhaps you add or terminate the right of use to one or more underlying asset, or you extend or shorten the lease term. Changing lease contracts after the inception date will trigger a reassessment of the lease parameters such as lease liability and ROU assets.

During the reassessment, the lessor must evaluate lease receivables based on the changed input data at the revaluation date to make changes in the lease payments. The following events would trigger a reassessment:

- Changes occur in relevant factors leading to a change of the terms of the lease, including the existence of significant economic incentives for the lessee.
- The lessee exercises an existing option to extend the lease term or purchase the leased asset *or* deliberately decides *not* to exercise a termination option in the lease.
- Changes occur in the index or interest rate during the reporting period that determine the lease payments used, with reference to the index or interest rate applicable during the reporting period.

### So what are the key changes brought about by ASC 842 and IFRS 16?

Table A.1 shows the key changes introduced by the new leasing standards.

| Item | IFRS 16 | ASC 842 |
|---|---|---|
| Definition | ■ Does not distinguish between finance and operating leases<br>■ Land can be included in the lease<br>■ Not necessarily a physical asset | ■ Separate guidance for finance and operating leases<br>■ Land is treated as a separate lease<br>■ Generally a physical asset |
| Supersedes | ■ IAS 17 | ■ ASC 840 |
| Measurement | ■ Assets valued under $5,000 are exempt<br>■ Allows the use of alternative evaluation models<br>■ Leases of shorter period, less than 12 months are generally exempt | ■ No explicit low-value threshold<br>■ Terms 12 months or less can be exempted from recognizing lease assets and liabilities when lessee opts to make an accounting policy election by class of underlying asset |
| Statement of cash flow | ■ Interest classed optionally as investing, financing, or operating activities | ■ Interest classified as operating activity<br>■ Amortization is a financing activity |

**Table A.1** Key Changes to IFRS 16 and ASC 842

### How do leases get classified under ASC 842 and IFRS 16?

Generally, you'd classify a lease as a finance lease if all risks and rewards incidental to owning an underlying asset are substantially transferred to the lessee; otherwise, you'd classify the lease as an operating lease.

Table A.2 shows how lease classification types differ between ASC 842 and IFRS 16. You should note that the classification criteria for classifying leases under ASC 842 are substantially similar to previous lease guidance.

In lessor accounting, a sales-type lease is a kind of finance lease, mostly provided by dealer and manufacturer lessors. Sales-type leases are often bundled together with additional non-lease components to make equipment financing more attractive. Unlike a normal final lease, with a sales-type lease, the lessor records operating profit equal to the difference between discounted minimum lease payments and the cost of the leased asset at lease inception. This scenario occurs only when the lease receivables (i.e., the minimum lease payments) are higher than the cost of the leased asset. With a normal finance lease, the lessor must record the interest portion of the lease payments as interest income for the duration of the lease.

| Accounting Model | ASC 842 | IFRS 16 |
|---|---|---|
| Lessee accounting | ▪ Finance lease<br>▪ Operating lease | ▪ Finance lease<br>▪ Operating lease |
| Lessor accounting | ▪ Sales-type lease<br>▪ Direct finance lease (operating lease) | ▪ Finance lease<br>▪ Operating lease |

**Table A.2** Lease Classifications with IFRS 16 and ASC 842

### Under ASC 842, entities are no longer required to assess some quantitative bright line test thresholds. Can we keep using these quantitative thresholds in classifying leases?

You can use quantitative bright lines test thresholds to determine a capital lease if the lease term is at least 75% of the remaining economic life of an underlying asset *or* if the sum of the present value of lease payments and the present value of any guaranteed residual value is at least 90% of the fair value of the underlying asset.

The quantitative result of the tests should then be diligently applied when undertaking lease classifications. If you decide to adopt bright line test thresholds, then apply these thresholds consistently across your entire lease portfolio.

### What are the lease exemptions for both standards?

As shown in Table A.3, a few lease exemptions are common to both standards, although a few lease exemptions are unique only either to IFRS 16 or ASC 842.

| IFRS 16 | Both Standards | ASC 842 |
|---|---|---|
| Licenses of intellectual property granted by a lessor | Intangible assets such as goodwill | Inventory |
| Rights held by a lessee under licensing agreements | Explore for or use of non-generative resources such as minerals, oils, or gas | Assets under construction |
| Service concession arrangements | Biological assets such as crops or timber | |
| Short-term lease less than 12 months | | |
| Leases for which the underlying asset is of low value (less than $5,000) | | |

**Table A.3** Lease Exemptions

### Will a capitalization threshold for low-value assets be established under ASC 842?

ASC 842 requires that entities recognize an ROU asset and lease liability for all leases (except for short-term leases) but, unlike IFRS 16, does not exempt leases of low-value assets. For leases that would otherwise be recognized under the new standard, lessees will be allowed to use an appropriate capitalization threshold to decide whether to recognize the lease on the balance sheet.

Be mindful of the materiality of these leases, since US GAAP does not apply to immaterial items when preparing financial statements. You should carefully evaluate the new capitalization thresholds instead of defaulting to existing ones for two reasons:

- Most existing capitalization thresholds for PP&E do not include the additional asset base that was introduced by the ASC. Take care that aggregated amounts of old and new assets are not material, and therefore require thorough analysis of the new off-balance sheet asset thresholds.
- Existing PP&E capitalization thresholds do not consider the effect on balance sheet liabilities. Examine the aggregate materiality of all ROU assets and lease liabilities that would be excluded from the balance sheet because of adopting the new threshold.

In determining a capitalization threshold, you may use whichever of the following measurements is lower:

- A capitalization threshold for PP&E inclusive of ROU assets determined in accordance with ASC 842
- A recognition threshold for liabilities that accounts for the effect of lease liabilities determined under the ASC

Another way to develop a capitalization threshold is to record all lease liabilities and adopt the threshold for related ROU assets only. You would expense any ROU asset valued below the threshold and amortize the lease liability in subsequent periods using the effective interest method. Part of the periodic lease payments would then reduce the liability, and the remainder would be recognized as interest expense.

Entities should consider the gross balance sheet effect of lease entries in assessing materiality, not just the net effect. Carefully determine the overall impact of omitting disclosures for assets not brought onto the balance sheet.

### When do IFRS 16 and ASC 842 take effect?

The two new leasing regulations will be applied for most entities at the beginning of the first annual reporting period, which is the date of initial application.

As shown in Table A.4, IFRS 16 is effective for annual reporting periods beginning on or after January 1, 2019. Note that an entity may adopt the standard early, but the standard must be applied after or at the same time as IFRS 15 (Revenue from Contracts with Customers) is adopted. An entity that opts to adopt IFRS 16 early is required to disclose that fact.

Under ASC 842, the effective date for public businesses is for annual reporting periods beginning after December 15, 2018. For all the other entities (e.g., privately owned companies), the effective date is for annual reporting periods beginning after December 15, 2019. Early adoption of the new standard is allowed.

| Item | IFRS 16 | ASC 842 |
|---|---|---|
| Effective date | ▪ Accounting periods beginning on or after January 1, 2019 | ▪ Accounting periods beginning after December 15, 2018 (public)<br>▪ Accounting periods beginning after December 15, 2019 (private, etc.) |

**Table A.4** IFRS 16 and ASC 842 Effective Dates

| Item | IFRS 16 | ASC 842 |
|---|---|---|
| Transition | ■ Early adoption allowed with the new revenue recognition standard | ■ Early adoption allowed |

**Table A.4** IFRS 16 and ASC 842 Effective Dates (Cont.)

### What are the disclosure requirements?

New disclosure requirements are particularly relevant for leases in which the entity is a lessee. The transition approach adopted by the entity will impact the disclosures it is required to make.

Let's look at lessees first. Table A.5 shows the information a lessee needs to disclose for both ASC 842 and IFRS 16. These disclosure requirements, which are described in ASC 842, paragraph 20-50-3 to 20-50-4, and IFRS 16, paragraphs 52–60, can help you evaluate your current business processes, as this information will be readily available for analysis as you generate the notes to be included in the financial statements.

| IFRS 16 | ASC 842 |
|---|---|
| A lessee shall disclose information about the leases for which it is a lessee in a single note or as a separate section in its financial statements | A lessee shall consider the level of detail necessary to satisfy the disclosure requirements |
| A lessee shall disclose qualitative and quantitative information about its leasing activities:<br>■ The nature of the lessee's leasing activities<br>■ Future cash outflows to which the lessee is potentially exposed that are not reflected in the measurement of lease liabilities<br>■ Restrictions or covenants imposed by leases<br>■ Sale-and-leaseback transactions | A lessee shall disclose all of the following:<br>■ A general description of those leases<br>■ The basis and terms and conditions on which variable lease payments are determined<br>■ The existence and terms and conditions of options to extend or terminate the lease<br>■ The existence and terms and conditions of guaranteed residual value provided by the lessee<br>■ The restrictions or covenants imposed by leases (e.g., those relating to dividends or incurring additional financial obligations) |

**Table A.5** IFRS 16 and ASC 842 Disclosure Requirements for Lessees

| IFRS 16 | ASC 842 |
|---|---|
| A lessee shall disclose the following amounts:<br>■ Depreciation charge from the ROU assets by class of underlying asset<br>■ Interest expense coming from lease liabilities<br>■ Expenses coming from short-term leases | A lessee shall disclose the following amounts:<br>■ Finance lease costs, separated between the amortization of the ROU assets and interest on the lease liabilities (lease payments)<br>■ Operating lease cost<br>■ Short-term lease cost with a lease term of 1 month or less, without expenses related to leases |
| ■ Expenses coming from leases of low-value assets<br>■ Expenses coming from variable lease payments that are not included in the measurement of lease liabilities<br>■ Income from subleasing ROU assets<br>■ Total cash outflow for leases<br>■ Additions to ROU assets<br>■ Gains or losses arising from sale-and-leaseback transactions<br>■ Carrying amount of ROU assets by end of the reporting period and class of underlying asset | ■ Variable lease cost<br>■ Gross income coming from subleases that are separate from the operating or finance lease expense<br>■ Net gains or losses arising from sale-and-leaseback transactions |

**Table A.5** IFRS 16 and ASC 842 Disclosure Requirements for Lessees (Cont.)

In contrast, Table A.6 shows the information that the *lessor* needs to disclose for both IFRS 16 and ASC 842. These disclosure requirements, which are described in ASC 842, paragraphs 30-50-2 to 30-50-13, and IFRS 16, paragraphs 90–97, can help you evaluate your current business processes, as this information will be readily available for analysis as you generate the notes to be included in the financial statements.

| IFRS 16 | ASC 842 |
|---|---|
| A lessor shall disclose these amounts within the reporting period:<br>■ Finance leases—selling profit or loss, finance income on the net investment in the lease, income from variable lease payments not included in the measurement of the net investment in the lease<br>■ Operating leases—lease income, and separately, income involving to variable lease payments that do not depend on an index or a rate | A lessor shall disclose lease income recognized in the specified report format which includes the following information:<br>■ For sales-type leases (finance leases) and direct financing leases (operating leases)—a profit or loss should be recognized at the commencement date together with the interest income that is either in combined or separated by components of the net investment<br>■ For operating leases—lease income coming from lease payments<br>Lease income involving to variable lease payments not included in the measurement of the lease receivable |
| A lessor shall disclose these information:<br>■ The nature of the lessor's leasing activities<br>■ How the lessor manages the risk associated with any rights it retains in underlying assets. In particular, a lessor shall disclose its risk management strategy for the rights it retains in underlying assets | A lessor shall disclose both of the following:<br>■ Information about the nature of its leases such as general description of the lease, terms and conditions on which variable lease payments are determined<br>■ Information about significant assumptions and judgments made in applying the requirements |

**Table A.6** IFRS 16 and ASC 842 Disclosure Requirements for Lessors

### What software does SAP recommend to quickly adopt and comply with the new leasing accounting standards?

For non-movable leases (real estate, warehouses), SAP recommends SAP Flexible Real Estate Management (SAP RE-FX), whether you are a lessor or lessee. SAP has completed a multiyear development effort to make SAP RE-FX compliant with the new leasing standards under ASC 842 and IFRS 16.

For movable leases (cars, planes, or equipment), SAP recommends SAP Lease Administration by Nakisa for both lessees and lessors. This product is a certified solution extension developed by an SAP partner that provides enterprise lease management and accounting functionality to accelerate your compliance with the new leasing standards.

# Appendix B
# The Authors

**Hanno Hofmann** has more than 20 years of SAP project experience in various industries, including the high-tech, telecom, financial, automotive, and aerospace industries. His focus for many years has been lease accounting with SAP RE-FX. Moving to accounting standards compliance in early 2015, he has been a trusted advisor for multiple IFRS 15 and IFRS 16 implementation projects in SAP around the world. He is a board member and cofounder at Walldorf Consulting AG.

**Louis Teunissen** is a solution architect and principal consultant with 18 years of experience in financials, banking, insurance, and leasing with SAP solutions. Since 2015 Louis has focused implementing the SAP solutions for compliance with IFRS 15 using SAP Revenue Accounting and Reporting and with IFRS 16 using SAP Flexible Real Estate Management for lease valuation. He also regularly delivers training for SAP on these topics, and is based in Singapore.

**Joy Mabborang** holds a bachelor's degree in accountancy and is a certified public accountant. To cope with technological advancement she changed career and gained experience in IT solutions at Lexmark International Inc. as a business systems analyst focusing on project implementation using SAP software for seven years. She now lives in Germany and works as an SAP functional consultant for Walldorf Consulting AG. As part of her role, she provides consulting services and designs leasing solutions for SAP clients to adopt the new standards for revenue recognition in contracts. Even though she works in IT, her passion for continuous learning keeps her abreast of what's new in accounting standards, especially for leases.

**Pamela Lim** is a certified SAP ERP Financials consultant who enjoys being in dynamic and challenging environments. Her leasing project portfolio includes several clients in the medical and pharmaceutical industry, where she has assisted in establishing and optimizing of a number of business processes. She is also experienced in customer training and stakeholder education for solutions pertaining to IFRS standards compliance. Pamela holds a bachelor's degree from the University of Melbourne.

## The Contributors

**Tom Anderson** is the global solution owner for SAP's Real Estate Management solution, which is used by commercial, residential, and corporate real estate organizations around the world. He is responsible for identifying trends in the increasingly complex real estate industry, working with customers to understand how they are impacted by these trends, and coordinating with SAP product owners to develop solutions. He supports sales teams globally by developing marketing materials, responding to information requests, and educating them on SAP's real estate solution.

**Zeina Dabbagh** is a technical accountant at the Center of Excellence at Nakisa. With more than 10 years of experience in corporate accounting and information systems, Zeina brings a breadth of knowledge when working with global organizations on compliance initiatives for financial regulations. Zeina's most recent experience has been in a consultancy capacity, where she has provided training, presentations, and workshops to organizations implementing SAP Lease Administration by Nakisa. Working closely with the Nakisa product team, Zeina ensures that all features and functionalities in the application meet the accounting regulations required by IFRS 16 and ASC 842.

**Puja Mehta** is a technical accountant in the Center of Excellence at Nakisa. Puja has many years of experience in corporate accounting and has specialized expertise in IFRS and US GAAP. Before joining the Nakisa team, she worked at the International Air Transport Association as assistant manager in the corporate finance team, where she led the implementation of IFRS 16. Puja now works closely with global companies across sectors to ensure compliance with the new lease accounting standards. A proficient user of SAP technologies, Puja provides insight into best practices for implementing SAP Lease Administration by Nakisa. Through her experiences with project specification and design, Puja has learned how to integrate lease accounting technology with SAP ERP while minimizing the disruption to existing business processes. She has been involved in the development of SAP Lease Administration by Nakisa, working in an advisory capacity to ensure that all new features and product enhancements are compliant with IASB and FASB regulations.

**Imran Mia** is the head of the Center of Excellence at Nakisa. With over 15 years of experience in corporate accounting and information system, Imran has helped develop best practices to enable organizations to plan, transition, and comply with financial regulations. He is a subject matter expert on the new lease accounting standards and works extensively with leading organizations around the world to help ensure compliance with minimal disruption to existing business processes. Imran has been closely involved in the development of SAP Lease Administration by Nakisa by advising and ensuring compliance with IFRS 16 and ASC 842.

**Heiko Roth** has been working for SAP consulting in Germany for 17 years, having started in corporate finance management and loans. He has extensive SAP project experience from various industries, such as financial services, automotive, telecom, and high tech. His primary SAP competence is within the areas of leasing, finances, and solution architecture.

In 2003, he entered the leasing business and has had many project assignments in Mexico, South Africa, the United

States, Australia, and various European countries. His SAP projects cover all aspects of the projects (blueprint, implementation, support, etc.), and he has served in roles as varied as solution architect, project lead, principal consultant, delivery manager, and steering committee member. Heiko headed SAP's EMEA leasing consulting department as consulting manager for seven years and was recognized for his high potential at SAP Germany. Since 2015, he has been a board member and co-founder at Walldorf Consulting AG.

**Pui Pui Wong** started in 2006 as a migration consultant for core ERP processes. She gained extensive experience in SAP CRM before she moved on to IFRS and SAP consulting. Having worked with the IFRS-related products since the new regulation's early stages, she supports customers on their journey worldwide.

# Index

## A



## B

## M



## N



## O

## S

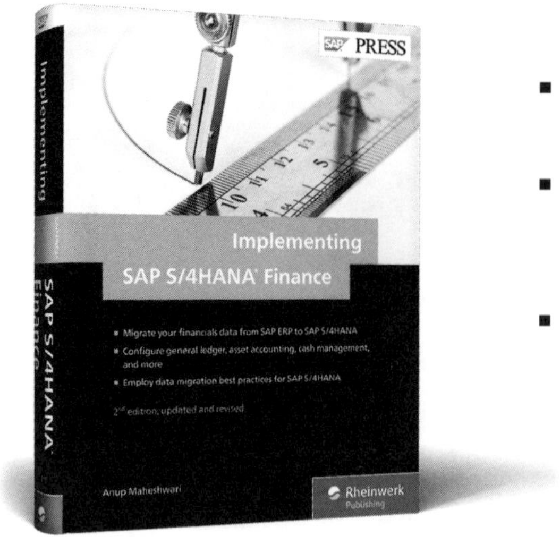
SAP PRESS
Implementing SAP S/4HANA Finance
Anup Maheshwari
Rheinwerk Publishing